Praise for *The Player*

"The most popular political biography of the year."
—Charlotte Gray, *The National Post*

"Geoffrey Stevens has finally captured, in *The Player*, the two sides of this contradictory and important figure, and revealed aspects of Camp's personality that until now have been largely hidden....Stevens has a seasoned journalist's eye and is at the top of his game when he is in the moment, detailing the layers that made up Camp's life....He weaves a tapestry of rich detail, offering penetrating insights into the complex and often tormented private man."
—Allan Gregg, *The Globe and Mail*

"A perceptive and no-holds-barred look into the life of the man most Canadians only remember in one of two ways: the man who engineered the demise of Diefenbaker, and the man who regularly debated politics on CBC Radio's *Morningside*. Camp became the witty voice of moderate conservatism, and in Stevens' capable hands, we are reminded why hard-core right-wing agendas have never taken hold across the country." —*Calgary Herald*

"Stevens rates [*Gentlemen, Players and Politicians*] as possibly the best book ever written about Canadian politics. I think he is wrong—this biography is even better."
—James Gillies, *Literary Review of Canada*

"In this highly readable account of Camp's turbulent life, Stevens describes a man who, although wedded to politics, was a renegade, a free thinker, a team player but one with an agenda of his own, a professional determined to put his small-l liberal stamp on Conservative political thought....Stevens, one of the country's most experienced political analysts, has fashioned the key components of Camp's chequered life into a scrupulously fair, well-researched and compelling biography. *The Player* is a page-turner, a book anyone interested in Canadian political history will savour." —*London Free Press*

"...revelations galore...Stevens' political savvy, married to a fine, raconteur-like prose style, does justice to Camp's contribution to Canadian politics." —*Winnipeg Free Press*

"Stevens does not hide admiration for his subject, and the pleasure he takes in the story is infectious. The author's comfortable and elegant prose gives us an authentic portrait of a complex man."
                    —Denis Smith, *Toronto Star*, author of *Rogue Tory*

"In *The Player: The Life and Times of Dalton Camp*, Geoffrey Stevens has deftly managed to revive the almost lost art of the compelling Canadian political biography. In the great tradition of Peter Newman's *Renegade in Power* or Richard Gwyn's *The Unlikely Revolutionary*, Stevens has latched onto a powerful, complex and often enigmatic personality who once loomed large in the life of many Canadians and transformed this life into a tale that has both historical fascination and contemporary resonance. The writing is spare and mercifully free of pop psychology clichés; the chosen anecdotes always fit cleanly into the overall strategy; and there is much evidence of care and concern to evoke a real human being and not just a political icon or punching bag. In short, a biography that delivers what it promises: a life drawn with sympathy, edge and a care for facts."
                    —2003 Drainie-Taylor Biography Prize Citation

"There's been an emptiness on the national stage since we lost Dalton Camp, but Geoffrey Stevens helps fill the void with a wonderful and insightful look back at one of the most engaging people in the history of Canadian politics and journalism. When Dalton wasn't in the middle of the story he was in the middle of the telling of it—*The Player* captures it all and makes us realize why he is now, and always will be, so missed."
                    —Peter Mansbridge

"Not only is Geoff Stevens' biography of Dalton Camp a serious and beautifully written account of one of Canada's most important political operators and columnists, it is such fun to read. It's all there—the lovers! the money! the intrigue! Who could resist?"
                    —Stevie Cameron

The Player

THE LIFE & TIMES OF

DALTON CAMP

Geoffrey Stevens

KEY PORTER BOOKS

Library and Archives Canada Cataloguing in Publication

Stevens, Geoffrey, 1940–
    The player : the life & times of Dalton Camp / Geoffrey Stevens.

Includes bibliographical references and index.
ISBN 1-55263-619-4

1. Camp, Dalton 1920–2002. 2. Progressive Conservative Party of
Canada—Biography. 3. Canada—Politics and government—1935–
4. Journalists—Canada—Biography. I. Title.

FC601.C34S74 2004   971.064'092   C2004-902900-2

THE CANADA COUNCIL | LE CONSEIL DES ARTS
FOR THE ARTS | DU CANADA
SINCE 1957 | DEPUIS 1957

ONTARIO ARTS COUNCIL
CONSEIL DES ARTS DE L'ONTARIO

The publisher gratefully acknowledges the support of the Canada Council for the Arts and
the Ontario Arts Council for its publishing program. We acknowledge the support of the
Government of Ontario through the Ontario Media Development Corporation's Ontario
Book Initiative.

We acknowledge the financial support of the Government of Canada through the Book
Publishing Industry Development Program (BPIDP) for our publishing activities.

Key Porter Books Limited
70 The Esplanade
Toronto, Ontario
Canada M5E 1R2

www.keyporter.com

Cover design: Jack Steiner
Electronic formatting: Jean Lightfoot Peters

Printed and bound in Canada

04 05 06 07 08 5 4 3 2 1

For the whole family:
Lin, Casey, Jamie, Alex,
Sean—and Jack!

Contents

Introduction

IN THE MONTHS BEFORE HIS DEATH in March 2002, Dalton Kingsley Camp was struggling to write the story of his life. It would have been an important book, a definitive chronicle, an insider's portrait of a dramatic swath of Canadian political history: from John Diefenbaker and Lester Pearson to Pierre Trudeau and Robert Stanfield to Brian Mulroney, John Turner and Jean Chrétien. For the first time, he would write about what *really* happened when he waged the leadership-review campaign that drove Diefenbaker from office, that democratized the Conservative party by establishing the paramountcy of party members over their chosen leaders—and that ultimately dashed Camp's own hopes of becoming a national political leader. And if the new book were anything like his first one, the magnificent *Gentlemen, Players and Politicians*, it would be written with elegance, grace and poise.

Writing the story of his life was probably the hardest thing Camp had ever tried to do, because it forced him to confront the demons of his private and political life. He was obsessed with detail and accuracy, knowing, for example, that every word he wrote about Diefenbaker would be scrutinized, as though under a microscope, by historians, political scientists and all the partisans who had fought stoutly with him and bitterly against him. He also found it painful, almost impossible, to reduce the passions, pleasures and disillusions of his complicated personal life to the black-and-white pages of an autobiography.

Tragically, he left the enterprise far too late. Hidden away in a hotel room in Fredericton, he searched for just the right words to assess and explain his long, productive and controversial life. He told friends he felt an immense pressure to get the writing done, and some of that pressure was monetary. Once a wealthy man, he was now virtually broke, his marriage was in ruins and he was unable to earn enough from his newspaper columns to carry his financial burdens. So he struggled, alone—an 81-year-old man with a heart transplant—with no research assistance, no computer (he had never taken to using one) and only a few files.

His will did not desert him, but his health did. With his eyesight deteriorating, his hearing failing and his memory beginning to betray him, he was unable—perhaps for the first time in his life— to finish a job he had set out to do.

When he died, he left a fragmentary draft manuscript that described episodes in his early life up to his undergraduate days at Acadia University in Wolfville, Nova Scotia. After his death, I looked through boxes of files in the basement of Northwood, his hilltop home in rural New Brunswick, and found an additional 27 manuscript pages in which he had set down some of his experiences in the Canadian Army in the Second World War.

For this biography, *The Player*, I have drawn on Dalton Camp's original, fragmentary manuscript. The bulk of the material comes, however, from scores of interviews I conducted with the people who knew him best. I was also able to draw on his letters, journals and speeches, on a number of oral history interviews that may be found in various public archives and, of course, on the thousands of newspaper columns that he wrote over a period of more than three decades. Not least, I have drawn on my own first-hand knowledge of Dalton Camp as a friend, source and inspiring colleague in journalism.

I first met him in 1965. He was running for the Tories in Toronto's Eglinton riding against Liberal frontbencher Mitchell Sharp, and I was a brand-new correspondent in the Ottawa bureau of the *Globe and Mail*. I interviewed him often during his battle with the Chief and in his years as guru to Robert Stanfield. He gave generously of his time and insights to help me when I wrote a biography of Stanfield and later when I co-authored, with John Laschinger, a book on backroom politics, *Leaders and Lesser Mortals*. During my eight years as the *Globe*'s national political columnist, Dalton was a friendly rival at the *Toronto Star*. I knew he was better plugged in to the Conservative party than I would ever be; for his part, he wondered why I wasted so much time talking to Liberals. Later on, as pundits sharing a page in the Sunday *Star*, we probably agreed more often than we differed. As managing editor of *Maclean's*, I hired him from time to time to write guest columns.

Even close friends sometimes wondered where he really stood politically; as the years passed, his columns were often more critical of his own party than of his presumed enemies, the Liberals and New Democrats. He admired the American liberalism of Franklin Roosevelt, John and Robert Kennedy, and Bill Clinton, but his own respect for tradition, his belief in political institutions, especially the party system, and his distrust of most forms of state intervention marked him in the Canadian context as both a conservative and a Conservative. His intense dislike of ideology—from either end of the spectrum—planted him squarely in the middle of the political playing field, which is where most Canadians want their elected representatives to be. Camp regarded himself as a Red Tory, as accurate a label as any.

In many ways, Camp was a pioneer. As he would reflect in later years, he came on the scene at just the right time with just the right skills, and he used them to build three successful, intersecting careers: in advertising, politics and journalism. As an advertising copywriter and agency executive, he changed political campaigns dramatically by exploiting the power of radio and, later, television. Before Dalton Camp, political advertising had consisted of text-heavy ads placed in local newspapers. The on-air commercials he crafted, extolling the virtues of his candidate and assaulting the weaknesses of the opponent, were instrumental in electing Progressive Conservative governments in New Brunswick, Nova Scotia, Prince Edward Island, Manitoba, Ottawa and, later on, Ontario. He used the government advertising contracts—mainly for tourism—that those victories yielded to build his own advertising agency and personal wealth. His success made him, for a time, the most powerful figure in the federal Conservative party.

Then he shifted gears, combining the skills he had learned in advertising with the understanding of political strategy he had developed in the backrooms to create a splendid career in journalism as a newspaper columnist, author and radio and television commentator. He had less success with fiction, over the years trying his hand at short stories, scripts for stage plays and an autobiographical novel—all of them unpublished (and perhaps unpublishable). He picked up honorary degrees from his three favourite universities—Acadia University, St. Thomas University in Fredericton and the University of New Brunswick—and was made an Officer of the Order of Canada. At age 72, he became the oldest person in Canada to receive a heart transplant.

Only one prize eluded his grasp in the course of his long, complicated and rewarding life. At a crucial juncture in the prime of his years, he wanted—briefly but intensely—to be leader of the Tory party and prime minister of Canada. He thought he had a shot at it, only to have circumstances deny his ambition.

In his 50s, Camp retreated with a new wife to his beloved New Brunswick, opting out of his former life with all its social obligations in Toronto, out of the advertising business and, except for a brief stint in the Prime Minister's Office in Ottawa, out of active involvement in high-octane politics. A public man who prized his privacy, he built himself a hilltop lair—he named it Northwood—on 80 acres of wooded land down a country road from Jemseg, a blink-and-miss-it hamlet south of Fredericton. He walked his dogs, chatted with the locals, fetched his *Globe and Mail* from the country store, bought berries and vegetables at the farmers' market on Saturday mornings, and in general lived the gentle life of a kindly, though somewhat reclusive, country squire. When he was not thinking, writing or talking (and drinking red wine) with friends at Northwood, he could be found at his modest cottage at Robertson's Point on nearby Grand Lake or holed up, hidden from the world, at the Clam Shack, a three-room cabin perched above the tidal flats of Passamaquoddy Bay, not far from St. Andrews.

Yet the more he tried to cut himself off from the world of politics, the greater his influence seemed to grow. Prime ministers phoned to talk about issues and to seek his advice—or simply to pass the time of day. Provincial premiers and other party leaders dropped in at Northwood or Robertson's Point. Backroom strategists came around to pick his brain. Every week, with a manual typewriter propped in his lap, Camp crafted two political columns, and they were read by hundreds of thousands of Canadians in the *Toronto Star* and in other newspapers across the country that subscribed to the *Star* syndicate. Thousands more tuned to CBC radio every Tuesday morning for those shining 20 minutes or more when Dalton Camp debated the issues of the week with Eric Kierans and Stephen Lewis. "Kierans, Camp and Lewis" was radio at its best and politics at its most engrossing. And for a time he wrote a column on New Brunswick politics for "the *TJ*" (Saint John *Telegraph Journal*) every Monday, until the paper's owners—the powerful and ubiquitous Irving family—had him fired for criticizing their friends in the provincial government.

Unlike some of his detractors, Dalton Camp was never a hater. He thought that yelling, ranting, accusing and attacking served only to demean politics and its practitioners. He was a firm believer in civil discourse and intelligent debate, and he demonstrated that belief in his columns and for the better part of a decade on "Kierans, Camp and Lewis."

Among his political contemporaries, the person he resembled the most was Pierre Trudeau. Like Trudeau, Camp had intelligence, style, independence of spirit, command of language and considerable charisma. Nancy Morrison, now a judge on British Columbia's Supreme Court, was a friend for 35 years. She tells of a day, many years ago, when she and two female friends were taking one of their regular brisk walks around the seawall in Stanley Park in Vancouver. As they walked, they talked about a magazine article they had just read about the 10 most interesting women in Canada.

"We said, 'What about men?'" Morrison remembered. "God knows, we all loved men." They decided to write about the 10 most interesting men in Canada—"that included everything attractive: brains, humour and sex, all rolled into one great package." Their enterprise foundered, however, when they were unable to come up with the names of 10 truly interesting males. But the three women, political junkies all, were absolutely agreed on one thing: the name at the top of the list had to be Dalton Camp. "Sexy? Oh, yes," Morrison said. "Dalton had it all. He was *the* icon and he remained that way. I never told Dalton that. When someone dies, you wish you'd told him. He was wonderful. He really was."

He truly was The Player.

THE EARLY YEARS

CHAPTER 1

An American Canadian

IRST BAPTIST CHURCH in Oakland, California, was filled to
capacity on that August day in 1937. Even the galleries were
jammed, and many mourners were forced to stand at the rear. The well
of the church, beneath the pulpit, was a wall of flowers. The second
son of the great Protestant preacher Harold Brainard Camp—the
man who would come to be thought of as the Billy Graham of his
day—could smell the heavy scent of the blooms. "When I sat up
straight, pressing my back against the pew, I could see over the
heavy bronze coffin to my left and glimpse, in profile, part of my
father's face. He was dead at 43; one week later, I would be 17,"
Dalton Kingsley Camp recalled years later.

> After the choir had sung my father's favourite hymn—"He Leadeth
> Me"—I broke down, sobbing uncontrollably. A great sigh of sympathy
> rose in the church behind me, like a wind stirring among leaves. One
> of Father's colleagues delivered the eulogy, meant to uplift, comfort
> and console. Beyond consolation, feeling anger, hurt and betrayal, I lis-
> tened but did not hear.
>
> After the service, still tearful, shaken with grief, I climbed in the
> front seat of the limousine, my mother and older brother in the back,
> and we drove off behind a convoy of police motorcycles. I had seen the
> last of my father and the last of his church. We would soon accompany
> him on the long rail journey home to his waiting grave in Woodstock,
> New Brunswick, Canada.[1]

Harold Camp's death, of a heart attack, was a significant event
in California and beyond. The *Oakland Tribune* ran his portrait on
the front page and *Newsweek* published an item on his passing. He
had been larger than life: a spell-binding orator who packed
churches and meeting halls wherever he spoke; president of the
Northern Baptist Convention; a confidential adviser to Franklin
Roosevelt who briefed the President on the deepening Nazi menace

and mistreatment of Jews in Germany in the 1930s; a friend of some of the most influential figures in America, including Earl Warren, later to be governor of California and chief justice of the United States Supreme Court; a prominent pacifist; and even a member of the California state boxing commission.

Although Harold's death at such an early age had a deep impact on the lives of Dalton's mother, older brother, Sanborn (called "Sandy"), and their mentally handicapped younger brother, Harold Jr. (nicknamed "Red"), it was especially traumatic for Dalton. He adored his father, even though he was never able to reconcile his adulation with his knowledge of the more tawdry side of Harold's life. Six decades later, Dalton would describe his father's death as the most significant happening in his own life:

> It completely changed my life, where I lived, who I was, where I was going, how my life would turn out. A good deal of life is made up of luck and happenstance and a little bit of bad planning. That was a momentous and entirely unexpected event. He was very young, a very young man. And as a result of his death we moved back to New Brunswick and I was moved out to a private school in Nova Scotia. That was in '37. Two years later we, as Canadians, were at war. Not the Americans: had we been living in the United States the war wouldn't have touched us for another two years.[2]

If Harold had lived even a few years longer, until his middle son was in college, chances are Dalton Camp would have remained in California and become an American, as Sandy, four years his senior, did. He would not have made that long cross-continent trek by train from Piedmont, a prosperous suburb of Oakland, back to New Brunswick, where Harold, his wife Aurilla and all three of their sons had been born. He would not have gone from a life of status and affluence as the son of one of North America's best-known clergymen—Harold Camp commanded an annual salary of $10,000, a princely sum in the Depression, not to mention the envelopes of cash that grateful parishioners gave him for presiding at marriages, baptisms and funerals—to a relatively modest existence in threadbare Woodstock, New Brunswick.

He might never have met and impressed Lord Beaverbrook, the

most powerful press baron of his day, who handed him a Beaverbrook Overseas Scholarship to the London School of Economics; there, he came under the intellectual spell of Harold Laski, a brilliant teacher and radical who was considered to be the leading socialist thinker in post-war Britain. If he had stayed in the United States, Camp might well have joined his great friend Frank Mankiewicz in directing presidential election campaigns for Democrats Robert Kennedy and George McGovern. But if so, Canadian politics would have been denied one of the most pivotal figures of the second half of the twentieth century, a charismatic loner who became a guru to leading politicians at both the federal and provincial level. Would anyone else, in the name of party democracy, have mounted the crusade that drove John Diefenbaker from office? And who would have filled the place that Camp occupied with grace and eloquence for the last 30 years of his life as journalism's voice of political moderation and common sense—a conservative thinker with a liberal conscience?

When Harold Camp died, Rilla certainly felt the loss of status and the diminution of the family's financial circumstances. Although she had loved her husband, theirs had been a stormy and at times unhappy union. Harold's passing at least meant a return to the place she loved above all others: Woodstock. After a few years back in New Brunswick, she took a second husband. Coincidentally, he was another Camp: John Camp, a dentist in New Haven, Connecticut, who was probably a distant cousin of her first husband. Although John Camp was already married, Rilla was as strong-willed as she was attractive, and, as Dalton told it, she took the dentist away from his wife and two children. She brought him back to Woodstock, where she sold her home and built a new log house. Not much is known in the family about her second husband, suggesting the union may not have lasted long.

Meanwhile, Sandy, tall, handsome and athletic, stayed behind in California, attended college on a basketball scholarship, married a girl from Oregon and joined the United States Air Force when the Americans entered the Second World War. After the war, he ran a successful Ford dealership for a while and acquired a yacht, but he fell on hard times, divorced, lost all contact with his Canadian family and apparently ended up an alcoholic. He died before his time and in debt. It was not until years later that Dalton learned of the death of his older brother.

The third brother, Red, five years younger than Dalton, had suffered brain damage as the result of a serious illness when he was a child; the family was never sure, but they thought it might have been polio. It left Red as an adult with the intelligence of an eight-year-old. He could perform simple tasks and he had a prodigious memory, but he was never able to look after himself well enough to live on his own. In that August of 1937, Red was unable to grasp the implications of his father's death. Early in the morning after the service in Oakland, Dalton went to Red's room, lay on his bed beside him and told him, "Dad is dead." "Oh, that's too bad," was Red's only response.[3]

The little family arrived in Woodstock on the noon train. They watched as Harold's coffin was transferred from the baggage car to a hearse for the short trip to the Protestant cemetery where an open grave awaited. Dalton was desolate. He had loved California and had felt completely at home in the culture, the climate and the lifestyle. He had been attending a high school where everyone came from a well-to-do family and virtually everyone was white and English-speaking. Although the family—at Rilla's insistence and usually over Harold's loud objections—had returned to New Brunswick for most summer holidays, Dalton realized he knew nothing of Canada beyond Woodstock:

> The sense of melancholy was overwhelming. All that I had loved and held dear had been wrenched away. Not only had I lost my father, friends, school, the family home, my room and the pleasures and comforts that had surrounded me, but, as well, I was leaving America for an unknown country where I would be a stranger.
>
> What I knew of Canada was represented by Woodstock, a town of ten churches and one theatre, a main street, no streetcars, university or professional sports, one fading hotel with brass spittoons in the lobby, two weekly newspapers of no interest and a one-crop economy—

potatoes. These dour presentiments accompanied my journey from California to New Brunswick, from the light that had been America to the shapeless shadow that loomed ahead: I was inconsolable.[4]

"The light that had been America" was never extinguished in Dalton Camp. He became a passionate Canadian, ardent economic nationalist and fierce critic of many American policies in the world—especially when they were imposed by Republican administrations in Washington. But he never lost his love for the American people, for many of their institutions and for their diversions. In baseball, he cheered for the San Francisco Giants, never the Toronto Blue Jays or Montreal Expos. He had no interest in hockey (perhaps because he never learned to skate well enough to play it) and he found the Canadian Football League "too complicated" to be worth following. But he loved basketball (which he had played in school), U.S. college football and the National Football League, never missing a game on television if he could avoid it. He cheered for the Cleveland Browns—the mark of a diehard football fan. His favourite newspaper was the *New York Times*, especially its sports pages.

And he devoured American politics. He attended every political convention he could—Democrat or Republican, it did not matter. He wrote about them, commented on them for television, or just sat and soaked them in. Although he was, improbably perhaps, a Conservative in his Canadian context, he would have made an impossible Republican. He admired Roosevelt and his New Deal. He loathed Richard Nixon and preferred Bill Clinton, with his human faults, to either of the George Bushes, with their lack of humanity.

He was a unique commodity on the Canadian political scene— a nationalist who did not feel himself any less of a Canadian because he admired the United States. He can best be described as an "American Canadian," in contrast to the "British Canadians" who had governed Canada in most of the twentieth century. While most Tory politicians of his generation looked first to Britain, venerated Westminster as the "Mother of Parliaments" and cherished the royal connection, Camp had no interest in the monarchy, the Union Jack or faded memories of a defunct empire. He found the United States and its politics, sports and theatre more interesting, more vibrant and more relevant. He was a true North American who knew and appreciated the United States just as thoroughly as he came to appreciate and love Canada. Yet knowing the United States as well as he did made him aware of its idiosyncrasies, alert to its shortcomings and wary of the dangers that American hegemony poses for Canada and the world. He did not realize until he returned to Canada following his father's death, "how deeply the American values are imposed or taught or imbedded in the minds of the children. It goes with the educational system. It's the hero system."

> When I came to Canada, I found there just weren't any heroes. In America we had one a week. People like Lindbergh, for example.... [E]xposure to American history is so profound that you don't lose it even when you leave. It's very uncritical. It tends more to propaganda than to reality. It's more mythology than reality. I really had a different view of the States because of the Canadian experience. I had something to compare it to. That's very valuable: living next door to these people and having them so inextricably bound up in their own lives. I don't think I'm antagonistic. There are parts of America I still love. I enjoy the culture, some of it at any rate, and I cling to the memory of it. But I know it's now the dark side. You can see it clearly from here. When I went to school in California, there were no blacks, there was one Jew and yet we were surrounded by Oriental people and the Mexicans were not that far away. Racism was very much a fact of life. It was in the language. It was in the humour. It was in the culture.... I consider the Americans as dangerous right now. I mean it's too much of a good thing. They're too powerful. They're too deeply lost in their mythology. They've deceived each other for too long. They really believe God gave them special entry into the world.[5]

The thing that distressed Camp most about Brian Mulroney— who began as his apprentice in Tory politics, became his friend and ally and was ultimately his boss—was not his tendency to exaggeration and rhetorical overkill (though the hyperbole did cause Camp to cringe), it was the unabashed way, as prime minister, that Mulroney romanced presidents Ronald Reagan and the first George Bush. Camp described an incident in Washington when he accompanied Mulroney to visit Reagan. Mulroney and Reagan were strolling on the White House lawn with the President's dog, which loved to chase Frisbees. Reagan threw the Frisbee. "For a moment," Camp reported, deadpan, "we weren't sure which one was going to fetch it."[6]

CHAPTER 2

The Camps of
New Brunswick

THE FIRST EUROPEAN TO SET EYES on New Brunswick, historians say, was the French explorer Jacques Cartier, who sailed into Chaleur Bay in 1534 on the first of his three voyages to the Gulf of St. Lawrence. Seventy years later Samuel de Champlain and Pierre du Gua de Monts established the first settlement in what was then known as Acadia when they built a small community at the mouth of the St. Croix River. In the Treaty of Utrecht in 1713, France ceded Acadia to Britain, which called it Nova Scotia.

The modern history of New Brunswick can be traced to 1783, when 14,000 United Empire Loyalists, faithful to the British crown in the American War of Independence, poured into the colony. It was a huge influx for the tiny colony. Many of the newcomers took up crown grants of building lots in Parr Town (now Saint John) and in the fertile farmlands along the beautiful valley of the Saint John River. The following year, Britain split Nova Scotia into two parts at the Chignecto Isthmus, with the west and north portion becoming the separate colony of New Brunswick.

Dalton Camp's ancestors—his great-great-great-great-grandfather Captain Abiathar Camp, wife, Rebecca, and their two sons and one daughter—were part of that great 1783 immigration. They came to Parr Town from Connecticut, where the family had settled from England nearly 150 years earlier.[1]

Born in 1732 at Durham in Middlesex County, Connecticut, Abiathar Camp moved his family in about 1766 to New Haven, where he quickly became an exceedingly prosperous merchant. His holdings included a brewery, sawmill, farms, properties in town and part ownership of several sailing ships. He and his family were pro-British Tories down to their socks, and Abiathar became an increasingly prominent opponent of American independence—so much so that his elder son, Abiathar Camp Jr., was expelled from Yale College in 1775 because of the family's political views.[2]

Abiathar Sr. infuriated the Whigs, who controlled the Connecticut Assembly, when he refused to swear an oath of fidelity to the cause of independence shortly after the Battle of Lexington in 1776. That fall, the assembly declared Abiathar guilty of acts "unfriendly and inimical to the rights and liberties of the state, and dangerous to the said town of New Haven," and banished him to the town of Eastbury, Connecticut, to remain there under house arrest (at his own expense). The depth of the assembly's anger may be judged by the fact that it denied his petition to be permitted to leave Eastbury to attend religious services in Middletown, the location of the nearest Anglican church. The next year, Abiathar's attempt to change his place of residence to Wallingford was frustrated when the selectmen of that town refused to have him. Finally, in January 1778, Abiathar gave in: he presented his oath of fidelity and was allowed to return to New Haven.

Swearing the oath, however, in no way dampened Abiathar's Tory fervour. Over the next year and a half, he met or renewed an earlier friendship with Benedict Arnold, the American general who had distinguished himself in the revolutionary cause in the early stages of the war. According to Camp family lore, Abiathar was instrumental in "turning" Arnold from the side of the revolutionaries to the loyalist cause (thereby making the name of Benedict Arnold synonymous with treason for generations of American school children).

Abiathar Camp and Benedict Arnold were certainly friends, both in New Haven, where Abiathar was a captain in the loyalist militia and where Arnold had established a trading business, and later in New Brunswick, where Abiathar sold his friend a building lot in Parr Town for 30 guineas. A few years later, when Abiathar submitted a claim to the British government for compensation for his Connecticut properties that had been confiscated during the war (including the brewery), Benedict Arnold was one of those who testified to Abiathar's loyalty and service to the crown.

Arnold may not have required much "turning" by Abiathar or anyone else. Passed over for promotion in the military and resentful about his treatment by his superiors, he may have been ripe for conversion, and he would have found sympathy and support from Abiathar Camp and others in New Haven's Tory enclave. Whatever his motives, he changed sides, cast his lot with the British and ultimately joined the growing community of loyalists in New Brunswick. (Arnold stayed in Saint John for just five years before moving on. He died in England in 1801.)

Dalton Camp was descended from Abiathar Camp Sr. through George Camp, the third son (among nine children) of Abiathar Jr. As the family grew, it spread up the Saint John River Valley with land grants at Gagetown, Jemseg and other communities in Queen's County. Late in life, when he developed an interest in his family's history, Dalton took to exploring cemeteries in the vicinity of his rural New Brunswick home near Jemseg. He was often successful in locating the grave of at least one Camp.

By the time Dalton's father, Harold Brainard Camp, was born, the family was established in Woodstock, New Brunswick. Harold's father, Hezekiah Harris ("Harry") Camp, was a fireman on the railway and lived in Sucker Flat, a working-class area on the edge of Woodstock. By all accounts, Harry Camp was an irascible sort. In winter, as he fired the steam engines on the run from Macadam Junction north along the Saint John River to Edmundston near the Quebec border, school children would stand by the tracks and throw snowballs at the engine. Dalton's grandfather would fire back lumps of coal.

As far as is known, his son Harold, Dalton's father, did not finish high school. "Hal," as he was known in those days, took a job as the operator of the film projector at the Gaiety Theatre, Woodstock's only cinema. Changing reels during the movies may have been boring work, but at least it enabled Dalton's father to see every film that came to town.

As a youngster, Dalton himself would attend Saturday matinees. He would sit in the front row, near the piano player, and watch Tom Mix, Hoot Gibson and other cowboy heroes. Every Saturday good would overcome evil and virtue would triumph over vice. It was all,

Camp remembered, "appropriately, unmistakably, in black and white, including hats, shirts and horses. No villain, in my long experience at the movies, ever rode into town on a white horse."

> More than in any other childhood venue, the Gaiety Theatre Saturday matinee schooled and steeped its audience in the values of goodness, did so unambiguously, with perfect clarity, more clear and transparent than dogma or scripture. One thing to be taught the wages of sin, another to see how cheating, calumny, horse stealing, train robbery and cruelty brought certain retribution, shame and public rebuke, a hell on earth, whereas goodness, kindness and valour brought their own rewards, which included public approbation, the respect of friends and the admiration of women of demure, flawless beauty and character. Goodness was the certain augury of happy endings; often the theatre audience cheered the climax, after the hero had neatly shot the gun from the menacing hand of the villain, thus ending the chase and the confrontation with the forces of darkness. The inevitable victory of good over evil unfailingly stirred the heart and confirmed a world of heroic dimension.[3]

His work in the projection booth at the Gaiety gave Harold Camp the time, and perhaps the opportunity, to meet and fall in love with Aurilla Sanborn, a young woman from a higher social station in Woodstock; her father was a chemist with a local pharmaceutical company, and the family lived in a large house on Upper Queen Street. The middle-class Sanborns were not at all pleased about the infatuation of their beautiful, lively daughter—people would later describe her as a Helen Hayes look-alike—with the school dropout from Sucker Flat. Although they did not withhold parental consent when their independent-minded daughter, at 18, married Harold Camp, then 21, in October 1914, there is no indication that her mother or father attended the nuptials, which were performed in the home of a local clergyman. There was apparently no honeymoon trip, and the young couple started married life by moving in with her parents.

Before that, however, there occurred an event that would be the first of two turning points in the lives of Harold and Rilla and, ultimately, of their family. One evening, in the darkness of the projection booth at the Gaiety Theatre, Harold heard the voice of God commanding him to quit his job and enter the ministry. So powerful was the call that Harold fell to his knees in prayer. In later years, he would recount the experience from the pulpit for the benefit of his parishioners. The projectionist's cramped space in the balcony of the Gaiety, he would relate, became a "whole room full of God." The revelation—this being an age when divine "interventions" were taken a good deal more seriously than they are today—saved Harold from certain obsolescence as a movie projectionist and his family from a probable life of hardship, even penury.

The second turning point came when Aurilla's father decided, however reluctantly, to put his son-in-law through Acadia University, a Baptist college in Wolfville, Nova Scotia, where Harold studied divinity. While still a student at Acadia, Harold preached in Baptist churches throughout the Annapolis Valley, quickly building a reputation as an outstanding orator. After Acadia, he went on to a graduate school of divinity in Massachusetts. His first church after graduation was outside Boston. He then accepted an offer to move to Calvary Baptist Church in New Haven, Connecticut, the home of his ancestors. Located just off the Yale campus, Calvary Baptist was known as the "Yale Church," and Harold and Rilla moved in the same intellectual and social circles as Yale faculty members. Dalton and Sandy regularly attended services at their father's church and, on occasion, took part in the service. One Sunday Sandy read some scripture and young Dalton was to follow with a few words before the offering was taken. Instead, he told a joke that brought the house down:

> There were three boys, and they were boasting about how rich their fathers were. One boy said, "My father's a doctor, and all these rich people come to him, and he cures them, and they send him money. He's very rich." The second boy said, "Well, my father owns a store, and all these people come to him, and he sells them food. And every day he makes money selling food." And the third boy said, "My father is a minister, and on Sunday, he asks them for money, and it takes seven men to bring it all down to him." And then I said, "Will those seven men please come forward?" They were the ushers who take up

the collection. It was kind of an inside joke, but of course they got it. I was so pleased with myself.[4]

Dalton was beginning to be noticed by others as well. One day an English professor at Yale came for dinner at the Camp home. A proud Rilla produced some children's stories that Dalton had written when he was not much more than five years old. The professor was, or professed to be, impressed by the little boy's prose. "Take my word for it, this boy's going to be a famous writer," he told Dalton's parents. When he was nine, Dalton produced a newspaper he called the *Palooka Press*, two to four mimeographed pages of neighbourhood news and sports. At five cents a copy, he managed to attract between 10 and 15 customers.

Meanwhile, Harold Camp's reputation as an orator was increasing. He was in constant demand as a speaker in the United States and in New Brunswick when the family returned in summer. He was so highly regarded in Woodstock that whenever it was known he would be preaching, the church would be filled beyond capacity. One Sunday, in an effort to accommodate everybody who wanted to hear him, the organizers moved the church service to the local racetrack. They still could not find room for everyone.

When Dalton was nine years old, the family left New Haven for California, where Harold was to be the pastor of First Baptist Church in downtown Oakland. They travelled by train, riding in a Pullman car with Rilla and Harold in a stateroom, Sandy and Red in the lower berths and Dalton in an upper, which pleased him no end because it gave him the privacy in which to read undetected at night. As the train crossed the Mississippi, Dalton could sense his father's growing restlessness; the days were long, there was little to do and there were not enough newspapers to read. But where Harold was elated by thoughts of life in California and impatient to get there, Rilla was uneasy at the prospect of being a continent away from her beloved Woodstock. For all seven years that the family was in California—until Harold's death in 1937—Rilla would insist that the family return to Woodstock in the summer. She usually got her way, often over the objections of her husband, who preferred staying in California to summering in New

Brunswick, especially as his celebrity increased and the demands on his time mounted.

The train carrying the Camp family to their new life on America's west coast had just crossed from Arizona into California when the passengers felt a bump. The train stopped and, looking out the window, they could see a truck lying upside down in a ditch. A little later, after the train was moving again, the conductor came through the car and one of the passengers asked whether anyone had been killed in the accident. "No," the conductor replied, "just a Mexican." The incident stuck in Dalton's mind. Fifty years later, he wrote: "What I remember most about the accident is how much better everyone seemed to feel when they heard that."[5]

To Dalton, Oakland "seemed a new world, an exotic, sunstruck balmy world of palm and towering eucalyptus trees, a city without a city's noise and bustle or inner tensions, but settled and unhurried, backed by foothills to the east and with a clear view of San Francisco to the west, across the bay. I had never seen or felt or smelled anything like Oakland."[6] While Harold and Rilla looked for a home, the family stayed at the Claremont Hotel, which resembled a country club, in suburban Berkeley.

Most mornings, Dalton and Sandy would work their way through the hotel lobby collecting cigarette butts. They would take the elevator to the top floor, then the stairs to the roof, where Sandy, then 14 and always the more audacious of the brothers, would smoke the butts they had gathered. Dalton had already tried smoking, in a barn during a summer visit to Woodstock. The experiment had left him dizzy, and he remained a non-smoker until he joined the Canadian Army in the Second World War and found that free cigarettes (along with condoms) were part of the ration kits issued to soldiers. He started smoking to help relieve the tedium of army life.

His parents soon found a suitable home on a hillside in Piedmont, a wealthy, lily-white suburb adjacent to Oakland. The house boasted a spectacular view of San Francisco across the bay and had palm, lemon and eucalyptus trees in the yard. But Rilla was always looking to move. A few years later, she and Harold arranged to lease another house higher in the Piedmont hills, but after Harold had signed the contract she found another, larger house in Oakland that she liked much better. She became very unhappy with the house they had just leased. Harold, who could not bear to see his wife miserable, got out of the deal by telling the real estate agent that if he did not tear up the lease, he would sublet the house to a Negro family.[7]

In Dalton's high school class, ethnic diversity was represented by one boy of Italian extraction and one Jewish girl (and he fell in love with her, briefly). Just about everyone was rich. Dalton rode to school every day in a limousine with the son of the family across the street; it was driven, glamorously in his eyes, by a chauffeur who packed a gun.

Not everything about California was glamorous. Dalton was horrified one night when, fiddling with the family radio, he came across a live report of a lynching in progress. Three farm labourers, almost certainly Mexican, had been arrested for the kidnapping and murder of a local youth in nearby San Jose. A mob seized them from the jail where they were being held and carried them off to be hanged from a tree in the town square. "I fled to the privacy of my room and lay in the darkness, wracked by incomprehension and fear," Camp recalled.

> I was 10, and beginning to learn what it seems to me every white American child inevitably learned, which was to look without seeing, to hear without listening.... There was not one nation, but two, one indivisible, the other invisible.... One took for granted, as being in the natural order of things, that Negroes were porters or maids (where they were not entertainers), Japanese were gardeners, Chinese were cooks and laundrymen, Filipinos were houseboys and Mexicans worked the fields.[8]

Once settled in California, Rilla threw herself into her role as "the minister's wife," as she had in New Haven. She entertained tirelessly at dinners for her husband's friends, benefactors and associates, took her three sons to church every Sunday, and generally anchored the family. As Dalton saw her, his mother was "an extraordinary woman and, as the wife of a clergyman, a frequent contradiction."

THE CAMPS OF NEW BRUNSWICK

She also rode, played golf with fierce intensity, smoked cigarettes, enjoyed martinis, loved the theatre, novels and the movies, and was a constant reader. She played the piano, sang popular songs of the day and loved cooking, as had her mother before her. She dressed fashionably, believed in exercise, and watched her weight.... For all that, she was shy, or—I sometimes suspected—pretended shyness as a mask. This gave her an aura of vulnerability that concealed a whim of iron and a stubborn will. She could be subtly manipulative and boldly complicit, conspiring with my older brother in ways of violating father's random edicts and prohibitions. What she seemed to want most was that her sons would have what they wanted, which could be a car, or clothes, or tickets to games and entertainments, or simply the freedom to make their own choices. She demanded, in return, strict adherence to her own values, which included grammatical speech, tidiness and personal cleanliness and a strict avoidance of vulgarity, slang, profanity, salt and sugar.[9]

As Harold Camp's fame grew, his opinions and advice were sought by prominent Americans, including President Franklin Roosevelt. Harold's views placed him at the liberal end of the Baptist spectrum. Long active on the fringes of politics, he became caught up in the peace movement of the early 1930s. His liberalism rubbed off on his second son. "Growing up," Dalton wrote, "I developed an instant sympathy for the underdog, for the put-upon, the unemployed, the disadvantaged and the luckless. And for the Spanish republicans and the German Jews."[10]

It was a sympathy that Dalton never lost. In later life, he often spoke out for the disadvantaged in his newspaper columns, he opposed the use of the War Measures Act in the Quebec crisis of 1970 and he was an active member of the board of the Canadian Civil Liberties Association.

Harold Camp worked with the Czech-born movie star Francis Lederer in the World Peace Federation, which Lederer founded in 1934. Harold was one of the exponents of a proposal that the United States and other countries amend their constitutions to require that plebiscites be held to obtain the people's approval before governments could legally declare war. Although the idea may seem half-baked today, Harold took it seriously enough to travel to Germany in 1936 to seek the support of the World Baptist Convention. His pacifist beliefs were badly shaken by the militaristic mood he witnessed in Germany. One day he and some of his fellow American Baptists went to a Nazi rally in Berlin. The crowd began to demonstrate against them, swarming them and trapping them in the centre of the mob. Storm troopers had to escort the clergymen to safety. Harold returned home convinced that Hitler was intent on war in Europe—a belief he passed on to Roosevelt and expressed in public speeches in California as he tried to alert Americans to the threat of war.

Harold's warning angered the Hearst newspaper empire, specifically the *Oakland Tribune* and the San Francisco *Examiner*, which attacked him for being a warmonger. In response, he decreed that no Hearst paper would henceforth be allowed in his home. Rilla Camp, however, was having none of that. She liked both the *Examiner* and the *Tribune* for their theatre reviews, so she made an arrangement with the paperboy to leave the *Examiner*, a morning paper, in the fuse box outside. Once her husband had gone to work, Rilla would retrieve it. The *Tribune*, which came in the afternoon, was delivered, read and presumably hidden or destroyed before Harold came home.

Although "Hal" and "Bill" (as he called his wife) had what appeared to be a solid marriage—a happy family with a gracious, devoted mother and a handsome, successful father—the appearance was deceiving. "There were times when I believed it myself, and other times I half believed it. Still other times, I knew better," Dalton recalled. Harold had a booming voice and violent temper, and he and his wife fought frequently. As often as not, it fell to Dalton to be the peacemaker:

> I was frightened, angered and humiliated by these outbursts. What frightened me was seeing my father out of control, aware of his strength and power, and [I was] angered because the rages interfered with the even tenor of my life. As I grew older—by the time I was 10 or so—I became a self-appointed intervener and referee in these disputes between my parents. I was often the only other person present, since the arguments usually began at night, after dinner, when my younger

brother would be in bed and my older brother would be at large, in the neighbourhood.... But it fell to me to maintain peace in the family, as best I could, and to contain the damage whenever the wars between my mother and father were resumed. As I grew more experienced, I developed my own technique for ending these outbursts of Father's wrath and Mother's defiance. I would cry, or shout, as loudly as they, so that it often ended in their trying to placate and silence me.[11]

During the Second World War, Dalton left Acadia University to enlist as a private in the Canadian Army. Before long, he was sent to take a course and face a board of examiners who would decide whether he was "officer material." The candidates were paraded before the board of senior officers, "to be grilled by them with the purpose of unnerving the candidate, or making him lie, be evasive, or otherwise demonstrate qualities unbecoming a leader of men." The grilling included such questions as, when did you last masturbate, or seek the services of a prostitute, or wet the bed? When it was Camp's turn, he was asked, "Did your mother and father fight?" He replied, "Fought all the time, sir." His examiners seemed entertained and impressed. "I knew, at that moment in my military career, I was seen as a leader of men, or, at least, eligible to become one."[12]

The greatest shock of Camp's young life was the discovery that his famous father, the great preacher, moralist, friend of the rich and famous and defender of family values, had a secret life. The discovery troubled Dalton so deeply that he could not bring himself to talk about it with anyone, not even members of his immediate family, until toward the end of his life, when he was struggling with problems with his second wife, Wendy. As he grew old, Camp began to reflect on personal morality, sexual ethics and people's behaviour in their private lives, and he talked guardedly about an incident in California when he was a boy. The Camp family had a cottage to which the Reverend Camp would repair for a couple of days each week, ostensibly to escape the demands of his congregation while he worked on his sermon for Sunday. The cottage was some distance from the city, but young Dalton decided one day to ride his bicycle out to see his father. He rode into the property, saw his father's car, threw down his bike, ran up the steps and banged on the front screen door, which was locked. "Dad, Dad," he called. Then, through the screen, he saw his father get up from the couch with a semi-clad woman. There was a delay while Harold straightened his clothes, then he came to the door and said, "What the hell are you doing here? Shouldn't you be at home? I'm not to be disturbed here. I've got important work to do." Confused and upset, Dalton rode his bicycle back to Piedmont.[13]

Relationships in the Camp family were a tangled web. The parents fought. Rilla clearly loved, and spoiled, her first son more than her second or third—to the extent that she secretly helped Sandy to buy a car (an old Ford coupe) in defiance of Harold's orders. Although his father frightened him when he lost control, Camp adored his clergyman father ("I thought he was a formidable man.... I loved him very much," he told an interviewer in 1998). But he struggled for years to come to terms with Harold's hypocrisy and infidelity. And Harold never quite trusted Sandy. They battled over all the usual teenage issues: girls, cars, beer and smoking. "[Sandy] had the hard life as a minister's son that I never had.... Sanborn got on his nerves, and my mother was always in between them."[14]

When Camp looked back on his seven years in California, his clearest memory, aside from his father's funeral, was the period of many months that he spent in bed with blood poisoning in both feet. He was a high school athlete who played football and basketball and fancied himself a track star. Suddenly, he found himself with a serious infection in his big toes—the result, he was told, of wearing track shoes that were too small. Those being the days before penicillin, the infection persisted. Camp was in and out of school, unable to play sports and forced to wear sneakers with the toes cut out. Inflamed from the infection, the toes oozed a ghastly looking yellow liquid. The doctors removed his toenails, but to no avail. They contemplated amputating the toes. In the end, a procedure of cauterizing the open wounds and frequently soaking the toes in hot water and Epsom salts defeated the infection.

For the better part of a year, however, Camp was out of school, mostly in hospital or at home in bed, lying with a "bird cage" over his feet to protect the toes from the weight of the blankets. He listened incessantly to popular songs on the radio, typing out the lyrics on a typewriter in his bed. His father exploded when he discovered how his son was passing the time. He went to his bookcase and pulled down Walter Lippmann's *A Preface to Morals*, telling Dalton if he was going to be stuck in bed, he should use his time profitably by reading the works of important thinkers. Dalton, who loved to read anyway, soaked up the books his father chose for him, including a biography of Abraham Lincoln. His lifelong interest in serious literature dates to that year in bed in California. He never did develop any interest in fiction, even though he tried years later to write an autobiographical novel.

If a passion for literature was the lasting byproduct of his blood poisoning, another effect probably had a more immediate impact on the teenage Dalton. It was the year when all his friends were taking dance classes and going to proms and parties. He alone did not know how to dance. "I was envious and complained to my older brother," Camp recalled.

> "Don't let it bother you," Sandy said. "I will teach you." I had watched him dance with Mother at home; he was masterful, graceful, poised. They danced the foxtrot. This would be especially hard for me to do, since I had retained a profound if subliminal fear of having anyone step on my toes. I confessed this limitation to Sandy. He was, in his familiar way, reassuring. "You don't have to learn the foxtrot," he told me. "Just hold the girl in your arms and move your body slowly. You hardly need to move your feet at all."
>
> "But that's not the foxtrot," I protested.
>
> "I know," Sandy said. "It's called the 'Walking F——.' Women love it."
>
> "I don't believe you."
>
> "You'll see," he said.[15]

Harold Camp's sudden death at age 43 left his family virtually penniless. His large salary and affluent lifestyle masked serious financial problems. The family could ill afford the extravagant house that Rilla had been so anxious to have. He had no life insurance. "He thought he was going to live forever," Dalton said. "Insurance was too sophisticated a thing for him. Financially, he wasn't very sophisticated. Money was so easy for him. He thought it would go on forever and could only get better.... He wasn't planning on dying at 43."[16] The church congregation raised a handsome sum of money for Rilla, and she lived off it for a number of years after she, Dalton and Red returned to Woodstock.

But first, Dalton had a particularly poignant task—to say good-bye to his California girlfriend, Carole, the daughter of the widowed president of a food packaging company. Carole had a head of thick blonde curls. "She was shy and dryly funny, and while our relationship was platonic, it was not without affection and warmth," Camp recalled. He went to see her on his last evening before leaving for Canada. They sat in the kitchen and talked. She began to weep. "Whenever I love someone, I lose them," she cried. He led her to a couch in the living room and held her in his arms. They sat silently, holding hands, for a long time. "Suddenly," Camp said, "a light went on and Carole's father appeared before us in his bathrobe. I made an unsuccessful attempt to stand up, but he motioned to me to stay where I was. 'Oh, Dalton,' he said agreeably, 'I'm glad to see you. Can I get you a Coke?' I did not leave until the dawn broke over my last day in Piedmont, California."[17]

Camp left California with a perspective on life that remained with him. Writing years later to his eldest son, David Camp, he said his father's sudden and unexpected death had convinced him that life really was a "fleeting, one-way run... and there was no time for the conventional, for self-suffocation and boredom." In other words, life is short and irreversible; live it your way and live it to the full. "[Dalton] really had a sense of his own mortality—and that was a kind of tuning fork for him," David said. "He was very honest about life, because he knew just how quickly life passes."[18]

CHAPTER 3
_____

Growing Up Canadian

RETURNING FROM CALIFORNIA in the fall of 1937, Dalton Camp quickly found that living in Woodstock, New Brunswick, was a very different experience from visiting the town for summer holidays. The summers had been a remarkable time for Camp: he had been a celebrity among the locals, an object of curiosity and envy, a unique phenomenon from an exotic locale, dressed in his Levi jeans, white sneakers and the stylish, colourful shirts that boys his age wore in the big cities of California.

He was the only boy in Woodstock in those idyllic summers who brought his own music with him to parties in town and corn boils at nearby Skiff Lake. He had a small portable gramophone that he carried in a case along with records from his private collection. His taste in music seemed the epitome of sophistication and worldliness to his friends in Woodstock. He knew the words to the latest songs, had seen all the new movies and had even been to the Chicago World's Fair. He had taken boxing lessons, played golf, seen the Yankees play in New York City. He was a strong swimmer who knew the Australian crawl. He had a father who was famous and a mother who possessed a wonderful singing voice and, in the eyes of small-town New Brunswick, dressed like a movie star.

All that changed with the death of Harold Camp and the family's return to the town where Dalton had been born 17 years earlier, but where he had not lived since he was a toddler. "It was no longer a universe built to order for me, revolving between town and cottage, friends, golf and the endless sunshine of summer days," he recalled. "I felt isolated and very much alone, with little to do." The memory of the spellbinding preacher faded quickly in the minds of the townspeople of Woodstock. "He would soon be forgotten. There was no one in my life who wanted to remember him, including, I was coming to realize, my mother."[1]

Dalton was bored silly. There was nothing to engage his intellect or satisfy his hunger for excitement. Woodstock was typical of thousands of small towns across North America. It was quiet, well treed, pretty enough, filled with well-maintained churches—and it was stagnant, with its one theatre, one rundown hotel and one-crop economy (potatoes). Its population in 1937 was around 3,500. (By the end of the century, it had barely reached 5,000.) Once they tore down the clock tower on the post office, the town had few striking architectural features. It boasted the L.P. Fisher Library, the L.P. Fisher Hospital and the L.P. Fisher School—all named after a local lawyer who was the town's principal benefactor. It was also a narrow, intolerant town. "There was hardly a Jew in Woodstock, but there were an awful lot of anti-Semites," Camp recalled.[2]

He worried about Rilla, her loneliness, her vulnerability and her lingering sense of rage over Harold's premature death, which had unalterably diminished her life. She was obsessively concerned about her eldest child, Sandy, who had stayed behind in California and who made no appreciable effort to keep in touch with his family in New Brunswick. She lost contact with her friends in California. By the time she died, the only vestiges of her earlier life consisted of a few letters from a cousin and a half-dozen Christmas cards from Earl Warren, the governor of California.

Rilla was a cultured woman. The social graces were important to her, and she loved the theatre, music, food and books. She and Dalton read plays to each other; they went to movies and listened to the radio together. A great baseball fan, she followed the Boston Red Sox religiously, listening to every game she could on the radio and later on television.

As her eyesight failed, she would pull her chair within two feet of the TV set to watch the game. Rilla had perfect musical pitch, which Dalton inherited, along with his father's command of the spoken word. "When Dalton spoke he could always hit the right notes, say things in just the right way," said his son David. "He used his voice like an organ. Maybe he got it from both parents."[3]

Rilla's life was burdened by the need to care for her youngest son Red. When they were living in California, she was able to send him off by taxi each day to a special school. In Woodstock, services for the handicapped barely existed. She put Red in a Roman Catholic school for a period of time. Although the sisters were wonderful with him, he needed more care than they could provide, and Rilla eventually had to look after him at home. Red had a prodigious memory and a passion for trains. His favourite activity was to go to the railway station in Woodstock to watch the trains—and one day he outdid himself: he hijacked a yard engine and drove it out of town.

Many years later, when Camp and his second wife were constructing Northwood, their retreat in the Saint John River Valley, they built an apartment in the house for Rilla and Red. Red lived on there after his mother's death, until Dalton had his heart transplant in 1993. At that time, the family moved him into a group home on a farm not far from Northwood. He still lives there, a cheerful, outgoing elderly man who wears railroad caps and loves to be taken into Fredericton for the farmers' market on Saturdays.

Dalton's closest friend in Woodstock was Buddy Chase, the son of his mother's best friend and stepson of the local pharmacist (Buddy's father was killed in a shootout in the United States, or so the story went). The two boys fished for eels off the bridge over the Meduxnekeag River, which joins the Saint John River at Woodstock. They swam and canoed at the Camp family cottage on Skiff Lake, played cards and engaged in petty larceny:

> I would go with him to his stepfather's drugstore, where he would stock up on "French safes," as they were mysteriously called, and cigarettes. This routine pilferage perplexed me: I knew he smoked cigarettes and always carried a safe in his wallet, which I assumed was to impress others. But what else? As it turned out, the boyish Buddy, with the auburn hair and spit curl, whom his mother would describe as "my darling baby," was a hellraiser in the countryside, enjoying a secret life of licentiousness and carnality that a schoolyard of braggarts could only envy.
>
> The incongruity still impresses me if only because, in matters of worldliness and sophistication, I believed myself to be his mentor. Reality required a period of adjustment in our relationship; I came to treat him with greater respect, since I had to conclude he knew more

about "the facts of life"—a catchall euphemism for knowing what the missionary position was, or a French kiss, or going all the way (in detail) or heavy petting to climax.[4]

Dalton found himself a girl in Woodstock. She was, he recalled, a lissome blonde with a radiant smile and an embracing directness. Her father had been a mink rancher, and when the bottom fell out of the fur market in the Depression, she left school to help support the large family. One day they walked out along Houlton Road and, on impulse, climbed up the ladder of a fuel storage tank. "Seated on top," Camp remembered, "looking down uneasily to the ground below, I said to her, 'I would like to kiss you, but I'm afraid you might fall off.' She replied, in her quiet, gentle way, 'I think you should worry about yourself.' I thus became both smitten and deeply enamoured and would remain so for years to come."[5]

Rilla Camp, worried about Dalton's education, insisted he leave Woodstock and go to a private school. He chose Ricker Collegiate Academy, a small boarding school in Houlton, Maine, just across the United States border from Woodstock, because it offered both a basketball program and American football (as opposed to the English rugby played at schools in New Brunswick in those days). He lasted two days, leaving after he discovered students were not permitted to go into town during the week.

His mother quickly registered him at Horton Academy, a boarding school located on the campus of Acadia University (which she and Harold had both attended) in Wolfville, Nova Scotia. Wolfville was another small town with one main street and no traffic lights, but it was a university town with shops and services devoted to the needs of its Acadia and Horton clientele. Camp set off for Horton with his emotions clothed "in an armour of stoicism and fatalism.... Come what may, I would remain calm, aloof, disinterested."[6] Yet Horton proved a comforting setting for a boy trying to come to terms with the loss of his father and his abrupt uprooting from the big cities and bright lights of California.

Something of a jock, Camp played on the school basketball team and later on, while a student at Acadia, he coached the Horton team.

Wolfville was a community with a profound Baptist tradition—which helped make it a difficult place in which to get into trouble, though some did manage the feat. One was Camp's roommate, a boy from Moncton who enjoyed minor celebrity at Horton because his sister had dated a member of the Toronto Maple Leafs. Handsome, withdrawn and unsmiling, he was also an alcoholic, the first one Camp had encountered. In those days, Camp neither smoked nor drank. But his roommate drank in their room almost every night and sometimes in the morning before lunch.

The Canadian winter was a new and unpleasant experience for the boy from California. The clothing list for Horton required students to equip themselves with three pairs of long underwear, an instruction Camp deliberately ignored. Most people at Horton and Acadia skated at the university rink and took their dates there, but Camp did not know how to skate and was too self-conscious or proud to learn. The recreational alternative in winter was Carver's pool hall, where members of the Acadia varsity hockey and football teams went to shoot pool and smoke cigarettes because smoking was not permitted in university residences. (Carver's was also known as the one place in town where students could buy condoms without attracting attention or gossip.) Camp and some of his Horton friends repaired to Carver's in winter, partly because it was warmer than the rink or standing around in the street.

He repeatedly ran afoul of the school's assistant principal, a florid-faced man named Edwards who lived in an apartment in Camp's residence. One evening, he was summoned to the home of the headmaster, Ernest Robinson, to answer a complaint that Edwards had laid against him. The headmaster reviewed the complaint, which centred on Camp's "attitude." "You know, Camp," he said, "there are as many trains leaving Wolfville as there are trains arriving. I think you should be on the next one out. I suggest you go back to your room and begin packing. We will help get your luggage to the station tomorrow."

Wondering how to tell his mother that he had been expelled, Camp returned to his residence, only to be called to the phone. Fearing it was his mother, he was almost relieved to hear the headmaster's voice. "Camp," he said, "I have given more thought to our talk. If you think you can improve your behaviour here, we might give you another try at things. It's up to you. You think about it tonight, and first thing tomorrow morning you let Mr. Edwards know your plans. If you stay, I will see you in class. But it's up to you."

Camp went to see Edwards in the morning and told him of his ardent wish to stay at Horton. The assistant principal told him he had a personality problem, that he was his own worst enemy. "I was obliged to listen to this until, at the end of his lecture, he produced a copy of Dale Carnegie's best-seller, *How to Win Friends and Influence People*, which he offered to sell me at a special price," Camp remembered. "I told him I had already read it. Silly bastard."[7]

Camp excelled in English at Horton, where he edited the school yearbook and was awarded a prize for proficiency and promise in English, along with a cheque for $75, which was a significant sum in the Depression years. He did well in the social sciences and managed adequate marks in math. But Latin was his Waterloo. Not even a sympathetic teacher could give him any sort of a passing grade in the subject. He was able to graduate from Horton and be admitted to Acadia (in science) because someone—Camp never knew who—gave him credit for three years of Spanish in California, courses he had never, in fact, taken.

The summer following his graduation from Horton Academy marked the end of innocence for tens of thousands of young people like Camp. It was the summer of 1939 and Harold Camp's worst fears were about to be realized. "War was coming," Dalton recalled. "You could sense the coming from beyond the earth's curve, not a distant thunder, but on an eerily silent wind, a light wind that turned the leaves over, their soft white undersides showing in the sun. People always said it was a sign of a coming rain...."

Walking along Lower Broadway [in Woodstock], on a still, airless afternoon, I recall hearing Adolf Hitler's voice on radio, coming out from behind a screen door. I heard the sounds of a crowd, and an American voice talking over it, explaining what Hitler was saying and why the crowd was cheering. People were beginning to talk about the possibility of war now, the way people might talk about being struck by lightning—something possible, yet unlikely.

It was a summer of heightened sensation, as though the ice cream were colder, the choke cherry bushes heavier with their berries, the sun higher, the shade darker, the nights longer. The music seemed more haunting, though we laughed longer, as if laughter were a treasure that might soon be spent. It was a season of small pleasures; life was anecdotal, time measured by the length of an embrace, a kiss, an early morning round of golf, by swimming naked under the railway bridge at Bull Creek, the water lit by a burning fire under a steaming kettle of fresh corn harvested from an unknown farmer's field. Seamless, sensuous, seemingly endless, one summer's day folded into the next while Italy invaded Albania and the Germans marched into Danzig and Vienna.[8]

The war was still a few years away for Camp as he prepared to enter Acadia. No country club college, Acadia was notable for its steadfast moral centre and its inflexible standards of right and wrong. Although few students, including Camp, actually lived up to the school's rigid standards, they knew what was expected of them and they understood the consequences of disobedience: family humiliation, parental wrath and private shame. In those days, some provinces tried to control the purchase and consumption of alcoholic beverages by requiring residents to obtain permits that they had to produce whenever they bought a bottle of liquor. When a student from Saint John lost his liquor permit and it was found on campus, he was unceremoniously expelled from Acadia.

Camp himself was placed on probation after he skipped 67 classes in one term. A prominent member of both the university football team and the basketball team, his passion was clearly sports and not academics. Acadia's president, F.W. Patterson, wrote to Rilla Camp, setting down five conditions under which her son would be permitted to stay at the university. These included attending class and giving up sports. "I am sorry this is necessary," Patterson wrote, "but if he is unwilling to do the work he is wasting his time and your money. You will see this at once."

Rilla called the president, listened to details of her son's misbehaviour, then replied: "All I can say to you, Dr. Patterson, is that he was a good boy when he left home." This maternal intervention, Camp believed, helped to stay the hand of those who wanted him thrown out of Acadia—"and, I hasten to add, not without cause."[9]

Life in Woodstock became kinder and gentler when he returned home for the summer holidays. Camp entered into an intimate relationship with a young woman he identified only as "C." They became inseparable, sleeping together each night in a screened sleeping porch at her house. "At dawn, I would leave for home, taking the shortcut through the Broadway schoolyard, then moving silently like a ghost through the cemetery to Queen Street South to let myself in and climb the stairs to my attic room, where I slept through much of the morning," Camp wrote. "Mother had no idea of this arrangement; in her diary there is a single entry reading, 'Dalt and C are off somewhere and I am alone.' This plaintive note characterized our relationship during the summer."[10]

Although Dalton was now the man of the house, the family's provider and nurturer in all ways other than financial, he was also fiercely independent, secretive and private. He followed his own agenda, reading Tolstoy and poetry, writing short stories and swimming in Meduxnekeag River. "I was seldom lonely, except in crowds," he recalled. "Since childhood I had sought my own space—on the upper limbs of trees, in the woods, drifting on tranquil waters in a canoe, finding secret corners of the house, in upper cupboards and empty attics. With Thoreau, I could say 'I love to be alone, and no more lonely than the loon in the pond that laughs so loud.' I enjoy silence; without silence one cannot hear one's voice. I do not talk to myself, but rather communicate with my own inner voice.... I sought solitude partly out of uncertainty about my own identity, anxious not to be known until I knew myself as someone I wanted to be."[11]

Years later, in a letter to his son David, Camp would reflect on the confused and troubled youth that he had been at that time: "When I was your age, I was reading everything except what I was required to read, challenging all authority, imposing my temperament on others, inflicting petty hurts on womankind, writing with more honesty, perception, depth and feeling than anyone else I knew of my age and company. I was not the best, fastest, strongest athlete in the school, but I was the quickest, and with a flair for dramatics, the most inspiring and resourceful. And I was terribly unsure about myself, where to go, how to escape the trap I saw so many older people [caught] in."

Although Camp did not know it yet, his life was about to change in more ways than one. First, he met and fell in love with Linda Atkins, a fellow student at Acadia. Linda's family had been Canadians who in the era of the sailing ship had been in the shipping and trading business on Canada's east coast. As steam replaced sail, the business gravitated south, away from ports like Halifax to such American ports as Boston and New York. The Atkins clan followed the commerce, but they maintained a strong Canadian connection, summering in Canada and sending their children back to Canada for high school and university. Linda was raised in Montclair, New Jersey, outside New York City, and she had her heart set on attending Smith College in Massachusetts. Her parents vetoed that. Linda would go to university in Canada—to Acadia, where her father and mother had studied.

She spotted Camp at a basketball game on her first day at Acadia, but did not get to know him until her third year. In the meantime, Camp was dating another girl, while Linda, a cheerleader and member of the school's gymnastics tumbling squad, was going out with the captain of the football team. She was the sort of girl men instantly noticed: she was small, shapely and very pretty, and she carried herself with a style that reflected her upbringing in a prosperous suburb of New York.

Linda remembered being at dinner at Acadia one night when she heard a bantering male voice from the next table: "That sweater's a little too tight, isn't it?" It was Camp, being a smartass.

"I was so mad that I looked over and I said, 'There are people at that table who wear their pants too tight,'" Linda remembered. "Right away, I felt bad about saying that. As it happened, we were having a Sadie Hawkins skating party that night. Dalton was standing there, and I said, 'Would you like to skate?' He had skates on, but he'd come from California and he really didn't know how to skate at all. We started around the rink and I thought, 'Hmm, he can't skate, but he has a sense of humour.'"[12]

Camp asked her for a date for the following day and took her to lunch in nearby Kentville. Linda quickly concluded she had misjudged the young man from California. Far from being the flippant jock that he had initially seemed to be, she found him earnest, intelligent, informed and highly articulate, as well as funny. Afterward, Camp excused himself, saying he had to get back to Wolfville to make a speech to students at Horton Academy. Linda tagged along, heard him speak for the first time and was bowled over. "I said to myself, 'Aha. This is somebody I'm really going to be interested in,' and it developed from there. I guess you could say I loved him for the rest of his life."[13]

Linda and Dalton would marry, but first the war intruded. An indifferent student at best, Camp knew he was not going anywhere academically at Acadia. In 1942, in his junior year, he followed the path taken by many of his friends: he dropped out of university to join the military. Impulsively, he chose the air force because he had read in the Saint John *Telegraph Journal* that there was an urgent need for tail gunners for bombers. What he did not realize was that the shortage was caused by the high attrition rate among tail gunners. "Even so, had I known, I would not have been deterred, since I believed in my own immortality, a conceit shared by many others."[14]

He was saved from his conceit by the air force's medical examiners: he flunked the eye examination. Bad eyesight had been a characteristic of the Camp clan since the days of Abiathar Camp in the eighteenth century. Camp had only 20 per cent vision in his right eye, and, shortage or no, the air force was not in the market for tail gunners with only one good eye.

The army did not want him, either. The deputy recruiting officer in Saint John, a colonel who was a First World War buddy of George Atkins, Linda's father, told Camp he was wasting his time trying to get into the army. Even if he succeeded, he would never be more than a private on account of his eyesight. But Camp persisted. However reluctantly, the army took him—and promptly assigned him to a desk job writing routine press releases at its public relations office in Saint John. It was not a happy time:

> [I was] relegated to the narrow confines of a crowded office, tasked with a relentlessly routine responsibility, a stranger in a dark, crumbling old city, lodged in a decrepit wood-frame house backing on a brewery whose operations emitted the stench of boiling hops during the long nights of silence and isolation. No radio, no telephone, no books, no papers or journals. By far, it was the hardest time of my life. I reminded myself of someone in solitary confinement.[15]

Camp neither smoked nor drank in those days, which was fortunate because on his private's wages of $1.20 a day he could afford neither vice. Instead, he saved his money for occasional visits to the Admiral Beatty Hotel, the leading hostelry in Saint John, where he would buy a Boston newspaper and sit in the lobby to read it, very slowly, while maintaining the air of a guest who had a room upstairs and was simply killing time while waiting to meet someone. Those dreary evenings were the highlight of his tour of duty in Saint John.

After a few months of this, Camp overslept one morning, was late for parade and was sent before the commanding officer for disciplinary action. The colonel, however, was more interested in why Camp was a mere private riding a desk. In those days, recruits who had been to university were expected to be officers, not enlisted men. When Camp explained his eye problem, the colonel sent him for another examination to see whether his eyesight had improved. This time the test was administered by an elderly ophthalmologist in private practice. In the darkened examining room, Camp covered his bad right eye with his right hand and read the chart flawlessly. "Very good," said the doctor. "Now, the other eye." On impulse, he put his left hand over the right eye and read the chart perfectly again. The subterfuge succeeded. "Very good," the doctor pronounced as he turned the lights back on. Camp was immediately posted to Fredericton for basic infantry training. Visions of European battlefields danced in his head.

CHAPTER 4

War and Marriage

I F EVER THERE WERE A YOUNG MAN who was singularly ill suited for military life, it was Dalton Camp. He was solitary, introspective, unsure of his expectations for himself and often uncomfortable in the company of others. He was probably beginning to experience his "Black Dog," a term Camp would borrow from his idol, Winston Churchill, to describe the periodic bouts of depression that afflicted both men as they grew older. He had already left one boarding school because he could not accept the rules, been threatened with expulsion by a second and been put on probation by Acadia University for, among other things, failing to show up for classes.

The military demanded conformity and obedience—neither of which was part of Camp's makeup. Something of an elitist, he had a high opinion of his own intelligence, individuality and talents. He found the army to be a no man's land of arcane protocol and arbitrary regulation. Officers and enlisted men both wore khaki uniforms during the day, but when off duty or on leave, officers were permitted to change to tailored uniforms made of lighter, more comfortable fabric, and they could wear shoes in place of military boots. Enlisted men had to stay in their heavy khaki and boots. Officers could wear ties; ordinary soldiers were not allowed to. Officers protected their fingers from the Canadian winter in lined leather gloves; the lower ranks wore wool mittens (and Camp was allergic to wool).

When he reported for basic training at No. 70 Infantry Training Centre in Fredericton, Dalton (or "Butch" as he was sometimes called by his fellow recruits) was issued a rifle, bayonet, ground sheet, package of field dressings, backpack, web belt, ammunition pouches and puttees. He learned to snap to attention, to shoulder arms, order arms, present arms, quick march, slow march and all the other commands, as recruits marched monotonously about the parade square or drill hall. He slept in a barrack of double bunks and took all his meals in a mess hall. During meals, a junior officer would appear, accompanied by a sergeant who called out: "Any complaints?" There never were any, the recruits having learned that in the military silence was golden and anonymity was protection against demands from superiors. This denial of personality was central to a recruit's strategy for survival.

Camp's most vivid memory of basic training had nothing to do with the mindless drills. It was the dental examination he was required to submit to before moving out for advanced training. Like poor eyesight, bad teeth ran in his family. The military dentist extracted two of his back teeth, without benefit of anesthetic; the pain was excruciating and he bled profusely. "The wound was neither wide as a church door nor deep as a well, as Falstaff said, but it was enough," he remembered.[1] The army gave him 24 hours to recover before shipping him for advanced training at a centre with the wildly misleading name of Camp Utopia.

Thomas More would have been appalled. Located in Charlotte County in the southern part of New Brunswick, Utopia was an isolated and cheerless place. Rows of huts and prefab offices stretched along treeless dirt roads; a raw chill and frequent fogs rolled in from the Bay of Fundy. The camp was in the middle of a blueberry bog, but the military being the military, the troops were forbidden to pick the berries. The nearest civilian life was in the village of St. George—too far to walk.

Every now and again, the soldiers would be rousted out of bed at two or three o'clock in the morning and sent out on four- to five-mile runs. At least that broke the tedium. Movies were infrequent, the most notable being films about venereal disease, which seemed in the minds of the camp's commanders to rank close behind the German army as a menace to Canada's fighting men. When they were not training, Camp and his fellows drank warm beer, smoked free cigarettes and played poker. Until Utopia, Camp had eschewed tobacco and liquor because he regarded himself as an athlete and wanted to keep fit, and because he simply was not interested in smoking or drinking. That changed at Utopia. "There wasn't much to do there except smoke and drink," said Fred Chase, who went through advanced training with Camp and was later his neighbour in New Brunswick.

Camp used his weekend passes to continue his courtship of Linda Atkins. Although she had graduated from Acadia in 1942 and taken a job in New York's financial district, she and her family continued to summer in New Brunswick, at their cottage at Robertson's Point on Grand Lake, south of Fredericton. Camp would check a motorcycle out of the motor pool at Utopia for the two-hour ride to Robertson's Point—a spot that would occupy a large place in his future family and political life. There was never much doubt that Linda would agree to marry him, but she did not make it easy for him. "I said to him, 'Dalton, my father's rather old-fashioned, and I am his only daughter, so you'll have to go and see him and ask him properly.'"[2]

While on a leave from his unit at Utopia, Camp went to Montclair, New Jersey, where Linda was staying in her family home, then took a commuter train into Manhattan to meet George Atkins for lunch near his office. They walked up and down Wall Street, and walked, and walked. Thoroughly intimidated, Camp was terrified to ask the question. Atkins, who knew perfectly well what the young man wanted, was getting worn out, wondering to himself, "Is this kid ever going to do it, or am I going to have to walk forever?" They were in the middle of Wall Street, when Camp finally blurted, "Mr. Atkins, I'd like to marry your daughter." Atkins replied, "Well, if she thinks she can put up with you for the rest of her life, there's not much I can do about it. Can we stop now? My feet are tired." This scene was replayed many times at Camp and Atkins family gatherings over the years. It always got a laugh.[3]

As it turned out, however, Linda's father was not the young couple's major obstacle. The Canadian Army was less obliging than George Atkins. It dictated that soldiers (including Lance Corporal Camp) needed permission to marry. Officers did not. Camp had assumed that the process of permission would be pro forma. It was not: "I appeared before Captain Palmer, whose family were shoemakers. A lean, sallow, dull man with a hesitant, barely audible voice, Palmer, sitting behind his desk, received me with palpable suspicion."

He proceeded to grill Camp. How long had he known Linda? Did he know her family? Was he aware the countryside was filled with young girls who sought to marry soldiers to get their hands on the $35-a-month marriage allowance? Insulted and humiliated, Camp said nothing, resisting an urge to kick the captain in the groin. Captain Palmer launched into a lecture on the perils of rushing into marriage in wartime. Saying Camp needed more time to reflect on the matter, he denied his request to marry.

Not about to be put down by "some tank town shoemaker," Camp went over the captain's head to—whom else?—the company sergeant major. "In the esteem of the lower orders of the military, the company sergeant major far outranked captains, whose duties were often obscure and who were uniformly suspect of being either unsuited for serious work or unfit to fight," he recounted. The sergeant major, in civilian life a plumber from Woodstock named Pickel, was sympathetic. He sent Camp to see the camp's padre, who quickly gave his blessing to the marriage.[4]

Camp wangled a 96-hour pass. He and Linda Atkins were married in Fredericton in August 1943. After the reception they took the train to Saint John for their honeymoon at the Admiral Beatty Hotel, the same establishment where not so many months earlier Camp had passed his evenings reading newspapers in the lobby and pretending he had the wherewithal to rent a room. This time, the hotel manager met the newlyweds in the lobby and welcomed "Mr. and Mrs. Camp" with a flourish. At the end of the 96 hours, Linda returned to her parents' home in New Jersey and her job in New York, while he returned to Utopia.

He rose through the ranks of non-commissioned officers: lance corporal to corporal to sergeant to sergeant-instructor. He felt comfortable as a sergeant, and he enjoyed being an instructor. But his commanding officer was pressing him to apply for officer training school. Camp turned to his father-in-law, George Atkins, for advice, writing to him from Camp Utopia about his dilemma:

It's about the first time I've been unable to make up my mind and come to my own decision. Usually, I like to decide for myself and then dive in. If I'm wrong, I can always blame myself.... But right now I'm stymied.... I'm fully aware of the financial compensations of a commission, and there are others who think that being a gentleman in His Majesty's Forces is equivalent to a seat in the House of Lords. I could never see it that way, having seen too many fools who were officers and so many gentlemen who were corporals.

He told his father-in-law that he was more than willing to undergo all the "grind and punishment" of the officer training course, but he dreaded being washed out at the end of the course by an eye examination that would reveal he should not have been allowed in the army in the first place. He would not make lieutenant. He would lose his sergeant's stripes. He would be busted to private, then be discharged because of his physical disability.

In the end, Camp set his fears and reservations aside and accepted assignment to officer selection school in Brockville, Ontario. He would take his chances with the inevitable eye test. Linda left her job in New York and joined him in Brockville. Successfully completing the six-week course, he was ready to be promoted to lieutenant. As he had anticipated, the army required every officer candidate to pass a medical examination before the graduation parade: "I was always just waiting to be nailed on a medical.... They'll find out I'm just as blind as I was when I came in."[5]

Miraculously, his luck held. Rather than stay in barracks on the base, Linda and Dalton, like many other couples, had bent the rules and rented rooms in town. The night before his medical exam, an earthquake struck Brockville, shaking the house and breaking a few windows. The Camps rushed into the street in their nightclothes, where they waited with neighbours until the aftershock of the quake had passed.

The next day, the earthquake was the subject of excited conversation at the base. The doctor who was to give Camp his examination was fascinated to learn that he had come from California and had experienced earthquakes there. They talked and talked. The doctor never did bother to examine Camp's eyes, and he returned to New Brunswick a newly minted lieutenant in the Canadian Army.

By then, he was growing increasingly impatient for an opportunity to put his military training to use. Many of his friends from Horton Academy and Acadia had already been posted overseas. Some had been killed (including his roommate from Acadia) and others had been grievously wounded. It looked as though the war in Europe might soon wind down, and, except for his stint in Brockville, he had not managed to get out of New Brunswick.

In later years, Camp would be infuriated whenever his good friend Finlay MacDonald would kid him about his failure to go overseas. "I used to introduce him as one of a small band of brave men who stood gallantly between the Hun and Summerside, Prince Edward Island," MacDonald said. "That would make him mad."[6]

"Dalton was a fighter," said his brother-in-law, Norman Atkins. "He wouldn't be satisfied with just having to be in Canada during the war."

His frustration turned to anguish when he learned that Buddy Chase, his best friend from his boyhood days in Woodstock, had been one of several Canadians killed by German mortar during a minor engagement in Italy at the end of 1944. The War Diary of the Westminster Regiment for December 28, 1944, recorded the details of the skirmish and went on to add: "The result must be counted a failure. The most obvious reason seemed a lack of adequate fire support, without which an attack into prepared positions was almost impossible in this coverless country." Camp was overwhelmed by grief and anger:

> And so he died, in a bloody, helpless firefight on a forgotten front, in the all but abandoned Italian campaign.... I could imagine him, in all that sudden overwhelming terror and pain and chaos, hearing him say what he had always said... "Jesus, Jesus, Jesus"... "Jesus," he would say, rubbing the hurt, or holding his sides, the voice compressed through his nose, a shrill cry. Even now, I can hear the voice.... What a fucking way to die—"lack of fire support."...
>
> Private Chase died carrying a Bren gun. The Bren would have been about his size, unless he had grown a foot since I last saw him walking

down Broadway [in Woodstock], on a summer night when the war was new and we were all immortal.[7]

With grief and anger came a sense of guilt that would remain with Camp for the rest of his life. As a result of some divine lottery, his friend had been taken, while he was spared to enjoy a life of prosperity, prominence and success in advertising, politics and journalism. Over the years, he ferreted out as many details as he could about Buddy Chase's war service and his death. He asked his friend Harry Bagley, a rare book dealer in Fredericton, to help him find out where Buddy was buried. Bagley knew the librarian at the National Defence Library in Ottawa, who found an account of the action that day in Italy and a photograph of the grave of Private Chase.

Near the end of his life, Camp told Bagley he would like to talk to someone who could remember Buddy or his family. Bagley drove him to Woodstock and tracked down an elderly schoolteacher who had known the family, and she and Camp talked about Buddy Chase's family and those early years in Woodstock. "I tried to fig-ure out this business about Buddy Chase," Bagley said. "Dalton thought of him as a surrogate. He was the kid he grew up with, and he's the one that paid the price in the war. And that could have been him. He tried to get overseas and didn't make it. But this guy who'd been his childhood friend went, and he paid for him. Maybe he thought he had an obligation to Buddy Chase. He was really hung up on that."[8]

Camp very nearly did get overseas. He had volunteered for another course, and when it ended he was entitled to a 96-hour pass. Linda took the night train up from New York to meet him in Montreal and the couple settled happily into a small hotel for a long weekend together. When it ended, they rushed off to Windsor Station so that Camp could catch a train back to his unit in New Brunswick while Linda got a train to New York. At the gate, Camp took another look at his pass and realized that the 96 hours did not include travel time. They approached a military policeman, who examined the pass and said, "No, you don't have to be back till tomorrow."

They checked back into their hotel and spent another day in Montreal. When he got back to his unit, he found it denuded of junior officers. While he and Linda were enjoying their extra day in Montreal, the officers had been scooped up and packed off to Europe, where many of them were killed or wounded in the final months of the war.

Abandoned in New Brunswick, Camp saw VE Day come and go. He applied for posting to the Pacific theatre and was waiting for assignment, ready to leave, when VJ Day came. As the end of the war neared, Camp knew just one thing: he wanted out. He had taken all the training the army could throw at him, he had volunteered for extra courses, he had chafed when his friends were sent overseas, and he had suffered when they were wounded or killed. He was ready and willing to serve, but the army, in its wisdom, had chosen to leave him behind. Camp had no intention of hanging around.

By now he was a father, Linda having delivered their first child, a daughter, Linda Gail (called Gail), just after the war in Europe ended. Linda had gone home to her mother in New Jersey to have the baby. Camp was stationed at the army base in Sussex, New Brunswick. He took a motorcycle from the pool at Sussex and rode to Robertson's Point to join his father-in-law and his brother-in-law, Norman Atkins. George Atkins, ecstatic over the birth of his first grandchild, cracked open the Southern Comfort, and they had a grand celebration.

But Camp still had some issues to address. He was about to turn 25. He was a husband and a father. He had no profession and no employment prospects. He had to complete his education. He knew he might not be welcomed back at Acadia; if he had not dropped out to join the army, he likely would have flunked out. It was time to get serious about school and about his future. It was time to have another talk with George Atkins. Atkins had been a classmate at Acadia of Milton Gregg, a New Brunswick boy who had become a First World War hero. Gregg had joined the Canadian Army as stretcher bearer and left it as a brigadier general, was wounded three times and won the Victoria Cross. Later on, Gregg would become a minister in the Liberal government in Ottawa. From 1944 to 1947, however, he was president of the University of New Brunswick in Fredericton, responsible for integrating returning servicemen into the university. In those days, servicemen who gained admission to a university could secure an immediate release from the military.

Atkins took his son-in-law to see his old friend Gregg. More interested in Camp's potential than in his academic record at Acadia, Gregg liked what he saw in the young veteran in front of him. He admitted him on the spot to third year at UNB. It was probably a gamble on Milton Gregg's part, but if it was, the gamble paid off spectacularly.

CHAPTER 5

Years of Self-Discovery

IT MAY HAVE BEEN THE DISCIPLINE implanted by the military, the responsibility of being a husband and father or simply the product of maturity, but the Dalton Camp who entered the third year of the arts program at the University of New Brunswick in Fredericton in the fall of 1945 was a transformed man. He found it intellectually stimulating to be out of the army and in university, to be challenged by ideas instead of constrained by protocol. He developed something he had never had when he was at Acadia: focus. In the next four years—two at UNB and one each at Columbia University in New York and the London School of Economics in England—he would discover and hone the interests, especially in politics and journalism, that would dominate the rest of his life.

At UNB, he became what they called in those days a BMOC—"big man on campus." He threw himself into university life. In the "one-way run of life"—the phrase he used to describe his perception of mortality when his father died—Camp was determined to squeeze every ounce of achievement from his precious time at university. Overnight, he became an exceptional student—so good that he graduated in 1947 with first-class honours and was voted class valedictorian. He became editor of the student newspaper, the *Brunswickan*, president of the Art Society and star of the university's production of Thornton Wilder's *Our Town*, for which he was voted best actor of the year.[1]

He represented UNB's veterans' club at a national conference in Montreal. He got involved in the New Brunswick Liberal party and its young Liberal organization, wrote highly coloured political columns for the publication *Liberal Review* and was invited to Ottawa to be wined and dined, stroked and flattered, by Liberal MPs and senators.

In later years, Camp would laugh at that memory. "Here I am, I'm a bankrupt student, and I'm travelling the rails and going into the Chateau Laurier," he said. "There's a bottle of rye on the table when I check in the room. Things like that. It never went to my head. It really didn't, it just mystified me as to what it was about. I thought maybe, you know, if I could find out—break the code—I would know something."[2]

Just about the only activity he avoided at UNB was sports. When he arrived on campus, he tried out for the rugby team, confident that although his head might be going bald, his body was as hard as a rock after his time in the military. But it was a 25-year-old body, not an 18-year-old one, and he quickly discovered that rugby uses very different muscles than the parade ground. He was knocked around, bruised and left black and blue. Hobbling back to his digs, he promised himself, "Never, no more of that."

The highlight of Camp's two years at UNB was his final act: his valedictory address to convocation in May 1947. The Fredericton *Daily Gleaner* reprinted it in its entirety. Ignoring the customary ritual on such occasions of thanking parents, professors and fellow students, Camp instead made an eloquent appeal for an expansion of the liberal arts in an era when universities, like society as a whole, were growing fixated on science and technology.

> In a thoroughly mechanized society, we stand to be manufactured in the image of the machine. We stand to lose our finest sensibilities, to see them as shavings heaped upon the floor. In a society so lavishly proud of its techniques in mass production, we ourselves have made a fetish of mass conformity. The independent and inquisitive mind finds itself compressed, confined, bounded on all sides by the eight-hour day and the double feature at the cinema house....
>
> I wonder what kind of a people we shall become if we continue to live in a world where we are urged to lubricate ourselves for our continued efficiency, as we lubricate our machines. I wonder how much we are influenced by the suggestion that by drinking a certain brand of liquor we can become men of distinction.

The liberal arts, he continued, "must be the fountainhead of our culture" even though an arts course might never put a nickel in a young person's pocket or serve as a useful reference for a job. He urged the university not to send graduates out into the world economically secure but culturally bankrupt. He was decades ahead of his time with a call for the school to amend its curriculum to recognize the French fact in New Brunswick. Nearly half of New Brunswick residents spoke French, he said, but the university in the provincial capital had as its only language requirement one year of Latin. "I suggest we render unto Caesar those things which are Caesar's and render unto Canada those things which are distinctly her own. Truly, we can never be Canadian citizens so long as we are unable to enjoy social intercourse with nearly half of our Canadian family."

Before he sat down, Camp made an appeal that must have endeared him to the student body if not to the university administration when he called for UNB to add 300 female students to bring the enrolment of women up to the level of men: "The qualities of social poise, gentility and manliness are vital necessities, and these qualities are the natural result of a campus society where men and women meet together in common endeavour, mutual respect and similar numbers."

Arthur Forbes, the minister of St. Paul's United Church in Fredericton, expressed the admiration of many of Camp's listeners when he wrote a letter of congratulation, saying, "It was one of the most brilliant valedictory addresses I have ever heard."

By one of those twists of fate that seemed to change the course of Camp's life, there was someone else in the audience who was equally impressed. He was New Brunswick's own Max Aiken, now Lord Beaverbrook, perhaps the world's most powerful press baron, who was being installed that day as UNB's chancellor. Beaverbrook was so taken by Camp and his speech that he issued an order on the spot that he be awarded a Beaverbrook Overseas Scholarship, good for a year at the London School of Economics; no need to apply, to write a test or to submit letters of reference.[3]

Dalton, Linda and little Gail would be off to London for the 1948–49 school year, but first New York and Columbia University's famed Graduate School of Journalism beckoned. As he neared graduation at UNB, Camp had applied to the law school there and to Columbia for its master's course in journalism. He had just about reconciled himself to law when Columbia's acceptance came through. The family was able to rent part of a very large house not far from Linda's parents in Montclair, New Jersey. Camp commuted every day to Columbia, by train or bus and subway.

At Columbia, students were exposed to instructors who included some of the finest writers and editors of the *New York Times*, *New Yorker* magazine and other leading publications. They were taught to lay out a newspaper, learned about television, then in its infancy, and were introduced to a balky, newfangled contraption that would ultimately revolutionize business communications: the facsimile machine.

Columbia sent its students out to play reporter at real-life news events, and Camp wrote a hilarious account of the arrival in New York of the governor of Alabama, "Kissin" Jim Folsom. He also interviewed Dwight Eisenhower, then president of Columbia, about how to run a major university.

And he met a classmate who would be his friend for life. Frank Mankiewicz came from one of Hollywood's talented families. He was the son of Herman Mankiewicz, the great screenwriter, who won an Academy Award in 1941 for co-writing (with Orson Welles) *Citizen Kane*, arguably the best movie ever made in the United States. Frank's uncle Joseph Mankiewicz won back-to-back Oscars for writing and directing *A Letter to Three Wives* (1949) and *All About Eve* (1950).

After Columbia, Frank Mankiewicz would go on to a career similar to Camp's own, straddling politics, print and electronic journalism, and advertising and public relations. He became a newspaperman, lawyer, regional director of the Peace Corps under John F. Kennedy, Democratic party guru, press secretary to Robert Kennedy, presidential campaign director for George McGovern, television anchor, twice-defeated candidate for political office, syndicated columnist, president of National Public Radio, author and, most recently, a lobbyist in his capacity as a Washington-based vice-chairman of Hill and Knowlton Public Affairs Worldwide.

Talking in his office in the Watergate complex, Mankiewicz remembered Camp as a kindred spirit. Both had come from California and both were veterans. They shared an irreverence about classes and instructors. Both loved newspapers, and they adored baseball. For less than 50 cents a day, they would buy eight or nine New York newspapers. He and Camp would start with the *Times* and the *Herald Tribune* in the morning, then move on to the *World Telegram*, *Journal American*, *Post* and *Sun*. Over coffee at midnight, they would read the early editions of the next day's *Mirror* and *Daily News*.

"Dalton and I did all that," Mankiewicz recalled. "We read all the papers, and commented on all of them, and talked about which writers we liked, and which ones we didn't like. I think what he was most interested in, even then, were columnists, analysts, feature writers—opinionating rather than reporting." They both liked Red Smith, Stanley Woodward and Jimmy Cannon. They did not much care for the *Times*' James Reston ("too heavy and self-important," they agreed), though Mankiewicz warmed to him later.

They did not go to many classes, but they did manage to get to a lot of ball games at Yankee Stadium—and when the Yankees were on the road, there were the Giants at the Polo Grounds or the Brooklyn Dodgers at Ebbets Field. Camp became a Giants fan that year and remained loyal to them even after they moved from New York to San Francisco. "They played baseball in the afternoons in those days, and there was pretty much always a game during the spring," Mankiewicz remembered. "Or maybe we'd go sit in a bar and drink beer, and talk about American politics, or maybe go to a movie. Anything that did not involve teaching, reporting or feature writing—things we thought we already knew."[4]

On weekends, Camp would travel with his father-in-law, George Atkins, and his brother-in-law, Norman Atkins, to West Point, New York, home of the United States Military Academy, to watch Army play Navy or other football rivals. U.S. college football was to be one of Camp's enduring passions.

Fortunately for Camp and Mankiewicz, the journalism school did not hold examinations. Both graduated with their master of science degree in journalism. They kept in close contact over the years as they pursued their shared interests in politics and journalism. "We were both fond of both professions and had a lot of respect for them," Mankiewicz said:

> To write a column and pop off, or be an anchorman and sound off the way I was doing, is not quite journalism, although it allows you to say you're in the business. But neither of us were day-to-day reporters. That made it easier. You had to know what you were talking about. It was also a way to get a bit of a reputation. I read a lot of his stuff, and I assume he read a fair bit of mine—and we talked from time to time, and whenever we got together at a convention or a meeting of some kind, we'd find plenty of common ground.
>
> Dalton was always more deeply concerned about American matters than Canadian in terms of public affairs. He had much more to say about Vietnam or Watergate or Richard Nixon than about equivalent Canadian matters. Maybe it was because, to us at least, in the newspapers we read, Canadian affairs were fairly calm.[5]

Camp attended U.S. political conventions with Mankiewicz, who in turn would join Camp for Canadian conventions and elections. Mankiewicz persuaded Robert Kennedy to accept an honorary degree from the University of New Brunswick in 1967 because he wanted to spend a few days with Camp. Kennedy made a speech about the Vietnam War to convocation, and over lunch and dinner he and Camp exchanged views on a subject of mutual interest: John Diefenbaker. Kennedy talked about the deep dislike that his late brother, President John F. Kennedy, had had for the former prime minister, and Camp explained why and how he had challenged Diefenbaker's leadership the year before.

On another occasion, Mankiewicz and his wife visited Dalton and Linda Camp at the cottage at Robertson's Point. He also remembered a memorable few days there with two of Camp's closest friends and political allies: Flora MacDonald and Richard Hatfield, then premier of New Brunswick. He got to know both of them well; Hatfield would visit him in New York or Washington and Mankiewicz would encounter MacDonald at various political gatherings, including a conference at Lake Couchiching in Ontario.

In October 1974, Camp invited Mankiewicz, a fellow fight fan, to Toronto to watch the Muhammad Ali–George Foreman heavyweight championship—the celebrated "Rumble in the Jungle" from Kinshasa, Zaire—on closed-circuit television at Maple Leaf Gardens. Two years later, the two spent the 1976 United States election night on-air with CBC host Peter Gzowski; Mankiewicz struggled mightily to explain the mysteries of the Electoral College to the Canadian audience as Jimmy Carter defeated Gerald Ford.

Mankiewicz went to Ottawa in February 1994 for a testimonial dinner for Dalton Camp at the Chateau Laurier Hotel when Camp was made an Officer of the Order of Canada. He met Robert Stanfield on that occasion—and was amused when the man whom Camp had helped become leader of the Tory party was introduced as "the best prime minister Canada never had"—along with Senator Wilbert Keon, the surgeon who had performed Camp's heart transplant operation the year before, and Jean Charest, then leader of the two-MP Tory caucus. Although Mankiewicz was unable to attend an eightieth birthday dinner and tribute to Camp that was held in Woodstock, New Brunswick, 17 months before his death, he sent a letter in which he reflected on their 53-year friendship:

> With his American educational background, Dalton needed no instruction in the infield fly rule or the third-strike bunt, or even how to compute the ERA. And the more Dalton and I talked about politics—particularly Canadian politics—over the years, and he explained his unique Tory positions compared to my orthodox U.S. New Deal liberalism, the more I became convinced Canada shared the British two-party system, as explained by two Brit comedians of the time. "We have two parties," they would explain to an American audience, "the Labour party, which you would call 'socialist,' and the Conservative party, which you would call—uh—'socialist.'"[6]

The year at Columbia did several things for Camp. It renewed his American roots. It deepened his understanding of American politics. It exposed him to daily debate and discussion of the news and the leading issues of the day. It fostered his interest in journalism as a career or, perhaps more correctly, as a way of life. And it rekindled his affection for American sports, principally baseball, football and basketball.

The only discordant note was money. Camp had a veterans' allowance for education, but it was not enough for him and Linda to live on, to pay their share of house costs and to entertain all the visitors who, as Linda discovered, were only too available to drop in to take advantage of a free bed on the outskirts of New York, which they all agreed was the most exciting city in the post-war world. Eventually, Camp managed to secure some financial assistance from Columbia to see them through the year. When the term ended, the family went back to New Brunswick, where he worked as a road surveyor while they waited for fall and London and the LSE.

They sailed from Montreal on the *Empress of Canada*, packed in steerage with hundreds of other students who were heading to Europe for their first look at England and the Continent since the end of the war.[7] The Beaverbrook Overseas Scholars received a handsome stipend, and Camp also had his allowance from the army. It was enough money to enable the Camps to live comfortably in London—a flat in an elegant old house in Notting Hill Gate, a playschool for little Gail, tickets to concerts at Albert Hall, with enough left over for vacation trips through Scotland, France, Belgium, the Netherlands and Spain.

The year in London brought Camp into contact with two people who influenced his life in important ways. The first was Harold Laski, the most famous teacher at the LSE in those days. Laski was a political scientist, economist, author and socialist, though some insisted he was closer to communism than socialism. He was an influence to be reckoned with in post-war Britain, as voters turned from the Conservatives to the Labour party, of which Laski was chairman in 1945–46. By all accounts, Laski was a brilliant lecturer. "Attending lectures rendered by Professor Laski is much like attending the theatre and, with the possible exception of the Old Vic Players, perhaps it is better theatre. It is at least a unique experience," Camp wrote in a feature article that he sent back to his old paper at UNB, the *Brunswickan*.

Students queue up for his lectures, standing outside the auditorium for as long as 10 minutes before the scheduled hour. They fill all available seats, sit in the aisles and stand at the doors. Once inside, there is a tumult of much conversation, scuffling of feet and jockeying for position. And then, from the wings, enters Laski. There is a kind of "curtain parts and houselights dim" atmosphere about it all. The conversation breaks off, the scuffling ceases, leaving a room full of throbbing silence. Professor Laski removes his spectacles, pours a glass of water, drinks, and then begins his lecture.

Harold Laski was the first bona fide political scientist Camp had encountered, and he took almost every course Laski offered. No teacher had a greater impact on him. Laski stimulated Camp to think critically, to challenge ideas and not to be afraid to dissent. Laski knew something about Canada. He had taught at McGill during the First World War where he became interested in Canadian politics. Later, Laski got to know such leaders of the Canadian left in the 1940s as M.J. Coldwell and Tommy Douglas. He had no use for the Liberalism of Mackenzie King, which Camp embraced in those years. He told Camp not to waste his time on Liberals. If he could not be a socialist, it would be better, he said, and more honest, to be a Conservative. He even advised him to go home to New Brunswick and use any means to overthrow the provincial Liberal government.

Laski also recommended that Camp read everything he could about Disraeli if he wanted to learn what was best about Conservatism; if he wanted to know about the worst of Liberalism, he should read about Gladstone. "I did some of both, but mostly I read and listened to Laski, reading all his published work and attending all of his lectures and seminars that I could," Camp told an Atlantic Studies conference in 1978.

As had Milton Gregg at UNB, Laski saw something special in the young man from New Brunswick. He invited Camp to his home, where the conversation could become so engrossing that Camp would lose track of time. On one occasion, he felt compelled to write to apologize to his mentor for staying too late.

Laski also taught a course on Marxism, and Camp asked to join it. Laski refused, telling him he was not ready. At mid-term, he asked again. Laski relented, and as Camp recalled:

> The first day I was in the class, Laski asked this fellow a question. The guy was from Yale, on a scholarship, and Laski asked him something about the dialectic or something. The fellow answered in French. I thought, I'm so far over my head that I'll just never see the light. There was a woman there who was a communist, and she got in an argument with him on Marxism, and he said this famous thing, which I've never forgotten. He said, "In Russia, they don't have that problem. The government says to people, 'You're happy, damn you.'" The class approvingly chuckled. It was just a great experience.[8]

Although he was in thrall to Laski's mind, Camp was not naive. As the year went on, he concluded that Laski's scholarship was flawed by a vivid imagination and that about half of what he said was pure invention. "It doesn't really matter. What one learned—what most of us, I think, learned from Laski—was the value of dissent, although perhaps nothing of its limits. He once described his function as a teacher of politics, which was 'to prick people into the insurgency of thought,' an observation both characteristic and true."[9]

Dissent became an important ingredient in Camp's makeup, first in his life in politics and later in journalism. He could never be comfortable as part of the pack. By the time Harold Laski and the LSE were finished with him, the seeds were firmly planted for his rejection of Canadian Liberalism and his embrace of the Conservative alternative.

The second person who influenced Camp significantly in his year in London was his patron, Lord Beaverbrook. Beaverbrook had no use for Laski or his politics, and the feeling was mutual: Laski once sued the press lord for libel, and lost. But year after year Beaverbrook gave scholarships to bright young people to study under Laski at the LSE. He was always curious as to what his scholars thought of their teacher, and was a bit disappointed if they seemed too impressed.

Beaverbrook was an intimidating force. He was the first truly powerful individual Camp had ever met. A member of the war cabinet, he had been, next to Winston Churchill himself, probably the most powerful person in Britain during the Second World War. As a Beaverbrook scholar, Camp was summoned one Sunday to lunch with his benefactor at Cherkley, Beaverbrook's 30-bedroom country house in Surrey. Camp took the train to Leatherhead, where a limousine was waiting for him:

> The driveway into the place was longer than the trip from the train station to the driveway. By the time I got there, I was thoroughly intimidated. Red, the butler, took me in through the dining room. I had to go around the porch because he was sitting on the porch looking out over the countryside. When I appeared before him, "Ah, Camp," he said. "There you are.... Would you like to go for a walk?" He was padding around. "What do you think of my sneakers?" He had a pair of Keds. I said, "Nice." Everything I said, he had a one-word answer. "What do you think of Harold Laski?" who was my teacher. I said he was a great teacher. He said "Anti-Christ." So I wasn't making much progress.... Then he picks up the phone and calls Lord Baldwin, and he says, "Has my bull finished servicing your cattle? When am I going to get it back?" Then some guy came out of the woodwork, and Beaverbrook said to him, "What's new?" And he gave a rundown of the world. Who was fighting whom and what troop movements there were, and so on. It was during the continual Berlin crisis, and Beaverbrook said, "There's going to be a war within a year in Germany."[10]

Although events would prove Beaverbrook wrong in his prediction, Camp never forgot that encounter with the press lord. "He was the first man that ever frightened me—and the last one," he said. "I was so terrified. It was incredible. Lunch lasted a couple of hours. It seemed like a lifetime."[11]

During his year at the LSE, he had other encounters with Beaverbrook, whom he found to be unpredictable and irascible. He thought it was alarming that people like Beaverbrook were loose in the world. "But it was a great lesson," he told an interviewer in 1993. "No one ever scared me again after that. I didn't give a damn who it was, I'd seen the worst."[12]

Two decades later, when he was waging his campaign against Diefenbaker's leadership, Tories who were terrified of the leader would tell Camp they could not understand why he seemed so unafraid of him. "A lot of people were just scared to death of him. But I thought, he's a pixie compared to this little fellow over there [Beaverbrook]."

Camp also came away from his year in England with an abiding interest in the man Beaverbrook called his best friend: Churchill. As a young man in New Brunswick, Camp, like many Canadians, had been thrilled by Churchill's wartime speeches on the radio, and as he grew older he read every book about Churchill that he could get his hands on, searching bookstores for the works about the man he called "my hero" and whom he regarded as "the greatest man in our century."[13] His children learned that if they gave him a book about Churchill for Christmas, they could forget about getting their father's attention for the rest of the day. He would sit on the sofa, locked in his own mental space and oblivious to his surroundings until he had read the entire book. He was also fascinated by Churchill's six-volume history of the Second World War, and he would reread one or more of the books in the summers when he was at Robertson's Point.

Camp may have seen parallels between Churchill's life and his own. Emotionally abandoned by both parents, Churchill had a hard childhood. Camp could relate to that: the father he adored had died prematurely, and his mother made no attempt to hide her preference for his older brother. In later years, Camp would remind friends that Churchill was in and out of politics throughout most of his adult life. In the periods when he was out, he supported himself financially as a journalist, writing for newspapers and churning out books to keep food on his table—just as Camp was still writing columns when he was into his 80s, and for the same reason: he needed the money.

He once told an interviewer he admired Churchill for three qualities: courage, perseverance and stamina. He was unafraid to dissent from conventional wisdom:

> He was really quite a radical, and he lived such a complete, enormous life that you can work your way through it and find all kinds of things that he did that were questionable or were wrong as colonial secretary—but there was always his great spirit and his great humanity. He was for prison reform, he was for pensions—he wrote Lloyd George after the war and said, "Now we have to do something for humanity."

He knew evil when he saw it—that's a large part of life, you know, knowing good from evil. I think he was a pretty good judge. And he loved the language.[14]

In 1995, Camp's friend Harry Bagley, the rare book dealer in Fredericton, came across a sample of Churchill memorabilia and letters being offered in an estate sale. At Camp's request, Bagley bid on some and bought them for Camp at a price of $10,500. These "letters and ephemera," as Bagley described the material, were among Camp's most prized possessions. The most valuable was a letter of condolence written by Churchill the day after Beaverbrook's death in 1964 to his widow, Christofor (the former Lady Dunn), whom the ailing press magnate had married just the year before:

> My dear Christofor,
>
> Words are vain, but I wanted to give you my true sympathy in your distress. I know how you loved dear Max and how wonderfully you sustained him and made his life a happy one.
>
> I, too, grieve for my oldest and closest friend, for whom my feelings of affection and admiration grew only stronger with the passing of time. It was heart-warming that he should have made such a splendid speech so recently, and that he then received justified tributes to his great stature.
>
> Clemmie and I so much hope that later you will come and see us whenever you can.
>
> Yours very sincerely,
> Winston S. Churchill

Camp did not keep any memorabilia from his years of supporting and opposing John Diefenbaker, except for one item that he displayed in his New Brunswick home, Northwood. It was a photograph, signed by Diefenbaker, of Diefenbaker and his wife, Olive, with Winston Churchill. It may have been a case of his taste for Churchill being stronger than his distaste for Diefenbaker.

As the LSE term drew to a close in 1949, Dalton and Linda decided to do some serious travelling before returning home. A savage cribbage player, Camp had won enough money from fellow students to finance the purchase of two bicycles. They were ready to cycle through Europe—but what to do with their daughter, Gail, who was not quite four years old? Never one to let children cramp his style, Camp decided that Gail would be sent to Linda's parents in New Jersey—by plane, alone, from London to LaGuardia Airport in New York, with refueling stops in Dublin and Gander, Newfoundland. Gail went bravely aboard the Pan American Flying Clipper, carrying a huge bag stuffed with presents, including a doll with red hair, a handbag for the doll, a plastic doll carriage and a toy wristwatch with a dazzling red strap. Her parents instructed her to open one present per hour, on the theory this would keep her busy and distracted during the flight.

The plan would have been fine, if it had worked. Gail, however, finding herself surrounded by adult strangers on the aircraft, was convinced they all had one thing on their minds: to steal her presents. She clutched the bag to her chest throughout the flight, prepared to fight off any adult who went after its contents. The flight went smoothly enough until the refueling stop in Gander, where the aircraft was grounded for several hours by mechanical problems, leaving Gail's grandparents, waiting in New York, frantically trying to find out what was happening. The Flying Clipper eventually made it to LaGuardia, and Gail spent the summer with George and Geraldine Atkins while her parents passed the next three months exploring France, Belgium, the Netherlands, Luxembourg, Italy, Switzerland and Yugoslavia.

Meanwhile, an election campaign was raging in Canada, and on June 27, 1949, the Liberals, under their new leader, Louis St. Laurent, rolled to an easy victory. It would be the last Canadian election Camp would miss for many years. At the end of the summer, he would return to Canada to look for a job and to find his political home. He expressed his misgivings in a letter to Linda's parents. He admired St. Laurent's mind and integrity, he wrote, but he questioned how progressive the new prime minister was. "There is no party represented for whom I could speak with any great warmth at any great length," he said. "Liberal still I am, but liberal, too."

The liberal Liberal was about to become something new to Canadian politics: a Red Tory.

CHAPTER 6

The Young Politician

WHEN DALTON CAMP RETURNED from the London School of Economics in the late summer of 1949, he had some employment prospects but no firm job offer. *Time* magazine in New York was interested in him, and Camp gave the proposal serious thought. It would have meant prestige, a handsome salary and a chance to work as a journalist in the most exciting news centre in the English-speaking world. He went to New York for a job interview, and over lunch he asked an editor what it was like to work for *Time*. "If you want to work for the world's most expensive whorehouse, this is the place to be," was the candid reply. Camp decided to seek his future in Canada instead.

He knew, or at least suspected, that the future would include politics. He remembered something his friend Desmond Pacey, who had raved over his performance in a review of *Our Town*, had said to him as he left the University of New Brunswick: "You can be the next Stephen Leacock, but I know you won't. You'll go into advertising or politics or something like that."[1]

As a student at the University of New Brunswick from 1945 to 1947, Camp had become active in the Liberal party, both on campus and at the provincial level. His involvement began almost accidentally. As editor of the *Brunswickan*, he tired of writing editorials about campus issues. The country was going through one of its intermittent crises over federal financial support for the Maritime provinces, and Camp started writing editorials supporting the position of the New Brunswick government. One day, a stranger came to the door of his apartment in the converted barracks that passed for student housing for married veterans at UNB. He was Robert Tweedie, the private secretary (today we would call him chief of staff) to John B. McNair, the Liberal premier of New Brunswick. Tweedie told Camp that McNair had liked his editorials, and he invited him to visit Ottawa as the guest of the premier and Frank Bridges, New Brunswick's representative in Mackenzie King's cabinet. Before going, Camp went to see Milton Gregg, the university president. "Don't get too involved," Gregg warned. "Politics can be a terrible waste of time."[2]

Camp was feted as a person of importance on his visit to Ottawa. Within six months, Bridges was dead, at 45, and the Liberals, ironically, chose Milton Gregg to be their candidate in the by-election in York-Sunbury. Gregg enlisted Camp to help him, and the two men stumped the riding together. Gregg would make his standard speech, in which he promised vaguely to do something to help the veterans of both world wars, and Camp would follow by assuring the crowds that Milton Gregg certainly had the support of veterans and young people. Camp left for Columbia University before the by-election; Gregg won handily, and he served with distinction in the federal cabinet for the next 10 years.

When Camp returned to New Brunswick after his year in New York, he was caught up in the June 1948 provincial election campaign. McNair ran the Liberal campaign personally out of the premier's office. Camp campaigned with McNair, and he also assisted two admen whom McNair had imported from Walsh Advertising Ltd. in Toronto to run the party's publicity campaign. From a suite in the Lord Beaverbrook Hotel in Fredericton, they designed the party's newspaper ads and cranked out the copy to fill them. Camp watched and learned, as the Liberals swept back to power, winning 47 of the 52 seats in the legislature.

Later that summer Camp went to Ottawa as a member of the New Brunswick delegation to the national Liberal leadership convention to choose a successor to King. Camp voted for Chubby Power; Power ran third and last, while Louis St. Laurent won in a walk. The convention left Camp bitterly disillusioned with the Liberal party. He had watched in dismay as Nova Scotia MP Robert Winters (later to be a cabinet minister) adroitly quashed an attempt by delegates from the three Maritime provinces to push the party into embracing a package of pro-Maritime resolutions. And when Camp addressed the delegates himself with an appeal to the party to listen to its youth—"If you will not listen to the younger members of this party, then they will leave and join another party"—his plea fell on the deaf ears of the Liberal establishment.[3]

As he headed off that fall for the LSE, Camp did not know what his political future might hold, but he felt suffocated as a Liberal. The federal party, too comfortable in power, had no interest in new faces or fresh ideas, while the provincial party had no role to offer a young man who did not conform to his elders' expectations.

He might, Camp commented later, have bided his time and toughed it out as a Liberal, but he was young, impetuous and impatient. A year with Harold Laski at the LSE had given him the intellectual tools to question his political commitment even more critically than he had previously.

That he made the switch from Liberal to Tory when he did was more the product of inadvertence than design. He was in Montclair, New Jersey, visiting Linda's parents on his way home from England when he received a telegram from Ewart Atkinson, the president of the New Brunswick Progressive Conservative Party, a man he had never met, offering him the position of executive secretary of the Tory provincial party—"a prospect both alluring and forbidding, like a sudden invitation to climb Mount Everest."[4]

Camp consulted some of his New Brunswick friends. They advised him not to do it. So did Linda's parents. Linda herself was vociferously opposed. He sat down and made two lists: one of all the reasons he could think of for accepting the Conservative offer, and the other of all the reasons for refusing the job. The list of reasons for refusing was the longer by far. Perversely, Camp accepted the job. It was partly because he needed the work, partly because he felt thoroughly unwanted by the Liberals, and partly because the contrarian in him relished the seemingly impossible challenge of electing a Conservative government in New Brunswick.

The man who as a Liberal at UNB had written a column excoriating the Tories, saying he could never be one of them because he could never find out what they stood for or against,[5] now went on radio to denounce his former party: "[T]he professional Liberal will sell any principle, as he has done throughout history, and looks like doing today—if the selling will yield him increased power. If professional Liberalism means anything today, it means an ability to hold power by the subtle exploitation of fear and suspicion."[6]

The radio address created a sensation. Liberal friends crossed the street or ducked into stores to avoid talking to him. "It had earlier been suspected I had gone off to Britain and returned a socialist, or worse," he said. "Now it seemed confirmed; it was worse."

Camp had barely located his desk in the Tory offices when Premier McNair called a by-election in the Charlotte riding, a four-member constituency that had elected four Liberals in the 1948 election. Camp went with the party leader, Hugh Mackay, to meet the Charlotte riding executive. Mackay tried to discourage them from fielding a candidate: "If you want to contest this by-election, go ahead, but you won't get a goddamned cent from me. I'm still paying for the last election."[7]

The local Tories did nominate a candidate, however. They scraped up $100 for the deposit, and Atkinson dug into his own pocket to underwrite the entire campaign budget of $75. Camp got his first personal exposure to underhanded election tactics. On voting day, the Liberal poll chairman decided it was too cold in the polling stations in St. Andrews and St. Stephen, so he moved the ballot boxes to other locations. Liberal supporters found out where to vote; Conservative voters did not. To no one's surprise, the Tories did not win the by-election; but they polled a respectable vote, enough to recover their deposit.

That pyrrhic victory could not save the Conservative party from the lassitude of its members, or Camp from the consequences of empty party coffers. Broke, the party closed its office and laid off its executive secretary. At 29, Camp was out of a job.

He decided to try his hand at advertising. He had watched the men from Walsh Advertising at work in the 1948 general election in New Brunswick; he understood the power of advertising and its ability to drive campaign strategy. It was time, he concluded, to learn the business for himself.

Thinking back on this career decision later, Camp said he had been inspired by the example of Winston Churchill. "[If] you weren't a natural member of the Establishment and [if] you were going to be falling in and out of the favour of politicians and politics and political parties...you had to make your own way first and establish your own position of independence.... The advertising industry appealed to me as a way in which to establish a self-sufficiency soonest."[8]

He took a job for $200 a month as a junior copywriter at one of the big shops, J. Walter Thompson, in Toronto. Connie Ganong, from the New Brunswick chocolate family, had been a student at Acadia when Dalton was there and was now working for JWT. It was, she told him, a great place to apprentice, to learn the intricacies of the advertising business. His first two accounts involved writing ads for Wrigley's chewing gum and for a company that made milking machines. Later, he wrote copy for Labatt's and Bank of Nova Scotia, among others.

He also joined the Progressive Conservative association in Toronto's Spadina riding, not because he lived in Spadina (he did not), but because it, too, appealed to the contrarian in him: "It seemed to me on examination to be the most dismal prospect in the Conservative party in Toronto; that's why I decided that I'd take up political [involvement] in Spadina."[9]

At home, money was tight, as Linda had four more children in the next six years. But Camp counted himself lucky in one regard. Across the street from their rented house in Toronto lived a man who worked for one of the most fashionable and expensive men's clothing stores in town, a place where film star Cary Grant was said to have his suits made. Some customers would go in to be measured for suits, then decide they could not afford them and never pick them up. Camp's neighbour would go through the unclaimed suits, find ones that would fit Camp and sell them to him for a song. He might have been struggling to survive on $200 a month, but he was the best-dressed adman in Toronto.[10]

He was also the best copywriter in the Toronto offices of U.S.–based J. Walter Thompson. His salary increases reflected his progress, and after he had been at the agency for about two years, he was offered a promotion to creative director. Camp, who had been thinking of moving to a rival agency, told his boss that the other firm, Locke Johnson, had offered him $7,500 a year. The boss said JWT had a rule that no Canadian employee could be paid more than $6,000 without the express permission of head office in New York. That did it for Camp; not waiting for New York's verdict, he left and joined Locke Johnson as copy chief.

His big break came in 1952, when John McNair called a general election in New Brunswick. Ewart Atkinson proposed that Camp return to Fredericton to run the advertising campaign for the Conservatives. Camp went to see the newly chosen Tory leader, Hugh John Flemming, a calm, at times vague, businessman who owned a lumber mill where Camp had worked in the summer for 22 cents an hour while he was a student. He volunteered his services, proposing that the advertising be placed through Locke Johnson, which would give him a leave of absence for the campaign. Flemming knew next to nothing about advertising, was not persuaded it was a good thing in elections and would have been happier to get along without it. But he was shrewd enough to figure that if the other fellows were doing it, the Tories should probably do it too. Camp told Flemming's people he would need a budget of $30,000, and, to his mild surprise, they accepted the figure. The budget was not large—the Liberals would have three times as much for their friends at Walsh Advertising to spend—but it was a fortune for the penniless Tories. Still, they agreed to raise it, and they did.

Camp settled into the Lord Beaverbrook Hotel and laid plans for a three-week advertising campaign, which was all he felt his budget could manage. He and Ken Carson, Flemming's assistant, worked through the night to write the party platform; they barely had time to read it to the leader over the phone before they released it to the press and sent it off to the newspapers as a paid advertisement.

It was still the age of innocence in Canadian politics. Television was not a factor in 1952. "For all concerned, it was akin to life in the Garden of Eden," Camp wrote. "No one could then imagine television, know its impact upon politics, upon politicians and upon campaign financing—the snake had not yet been seen in the Garden."[11]

Camp was brilliant; no one doubted that. He demonstrated it in New Brunswick and in dozens of other campaigns over the years. But he was not a classic strategist. He was a great counter-puncher. His genius lay in his ability to see into his opponents' campaigns, to anticipate their actions. He could spot a foe's weakness and attack it before the foe could adjust. And when an opponent made a misstep, Camp would be on him in a flash. Speed was crucial. For the sake of immediacy, he always produced his radio scripts and newspaper ad copy at the last possible moment.

In New Brunswick in 1952, Camp was aided—as most successful campaigners are—by the seeming determination of the other side to inflict mortal injury on itself. He understood intuitively the first law of politics: when your enemies are trying to defeat themselves, get out of the way. He knew McNair and his party well, and he sensed that after 17 years in power the Liberals were imploding. "When men in power lose their touch, their facility in determining the political climate, the tragedy is always that they are the last to know it is gone," he wrote in Gentlemen, Players and Politicians.[12]

Camp was extremely fortunate to be running a campaign in a province in which the daily newspapers largely ignored politics. In that vacuum, the newspaper ads and radio commercials that Camp wrote had an extra impact; they attracted as much interest in New Brunswick as regular election news reports did in provinces that were better served by their news media.

He did several unique things that would serve as a template for later campaigns across the country. He commissioned a young Canadian cartoonist, Duncan Macpherson, to draw four cartoons for the Tory campaign. They were the first political cartoons Macpherson had ever drawn, and afterward Camp would lightheartedly claim credit for discovering Macpherson and propelling him to fame as the leading political cartoonist of his generation in Canada. Camp also determined who was the most popular radio announcer in the provincial capital—Jack Fenety, the voice of station CFNB—and hired him to read the one-minute commercials that Camp banged out on his portable typewriter. These commercial spots infuriated the Liberals, who had apparently never thought of using Fenety themselves.

And he took advantage of the lack of political reporting by writing his own daily opinion "columns" or "editorials," which he sent off to every daily newspaper in the province, to be run in space purchased by the Conservative party. They appeared under the pseudonym L.C. House—a play on the Tory campaign slogan, "Let's Clean House." The columns were controversial, provocative and fun. Readers read them with enjoyment and waited with keen interest to see what issue L.C. House would tackle next.

Those issues reflected Camp's counter-punching style. He did not try to promote Conservative policies or the virtues of the candidates. Instead, he attacked the Liberal record: an unpopular new 4 per cent sales tax; the mismanagement of road construction that had led to a public inquiry; the extravagance of the new Power Commission; and a feud between the minister of health and the York County Medical Association. There were plenty of issues to fuel the radio commercials and the columns of L.C. House. Camp recalled: "McNair, stung by the editorials, offended by Macpherson's cartoons, needled by Fenety's daily joustings, reacted in cold fury. Taking to radio, he sent me a personal message, referring to 'the Camp-following York County Tory machine.' I took it as a compliment."[13]

As he would do in subsequent elections in other provinces, Camp insisted that his leader stay above the fray. At one point, Flemming, both surprised and intrigued by the public response to the L.C. House columns, suggested that they appear under his name, instead, and perhaps include his picture. Camp refused. It was important, he believed, to wage battle on two levels. While Camp fought the Liberals tooth and nail in print and on the airwaves, Flemming did what he did best, amiably touring the province, greeting voters and making bland little speeches in which he set out cautious policy proposals. He did not promise to eliminate the sales tax, but rather to "proceed toward the abolition" of the tax, a distinction that escaped many voters. He promised to "put the province on a sound business footing"—but without reducing important services.

Camp's strategy worked. On September 22, 1952, the Liberals were swept aside as Hugh John Flemming's Conservatives took 36 of the 52 seats. "Congratulations," Camp said to the premier-elect. "Well," Flemming replied, "congratulations to *you*, young man." The Tory triumph was so unexpected that Canadian Press declared the New Brunswick election to be the second biggest news story in Canada in 1952. It was Camp's first triumph, and it became his talisman. It made him a player. It gave him a certain celebrity in political circles across the country. Liberals in other provinces would become nervous when they heard Dalton Camp was in town. "I became after that a kind of good luck charm to the Conservative party," he said. "Whenever they had anything going they would always call me."[14]

Gordon Fairweather was elected for the first time in that 1952 election; he would go on to become the province's attorney general, a federal MP and, after he left elected politics, head of the Canadian Human Rights Commission. A Red Tory, he became one of the leading caucus opponents of John Diefenbaker and an early Camp ally in the leadership review campaign. But in 1952, Fairweather was intimidated by Camp. "I was just an MLA and we were in Fredericton and there was a certain mystique about this Toronto man," Fairweather remembered. "He'd made it, and down he comes and runs the election and we win! [We asked ourselves] 'What does Dalton think? What does Dalton say?'"[15]

The New Brunswick campaign established a formula that Camp would use in the next few years to orchestrate the election of Conservative governments in Nova Scotia (Robert Stanfield, 1956), Manitoba (Duff Roblin, 1958) and Prince Edward Island (Walter Shaw, 1959). Camp reckoned that he employed the lessons he learned and techniques he developed in New Brunswick to no fewer than 28 election campaigns, federal or provincial, over the next two decades.

The 1952 election in New Brunswick also set Camp's course in business. A grateful Premier Flemming took the province's tourism advertising account away from Walsh Advertising, the Liberal agency, and gave it to Camp and Locke Johnson. It was just the beginning. Tourism accounts in other provinces followed on the heels of election successes, and Camp used those accounts to launch his own advertising agency, Dalton K. Camp and Associates—a business that made him a wealthy man in relatively few years.

He was almost irrationally happy to be a Tory: "I found myself among kindred spirits, disarming in their innocence of power, uncorrupted by arrogance or cynicism, endearing in their stoic perseverance and uncomplicated in their loyalty to that mysterious meaning of Conservatism."[16]

CHAPTER 7

Not Bright Enough for Two

N O REGION OF CANADA was a bleaker wasteland for Conservatives than Atlantic Canada in the early 1950s. Until the great upset in New Brunswick in 1952, all four Atlantic provinces had been solidly Liberal, and seemed destined to stay that way indefinitely.[1] New Brunswick and Prince Edward Island had been Liberal since 1935 and Nova Scotia since 1933. Liberal Joey Smallwood took an iron grip on Newfoundland when the province joined Canada in 1949, a grip that would not be broken for 23 years. It was such hostile territory that Camp was warned by Newfoundland Tories not to let the Liberals find out when he was visiting the province, lest his body be found floating in a river one morning.

They were not being wholly facetious; Smallwood was known to have informants at the airport who kept him personally posted on the arrival of suspicious strangers from the mainland. Flora MacDonald, for one, was convinced she was at risk when she went to Newfoundland on Tory party business; she would always stay anonymously with relatives, telling as few people as possible that she was there. When Camp went to St. John's, he stayed in a hotel registered under the name of James McGrath, a Tory MP (and future lieutenant-governor).

When a contrarian like Camp looked at Atlantic Canada, however, instead of a wasteland he saw fallow fields that with careful cultivation would one day sprout Tory governments. And he reasoned that no matter what he did, he was bound to improve the plight of the Conservatives. He could not make it any worse than it already was, could he?

Well, yes, he could. The P.E.I. election of 1955 proved that. Camp learned a valuable lesson: just as all provinces are different, so are their electorates. They have unique views of the political process, and they respond in different ways to the issue of what is fair or unfair when they encounter a hired gun like Camp. Unaware of these subtleties, Camp made the mistake of applying precisely the same campaign formula that had worked so well in New Brunswick in 1952 to P.E.I. three years later. As he conceded afterward, the election might have gone better if he had stayed in Toronto.

When the election was called for May 25, Camp booked into the Charlottetown Hotel, the principal hostelry in the capital, and checked out the local news media. He was delighted with what he discovered. There were only two daily newspapers on the Island, the Charlottetown *Guardian* and the *Patriot*, published in Summerside. They were small papers, thin on news content, and each could be read comfortably in 10 minutes or less. They were perfect for his purposes. The only other media operation that mattered was the Charlottetown radio station, and it was conveniently located next door to the hotel.

Camp was particularly attracted to an unusual advertising buy offered by the *Guardian*. He could purchase a banner headline on the front page, across the top or bottom, or both. This seemed an ideal way to publicize party slogans. As he had in New Brunswick, he also bought advertising space inside both newspapers for the political "columns" that he wrote in his hotel room. As in New Brunswick, the columns created a minor sensation among readers; Islanders had never encountered anything like them. Unlike New Brunswick, however, the reaction was largely negative. Islanders did not like the nasty edge to Camp's writing, which became increasingly strident as he saw the election slipping away from him.

It probably did not help that he was viewed as being too clever by half. In New Brunswick, he was at home, campaigning in the province where he had been born. In Prince Edward Island, he was an outsider—a slick adman come from Toronto to tell the locals how to vote.

It certainly did not help that he did not understand the intricacies of P.E.I.'s arcane electoral system. The province had a voting population of about 40,000—equivalent to a large town in other parts of Canada. It was divided into 15 constituencies, each of which sent two members (known as a councillor and an assemblyman) to the legislature. In those days, property owners were entitled to cast votes for both councillor and assemblyman; non-property owners could vote only for assemblyman.

There was another wrinkle. A property owner was permitted to vote in any and all constituencies where he owned property. A person who owned a home, business and cottage in three different constituencies, for example, could legally cast six votes, whereas a poor person would have only one vote. It was not at all unusual in 1955 to come across residents with six or more votes. In these 15 small constituencies, where a few dozen votes could be the difference between defeat and comfortable victory, it was vitally important that a party be able to identify the multiple vote holders, to know which ones were its supporters and to have the organization ferry them to the various polling stations on election day. The Liberals had the voter intelligence, the workers and the financial means to provide election-day transportation. The Tories did not. Without these other necessities, even the best advertising in the world would not have produced victory for the Conservatives.

Camp knew his campaign was surely doomed a few days before the balloting, when he got a glimpse of the Liberals' preparations for their voting-day "treating." "Treating" was a time-honoured, and corrupt, practice throughout the Maritimes in those days. In Nova Scotia, he knew, whole families, especially in rural areas, would refuse to go to the polls until they had been "treated" by one party or another. The "treats" did not have to be large: perhaps chocolates or stockings for the women, a pint of rum for the men, candies for the children. In close elections, two- or even five-dollar bills might change hands. The bribes might be proffered to purchase votes, or simply to persuade supporters of the opposing party to stay at home on election day.

In P.E.I., on the weekend before the 1955 election, Camp and David Stewart, the mayor of Charlottetown, had driven to Stewart's club. While Stewart went inside, Camp stayed in the car listening to the news on the radio. As he described the scene in *Gentlemen, Players and Politicians*, another car pulled alongside and the driver began loading cases of liquor into the trunk.

"Hello," the man said. "I know who you are. You're that fellow Camp." Camp acknowledged that he was and asked the man who he was. "It doesn't matter," was the reply. "But I know all about you. You're a bright fellow, Mr. Camp. Heard all about you."

He took my hand and shook it.

"I like you, Mr. Camp," he said.

I decided he was sober, nonetheless, and also that he was a Liberal. "See that stuff?" He pointed to the trunk, stuffed with booze.

"That's election ammunition," he said, with pride in his voice. "And because I like you, Mr. Camp, I want to say to you that I'm sorry for what we are going to do to your Tory friends on election day. I really am. I'm sorry for you because I like you, Mr. Camp."

He closed the trunk, entered his car and drove away.[2]

The results on May 25, 1955, were even worse than Camp had feared. The Conservatives, who in the previous election in 1951 had won six of the 30 seats without the benefit of his guiding hand, managed to take only three seats. When he reflected in later years on the beating he took in P.E.I., Camp was sometimes reminded of an observation that Hugh John Flemming once made about him: "Too smart for one, but not quite bright enough for two."

He was bright enough to keep his distance from the next Island election. In 1959, Camp sent Fred Boyer, one of his associates in the advertising agency, to Charlottetown, while he stayed in the background, pulling strings from Toronto. It worked. The Tories won 22 seats to the Liberals' eight, and the new Conservative leader, Walter Shaw, became premier of Canada's smallest province at the age of 71.

CHAPTER 8

The Alter Ego

SIX MONTHS AFTER THE CONSERVATIVE victory in New Brunswick, Camp received a call from the Tory national president, George Nowlan, who was an MP from Nova Scotia (and would later serve as a minister in the Diefenbaker cabinet), to ask if he would mind popping down to Halifax to have a word with the party's provincial leader, Robert Stanfield. Although a provincial election was in the air, the Tories were labouring under no false hopes. Nowlan cautioned Camp that Nova Scotia was not going to be as easy as New Brunswick—and the reticent Stanfield was no Hugh John Flemming. No one, he said, was going to beat the Liberal premier, the legendary Angus L. Macdonald.

When Camp caught up to Stanfield at his law office in Halifax, he found him to be as diffident as Nowlan had warned he would be. The Tories had had no members in the legislature when he was elected leader in 1948, and he had nursed it up to eight seats by the time he met Camp in 1953. "This is not New Brunswick," Stanfield warned him. "The Grits are pretty strong here."[1] Although he did not expect to win, he did think he would do better than the last time. Not a whole lot, but "somewhat" better. No one, he confirmed, was going to beat Angus L.

It was an inauspicious beginning to a remarkable relationship. Over a period of nearly five decades, that relationship would develop and deepen, surviving periods of estrangement, until it bound Dalton Camp and Robert Stanfield together in the minds of politicians, journalists and most Canadians who paid attention to politics. Whenever people thought of Dalton Camp, they thought of Robert Stanfield, and vice versa. They were each other's alter ego.

Stanfield would be proved right in 1953. Despite Camp's help, he did not win, though he did do somewhat better (a total of 12 seats). But Camp was there to guide him to victory in 1956 and to help him get re-elected three times—"I don't think we'd have made it without Camp," Stanfield said.[2]

In 1966, Stanfield supported Camp's successful campaign to force a review of John Diefenbaker's leadership, delivering Nova Scotia delegates to Camp's side. Camp, in turn, was the key player in persuading Stanfield to leave provincial politics to seek the national leadership the following year. He plotted the strategy and wrote the speeches that carried Stanfield to victory at the convention in Toronto's Maple Leaf Gardens. Despite a period of strained relations in the late 1960s and early 1970s—Camp felt betrayed because Stanfield did not acknowledge his contributions and sacrifices, while Stanfield was worried that any overt association with Camp would further alienate Diefenbaker loyalists in his tinderbox caucus on Parliament Hill—they never lost their respect for each other. Each man remained the other's most fervent supporter.

Camp did not often meet people whom he regarded as his intellectual equal. Stanfield was that. Both were extremely bright. Both were students of political history. Both had a grasp of serious issues. And both were involved in politics because they thought they could make a difference. The two men were very different in most other ways, however. Stanfield was thoughtful, reflective, realistic, cautious, a master of understatement and almost painfully deliberate in word and deed. (They used to say in Nova Scotia that when Bob Stanfield made a speech, he spoke so slowly and carefully that his listeners could slip out for a beer between sentences.) Camp, on the other hand, was quick, impulsive, optimistic and highly articulate—glib, his detractors would say—in print and in speech.

Camp loved language; to him, it was an art form, a tool of persuasion. Stanfield liked his language plain; he was uncomfortable appealing to the senses or feelings. Yet the two men complemented each other. Camp understood that people vote as much with their emotions as with their minds, that there has to be an element of theatre to politics. He taught Stanfield to inject passion and enthusiasm into his speeches, helping to lift him from the plodding provincial politician to an articulate, if not dynamic, national leader—a man who would come within two seats of winning the federal election of 1972. For his part, Stanfield taught Camp a greater appreciation of the values of introspection, self-discipline and restraint.

Stanfield also radiated honesty—a quality that appealed greatly to Camp who, as a son of the manse, had been appalled by the corruption he had seen in the New Brunswick Liberal party. Flora MacDonald was a close friend of both men. "He met Stanfield, and Stanfield made a real impression on him," she said. "Here was somebody who couldn't be bought, and wouldn't try to buy others. And that meant a lot to Dalton—he didn't like to be arm-twisted."[3]

Camp's initial reaction on meeting Stanfield in 1953 was restrained. "God knows he needed help; I don't believe I ever saw anyone who needed more of it," Camp wrote in *Gentlemen, Players and Politicians*.[4] Puzzled by Stanfield's diffidence and worried that he would simply get on the leader's nerves, Camp flew back to Toronto, half hoping Stanfield would look elsewhere for campaign assistance.

When the writ was issued for a general election on May 26, 1953, however, Stanfield wired Camp, asking him to return right away. Camp checked into the Lord Nelson Hotel, known as the "Tory hotel" in a town that took its partisanship seriously (the Liberals used the Nova Scotian, which was owned by Canadian National Railways and was deemed to be the "government hotel"). He began to address the same issue he had faced in New Brunswick: how to fight an election everyone believed was lost before it had started. The Nova Scotia Liberals, in office for 20 years, should have been an easy target. There was corruption, there was scandal, and aside from the premier, the cabinet was a dreary collection of mediocrities. But Angus L. Macdonald towered above his caucus. He was a far more formidable foe than John McNair, who had been the Liberal premier of New Brunswick until he was ousted in the 1952 election there. To his core voters—the Liberal Catholics of Cape Breton and the city of Halifax—Angus L. was a secular saint.

Because Macdonald's integrity was deemed to be above question, Camp went into the campaign with one hand tied behind his back: he was repeatedly admonished by anxious Tories not to attack the premier. He was not even supposed to mention his name. He expressed his frustration: "So, if the bishops were bunglers and the priests corrupt, the Pope was sacrosanct, leaving the Tories in eternal purgatory."[5]

Camp tried to use the same weapons he had employed in New Brunswick the year before. The obstacles were higher, however. The only Nova Scotia newspaper with province-wide distribution was the Halifax Chronicle-Herald (known to its legions of detractors as the "Chronically Horrid"). As in New Brunswick, Camp began writing a series of editorial-style advertisements. The provocative ads quickly caught the eye of the Chronicle-Herald's managers. They were alarmed and served notice that they would not publish any more of Camp's copy unless they received it 48 hours in advance of publication, ostensibly to have it checked for libel, though Camp suspected the true intent was to give the Liberals advance notice of Conservative tactics. The 48-hour requirement robbed the ads of their immediacy and prevented Camp, the counter-puncher, from responding effectively to Liberal promises and gaffes. Camp appealed to the publisher, to no avail. His editorials or columns had, in consequence, more bark than bite.

His problems with CHNS, the radio station owned by the newspaper, were even more vexing. The station diligently applied a set of broadcasting regulations that were seemingly designed to keep all political broadcasts as sterile and uninteresting as humanly possible. Camp looked for a Nova Scotia equivalent to Jack Fenety in New Brunswick. He settled on John Funston, a popular sports announcer at CHNS. The station management objected. To Camp's fury, it decreed that if Funston did commercials for the Tories, he would have to be available to the Liberals as well. And that's what happened. The Liberals woke up. Angus L. Macdonald complained about "Mr. Stanfield and his Toronto advertising writer," and the Liberals booked a series of commercial on CHNS, to be recorded by John Funston.

The Liberal commercials infuriated the Tories and confused the voters, who could not fathom why Funston had suddenly become the voice of the Liberals, too. Neither could other radio stations in the province to which CHNS supplied tapes of political commercials; some refused to broadcast the Liberal tapes. Although CHNS reversed its policy and agreed to let Camp have exclusive use of Funston, the station found another way to harass the Conservatives. It refused to accept a 15-minute free-time address by G.I. "Ike" Smith, Stanfield's running mate in Colchester riding, unless it was rewritten. Substantial portions of Smith's text were not suitable for broadcast, Camp was told.

Thoroughly frustrated, he went around to the other private radio station in Halifax, CJCH, which he had learned was managed by a young, prematurely grey Cape Bretoner, Finlay MacDonald. MacDonald's father had been a Tory member of Parliament but Finlay himself appeared to be a Liberal; he had signed nomination papers for his friend Angus L. Macdonald in the riding of Halifax South. Camp poured out his complaints about CHNS, culminating in the censorship of Ike Smith.

"Wait a minute," MacDonald said. He marched down the hall to the studio, flipped open the microphone and announced to CJCH listeners that all politicians and political parties were welcome at his station. The air was free and politicians could say whatever they wanted without interference or censorship from the radio station. He returned to his office, sat down and said to Camp, "Now, what else can we do?"

"It was the beginning of a beautiful friendship," Camp wrote. "Finlay MacDonald became a formidable political ally: decisive, resourceful, fearless, and intelligent. I would not have wanted him as an adversary."[6]

Camp had not been impressed with Stanfield's organization. He found it composed largely of genial, well-intentioned survivors; urgency was unknown to them and they moved at a glacial pace as they contemplated the prospect of yet another electoral defeat. There were a few exceptions, and Camp found one of them in Halifax South directing the Tory campaign against Angus L. Macdonald. He was Rod Black, the son of a former highways minister. Rod Black was a superb organizer, with a capacity for detail, the ability to delegate responsibility and the patience to listen to the opinions and advice of others. Just as important, Black knew the territory; he knew politics where it was really played—on the street corners and at the polling booths. As Camp wrote, "Black knew about false enumeration, impersonation, telegraphing, bribery, and intimidation, and all the arts and practices of party machines; but unlike his Tory contemporaries, he was not afraid to meet the practices of machine politics head on."[7]

The Conservatives did not win Halifax South in 1953. Angus L. died the next year, however, and Black and Camp returned to the trenches for the by-election to help the Tory candidate, Halifax Mayor Richard Donahoe. Donahoe won, breaking the Liberals' hold on Halifax and demonstrating that the Conservatives could win a predominantly Catholic seat. The 1954 Halifax South by-election was the harbinger of Tory triumphs to come. Rod Black became a staunch ally to Camp and a crucial player in Stanfield's victory in 1956 and subsequent re-elections. By 1960, Black was running the gritty organizational side of the Stanfield campaigns while Camp looked after the so-called intellectual side: planning, strategy, speeches and advertising.

Finlay MacDonald was Camp's other key find in that 1953 election. His skills were quite different from Black's. He did not know much, or care, about politics at the polling subdivision level. But he was, Camp discovered, both an innovator and an activist, which made him a uniquely valuable commodity in a Conservative organization that was singularly short on inspiration and new ideas. MacDonald was the dynamo Camp and Stanfield desperately needed; he organized rallies, testimonial dinners and network radio and television productions.

In *Gentlemen, Players and Politicians*, Camp wrote a remarkable paragraph about MacDonald. It was remarkable because it captured the essence of the man. But it was also remarkable because the very same words could have been written, with equal perception and accuracy, about Camp himself:

> Articulate, sophisticated, and self-sufficient, Finlay MacDonald and men like him make politicians uneasy. Such men are likely to be held suspect, since the simple family traditions of Toryism and the familiar tribal loyalties of politics are plainly not much a part of them.

Furthermore, such men are as complex, in themselves, as the system in which they operate. Their lifestyles are different, as are their values. Often their personal independence makes them seem unreliable, while at other times their catholicity of outlook makes them appear indifferent.[8]

As self-analysis, that would have been brilliant. Camp was every bit as complex as MacDonald. He possessed the same qualities of articulateness, sophistication, self-sufficiency and independence. His lifestyle was very much his own and, like MacDonald, he made other politicians uneasy. Neither of them would ever be fully accepted by some of their peers—even by some who owed their careers to Camp.

Camp and MacDonald became close friends—so close they almost seemed like brothers. "Dad liked people who could make him laugh, and Finlay made him laugh," David Camp, Dalton's eldest son, recalled:

> I remember the two of them doing this skit about the FBI. There'd been a report about J. Edgar Hoover taping the private life of Martin Luther King, and the tapes recorded an awful lot of sexual activity, not with his wife. The two of them started to act out the parts of FBI agents, getting the assignment, listening with water glasses at the wall—"Whoa, are you getting this stuff?" It was hilarious. They could take small material and improvise on the spot. They were great actors and entertainers—very, very funny.[9]

In the 1960s, a third Tory joined the group: Richard Hatfield, who became premier of New Brunswick from 1970 to 1987. Hatfield spent so much time at Camp's home and cottage in New Brunswick that Camp's family regarded him as just another member of the household. One of MacDonald's lovers recalled that in the time she was with him a day seldom passed when MacDonald, Camp and Hatfield did not talk on the telephone. Hatfield died in 1991, with Camp and MacDonald at his bedside.

MacDonald and Camp died within weeks of each other in 2002. Shortly before his own death, Finlay MacDonald was interviewed by Hugh Winsor of the *Globe and Mail* about his friend Camp, who was then in hospital in Fredericton after suffering a stroke. "He introduced me to Bob Stanfield, which was the greatest favour he could ever have done for me," MacDonald said. "Dalton and I ran all of Stanfield's campaigns. We used to argue a lot. Dalton was a difficult person to work with, but I prided myself on really getting along well with him. I knew what made him tick. I always deferred, particularly in matters of strategy. We complemented each other very, very well."[10]

If the New Brunswick victory established Camp's reputation, Nova Scotia became his hallmark. It was partly winning the election there in 1956 (and 1960, 1963 and 1967). It was partly the enduring Stanfield connection. And it was partly the talent that Camp found in Nova Scotia for the political wars that lay ahead of him across the country. Finlay MacDonald in 1953 was the first. The 1956 provincial election brought Flora MacDonald (also from Cape Breton, but no relation to Finlay). During the 1958 federal election, Camp discovered Lowell Murray, a bright recent university graduate who was working at a television station in Sydney on Cape Breton. And the 1960 Nova Scotia election added to Camp's forces a student from St. Francis Xavier University in Antigonish who was preparing to enter law school in Halifax. Self-confident, smooth talking and fluently bilingual, his name was Brian Mulroney.

It was an amazing group. Although they all pursued separate careers, they worked to the same end in politics. Among them, they would write much of the history of the Tory party for the rest of the century.

PART 2

THE PLAYER

CHAPTER 9

On to Ottawa

CAMP'S PROWESS IN THE MARITIMES inevitably brought him to the attention of the power brokers in the federal Progressive Conservative party. He was invited to Ottawa to advise on advertising strategy for the general election expected before the fall in 1953 (it came in August). Stopping only long enough to buy a new grey flannel suit, Camp went directly to the capital from Nova Scotia, where he had been working in Robert Stanfield's campaign.

No one would have blamed him if he had declined the invitation. The federal Tories were a party on life support. Out of power since 1935, they had been crushed in four successive general elections and would surely face a fifth humiliating defeat whenever Louis St. Laurent chose to go to the polls in 1953. The Liberals had made a relatively seamless transition from Mackenzie King to his heir apparent St. Laurent. Under "Uncle Louis"—an improbable sobriquet for a former corporation lawyer and Laval University law professor—the Liberals were formidable, winning 191 of the 262 seats in the House of Commons in the 1949 election. They dominated in every region of the country. They even held two-thirds of the seats from Ontario, despite the fact that George Drew, the former premier, was now the Tories' federal leader.

Drew had image problems throughout his years as national leader. Where St. Laurent was able to shed the skin of a boardroom lawyer to be remade as everyone's favourite uncle, Drew was never able to escape from the popular perception that he was devoid of warmth and humour, that he was bombastic and partisan, a mouthpiece for business, and an insufferable stuffed shirt to boot. That stereotype was wrong, Camp decided. As he got to know Drew, he concluded that the leader did indeed lack the common touch, but not because he was arrogant or indifferent to the concerns of others, but because he was painfully shy and often wracked by self-doubt.

The Conservatives were obsessed with Ontario—for three reasons. First, the province accounted for 25 of the 41 seats they had won in 1949 (the only other province where they won more than two seats was British Columbia, which had elected three Tories). Second, Ontario was the only jurisdiction where the Tories had enjoyed consistent success at the provincial level, even though Leslie Frost, the premier, would not raise a finger to help Drew or the federal party. Third, Ontario was the only significant source of funds for the Tories. Not surprisingly, the party's policies were skewed heavily toward Ontario—and especially toward the interests of Bay Street—to the virtual exclusion of the rest of Canada. In short, the federal Progressive Conservatives were an orphan from Upper Canada masquerading as a national political party.

Camp knew, or at least suspected, all this on that spring day in 1953 as he made his way to his first meeting of the party's campaign planning committee, held in a private dining room tucked away behind the band platform in the Canadian Grill, the pretentious main dining room of the Chateau Laurier Hotel. The other members of this inner circle were: Richard A. Bell, the party's national director and a decent man whom many Tories thought arrogant; Cappé Kidd, the executive secretary, who had the only sense of humour in the national office; Kathleen Kearns, the indomitable office manager; Grattan O'Leary, a confidant to leaders who became editor of the *Ottawa Journal* and eventually a senator; J.M. Macdonnell, the party's finance critic; and Allister Grosart, a Toronto adman who shared with Camp the distinction of being the only person in the room who had ever managed a winning campaign—Grosart having done it for Drew and Frost in Ontario.

There was a natural tension between Camp, who was determined to control the advertising campaign in the impending election, and Grosart, whose McKim Advertising had mounted an extravagant and ineffective ad campaign in the 1949 election. The tension was exacerbated by a sharp difference of opinion over issues and strategy.

Over many drinks, Camp was asked how the New Brunswick election had been won. He told them the Conservatives won by consciously not sounding like Conservatives. They had won by attacking the Liberals on Liberal grounds, on social welfare issues, and they won by not declaiming constantly about high taxes and government spending, as Tories were wont to do. He urged the federal party to adopt a more human approach, to show compassion, to demonstrate understanding of the everyday concerns of ordinary Canadians.

The others patted Camp on the head, metaphorically, and moved on to the issue they really wanted to campaign on: a promise to cut taxes. Seeing Camp's dismay, Grosart announced he would arrange to have McKim take a public opinion survey. It was the kind of poll that gives polling a bad name. Respondents were asked if they thought taxes were too high. Not surprisingly, 85 per cent said they were. They were then asked whether they agreed that high taxes were to blame for high prices. Thus prompted, 66 per cent agreed. When asked what kept taxes so high, 57 per cent cited government waste and extravagance.

There, in a nutshell, was the Conservative campaign as far as Grosart and most of the other committee members were concerned: attack waste and extravagance and pledge to cut taxes.

The only question to be resolved was the size of the tax cut to be promised. "Let's be specific, let's say $500 million," said O'Leary, pulling a number out the air. Camp did not like it because he knew the damage that a massive reduction in federal spending would cause in poor provinces like the Maritimes. Macdonnell, the finance critic, did not like it either, because he knew it could not be done—"And if we by any chance got elected, I would be the one who would have to do it." To which O'Leary replied, "Jim, for God's sake, what are you worried about? If you win, you'll think of something."

The $500 million tax cut was enshrined in the program, and not long afterward Drew opened his election campaign in London, Ontario, where he unveiled the tax plank. For all practical purposes, the election ended that night for the Tories. The press and the Liberals seized with glee on the Conservative promise. The Liberals crucified Tory candidates across the country by telling voters that the tax-cut policy of the Tory party—already viewed by many Canadians as the voice of Bay Street and corporate Canada—would mean reduced old age pensions, smaller family allowances, no increases in welfare payments or military salaries, and fewer new post offices, wharves and other public works. The Liberals did exactly what Camp would have done if the roles had been reversed: they attacked the Tories on the Tories' own ground, and they demolished them.

Any Conservative who was not running in a safe riding knew his or her chances had probably been snuffed out. In Saskatchewan, John Diefenbaker, the party's sole sitting MP, was furious. He disassociated himself and the party's other candidates in the province from the national campaign, informing headquarters that no advertising from Ottawa would be seen in Saskatchewan without his prior approval. The results in the 1953 election mirrored those in 1949 as the Liberals took 170 seats to the Conservatives' 51, and 33 of those 51 seats came from Ontario.

Political scientist Denis Smith asked Camp in 1968 whether he felt he had had any discernible influence on the 1953 campaign. "Absolutely none," was the reply.[1] In fact, Camp did not wait around to witness the carnage. Two weeks before the election, he walked out of headquarters, left Ottawa and returned to his cottage at Robertson's Point in New Brunswick. On election day, he and his wife drove to Wolfville, Nova Scotia, to drown their sorrows in Scotch with Tory MP George Nowlan as the results came in. "Dear God," he said to Camp, "where did we ever get that platform?" Camp professed surprise at Nowlan's question: "He was, after all, the party's national president."[2]

With the exception of the disastrous 1955 Prince Edward Island election, the 1953 federal campaign was the worst one Camp was ever involved in. His efforts to orchestrate an effective national publicity campaign had been doomed from the moment the disastrous platform was unveiled, and Camp knew it. He returned to Toronto to bury himself in his advertising work. In the spring of 1954, however, William Rowe, a sometime Tory troubleshooter and son of Earl Rowe, a Conservative MP and later lieutenant-governor of Ontario, called and suggested they meet. Over lunch at Simpson's Arcadian Court in Toronto, Rowe told Camp he had been offered the post of national director, replacing Richard Bell. He would accept only if Camp would go to Ottawa, too, to run the party's public relations. Camp had an intense dislike of Ottawa as a place to live and work. He found it a dreary, soul-destroying city— a view that was not moderated by the passage of time. He hated the endless round of meetings on which the capital thrives. In *Gentleman, Players and Politicians*, he described his feelings about some of the meetings he had sat through during the 1953 campaign:

> Sitting in airless, smoke-filled rooms in the company of grown men, hearing them pondering these words, chewing over each phrase, holding sentences of almost total vacuity up to the light of serious consideration, all conspired to make me physically ill. I found myself palpitating with suppressed rage, gripped by massive, throbbing headaches, stuttering and incoherent in speech, and I would again and again lapse into truculent silence.[3]

This almost irrational dislike of meetings was a Camp characteristic throughout his life. He preferred to think and work on his own. Even during the intense period when he was campaigning for a review of the Tory leadership in 1966, he tried to avoid formal meetings. He let others who enjoyed meetings more take care of them. Later, when he worked in Ottawa for Brian Mulroney, he would skip the morning planning meeting in the Prime Minister's Office whenever he could. He was not an organization man. He functioned best without a title or agenda.

Even so, Camp found himself drawn back to Ottawa. He and William Rowe agreed that Rowe would become the full-time national director and Camp would be his part-time publicity director, dividing his time between Toronto and Ottawa. He became a regular on the overnight train between the two cities. At 34, Camp had surrendered a large part of his life to the Tory machine, and he would not get it back until 1968, when he resigned as the party's national president.

By 1954 he was convinced that the only way to rebuild the federal structure was to develop support in the provinces, to help provincial Tories increase their strength, to elect provincial Conservative governments, and to use the organizational base and popular support of the provincial parties to create a stronger, more representative federal party. The Liberal party was just the opposite. It was centrally organized and controlled. Power flowed down from the top, from the Prime Minister's Office to the cabinet and caucus to the rank and file (as Camp had discovered to his dismay when he tangled with Robert Winters at the Liberal convention in 1948). The Tories were going to try to reverse that by building from the bottom up.

Camp and Rowe worked with Drew to develop their strategy to reinvent the party by strengthening the provinces. They already had Hugh John Flemming in New Brunswick; Bob Stanfield was coming on in Nova Scotia; and 37-year-old Duff Roblin was elected leader of the Manitoba Tories in June 1954. Camp and Rowe spent much of the rest of 1954 and 1955 travelling the country, getting to know provincial organizers, recruiting smart young people to stand as candidates or to work in the party backrooms, and offering such support as they could—advice on advertising and campaign strategy, a little money, a few warm bodies to help out—to provincial parties as they prepared for elections. They reasoned that as provincial parties came to power, the federal party would be able to tap them for money and manpower for national campaigns.

Camp proposed that the party make something special out of the one hundredth anniversary of its founding by staging a series of Second Century dinners in 1955. The idea was to raise some money, stress the party's long history, provide a national stage for the leader, display some of its national figures to people in the regions and generate some press interest. Four dinners were held in different cities, and they got a good response. The dinner in Winnipeg was important because it marked Camp's first encounter with John Diefenbaker; he had gone through the 1953 campaign without actually meeting the maverick MP from Saskatchewan.

In Winnipeg, as elsewhere, head table arrangements preoccupied the organizers. They had to accommodate national, regional and local luminaries and make sure that MPs and members of the

party executive were suitably seated. They had to find appropriate places for the spouses of the dignitaries. And they had to deal
with the uncertainty caused by some VIP guests who would not
let them know until the last moment whether they would attend.
Diefenbaker, in particular, was notorious for not responding to
invitations. The Winnipeg arrangements were further complicated by the fact that George Drew had been taken temporarily
to hospital suffering from chest congestion—an early manifesta-
tion of an illness that would cause him to resign as leader the
following year.

Camp was in his hotel room writing a speech for Drew when
Diefenbaker phoned to announce he was in town, would be attending the dinner with his wife and, yes, he would speak. No, he would
not tell Camp what he intended to talk about. No, he would not
have a text for the press.

Camp and Rowe decided that only three women could be
accommodated at the head table: Fiorenza Drew, the wife of the
leader; Ellen Fairclough, the MP from Hamilton, Ontario, who in
1957 would become the first woman cabinet minister in Canada;
and the wife of the mayor of Winnipeg. This meant Olive
Diefenbaker would be seated at a special table reserved for the
spouses of head table guests.

The dinner went off without any serious hitch. Diefenbaker was
superb. He made a brief, witty speech laden with anecdotes that
delighted the audience. Camp figured Diefenbaker was the star of
the evening. He breathed a sign of relief.

A year or so later, Camp wandered into the parliamentary cafeteria in Ottawa, where John and Olive Diefenbaker were eating.
Diefenbaker beckoned Camp over and told him to sit down. "His
opening words," Camp recalled, "were, 'I just want to tell you one
thing, young man, if you ever put my wife below salt, or if you ever
put her off the head table, you won't have me there, either.'" As
Olive tried to shush him, Diefenbaker dressed Camp down for what
seemed like five minutes: "I want to get this clear. I realize it wasn't
his fault. I know how these things happen." His eyes flashing, he
added, "You just keep that in mind."[4]

It was the first time Camp had been exposed to Diefenbaker's capacity to nurse a grudge. He wondered if he was paranoid. He became wary of the man who, with Drew's health failing, seemed destined to be the next leader of the party.

The year 1956 brought the infamous pipeline debate in Parliament, valiantly waged by Drew, followed by Drew's resignation on the advice of his doctors—and then, in December, the convention that finally made Diefenbaker leader after two earlier failed attempts. Camp was a marginal player in the leadership process. He assumed Diefenbaker would win easily—an assumption that became an ironclad certainty when Ontario's Leslie Frost declared his support for the Saskatchewan MP and instructed his key people, including Grosart, to campaign for him. Camp could not bring himself to support Diefenbaker; nor could he bring himself to oppose him. In the end, he did not vote.

In truth, he was less concerned that year with the national leadership than he was with the October 30 provincial election in Nova Scotia in which Stanfield was elected premier. Camp talked the organizers of the leadership convention into inviting Stanfield, rather than Grattan O'Leary, to be the keynote speaker. The new premier agreed to do it, on the condition that Camp write his speech. Camp did, and he put some of his own convictions into it. Sitting at the back of the hall, he listened as Stanfield read his words, urging the party to pay new attention to the sort of Canadians to whom the Tories had had little or nothing to say for many years:

> There are many Canadians who, despite this rich abundance, live in mean and helpless circumstances. There are those who are in want, those handicapped by grinding poverty, those deprived of good fortune by the simple lack of opportunity. There are those made helpless by circumstances beyond them, the infirm and the sick. There are slums and depressed areas, and in them there is suffering and despair enough to be a blight upon any democracy.
>
> And yet there are those in public life today who believe they have exhausted government's capacity to uplift and elevate the state of mankind in this society. There is no sadder spectacle than the politician holding office who truly believes his own propaganda.

Those were heartfelt words. They would have been jarringly out of place if anyone had dared to utter them from a Conservative platform in the 1953 election, when the party had been fixated on tax cuts and spending reductions. They were words for a new party, a new leader and a new campaign. The next election was going to be very different.

Initially, however, Camp was reluctant to get too involved. He was tired. He was concerned that Diefenbaker's people were conducting a purge of Drew supporters. And he found Diefenbaker himself unsettling—erratic, temperamental and a loner. As far back as 1956, a lot of loose talk was making the rounds. "I think I could say from memory that people said to me that he was mad; he was a dangerous fellow," Camp reflected in a 1969 interview.[5]

After the leadership convention, he stayed around long enough to tidy up loose ends at headquarters, then headed back to Toronto, to his family and his advertising job at Locke Johnson. Diefenbaker, however, wanted him in Ottawa, and he passed that wish to Camp via Allister Grosart, Winnipeg MP Gordon Churchill and other intermediaries. Camp told them that if Diefenbaker wanted him, he would have to ask him himself. Camp described to Denis Smith this encounter at the 1957 Parliamentary Press Gallery dinner: "I walked into the Railway Committee Room, and Diefenbaker was standing by the door.... I walked up to him, or I walked right past him, rather, and he reached out his arm and put it around me and grabbed me by the neck and held me against his chest, and said something like, 'You and I are going to be in this [together]'—something like that—'aren't we?'"[6]

As would happen nearly 30 years later when Brian Mulroney asked him to move to Ottawa and help him in the Prime Minister's Office, Camp would find it impossible to say no to his leader. That night in 1957 he and a few others liberated a case of champagne from a journalist's home and polished it off before dawn. He returned to Toronto the next day with a terrible hangover, but Diefenbaker had softened him up. When the call came to prepare an advertising plan for the 1957 campaign, he agreed.

That election was a far cry from the disastrous one four years earlier. For one thing, Camp was put in complete charge of the party's national advertising effort and given a free hand in designing it. For another thing, the Liberals handed him issues to use against them.

The biggest issue came out of the debate that had dominated Parliament Hill from May 14 to June 5, 1956. C.D. Howe, St. Laurent's most powerful minister, tried to ram a bill through Parliament to authorize the government to loan TransCanada PipeLines Ltd., a U.S.-owned company, $80 million toward the cost of building a natural gas pipeline from Alberta to Winnipeg. It would then plug into the eastern Canadian grid, which would in turn carry gas to export to the eastern United States. The problem was not the pipeline project itself, although its foreign ownership was an issue to the Tories. The real problem was the haste with which Howe wanted to rush the bill through the House of Commons; the government was anxious that the pipeline be built before it called an election in 1957. It decided to restrict debate by using "closure," a procedural device that had been employed on only seven occasions in Canadian parliamentary history. This time, the Liberals did something that had never been done before: they used closure to cut off debate at all five stages of a single bill—resolution, first and second reading, committee and third reading. Bedlam reigned. At one point, Tory frontbencher Donald Fleming was expelled from the House. The climax came on Friday, June 1, when the Speaker of the House, under intense pressure from Liberal ministers, reversed a previous ruling and disallowed a motion by the Cooperative Commonwealth Federation, forerunner of the New Democratic Party, that would have enabled the opposition to extend the debate. It became known as "Black Friday."

As the election neared, Camp and his associates at Locke Johnson—Bill Kettlewell, the creative director, and Hank Loriaux, an account executive—set to work designing the two principal print ads for the Tory campaign. They took a *Globe and Mail* cartoon by James Reidford as the motif for one full-page ad. It depicted the Peace Tower as a guillotine and carried the stark headline,

"Black Friday." The other, equally powerful ad was an uncluttered full page with a square-cut photo of Diefenbaker, a block of type containing testimonials from various newspapers and a blank space at the bottom for a slogan. They wanted a slogan that would convey the message that it was time to get rid of the Liberals. As the admen brainstormed, they knew they should not emphasize the name "Progressive Conservative" because of the negative connotations it had for voters after so many years of futile opposition. They wanted something that would do for the federal Tories what "Let's Clean House" had done for Hugh John Flemming in New Brunswick in 1952. It was Loriaux who finally came up with it: "It's Time for a Diefenbaker Government." It was perfect, Camp told them.

The two ads—"Black Friday" and "It's Time for a Diefenbaker Government"—formed the core of the Conservatives' $200,000 advertising campaign. They appeared in newspapers and magazines across the country and were turned into brochures for candidates to distribute.

In addition to his responsibility for national advertising, Camp ran Diefenbaker's campaign in the Maritime provinces from offices in Halifax. Thinking back to his days as a student Liberal, when he had been frustrated in his efforts to get the Liberal party to act on a package of Atlantic resolutions, he came up with the idea of having Diefenbaker endorse an Atlantic Manifesto, the central element of which would be a commitment that a Diefenbaker government would provide grants to the four cash-strapped eastern provinces above and beyond the federal-provincial funding formula. He arranged to have many of the senior Conservatives from the Atlantic region assemble in Moncton. Camp and Ken Carson, from the New Brunswick party, worked in a hotel room, writing resolutions. As they finished each one, Nova Scotia MP George Nowlan would take it downstairs to be debated by the assembled Tories. At the end of the exercise, they had their manifesto, a set of unanimously approved Atlantic resolutions.

The only hurdle now was Diefenbaker, who knew nothing about the resolutions and who, as Camp well knew, could be temperamental and unpredictable. Camp took the manifesto to Saint John, where the leader was campaigning. Diefenbaker read the resolutions but said he could not accept them. Camp's hopes seemed dashed. Later that day, however, while Diefenbaker was being interviewed on local television, he was asked by Tom Bell, the Tory candidate in Saint John, whether he had seen the Atlantic Manifesto. "Well, I think those Atlantic resolutions are marvelous," he replied. "If we get elected, this is what we are going to do." Camp was dumb-founded, but delighted. The Atlantic Manifesto became the centrepiece of the Tory campaign in Eastern Canada. National headquarters in Ottawa paid for some of the promotion, and Camp arranged for the Conservative parties in New Brunswick and Nova Scotia to cover the rest of the cost. "I think they probably were effective in the campaign in the sense that they gave a cohesiveness to the party there and were good for morale," he said.[7]

Camp made a point of meeting Diefenbaker whenever he entered Atlantic Canada and travelling with him as long as he was in the region. He wrote his speeches, supplied local colour and issues for Diefenbaker's extemporaneous remarks and briefed him wherever he went, providing lists of the names and duties of the people he would meet at each stop. It was his first sustained expo-sure to the new leader, and Camp could feel many of his early doubts begin to dissolve. "Diefenbaker was absolutely superb in the campaign of '57, in many ways at his best," he said. "He was agree-able, and he gave the impression of being flexible."

Diefenbaker the campaigner was totally unlike George Drew as he reached out to ordinary voters—the sort of people Stanfield had talked about in his Camp-ghosted keynote speech at the leadership convention. "[Diefenbaker] was so clearly non-establishment, and he was so clearly able to identify with people who had never really had a chance in life," Camp said. "They sud-denly saw something in him, and he had an easy way with them, and it was very, very impressive."[8]

All speechwriters fret about the way their clients use or abuse their material. Will they use it all? Will they emphasize the right sections? Will they deliver the words with outrage, incredulity, pas-sion, concern, humour or whatever the speech calls for? Will they recognize the punch lines? Most politicians disappoint their ghost-writers. Diefenbaker was one of the exceptions. "He was one of the few people that ever improved on my material," Camp said.

> He seemed to know where the knife met the bone and he knew how to get it out and put it over [to the audience], and he had a way then, in that particular year, of touching people, of reaching people.... [He] made Conservatives feel good and made people hopeful, especially in this godforsaken part of the country....
>
> He had time for everybody. He had time for waitresses, and he had time for taxi drivers, and he was just an amazing man. [It was as though] the whole country was Prince Albert.[9]

Four decades later, Camp still had a vivid memory of getting off the Diefenbaker train in Moncton and standing on the platform while he waited for it to pull out of the station. Olive Diefenbaker was late because she had been campaigning separately outside the city. When Diefenbaker saw her approaching, he picked up a loud-hailer and shouted a mock rebuke: "You've kept all these people waiting. A terrible thing. Hurry up." She got aboard, and as the train pulled out, Diefenbaker said to his wife, "Olive, wave to Dalton." She waved and he waved back. "I suddenly found I had tears in my eyes and it just suddenly struck me—You're gonna win!"[10]

As he watched the train disappear in the distance, Camp knew he had been won over. "I can't say that I kept any reserve," he reflected. "I think standing on the platform I decided I'd forgive him, you know, for all the things that I had felt about him in the past. [They] were just washed away in that one Maritime swing."

The doubts would return later. For the moment, however, he was swept up in the joy of being a Tory. After 22 years in office, the Liberals were finished. "Uncle Louis" St. Laurent would retire, a broken man. John Diefenbaker would become prime minister at the head of a minority government as the Conservatives elected 113 members to 103 Liberals. The Maritimes did their bit, and more. New Brunswick, long a Liberal stronghold, split its 10 seats evenly between the two parties. Prince Edward Island gave all four of its seats to the Tories, while Nova Scotia, with 12 seats, elected 10

Conservatives, up from just one in 1953. Only Newfoundland, in the tight control of Joey Smallwood, resisted the Diefenbaker trend. It elected five Liberals and just two Conservatives, but that was two more seats than the Tories had won in the previous election.

Camp could not have been prouder—of his beloved Maritimes, of his own contribution or of John George Diefenbaker.

CHAPTER 10

Kempton

SELDOM HAS A CANADIAN POLITICIAN generated such strong and enduring emotions as Dalton Camp. In the eyes of his admirers, he wore a halo. He was brilliant. He breathed life into the Progressive Conservative party in regions where it was feared extinct. He plotted the strategy that made John Diefenbaker prime minister, and when it was time for Diefenbaker to go, he had the courage to lead the fight to bring internal democracy to the Tory party, sacrificing his own political ambitions in the process. He empowered ordinary party members to change leaders when they, not the leader, deemed it necessary. He attracted scores of previously uncommitted young people who became involved in public life because he made them believe that they, too, could make a difference. In the process he raised the level of politics in Canada.

Camp's enemies were legion. They considered him a devil. They blamed him for everything they believed had gone wrong for the Tories in the 1960s and 1970s. He was guilty of the sin of disloyalty to his leader and, by waging a vendetta against the leader, he split the party into two irreconcilable factions. He claimed to be a Conservative but he gave comfort to the Tories' opponents, sounding at times more like a socialist than a Tory. To his antagonists, Camp was an egoist and a hypocrite: he preached a new politics of openness and transparency, yet he enriched himself with the spoils of patronage—fat contracts for his advertising agency in Toronto. When he died in 2002—three and a half decades after the Diefenbaker battle—there were still Conservatives who could not say the name of Dalton Camp without spitting.

Although they would never admit it, his followers and detractors had something important in common: both laid too much at Camp's doorstep. His supporters gave him too much credit for reviving and modernizing the party. His foes assigned too much blame for, as they saw it, destroying the party. Whatever he did, good or bad, however, Camp did not do it alone. He was the leader, the catalyst. He was the one with the charisma. But the people who believed in him, followed his lead and took his ideas and put them to work deserved generous lashings of the credit, or blame, as the case may be.

The first among the followers, the leader of the spear carriers, was Norman Kempton Atkins, Camp's brother-in-law. Known as "Kemp" in the family, Atkins was the youngest of three children of George and Geraldine Atkins, whose first born, Linda, Camp's first wife, was 14 years older than Kempton.

Atkins was still in high school when he started working for Camp as a gofer in the 1952 New Brunswick election. He became a key player in all of his brother-in-law's political battles. The two men were exceptionally close, and they complemented each other almost perfectly. If Camp was the inspired designer of the fanciest automobile in the showroom, Atkins was the skilled mechanic who kept the temperamental vehicle on the road. Where Camp was solitary by nature, Atkins was collegial. Where Camp was creative, Atkins was managerial. Camp hated meetings; Atkins thrived on them.

As Camp's focus shifted from politics to journalism, Atkins moved out of his shadow. He assembled the organization that became known as the "Big Blue Machine," which won four consecutive elections for Ontario's William Davis—an organization that *Saturday Night* magazine with only a little hyperbole called "the most successful democratic institution in the Western world."[1] When Brian Mulroney asked for help, Atkins transferred the Big Blue Machine to Ottawa. He ran the campaigns that elected majority Conservative governments for Mulroney in 1984 (in the biggest landslide in federal political history) and in 1988. He became the greatest campaign manager the Tories ever had. What Keith "The Rainmaker" Davey was to the Liberals in the 1960s and 1970s, Atkins was to the Conservatives in the 1970s and 1980s.

Kemp Atkins's first memories of Dalton Camp date back to the family cottage at Robertson's Point, New Brunswick, in the summer of 1942, when Camp, then a private in the Canadian Army, came courting his sister. It was obvious to young Kemp that Dalton was serious about Linda and anxious to impress her parents. Why else would he spend so much time playing with eight-year-old Kempton, tossing a baseball and pulling him in a wagon around the Point? "I immediately liked Dalton. He was fun, and he certainly made an impression on me, because he gave me the attention that a little boy likes to have," Atkins recalled. He had a severe case of hero worship toward his future brother-in-law. "He always encouraged me to reach beyond what I could do. I started with him as a snivelling little kid. We ended up partners in business and in politics."[2]

Camp impressed Linda's father, too. They had shared interests in sports—both were huge college football fans—and in public affairs. The fact that Camp had attended Acadia University before joining the army probably clinched it for George Atkins, an expatriate Canadian who had been a star athlete in his own undergraduate years at Acadia. It was at Acadia that he met his future wife, Geraldine Reid. Born in Cumberland County, Nova Scotia, George was the son of a sea captain who drowned when George was a boy and the stepson of an entrepreneur who had left the Maritimes and moved to Boston, where he prospered in the stevedoring business.

After Acadia, George enlisted in the Canadian Expeditionary Force and served overseas in the First World War; he was at the Battle of the Somme in 1916 and Vimy Ridge the next year. When he was discharged in 1918, he went to visit his mother and step-father, who by then were living in Brooklyn, New York. He was offered a job there and, having already discovered there were few openings for returning servicemen in Atlantic Canada, he accepted it, stayed in the United States, acquired U.S. citizenship and became a prosperous insurance broker in Manhattan. But every summer from 1921 on, the Atkins family would migrate from their home in New Jersey to New Brunswick, where, in 1937, George built the first family cottage at Robertson's Point. They had no car radio in those days, and on the way back and forth to New Brunswick, he would regale his family with army songs and Acadia school songs.

Robertson's Point—named for the farm family that owns the land and leases lots to cottagers—was a magical place for the Atkins family and, later, for Dalton and Linda and their five children. Located on the shore of Grand Lake, which locals claim is the largest body of fresh water east of the Great Lakes, Robertson's Point is a collection of 55 unpretentious cottages built along a gravel road that winds around the farmyard. It is a true community; some of the families have been returning for four generations. The youngsters learn to play tennis on a shared clay court and to swim at a communal beach. No one locks their doors, everyone knows everyone, and they all know everyone else's business. Marriages may fall apart and new lovers appear, but however much the residents of the Point may chatter among themselves, they generally keep their gossip within the Point. For years, the only telephone was in the Robertson family's farmhouse; Norvel Robertson, who grew up there, remembered as a youngster running messages to the white cottage near the end of the road, messages for Dalton Camp to please call some of the biggest names in Canadian politics. Thirty or more years after the fact, Robertson was still too discreet to tell an outsider who those callers were.

Camp would walk to the farmhouse and return the calls. Frequently, the callers would end up coming to Robertson's Point for a visit, for a few martinis, a bottle or two of wine and some earnest conversation about the political issues of the day. It was the refuge where Camp did his best thinking and writing, a place where he could hide to read, talk to friends and generally unwind from the pressures of advertising in Toronto or politics in Ottawa. It was where he and Atkins organized the Tory leadership review campaign of 1966 and where, a year later, they charted Robert Stanfield's leadership campaign.

The cottage that George Atkins built in 1937 was one of the first permanent dwellings at Robertson's Point. Over the years, as children and grandchildren put in appearances, additional cottages were added. Family members today occupy a cluster of five cottages at the end of the road. Linda Camp has a two-storey white cottage, her children have two cottages and her brother,

Kempton, now a senator, has two—a yellow one that he uses year-round whenever he can escape from the capital, and a brown one (the original Atkins cottage) that he rents or loans to friends and family. For a number of years, Camp and Atkins staged a more or less annual tennis weekend for members of their political organization. They would hit a few tennis balls, do a lot of talking and, as Finlay MacDonald liked to say, do some serious damage to the grape. They called it the "Robertson's Point Rough-In," and invitations were highly prized among Tories across Canada.

Norman Kempton Atkins was born in New Jersey; after attending Appleby College in Oakville, Ontario, he followed in his father's footsteps to Acadia in Wolfville, Nova Scotia, where he was the star tailback on the football team. On graduation in 1957, he took a job in the accounting department of Canadian Pacific Railway in Montreal. As a U.S. citizen, however, he was liable for the draft. One day, he received his greetings from President Dwight Eisenhower with a notice to report for military duty on September 9, 1957. Atkins had to make a choice: he could serve a two-year hitch in the United States Army or he could seek a deferment to continue his education.

Quitting the CPR, he went to Halifax, where he met Camp and Finlay MacDonald. They took him to see the registrar at the law school at Dalhousie University. MacDonald was well known in Halifax and at the university. He and Camp had just helped elect Bob Stanfield as premier of the province. A few names were dropped. Atkins's eagerness to play football for Dalhousie was mentioned. The law school, it quickly transpired, would be delighted to admit young Atkins. Atkins, however, was not sure he wanted to be a lawyer. He did not think he wanted to spend another three years in school, but he had no idea what he did want to do. All he knew was he was due to report for military service in 48 hours. That evening, the three men went for a few drinks at the home of the mayor of Halifax. The few became too many as they wrestled with Atkins's dilemma. It was resolved when Camp said, "I don't know what I'll be doing in two years, but whatever it is, you can be part of it."[3]

That was good enough for Atkins. Horribly hung over, he caught a plane at 6:30 the next morning, collected his clothes and headed back to New Jersey, where he reported for service at Fort Dix. After two weeks at Fort Dix, he was posted to Fort Benning, Georgia, for basic and advanced training. An acting lance corporal, he was shipped off to the U.S. Army forces in Germany, where he spent the balance of his two years in the military. He worked in the quartermaster's corps, where, among other things, he learned the science or art of organization.

While Atkins was in the army, Camp and two of his advertising agency colleagues, Bill Kettlewell, who had designed the "Black Friday" and "It's Time for a Diefenbaker Government" ads in the 1957 election campaign, and Fred Boyer decided to go out on their own. They established Dalton K. Camp and Associates Limited in September 1959, taking with them the tourism accounts from New Brunswick as well as a federal travel bureau account that had come Camp's way after Diefenbaker's victory in 1957. They quickly added Nova Scotia, Manitoba and Prince Edward Island.

True to his word, Camp hired Atkins as production manager of the new agency, paying him $250 a month, considerably less than he had been making at the CPR. Camp's partners were dubious; Atkins knew next to nothing about advertising and nothing at all about advertising production. But he was a quick study, with a capacity for detail and a talent for organizing complicated tasks. He was a born manager, and within six months he had mastered the job. He also made a change in his name. Up until then, everyone had called him Kempton or Kemp. The agency's receptionist, however, found it confusing to distinguish between callers who were asking for "Camp" and those who wanted "Kemp," so he switched to using Norman, his first name.

Atkins would stay with the agency for 27 years, and as Camp became increasingly involved in politics and journalism, his brother-in-law gradually assumed control of the agency, hiring the staff, pitching prospective clients and making sure their needs were met. Although the firm's specialty was government and other institutional advertising, they picked up a number of blue-ribbon corporate clients, including Clairtone Sound Corporation (co-founded by Peter Munk, later of Barrick Gold), Labatt's, Inco and Telus. It was a highly profitable business. As Atkins recalled, it lost money in only one year between 1959 and 1986; that was in 1970, when a change of government in Manitoba cost the company the provincial tourism account.

As the business grew, Camp bought out Kettlewell and Boyer, assuming sole ownership of the agency. In 1968, Atkins became president, taking over Camp's big office and changing the name from Dalton K. Camp and Associates to Camp Associates Advertising. But it was not until 1972—after he landed the Ontario government tourism account from the newly elected Davis government—that Atkins finally became a full partner with his brother-in-law. As the years passed, Camp spent less and less time on the advertising business, but he kept an office at Camp Associates, dropped in occasionally and received half of the profits.

They owned the business until 1986—the year both went to Ottawa: Atkins to the Senate and Camp to the Prime Minister's Office—when they sold it to a group of senior employees. Camp signed a photograph for Atkins with the inscription, "From the first president, C and A, to the best." Atkins hung it proudly on the wall in his Senate office. Camp pocketed about $1.2 million in the sale—a sum he would often refer to as his "fuck-you money," meaning that it enabled him to be financially independent for, as he thought then, the rest of his life.

Although Finlay MacDonald and Richard Hatfield were probably Camp's best friends, Atkins was the most important. Marriage was one of their bonds. The advertising agency was another. Politics was a third. When he started in the 1952 New Brunswick election that brought Hugh John Flemming to power, Atkins's job was to drive Camp around and run advertising copy to the newspapers and radio stations. As the years and campaigns passed, his responsibilities increased: student organizer, assistant campaign coordinator, production communicator, communications coordinator. He was the on-site organizer of the Tories' 1964 Fredericton thinkers' conference (assisted by a young Tory named Joe Clark) and campaign manager for Camp when he ran for national president of the party in 1964 and 1966 and for Parliament in 1965 and 1968. He managed the leadership convention organization for Robert Stanfield in 1967 and the 1971 Ontario leadership campaign of Allan Lawrence, who was narrowly defeated by William Davis.

After the Ontario convention, Davis put Atkins in charge of the provincial Tory apparatus, and he made it into the most successful political organization in the country. Throughout Davis's years in power, Atkins was a key member of the premier's kitchen cabinet, which met for breakfast every Tuesday at the Park Plaza Hotel in Toronto. Mulroney's shrewdest move after he won the national leadership in 1983 was to convince Atkins—who had supported Joe Clark at that convention—to take over the federal campaign organization.

One of the most prominent Conservatives in Canada during that period recalls receiving a phone call in 1986 from Mulroney, who asked what he would think of Mulroney appointing Dalton Camp to the Senate. The answer: while Camp was undoubtedly deserving, Mulroney would be better advised to appoint Atkins because he had earned the appointment with his backroom service to the party in Ontario and Ottawa, because he would relish the Senate and because he would be a committed, effective senator. Mulroney agreed, and appointed Atkins.

He was a born organizer. Only rarely, as Camp once noted, was Atkins interested in grand strategy:

> It's hard to get a handle on his true genius, but it has something to do with administrative detail. He gets people to confront particular problems, not to generalize or woolgather. He cares that when the leader gets up the hall is full, everyone has been consulted, the plane has arrived on time, the baggage is there, the bar is set up, the leader is rested and watered and fed and has something in his hands to read. What that something is, isn't Norm's business.[4]

Atkins's preoccupation with administration and logistics tended to bore Camp, who also found his brother-in-law's unrelenting loyalty and deference suffocating at times. On occasion, Camp would break away and give himself some breathing space by heading off somewhere on his own, deliberately not telling Atkins where he was going or what he was up to. "Don't tell Kempton what I'm doing," he would caution other family members.

When he was not directing political campaigns, Atkins delighted in organizing events of all sorts—testimonial dinners, birthday celebrations, tennis tournaments, charitable campaigns or simply beer and pizza gatherings for workers. In the last decade of Camp's life, Atkins increasingly became the go-to person in the Atkins/Camp family—this, despite his own health problems (diabetes and a heart bypass, brought on, he readily admitted, by an incautious lifestyle). He made arrangements, solved problems, sorted out details and helped other family members with the minutiae of daily life. When Camp was no longer able to look after his mentally handicapped younger brother, Red, Atkins arranged for him to be cared for in a group home close to Northwood, the Camp home in New Brunswick. After Camp died, Atkins organized a campaign to raise $1.5 million to endow a journalism program in Camp's name at St. Thomas University in Fredericton.

The hero worship that Atkins felt when Camp was pulling him in his wagon at Robertson's Point in the 1940s never abated. It survived the vicissitudes of partnership in business and politics. Atkins's loyalty was unbreakable. Their relationship remained close even after Camp divorced Linda Atkins in favour of a younger woman. "Norman gave Dalton the respect that one would traditionally give a father," said Dianne Axmith, who worked with both men at Camp Associates and who became one of the agency's principals when they sold out. "Norman admired him, but I think he also felt that Dalton had gone out of his way to take care of him when he was a kid. Norman always had a loyalty to Dalton that almost went beyond being reasonable. Even if others thought Dalton was wrong sometimes, I'm not sure Norman ever thought he was wrong."[5]

CHAPTER 11

Disillusion and Alienation

THE FALLING OUT BETWEEN DALTON Camp and John Diefenbaker that culminated in Camp's dramatic 1966 campaign to oust the Chief from the leadership of the Progressive Conservative party was precipitated by the firing of Flora MacDonald, Camp's friend and ally, from her job at party headquarters in April 1966. But the seeds of disenchantment were planted as far back as the 1958 election campaign—the one that gave Diefenbaker an astonishing 209 of the 265 seats in the House of Commons.

Camp's duties in the 1958 campaign were the same as they had been in the first Diefenbaker election the year before: he was responsible for the Conservative party's national advertising, and he was in charge of the full campaign in the Atlantic provinces, travelling with the leader, writing his speeches and briefing him on local personalities and issues.

Diefenbaker was prime minister now, not the opposition leader, and the difference showed. After a career spent attacking governments and their records, he was ill at ease campaigning as an incumbent with a record of his own to defend and promote. He did not have what Camp called "the power of positive speaking."[1]

"You know," he said to Camp, "your stuff is not as good now as it was last time." Camp had to concede that Diefenbaker was right. It was easier for a speech writer, too, to flail away at the transgressions of a government in power than it was to defend the achievements of one. He understood why Diefenbaker felt disoriented: "In his mind, he was always in opposition. He was always campaigning as though the Grits were in power."[2]

The fun and warmth that had marked the 1957 campaign were gone. Diefenbaker was more demanding, more remote, more imperial in his attitude. He was less interested in the concerns of waitresses, taxi drivers and other ordinary voters. His relations with the press began to erode. Camp reported from the Diefenbaker train to Allister Grosart back at campaign headquarters in Ottawa that the Chief was becoming more querulous and less patient with the people who were trying to help him.

He was a changed person. Camp reminded the leader how he had made voters laugh at rallies in the 1957 campaign. "Recession," Diefenbaker replied. "A lot of people are unemployed, and it's not a time for jokes." So he stopped telling jokes.

Camp was troubled by an incident that began in the Lakehead in Northern Ontario when Tory frontbencher George Hees publicly criticized the award of the Nobel Peace Prize to Lester Pearson, the new Liberal leader. The Nobel, Hees declared, should have gone to Diefenbaker, instead. Columnists and cartoonists had a field day with that. In Halifax, the *Chronicle-Herald* ran a savage cartoon that depicted Hees leaping on Pearson and trying the rip the Peace Prize away from him. People were laughing. Camp was concerned, and he went to Diefenbaker to suggest that he tell Hees to shut up. Diefenbaker nearly bit Camp's head off. When he checked in later with Grosart, he learned why: Diefenbaker was delighted with Hees's initiative. In fact, he had put Hees up to it. Diefenbaker shrank in stature in Camp's eyes.[3]

"He was just paranoiac," Camp recalled. "He imagined things that never happened. He didn't want to see people. He didn't want to hear [negative] stuff.... He said the reason for that [is] he's prime minister and [has] to be careful. He had to see all of the people or see none of them."[4]

In the end, Diefenbaker's eccentricities, as they seemed to be, made absolutely no difference to the election. Camp's antennae had told him from the outset that the Conservatives were going to win easily: "It was one of those extraordinary campaigns when it was almost criminal to do anything."[5]

The 1958–1962 Diefenbaker government was itself an extraordinary exercise in reverse alchemy—it managed to turn electoral gold into lead. The Tories blew the biggest majority in Canadian history to that time; they lost nearly 100 seats in the 1962 election, yet, incredibly, managed to hang on to power. Where the minority government of 1957 had been responsive, moving quickly to address problems and introduce programs, the sluggish, oversized administration that emerged from the 1958 election seemed frozen in inaction.

Camp found himself travelling to Ottawa frequently after 1958 because of the government travel bureau account that his agency had acquired in the spoils of victory. He was appalled by the mood and shocked by the change that had come over the Tories with whom he had worked closely during the previous five years: "There was now no longer any room for any kind of objective examination of any kind of problem, because the answer from Grosart or anyone else was: 'Look, [Diefenbaker] knows what he's doing. He's a genius. Leave him alone!'"[6]

Some ministers were shut out of decision making entirely. The government had become a one-man show, and all the people around Diefenbaker had acquiesced in the view that the party had reached its high station solely because of the energy and talent of its leader. This was nonsense, Camp knew. The 1957 election had been a very close thing. And it had taken the hard work of Tories across the country, and the leadership of Leslie Frost in Ontario, Bob Stanfield in Nova Scotia and Hugh John Flemming in New Brunswick, among others, to achieve the massive victory of 1958.

But that was not what he heard on his visits to the capital. "All you got was this great, obsequious, you know, relationship with the great Chief. Nobody else mattered and nothing else mattered, and you couldn't help but shrink from that.... I felt, well, if he's right and it's all about him, then who needs me?" In Camp's view, Diefenbaker was "surrounded by a lot of fools." One of them, he concluded, was Grosart, the leader's chief political adviser—"I always thought Grosart had appalling judgment. He had no assessment of people, and he developed... a deaf ear."[7]

For the next few years, Camp had no direct communication with Diefenbaker and very little with the federal party. He established his own advertising agency, Dalton K. Camp and Associates, in 1959; helped Duff Roblin and the Conservatives win a majority in

Manitoba the same year; and returned to Nova Scotia for the re-election of the Stanfield government in 1960. Even so, he was aware of the vicious battles that were raging in Ottawa over patronage, or the lack of it. Senate appointments were not made; Public Works Department contracts did not go to Tories who felt they were entitled to some federal largesse after years of pork barrel denial; and across the country Conservative small businessmen were enraged when they discovered that victory at the polls had changed nothing—federal purchase orders still went to their Liberal competitors. "The feedback was terrible," Camp recalled. "But Diefenbaker always was above all this. He was the god-like father out there on cloud nine saying, 'If you have a problem, write me.'... And nobody dared go to Diefenbaker, lest they get blown out of the room."[8]

Flora MacDonald, who for all practical purposes was running party headquarters, also noticed the change in the leader. She was, she said, turned off in the 1958 campaign, "because of the way in which people were idolizing Diefenbaker. It wasn't really human—you don't set somebody up on a pedestal. People would come and just touch him.... I had to convince myself to vote for him."[9]

As a party employee, she was witness to Diefenbaker's tendency to make impossible demands. He gave a campaign speech one Friday night in Cornwall, Ontario. MacDonald was working alone in the office the next morning when Diefenbaker called. He had been walking about in Cornwall, talking to local citizens and found that none of them had a copy of his speech. Diefenbaker seldom worked from a speech text, and when he had one, he would not follow it. That did not matter. He wanted copies prepared forthwith for the eager people of Cornwall.

MacDonald was also appalled by the way Diefenbaker dealt with some of his senior cabinet ministers. Somehow, he had come into possession of documents that established—to his satisfaction, at least—that two ministers, George Nowlan and Gordon Churchill, had been involved in affairs with secretaries on Parliament Hill. According to MacDonald, Diefenbaker kept a file on the two liaisons in the top drawer of his desk in the Prime Minister's Office, pulling it out from time to time to threaten the ministers.

In two extended oral history interviews taped in the late 1960s and opened to the public on his death, Camp talked about his gradual alienation from Diefenbaker. One interview was with York University historian J.L. Granatstein and two colleagues, Paul Stevens and Peter Oliver, and is archived at York in Toronto. The other interview, with political scientists Denis Smith and William Neville, is in the archives at Trent University in Peterborough, Ontario. Reading the interviews, one is struck by the depth of Camp's feelings.

Camp became sufficiently alarmed by Diefenbaker and disenchanted with the people close to the Chief that he did not want to be involved in the re-election campaign of 1962, although he kept his concerns to himself at the time. Whatever his inner apprehension, he managed to remain publicly loyal to Diefenbaker until the early months of 1966. He was certainly not one of the first members of the dump-Diefenbaker movement.

One other thing is clear from the oral history interviews: Camp developed a shrewd appreciation of the flaws in Diefenbaker's complex character. "It seemed to me Diefenbaker was very uneasy with people who he felt were equal in his intelligence, or had a leg up somewhere," he told Smith and Neville.

He was very much at home with his inferiors—either, let's say, social inferiors or intellectual inferiors.... He had to dominate every confrontation, he had to dominate every argument, he had to dominate every gathering. And if anyone began to rise and shine, it became a contest, and he had this in his nature: somehow or other, he had to win in his own eyes....

To me, Diefenbaker's great failing was his absolute inability to sustain or maintain or achieve an adult relationship. It was authoritarian or it was nothing.... You know, 'I'm prime minister, you're subject; I'm leader, you're follower.'... If anyone disagreed with him, there had to be another reason. It couldn't be a matter of intellect or principle. It had to be something else. My chief difficulty with him was deciding whether or not he was ever a real person, whether he ever said anything he meant, ever.... There wasn't a genuine bone in the body. I can't remember a conversation with him when I felt that he meant what he said.

Camp's disquiet extended to the leader's wife, Olive, and her influence on her husband. She seemed less a wife and more a mother to a man incapable of normal human affection, he thought. To Camp, Olive Diefenbaker was a "whiner" who brought out the worst in her husband:

> She was the repository of all his hallucinations and his frustrations and so on. I think she fed his ego and she fed his prejudice and she carried his personal causes, too. If he disliked somebody, she hated him.... She had a very discernible brooding mistrust and dislike of French Canadians and was very uncomfortable with them.... She would say from time to time disparaging things about Quebec, about French Canadians in Quebec. She was far more malevolent than he was.... He could conceal it.[10]

Flora MacDonald also witnessed the bigotry of Olive Diefenbaker when she spent a day with her during the campaign in a deferred election in the Stormont-riding in eastern Ontario. One of the candidates had died before the 1962 general election, and the vote in the riding, which included the city of Cornwall, was postponed. The local Conservatives had asked party headquarters not to send Diefenbaker, fearing the presence of the Prime Minister would hurt their chances. "So I went down with Mrs. Diefenbaker, to take her as the surrogate for the Chief," MacDonald said. "She spent the whole time in this chauffeur-driven car, talking of these terrible Quebeckers who had voted against her husband, these French, and never to trust them. And I could hardly say anything, knowing we were going into a French-speaking riding—and our driver was French Canadian. It was just awful."[11]

Given the strong dislike and distrust that Camp was developing toward Diefenbaker, why did he remain loyal to him? Why did he, after initially refusing, agree to run the Tory advertising campaign again in the 1962 election? Why did he consent to manage the entire national campaign in the 1963 election? Why did he defend Diefenbaker at the time of the Bomarc missile crisis in early 1963? Why, in 1964, did he run for national president of the party (with, ironically, the tacit support of Diefenbaker) and help fend off at least two attacks on his leadership? And why did he run for Parliament in 1965 under Diefenbaker's leadership?

The answers are as complex as Dalton Camp himself. He felt a powerful loyalty to the Progressive Conservative party, and that meant being loyal to its leader. He had been loyal to George Drew—whom he knew could never win—and he intended to be loyal to Diefenbaker, despite deep reservations. He hoped, however improbably, that the John Diefenbaker he had campaigned with in 1957—warm, human, concerned and funny—would reassert himself. Like many Tories, Camp was prepared to blame the confidants, advisers, apologists and time-servers in the leader's inner circle for isolating and misdirecting him before he would assign blame to the leader personally. At that time—1962 to 1965—he believed implicitly that he should protect the party and try to save it from a bloody leadership battle. It had taken the Tories 22 years to turn the Liberals out of office in 1957; he did not want to give the Grits the keys to Parliament Hill for another 22 years. Far from abating, his dislike of the Liberals had intensified over the years. He had nothing but contempt for Liberal leader Lester Pearson, whom he considered to be weak and dishonest.

Finally, Camp knew Diefenbaker's time would eventually come, and he calculated that if he positioned himself carefully—loyal to the leader but not part of his circle—he might one day have a shot at the leadership himself. Camp was not actively contemplating the leadership as early as 1962—that would come a few years later. But he was not without ego or ambition. The more he saw of the senior politicians on both sides of the aisle in the House of Commons, the more clearly he realized that he could do as good a job as most of them if he had an opportunity to run a department, or even the entire government.

The 1962 federal election ranked with the 1955 Prince Edward Island election as Camp's worst nightmare in politics. He had no intention of getting involved. Repelled by Diefenbaker and distressed by the performance of his government, he had stopped paying close attention to what was going on in official Ottawa. He knew from the Gallup Poll that Tory prospects looked bleak, but he told himself that the country was in a recession and the polls were subject to fluctuation. The Conservatives' numbers would go back up, he thought, or maybe they would not. Whatever, it was not his problem.

Early in 1962, Allister Grosart invited him to a secret meeting in Montreal of key Conservatives from across Canada to assess the state of the party and the government. They met in a suite at the Queen Elizabeth Hotel and as Grosart went around the room polling the participants, the gloom deepened. Everyone agreed the party was in critical condition and would lose the next election. The consensus was that Diefenbaker was the problem, and every time he appeared on television, the problem got worse. After four or five hours of this, Grosart said he would convey the group's assessment to Diefenbaker—which the others all knew he would never dare to do.

Possibly worse, there had been nothing to drink during the meeting, not even coffee. "I remember afterward they opened the bar and everyone immediately got stoned—almost instantly," Camp said.[12]

He went out for dinner that night in Montreal with Grosart and a few others. Grosart ordered the wine. "He was an expert on wine and when he finished the first bottle, he threw it over his shoulder on the floor. Such a clatter! Allister said this was a fine tradition, a gourmet tradition, but the rest of us concluded that he was simply boiled."[13] The powerful advertising man who had become the political right arm to the Prime Minister of Canada—Peter C. Newman described Grosart as a "remarkable political manipulator" and "the main creator of the Diefenbaker legend"[14]—seemed to have been physically diminished by the meeting at the Queen Elizabeth. "For the first time in my life, I felt sorry for him," Camp recalled. "A pathetic figure. He had staked his life, I think, on Diefenbaker's power and influence. He'd now been told that [Diefenbaker] had become a liability and no one any longer feared Allister."[15]

About two months later, Parliament was dissolved as Diefenbaker called an election for June 18 (which, as Flora MacDonald observed, happened to be the anniversary of the Battle of Waterloo). Grosart called again and asked Camp to handle the campaign advertising and publicity. Stalling for time, Camp said before he would do anything, he wanted to take a national survey of public opinion. The survey confirmed his worst fears. Everything the group at the Montreal meeting had said about the party and about Diefenbaker was echoed in the poll. There was an overwhelming lack of confidence in Diefenbaker and, for the first time since he became leader, the Tory party placed ahead of him in public esteem. Diefenbaker, who only four years earlier had been the Tories' greatest asset, was now a liability. Camp sent Grosart a copy of the poll, which Grosart almost certainly never showed to Diefenbaker. Hoping to duck any further involvement in the election, Camp took off for Bermuda—he tended to head there, or Antigua, when he wanted to escape.

Flora MacDonald tracked him down to say that Grosart had called a meeting of the national campaign committee and would Camp please prepare an analysis of the party's situation, as revealed by the survey, and provide his thoughts as to how the party might fight the election. He wrote a three-page memorandum, which he dictated over the phone to MacDonald in Ottawa. "It could have been and probably was wrong and the opposite of what I really thought," he reflected. "But at the time I'd led myself to the belief that it was the only thing to do, and I made the assumption that Diefenbaker would be manageable because he might be scared. You know, he might be like he was in '57."

The Tory campaign, Camp advised the committee, would have to make the most of Diefenbaker's strengths and exploit Pearson's weaknesses. The Liberal leader had come off as an amiable nonentity in Camp's poll, and the Tory task would be to tell Canadians that the one thing the country did not need in 1962 was a Lester Pearson who had no mind of his own. Diefenbaker's special assistant John Fisher, the former broadcaster who had been dubbed "Mr. Canada," read Camp's memo to the campaign committee members. They all cheered. Perhaps they were clutching at straws, or perhaps they actually believed that Camp's memo, which was meant as a discussion of tactical options, was a blueprint for victory.

He returned to Canada to find that no one was prepared to take on the publicity job. Finally, knowing he had no real choice, Camp gave in to Grosart's pleas. He decided at the outset never to present Diefenbaker alone in advertisements. He would be portrayed in the company of other Tories for whom the public had more favourable opinions. The first major print ad was a supplement in *Weekend Magazine*, which was carried by newspapers across the country. It showed the leader surrounded by his entire cabinet.

The election of 1962 was the first true "TV election," as television replaced print as the most important (to the politicians) vehicle for election news and television commercials began to supplant newspaper and magazine ads as the preferred means of reaching voters scattered across the country. Until that election, political parties had been sorely constrained in their TV advertising. They were permitted to use talking heads to read their campaign messages, but they were barred from using motion in their film clips. That barrier came down in 1962; motion was now acceptable. The Liberals took advantage of the change to air commercials that showed Pearson's campaign bus rolling into towns; at each stop, attractive young candidates would be seen getting off.

Camp had a more ambitious idea. Diefenbaker was notorious for never following the text that Camp or other speechwriters wrote for him. He rambled. He introduced topics, dropped them and then picked them up again. He tied his syntax in knots. Camp's idol, Winston Churchill, who had a lifelong love affair with the English language, would have been heartsick to hear Diefenbaker. The trick would be to turn the Chief's unique speaking style into a campaign asset in the new television age. Starting with a speech in Edmonton early in the campaign, Camp arranged to have every Diefenbaker appearance filmed (this being long before videotape). Flora MacDonald's job each night was to type a transcript of Diefenbaker's speech from the audiotape. Camp marked the passages he wanted made into two-minute TV clips. The marked transcript and film were sent to a firm in Toronto, which packaged the clips and shipped them to television stations all over the country for inclusion in newscasts. Quite a few stations made use of this Tory service. "When you read his speeches, the sentences didn't make sense," MacDonald said. "But when you heard them, it was electrifying. It was his showmanship that put them across."[16]

Most of the news in the 1962 election, however, was bad news for the Tories. The campaign was barely underway when the finance minister, Donald Fleming, seeking to strengthen Canada's export performance in the teeth of a recession and a monetary crisis, decided to devalue the Canadian dollar. The dollar, which had been floating above par with the United States dollar, would be pegged at 92.5 cents U.S. The Liberals could hardly believe their good luck. They attacked the Diefenbaker government's management of the economy. They mocked the "Diefendollar." They distributed "Diefenbucks"—play dollars worth 92.5 cents. They told voters, quite misleadingly, that the dollar they were accustomed to spending in the supermarket would henceforth buy only 92.5 cents worth of produce. A Liberal advertisement in Nova Scotia stated that an apple from the Annapolis Valley that formerly cost 10 cents in Halifax would now cost 12 cents.

Camp wanted to counter that with a print ad that would show a basket of fruit and explain how its value had not been affected by devaluation. But the advertisement was rejected. "Diefenbaker said, 'I will personally supervise every ad,'" MacDonald recalled. "And we could never get his approval."[17]

The 1962 election was also marked by angry demonstrations against Diefenbaker in various parts of the country. The riots would be much worse in the campaign that followed in 1963, but in 1962 Camp saw a chance to turn the protests to the Tories' advantage. Diefenbaker was usually at his best when confronted by hecklers. In Vancouver, one of his appearances degenerated into a mob scene, with the Prime Minister left alone to stand his ground on the platform. Even the operator of the Tories' TV camera fled for safety. But he had the foresight to tie his camera in place, and it captured all the action. Camp wanted to turn that film into a documentary-style 15-minute broadcast for a CBC free-time telecast. He was sure it would generate sympathy for Diefenbaker when Canadians saw how badly the leader was being treated by loutish partisans of the opposition parties. But Grosart and some of the others close to the leader lost their nerve and overruled Camp. "You should never show the Prime Minister of Canada being heckled," Grosart said.[18]

Camp felt so alienated from Grosart and the rest of the palace guard that he did not travel to Ottawa even once during the 1962 election. He ran the publicity and advertising out of his Toronto office, although he did accompany Diefenbaker in the Atlantic provinces, as he had in 1957 and 1958. It was a dreadful campaign, and the leader was frequently irrational: "He was unable to respond to the challenge. He'd lost. He was out of touch with the country. He could no longer reach people. Nobody believed him. He wasn't credible. And we were in for a very bad time."[19]

A hypochondriac at the best of times, Diefenbaker was given to psychosomatic illnesses, usually chest congestion, when the going got tough or when he was called on to do something he did not want to do. He was in Halifax and was scheduled to go on to Newfoundland—the place he hated most to campaign—when he announced he was ill. Camp knew a doctor in Halifax who was rabidly anti-Diefenbaker. He made an arrangement with him. The doctor would examine Diefenbaker and, no matter what he found, he would tell him he was in excellent shape. Then he would meet Camp and tell him precisely what the leader's condition was; they would figure out what to do from there. Afraid to let the press get the scent of a possible medical problem, they waited until after midnight before sneaking the doctor on board Diefenbaker's campaign train in Halifax Station. The doctor examined the leader, assured him he was a magnificent specimen and, other than a bit of congestion, he was in remarkable shape. "I don't know how you do it," he told Diefenbaker.

The doctor got off the train and huddled with Camp in a corner of the deserted train station. "Really, he's not too good," the doctor said. "He's got some congestion there in one side of his chest." He told Camp Diefenbaker's condition was not serious, but could become serious if he took any risks. He thought Diefenbaker could continue campaigning so long as he was not overtaxed—"My advice to you is not to give him any more to do than he has to do." Camp sent the Chief off to Newfoundland, as scheduled.[20]

Diefenbaker survived, and so, to Camp's surprise, did the Conservative government. Sitting in his office in Toronto on election day, he wrote a memo in which he predicted the outcome would be a minority government—a minority Liberal one. He had not expected the Tories would hold as many Atlantic seats as they did (they won 18 seats to the Liberals' 14 in the four eastern provinces). He had mistakenly assumed the Conservatives were in as much trouble in the rest of Ontario as they were in Toronto. Camp's political antennae had never been much good in Quebec; he once dismissed politics in that province as just one of the costs of doing business, like pilferage on the docks. In 1962, he, like most others, misread the situation there, and he was astonished when Social Credit came out of nowhere to take 27 Quebec seats. Those Socred seats alone denied Lester Pearson the victory he had expected.

The Conservatives suffered the greatest reversal of fortune in Canadian political history. Their popular vote dropped by 17 percentage points, compared to 1958; they actually polled 4,815 fewer votes nationally than the Liberals did; and they won 93 fewer seats than they had four years earlier, winding up with just 116. But it was enough to cling to power a little longer.

On election night, Camp, his brother-in-law, Norman Atkins, and Bill Kettlewell, a partner in Dalton K. Camp and Associates, and their wives gathered in the offices of the advertising agency to listen to the election returns. Once the Ontario results were in, they knew the Tories would be coming back with a minority government. They did not bother waiting for the returns from Western Canada. "There was never any doubt that we were going to win the West," Camp recalled.[21] The group went out for dinner, but it was a wake, not a celebration.

The only happy note for Camp in 1962 was a provincial election in the fall in Newfoundland. He and Flora MacDonald went east to help the Newfoundland Tories. They knew they could not beat Joey Smallwood and the Liberals, but they were determined to make life as miserable as possible for them. By 1962, Smallwood was running Newfoundland as his personal fief, which he controlled absolutely with the twin weapons of intimidation and corruption. Richard Gwyn described the atmosphere brilliantly in his book, *Smallwood: The Unlikely Revolutionary*:

> Political debate, once a bawdy Newfoundland art form, was driven underground, to be voiced only in taverns and private homes. The Official Opposition, resigned to perpetual defeat, lapsed into silence. The miasma of fear pervaded everywhere: in anti-government letters to the editor that were signed only by 'Interested Citizen,' 'Terra Nova' and 'Housewife'; in pallid newspaper editorials and, even more tellingly, in the timidity of the local outlets of the CBC.... Businessmen, once the community's natural leaders, withdrew themselves from involvement in political affairs.[22]

In James Greene, the Conservatives had an outstanding young leader who was, as he himself knew, in a hopeless situation. "I have detected for some little time now and seen instances in many places of a fear coming over our people, a fear of many people in many walks of life that they cannot stand up publicly and take their place in the public life of this country, cannot make their voices known for fear of repercussion," he told the legislature in early 1962.[23]

Greene and his party had no money for a campaign, but Camp and MacDonald managed to scrape up $15,000, $10,000 of which Grosart obtained, ironically, from Smallwood's pal John C. Doyle, the head of Canadian Javelin Ltd. Doyle, who was also a friend of Grosart's, later fled to Panama, a fugitive from Canadian justice. "It was a fascinating election!" MacDonald remembered. "It was, of all of them, the most interesting and the most fun. We had three seats in the legislature, and we ended up with seven seats. Dalton was brilliant."[24]

Newfoundland was a study in contrasts. MacDonald was at a Tory rally in a fishing outport one evening when she glanced up at Greene and the three other men sharing the platform. All four, she realized with a start, were Rhodes Scholars. And yet some of the Tory candidates in rural areas in that election were illiterate. One of them, from Ferryland, a village south of St. John's on the Avalon Peninsula, came to Tory campaign headquarters in the Newfoundland Hotel. In his hands he had a glossy booklet that the Liberals had prepared for election use. The candidate was bubbling happily because the book was filled with pretty pictures. What, he wondered, did the words say?

Camp and MacDonald realized immediately what had happened. The book not only recounted Smallwood's achievements, it set out the planks for his re-election campaign. The Liberals had printed it in advance and sent it out to post offices around the province with instructions that it not be distributed until a certain date. But the postmaster in Ferryland, also unable to read, had distributed the booklet prematurely. "On the back cover it had what Joey was going to do, all the steps he was going to take in his fisheries program in the election—"'We are going to build 1,800 new fishing craft,' or whatever it was," MacDonald said.

Broadcaster Don Jamieson, who would later be a Liberal cabinet minister in Ottawa, was the owner of the private television station in St. John's. Although he was a partisan, he was determined to be fair. He offered each party a 15-minute free-time slot once or twice a week. His only condition was that the broadcasts be live. The Conservatives would go first one time, the Liberals the next, and so on. With the Tories leading off, Greene went on the air and started telling the people what his party would do for the fishery—"We will build 1,801 new fishing craft—"

"Joe was sitting outside, waiting to go on and read his own plank. And he came in sputtering and stuttering, 'They've stolen it!' We just were in stitches," MacDonald recalled, still laughing at the memory four decades later. The next time the Conservatives went first again, they did the same thing, upping the ante and declaring that they would supply 1,201 of something else.

A couple of weeks later, Camp, the counter-puncher, came up with another tactic to keep the Liberals off balance. St. John's was divided into a number of canvassing districts. In each district, the Liberals had an agent in charge of patronage. As MacDonald explained, "Each one had a bunch of coloured slips: the north end might have blue slips, and the centre might have green slips. The south end, on the other side of the harbour, had pink slips. And if you came in, and said you were going to vote Liberal—this is before the election day—you would be given a slip. And you would take that to a grocer, and he would give you $10 worth of groceries. So this man and his wife came in from the south-side hills, the pink slip area, and said they were going to vote Liberal. They got a pink slip, and they went back to the grocer, and they got $9.97 worth of groceries, and three cents change."

The couple, in fact, were Conservatives. They went to a lawyer and swore an affidavit about what had happened. James Greene, the leader, heard about this and went to Camp. "We'll take the affidavit," Camp told him, "and we'll take the bag of groceries, and we'll go on television, and you can be reading the affidavit while you're unpacking the bag of groceries."

"Joe was sitting out in the waiting room, ready to go on again. It was such fun that campaign. It was great, because it was Dalton at his calculating best," MacDonald recalled.[25]

As expected, the Conservatives lost the election, but they did elect seven members, all of them in St. John's and in other centres where voters had access to television. It was a beginning—barely. It would be another decade before the Tories were strong enough to chase Smallwood from office.

CHAPTER 12

An Uncivil War

THE 1962 ELECTION PRODUCED the worst of all possible outcomes for the Progressive Conservatives. The party was in disarray. It had a leader who could no longer command support in the country or, increasingly, in his own cabinet. Although the Tories had managed to hang on to enough seats to retain office, the opposition parties smelled blood; they would bring down the government at the first opportunity. But because John Diefenbaker was still prime minister, the Tories were hamstrung: they could not do the one thing that might save them in the next election—rebuild the party around a new leader. They all knew they would surely lose with Diefenbaker. They hoped he would decide to leave voluntarily, but they were sure he would not. They also knew that if they tried to force him out, they would probably tear the party apart and consign it to the opposition for years to come.

Some years later, Dalton Camp explained to Robert F. Kennedy, who was then preparing to challenge President Lyndon Johnson for the Democratic party nomination, how he and his Tory allies had organized the 1966 putsch that finally drove Diefenbaker from the leadership. Kennedy was impressed, but he noted that Diefenbaker was in opposition by then. The coup would never have succeeded if he had still been prime minister, Kennedy said. He was right.

The Conservatives would spend the period from 1962 to 1966 in a state of civil war. Brush fires would break out in the caucus, in the cabinet and in the party's 140-member national executive. One blaze would die down and another would flare up. The public got into the act, too. Angry demonstrations, many of them over the issue of acquiring nuclear arms for Canada, greeted Diefenbaker on the campaign trail in 1963; one, at Queen's University in Kingston, Ontario, got so badly out of hand that the fire department was summoned to hose down the angry students.

Prominent Conservatives could not agree on what to do. New Brunswick MP Gordon Fairweather was a hardliner among the "termites" (Diefenbaker's derisory name for his enemies in caucus). Getting rid of Diefenbaker took precedence over the future of the party, in Fairweather's view: "I thought that it was in the national interest to prevent him ever becoming prime minister again and that, party or no party, this was essential."[1]

On the other hand, Toronto lawyer Edwin Goodman, a party vice-president and key backroom organizer, who was just as anxious to be rid of Diefenbaker, put the party ahead of the leadership. At one point, when he was unable to get Diefenbaker to commit to a retirement date, Goodman decided against trying to push him—"I did believe it was possible we could just disintegrate into nothing."[2]

One Tory frontbencher, George Hees, bounced from side to side. He broke with Diefenbaker, reconciled with him, resigned from his cabinet over nuclear arms in 1963 and returned to be a candidate for him again in 1965. Another, Davie Fulton, dithered and dissembled. He was "convinced that with Diefenbaker as continuing leader, we were headed straight for suicide, extinction." Yet Fulton, the prisoner of his own ambition, kept his powerful feelings to himself, "because I wanted to be leader of the Conservative party, and I wanted to be leader of [a] united party, and I felt that any man who identified himself with a movement to unseat the existing leader had a very bad strike against him."[3]

Camp's dismay over Diefenbaker's leadership was unabated, but he was equally appalled by the quality of some of the caucus rebels, dismissing them as "a group of despairing incompetents." The party, he argued, owed it to itself to hang together, to try to get through the next election as a "credible unified whole and keep the Grits from forming a majority [government]."

He soon had a chance to put his theory into practice. Three months after the election in 1962, Diefenbaker appointed Allister Grosart to the Senate. Using Winnipeg MP Gordon Churchill as an intermediary, as he often did, Diefenbaker proposed that Camp succeed Grosart as national director of the party. The proposal created several problems for Camp, including a conflict of interest. By this time, Dalton K. Camp and Associates was doing hundreds of thousands of dollars worth of advertising business with the federal government. It would not be appropriate for this untendered business to be going to a firm headed by an employee of the governing party. Besides, the advertising agency was in the process of expanding, and it needed his time.

He hated Ottawa and had no desire to move there—"I had lived there enough. It was a dismal place."[4] More important, Linda Camp was dead set against him taking the job, because she knew it would mean she and the family would hardly ever see him. Angry and upset, she told Camp she wanted to see a divorce lawyer. "She just wasn't going to have it, and suddenly I realized that I didn't want to do it, either."[5]

Camp and Churchill negotiated an accommodation. The position of national director would be left unfilled. Camp would have a new position: chairman of the national organization committee, reporting directly to the leader. He would run the next campaign as he saw fit. He would not be a party employee. He would not receive a salary, just expenses. By being a volunteer, he would, he thought, enhance his moral authority in the party. He would be free to live in Toronto and commute to Ottawa. He would not work weekends. And the job would end the day after the next election.

Churchill assured him that his conditions would be acceptable to Diefenbaker, but Camp knew better than to rely on anyone who claimed to know the unpredictable mind of the leader. Typing out his conditions on a sheet of yellow copy paper, he went to see Diefenbaker, half hoping he would reject them. The Prime Minister had slipped unannounced into Toronto to have a doctor give him a medical checkup aboard his train. Diefenbaker read Camp's list and agreed to all of the conditions—"I suppose maybe he knew more about his vulnerability than I did."[6]

That vulnerability was only too apparent at the time of the Cuban missile crisis in October 1962. Livingston Merchant, a former United States ambassador to Canada, flew to Ottawa with a personal message for Diefenbaker from President John F. Kennedy. In it, Kennedy presented the evidence he would disclose on national television that night to demonstrate that the Soviet Union was constructing missile sites in Cuba. He wanted to be assured of Canada's support.

Although most of his ministers assumed that support would be automatic, Diefenbaker could not make up his mind. He distrusted Americans, disliked Kennedy and believed the United States administration was hostile to the Tories to the point of interfering in Canadian political affairs so as to advance the cause of Washington's favourite, Lester Pearson and the Liberals. Confronted with Kennedy's request for support, Diefenbaker wavered and procrastinated. He proposed that an independent inspection commission with representatives of eight non-aligned countries be sent to Cuba for an on-site check of the alleged missile bases.

Kennedy was furious. Even French President Charles de Gaulle, no fan of the United States, had accepted his word on the missile sites, but Diefenbaker, who was supposed to be a friend and ally, would not. Camp, too, was outraged by Diefenbaker's failure to back Kennedy. The cabinet was split. Howard Green, the foreign affairs minister—who, in Camp's view, was "stubbornly anti-American"—wanted the government to resist pressure to follow Kennedy's lead. The hawks, led by Defence Minister Douglas Harkness, insisted that Canada support the United States unconditionally. George Hogan, a national vice-president of the Tory party who managed to be a close friend of both Diefenbaker and Camp, upset the leader by making a speech in Toronto condemning his procrastination. Although Diefenbaker finally did come out in support of the Americans—three days after Kennedy had asked him—the damage had been done.

The stage was set for the nuclear weapons crisis of January–February 1963, which would destroy his government. The Cuban crisis had revealed to all Canadians Diefenbaker's inability to make up his mind. When the military was finally put on alert during the crisis, it became obvious that Canada's newest, most sophisticated weapons systems were impotent. The Canada-based CF-101 Voodoo interceptors and Bomarc B surface-to-air missiles, along with Canada's Europe-based CF-104 Starfighters, were designed to carry nuclear warheads. His government had bought the delivery systems, but Diefenbaker—alert to anti-nuclear sentiment in the country and anxious not to be seen to be a slave to American military policy—could not make up his mind. He would not give the order to acquire the warheads; nor, however, would he refuse to accept them. In fact, his administration had clearly made a commitment to accept the warheads from the United States. At times the Prime Minister seemed poised to honour the commitment. At other times, he seemed to be vague, to be reconsidering, or to be opposed to taking the nuclear warheads.

The acquisition of nuclear weapons was a legitimate issue for public debate in Canada, although it was a debate that might better have been conducted before, not after, the purchase of the aircraft and missiles. Diefenbaker's vacillation simply confused the issue, and once the opposition leader, Lester Pearson, had declared that a Liberal government would acquire the warheads, the Prime Minister's indecision became an acute embarrassment.

His caucus and cabinet were in upheaval. For a while, there seemed to be as many plots in various stages of gestation as there could possibly have been plotters. One of the most popular plotlines had Diefenbaker stepping down and being appointed chief justice of the Supreme Court of Canada; meanwhile, the caucus would make George Nowlan interim leader and acting prime minister; Nowlan would strike a deal with Social Credit leader Robert Thompson to prop up the minority government for six or eight months (some of the plotters actually went to Thompson to discuss such an arrangement); a leadership convention would be held at which Nowlan, by prior agreement, would not be a candidate; and the party would elect George Hees as its new leader.

Camp thought this was madness. He stumbled on one plot by accident. He dropped in on the "Four O'Clock Club," which was simply a group of anti-Diefenbaker MPs who liked to drink strong liquor and gathered for that purpose in the office of Ernest Halpenny, the secretary of state. Richard Bell, Wallace McCutcheon, George Nowlan and a few others were there that day. As the booze flowed, they started denouncing the leader, saying things like,

"Diefenbaker's insane." Camp feared they might actually try to mount a serious challenge to the leader—"and if it was carried out by this bunch of bunglers, it would not only destroy the government, it would destroy the party. And I had a kind of a different attitude toward the party than I had toward the government."

He went to see his friend Nowlan privately to ask as discreetly as he could whether something was going on. "You're damn right there is," Nowlan replied. Camp tried to caution him, warning it would be extremely dangerous to the party if the talk went too far. "I got mad," Camp remembered. "It seemed to me that they were like children. They were the government of Canada. They had, I thought, responsibilities to the party. There was no question that we were nearing an election; the government couldn't stand much longer."[7]

Camp felt a strong urge to try to save his dysfunctional party from itself: "I felt that maybe in a funny way this was the hour that I was meant for, that maybe I could hold the thing together because I had oars in a lot of boats, and friends on both sides, and I realized the difficulties of anyone [else] having any kind of relationship with Diefenbaker."[8]

The party's national executive happened to be meeting in Ottawa in early February 1963 when the wheels fell off the Diefenbaker government. Harkness resigned over Diefenbaker's failure to acquire nuclear warheads. The government was defeated in the House on a supply motion—a routine vote to advance money to the government to finance its operations—when the opposition moved an amendment that cited the administration's failure to enunciate a clear defence policy. Pierre Sevigny, the associate defence minister, and George Hees, the trade minister, both resigned, as did Eddie Goodman, a Hees ally, who quit as a vice-president of the party.

With Camp trying to steer a course between the pro- and anti-Diefenbaker forces, the executive made an attempt to control the damage caused by the resignations by passing a motion of loyalty, confidence and support for the leader. The vote was unanimous, but no one was fooled.

"If the revolt had carried, I think the party would have been beyond salvation," Camp said. "I think it would have taken us years to recover. . . . The vast majority of the party would not have understood it, would not have supported it, would have wanted Mr. Diefenbaker to have another chance. This was very much my feeling—that you couldn't possibly do this to a prime minister."[9]

The government's defeat in the House forced Diefenbaker to call an election for April 8, 1963. For the first time, Camp was in complete charge of a federal campaign, and he knew he faced impossible odds. The country was mired in recession. Unemployment levels alarmed Canadians. The dollar had been devalued the year before, and now the country was staggering under an economic austerity program that the Tories had imposed almost before the ballots had been counted in the June 1962 election. Diefenbaker's response to the Cuban missile crisis had exposed his inability to act decisively. The nuclear arms issue had split both the cabinet and the Conservative caucus and had caused the government to be defeated in Parliament. Diefenbaker was an albatross around the neck of many Tory candidates, especially those in urban areas.

Flora MacDonald recalled Camp being moody and deeply depressed during that campaign. "He was really down in the dumps," she said. "It was a hard one for him, because I think he felt Diefenbaker was owed allegiance, but his heart wasn't in it. It was not a happy time."[10]

Money was tight. Camp saw an ominous warning sign when Lady Eaton, the matriarch of the department store family, wrote a short, strong anti-Diefenbaker letter to the *Globe and Mail*, and for the first time ever Eaton's refused to give a cent to the Conservatives, nationally or at the constituency level. And the Liberals campaigned enthusiastically along the low road. They produced a tasteless comic book that ridiculed Diefenbaker. They created a "Truth Squad," headed by Liberal MP Judy LaMarsh, which trailed after Diefenbaker, looking for misstatements and errors of fact in his speeches.

Camp's challenge was to try to recreate in 1963 the rapport that Diefenbaker had had with ordinary Canadians in the 1957 election.

He decided at the outset not to take Diefenbaker into Metropolitan Toronto at all during the campaign. Not only did the Conservatives have little chance there, antipathy toward Diefenbaker was so profound that Camp was afraid that his appearance would ignite demonstrations by groups angry with the government for a whole range of reasons, and possibly produce mob scenes even worse than the ones the leader had encountered in Hamilton and Toronto in the election the year before. An anti-Diefenbaker riot in Toronto would lead the news across the country, Camp knew, and could only hurt the Tory campaign everywhere. The closest Diefenbaker came to Toronto in 1963 was Richmond Hill, north of the city.[11]

Camp also decided that Diefenbaker would campaign by train rather than by aircraft. He was more at ease in a train, and the more comfortable he felt, the better he campaigned. Olive Diefenbaker also was happier in a train than on a plane; her happiness or unhappiness was invariably reflected in her husband's performance. And Camp wanted to see if they could rekindle the spirit of 1957 by opening the campaign with a long, sentimental whistle-stop tour of the Prairies.

It was a fine idea—but it nearly went off the rails before the special campaign train, leased from Canadian National Railways, pulled out of Ottawa. The train was scheduled to depart at 8:00 p.m. At 6:30 p.m., Olive Diefenbaker phoned. "Mr. Camp," she said, "I must tell you that John and I are very unhappy about the train." The Diefenbakers had a favourite private rail car, known as "Car 100." But it was in the shop for repairs. In its place, CNR had provided a newer, larger and more comfortable rail car. "Where is Car 100?" Mrs. Diefenbaker demanded. Camp told her it was in the shop. "There you go," she said. "They're conspiring against us. They just don't want to give us a car in which we'll be comfortable."

It transpired that CNR had sought to do the Diefenbakers a favour by transferring to the new rail car two long-term employees, a chef and a butler, who had served the Prime Minister and his wife on Car 100 and whom the Diefenbakers liked. The two men, however, disliked the new car because it was larger and involved more work. So they complained to Diefenbaker's valet that the beds were uncomfortable, the shower did not work and the kitchen was no good. These complaints were swiftly relayed to the Diefenbakers, and Olive insisted that Camp get Car 100 back for her. "I was just out of my mind," Camp remembered. "Of all the things I had to cope with, I had to cope with a foolish railroad car."[12]

He never liked to ask Allister Grosart for help, but he did on this occasion. They went to the train together and located the chef and butler. Grosart, a large man, backed them against the wall and angrily demanded an explanation. Along with Walter Smith, a CNR public relations official, they marched the two employees in front of the Diefenbakers and made them confess that it was a good car, a better car, that they would be happy working on it, and that the Diefenbakers would be happy, too. Olive Diefenbaker grudgingly agreed to try the new car, but before they had gone 300 miles she was complaining that the ride was rough and the beds uncomfortable. She said her back was sore, she could not sleep and she would not be happy until she got Car 100 back.

For the most part, though, Diefenbaker was easier to work for than he had been in 1958 or 1962. He was considerate of the people who were trying to help him, and his relations with the press were cordial. Camp and Donald Fleming wrote the party's election program, which Diefenbaker accepted without complaint and unveiled in Winnipeg in a speech Camp wrote for him. The campaign unfolded smoothly and Diefenbaker seemed to be doing better than Camp had expected. Waging a valiant one-man campaign, he attacked the Liberals with much of his old gusto. Sensing the passing of an era, huge crowds gathered on station platforms to see the Diefenbaker train go through. Diefenbaker ordered the engineer to stop wherever there was a crowd. "Diefenbaker was good," Camp recalled. "He was reasonably in control.... He was cooperative and he was aware of some of the mistakes he had made in '62. He was a better campaigner in '63."[13] If he had campaigned so well in 1962, Camp thought, he probably would not have lost his majority.

What might have been enough in 1962 was not enough in 1963, however. Diefenbaker had alienated urban Canada and driven away many of the people who had supported him faithfully through three elections. He had set Western Canada against the East. His vacillation had angered Canada's closest ally and created a rupture in his cabinet. His paranoia often made it impossible to deal with him on a reasonable basis. He had demonstrated how a great opposition leader can be an incompetent prime minister.

But he managed to do what Camp had hoped he could do: he denied the Liberals a majority government. He stopped them at 129 seats, four short of a majority. In Camp's view, George Hees and his co-conspirators in "that abortive stupidity" at the time of the nuclear uproar had cost the Conservatives the election. Diefenbaker, however, had saved the Tory party—"because he could have blown [it] right out the window"—and, Camp thought, had earned the right to lead the party into one more election.

As agreed, Camp resigned as national organizer, cleaned out his desk and returned to Toronto. Before going, though, he wrote a letter of congratulations to the leader, in which he drew an analogy between Diefenbaker's situation and that of Winston Churchill at the end of the Second World War. He told Diefenbaker that the young people in the party would be restless and hard to contain, but that he should do nothing to precipitate a confrontation and should not worry unduly about the inevitable recriminations. "My advice to him was just to hold up and let things heal and then reappraise the situation," Camp said.[14]

Others were not so sanguine. Anti-Diefenbaker whispering and manoeuvring continued in the upper reaches of the Tory party, and a few constituency organizations passed resolutions calling for the party's next annual meeting, scheduled for early February 1964, to be turned into a leadership convention. Camp, as he would concede later, played both sides of the street. He confused one national executive meeting when he accused the Tories of making a god of their leader and sheep of themselves. As he explained later, he was trying to avert a confrontation by sending a warning to both the "anti-Diefenbaker league," as he called it, and the "yahoos" (hardcore Diefenbaker supporters). His hope was to discourage the plotters without giving any encouragement to Diefenbaker to hang on to office.[15]

Just before the 1964 annual meeting, the Progressive Conservative Student Federation called on the senior party to conduct a secret ballot to determine whether Tories still had confidence in Diefenbaker. The student federation was headed by a young Albertan, Joe Clark, whose occasional irreverence and caustic humour irritated Camp but caused Clark to stand out from the grey cadres of desperately earnest student Tories. "I did not glimpse in him the shape of a putative prime minister," Camp wrote. "But, among the random shapes and sizes of Tory political fledglings, Clark stood apart. He was different."[16]

Camp advised Diefenbaker to relax, to let the students have their secret ballot, telling him he doubted if more than 25 per cent would vote against him. Diefenbaker refused to take the risk, however. Instead, he made an emotional speech to the delegates, and the PCSF's resolution was beaten back easily. However, the incident served notice that the leadership issue was not going to go away and that a significant element in the party did not share Camp's assessment that Diefenbaker had earned the right to fight another election.

The annual meeting in February 1964 would turn out to be a watershed for Camp and the party. Over Christmas, Camp had made the biggest decision of his political life—or, at least, the biggest since he decided to abandon the Liberals for the Conservatives after his return from the London School of Economics 15 years earlier. He decided to run for the office of national president of the party. Although many of his friends and associates were astounded—"I don't know why you'd want to do a damn-fool thing like that," Robert Stanfield told him[17]—they should not have been. Camp's motivation was consistent. He had agreed to take over the party organization and run the 1963 election campaign because he believed he was better able than anyone else to keep the party intact, to get the best out of Diefenbaker in the campaign and to keep the Liberals from electing a majority government. It was the same motivation that had caused him to put the party first when he opposed attempts by the mutineers to force Diefenbaker out of the leadership prior to the 1963 election.

In fact, Camp had been thinking for a year or two about seeking the presidency. He felt he could use the position to stop the party organization from imploding. He thought he probably enjoyed more personal goodwill than anyone in either the Diefenbaker or anti-Diefenbaker factions. He had a good rapport with younger Tories. He had close contacts and many friendships at the provincial level, where by 1964 much of the real power in the Conservative party was being wielded by premiers Stanfield in Nova Scotia, Walter Shaw in Prince Edward Island, Duff Roblin in Manitoba and John Robarts in Ontario. And he felt he could do what others could not do: bring back into the fold important Tories who had left at the time of the split over the acquisition of nuclear warheads. The return of these "prodigals," as he called them, including Hees, Harkness, Goodman, Toronto *Telegram* publisher John Bassett, Camp's friend George Hogan and Davie Fulton, who was in self-imposed exile in British Columbia, would be crucial to the survival of the party, Camp believed.

The Tories clearly agreed. By not opposing him, Diefenbaker lent his silent blessing to Camp's campaign. The incumbent, former Montreal MP Egan Chambers, withdrew, and Camp was elected by acclamation.

His first important move as president was to organize a conference that he hoped would have the same invigorating impact on the Conservative party that the Kingston thinkers' conference of 1960 had had on the Liberal party. Officially called the National Conference on Canadian Goals, but popularly referred to as the "Fredericton Conference," the Tory think-in was held in the New Brunswick capital in September 1964.

Camp had a number of objectives. He wanted to divert the party away from its preoccupation with the leadership issue, its election defeat and its internal feuding. He was anxious to give restless younger members of the party some mental nourishment. He saw the conference as a way to expose Tories to something they seldom experienced: informed opinion about French Canada. And he hoped to drag some intellectual heavyweights into the Conservative party or, at least, expose Tory members to them. If he achieved his objectives, he could start the process of modernizing the party and making it credible in urban Canada.

"This conference will, I trust, demonstrate our intent, so far as lies within our power, to purge from Conservatism that which is doctrinaire, obsolescent and irrational," Camp told the opening session. "While clichés are comforting, they do not really provide a refuge from facts, and while shibboleths can be worn and waved by partisans, they provide no defence against reality."

Diefenbaker was not amused, and he made his displeasure plain to Camp. "Damned intellectuals," he snapped. Camp knew where Diefenbaker was coming from. The Chief had mocked the Liberals' Kingston conference, and he feared Fredericton would be another Kingston, giving the hated Liberals a chance to mock him in turn. Camp tried a little song-and-dance number—telling Diefenbaker that, with his grasp of Canadian history, law, jurisprudence and Parliament, he qualified as an intellectual himself. The old trial lawyer had heard too many spurious arguments from too many opposing counsel to buy Camp's cant. He wanted to know who Camp was inviting to participate, but Camp refused to tell him, lest the leader try to veto his choices.

"I could tell by the people he wanted to have at the conference that he had in mind to sabotage the conference," Camp recalled. "He wanted to have all the party hacks there. He had a friend in Quebec who was just disgusting—a useless person—but he said, 'Unless he is invited, I won't be there.'" Although the Quebec friend was invited, Diefenbaker was not mollified. As was his wont, he kept the organizers on tenterhooks. He could not possibly tear himself away from the flag debate in the House of Commons to go to Fredericton, he said. At the last moment, consumed by curiosity about the conference and concerned about what Tories were saying behind his back, he put in an appearance, made a pedestrian speech and took off again. "He came to sneer," said Flora MacDonald.[18]

If Camp did not realize it at the time, he did before long: his relationship with Diefenbaker, patched together at the time of the 1963 election, had come unstuck over the Fredericton Conference, and the two men would never be on the same wavelength again.

As was his custom, Camp, the idea man, turned over the tedious details involved in organizing a successful conference to his lieutenant, his brother-in-law, Norman Atkins. Atkins was assisted by Clark, who invited the delegates, collected their conference fees and confirmed their travel arrangements, and by Flora MacDonald, who, working out of party headquarters, took charge of conference materials, distribution of position papers and preparation of verbatim reports of the proceedings. Lowell Murray, another of Camp's Nova Scotia finds, handled media relations.[19]

Camp cast a wide net in his search for speakers who might shock the Tories into an awareness of the Canada of the mid-1960s. The guests did not have to be Conservatives. It was actually better for his purposes if they were not; there was a whole wide world of ideas out there, of which the Tories comprehended only a tiny corner. So he invited historian W.L. Morton, who warned of the dangers of Quebec separatism, an utterly foreign notion to most Tories in 1964, and went so far as to imply that the use of force to keep Canada intact might be justified—an extremely controversial view in those days. Camp went to Montreal and landed Claude Ryan, publisher of the Montreal daily *Le Devoir*, who later became Quebec Liberal leader. He got Montreal lawyer Marc Lalonde, who actually had a tenuous tie to the Tories (he had worked in Ottawa for Davie Fulton) but went on to become a major minister in Pierre Trudeau's Liberal cabinet. And he secured the participation of financier Marcel Faribault, who would later be a constitutional adviser to the premier of Quebec.

Flora MacDonald got another name from Michael Pitfield, who was then on the staff of the governor general and would later be clerk of the Privy Council. The name was Pierre Elliott Trudeau. MacDonald passed the name to Camp and arranged for the two men to have dinner in Montreal. Their chemistry was terrible. "There was a complete clash of egos," MacDonald recalled. "Dalton phoned me the next morning and said, '*Never* send me to meet with that man again.' It was just not on."[20] Camp dismissed Trudeau as being too superficial—even for the tattered, battered, dispirited Tory party of 1964.

All of the other speakers at Fredericton paled next to the man Camp recruited to be his keynote speaker: Marshall McLuhan, the guru of the global village, who was then a little-known professor at the University of Toronto. Camp had become friendly with McLuhan in Toronto, was dazzled by his insights and was convinced he would be just the jolt the Tories needed to shock them into new ways of thinking.

McLuhan jolted them all right. Read four decades later, his speech is provocative, bizarre and mostly incomprehensible. The poor linear-thinking Tories of 1964 must have thought they were being addressed by a lunatic, if not an extraterrestrial. McLuhan began by asking the delegates if they knew what was purple and hummed. "A purple electric grape," naturally. And why does the grape hum? "[Because] it doesn't know the words."[21] That launched McLuhan into a dissertation on the importance of language, knowing the words if one wanted to communicate, and a discussion of what is "cool" and what is "hot." The humming grape, he said, is an example of cool humour, humour that involves the listener. He told a longish joke about an airline passenger with a bomb to illustrate hot or "uncool" humour—humour that does not involve the listener. Lest the audience manage to grasp his meaning too easily, McLuhan quickly elaborated: hot and cool had recently reversed meanings. What used to be hot was now cool, and vice versa.

Even Tories who had mastered all of the intricacies of the arcane plots against their leader and could explain them in their sleep were dumbfounded. They did not have the foggiest idea what McLuhan was talking about. They doubted whether even their university-age children could understand him. Flora MacDonald, however, was entranced: "He gave the most extraordinary lecture on what happens when you don't know the words to communicate, and it was brilliant, and I think it really was the start of McLuhan's prominence. Dalton always prided himself on the fact that he discovered him, or launched him."[22]

Camp, too, was delighted—"McLuhan was an absolute sensation"[23]—and his acolyte Richard Hatfield, a rising young Tory in New Brunswick, shared his enthusiasm. But other friends were skeptical. "This is the price we have to pay for losing the election," Finlay MacDonald grumbled in his speech to the delegates. Gene Rhéaume, a Tory MP and organizer, had been deputized to go to the airport to meet Diefenbaker on his arrival in Fredericton. He decided not to bother. "Marshall McLuhan taught me I could kiss his ass from here," he declared.[24]

Although the Fredericton Conference left no lasting mark on the party, it did enhance Camp's stature. To his previous reputation as a brilliant advertising man and campaign strategist, he added the image of a political intellectual, a creative thinker, a person who could see beyond the problems of the present to the glittering opportunities of the future. The conference left Camp feeling buoyant about the Conservative party and his role in it. The transfusion of fresh ideas would make the party more contemporary, more relevant and more attractive to younger voters and urban dwellers, he believed.

Diefenbaker, however, did not share Camp's satisfaction or his hope. He saw Fredericton as an affront to his vision of the party—and Camp as a growing threat to his leadership and his legacy. Their relationship grew progressively worse. And, as the spirit of Fredericton faded, the Tories returned like political homing pigeons to their preoccupation with the leadership. Camp, as national president, spent the next year in the role of a peacemaker, trying to keep challenges to Diefenbaker from blowing the party apart, thereby emboldening the minority Liberal government to call a snap election.

Three months after Fredericton, the leadership crisis came to a head again at a meeting of the full national executive. At that time, in early December 1964, Diefenbaker had succeeded in tying the House of Commons in knots with a filibuster as he tried to preserve the Red Ensign and prevent the adoption of Canada's maple leaf flag. Several members of the executive rose to complain about Diefenbaker's tactics and about the corrosive effect his leadership was having on the party's fortunes. Léon Balcer, Diefenbaker's Quebec lieutenant, proposed that the executive pass a resolution calling on the party's parliamentary wing to abandon the filibuster.

Although Camp was able to prevent Balcer's proposal from coming to a vote, he did try privately to persuade Diefenbaker to end the filibuster. "I went to Diefenbaker and told him that in my judgment the party wanted to see this thing ended in the first instance. It was now hurting us and hurting him," Camp remembered. "The second thing was that he was doomed to lose, and as a result of losing this, the people who were supporting the Red Ensign were going to lose a lot of things with it, more than they thought they were losing."

He suggested a compromise, one that he knew was acceptable to Balcer and the Quebec caucus: the Tories would agree to accept the flag with one maple leaf if the Liberals would agree to add a crown to the flag. This way, Diefenbaker would accomplish something, and he would preserve a vestige of the British connection—a connection that mattered deeply to Diefenbaker but not at all to Camp. "Otherwise," he warned the leader, "you're going to lose and you're going to get the maple leaf and you're going to have it, period. And then you're going to find the other things [monarchial symbols] under pressure and attack." Diefenbaker, Camp conceded, "thought that was a helluva poor way to go about things and he was bloody-minded about it. He didn't concede defeat. He thought Pearson would quit."[25]

Diefenbaker was dead wrong. Pearson persisted, and the flag with the single red maple leaf became the national flag of Canada— but not before the Tory party went through more convulsions. A few days after the national executive meeting, Balcer rose in his place next to Diefenbaker in the House and, on a question of privilege, attacked his own party's tactics in the flag debate. He invited the government to invoke closure to choke off the filibuster. Gordon Churchill, Diefenbaker's House leader, quickly jumped up to insist that Balcer did not speak for the party.

A lawyer from Trois Rivières who had been solicitor general and transport minister in Diefenbaker cabinets, Balcer was not finished with Diefenbaker. In mid-January 1965, he convened a meeting in Montreal of the eight-member Quebec caucus, along with a few other Tories from the province. The group approved a resolution proposed by Balcer that demanded that the party's national executive be convened before February 16, 1965, the day Parliament was to resume, to fix a date for a leadership convention. Balcer wrote to Camp to accuse Diefenbaker of making French Canadians feel "ill at ease and uncomfortable" in the party. His ultimatum was supported by the "termites" in the caucus, but Diefenbaker rejected it out of hand, claiming Balcer's complaints were the work of the Liberal propaganda machine.

Although he had as little respect for Balcer as he did for George Hees, the central figure in the abortive 1963 putsch, Camp knew the demands of the party's Quebec wing could not be so cavalierly dismissed. He also knew Diefenbaker would never agree to a meeting of the national executive to consider Balcer's ultimatum. Camp polled the members of the executive and, when 60 per cent expressed support for an early meeting, he knew he would have no choice.

The trick would be to get around Diefenbaker's objections. With the leader away in London attending Winston Churchill's funeral, Camp and Flora MacDonald came up with a stratagem. MacDonald found that Diefenbaker's flight back to Canada was scheduled to leave London at midnight Ottawa time. At midnight, she went to the telegraph office and sent wires to all of the approximately 140 members of the national executive, including provincial premiers, asking them to be in Ottawa for a meeting on February 6.

Diefenbaker was furious when he found out. His assistant, B.T. Richardson, accused Camp of "an act of perfidy."

But the old leader was not without a stratagem of his own. As he had done in 1963, he rescheduled the customary pre-session meeting of the Tory caucus. This time he moved it from its scheduled date in the week after the national executive meeting to the day before the executive was to meet. He still controlled a majority of MPs. He would go to caucus, face down his enemies again, gather the support of his loyalists and proceed the next day to confront the executive with the wind in his sails.

Desperately anxious to avoid a confrontation that would split the party, perhaps irreconcilably, Camp and the other principal members of the executive came up with a plan. Rather than permit an open debate on a motion to order a leadership convention, they would distribute a questionnaire to the executive. It had two key questions: Should there be a leadership convention? and Should the leader resign?

Joining Diefenbaker for breakfast before the executive meeting, Camp explained the questionnaire and the procedure he proposed to follow. It would be a secret ballot. As national president, he would collect the completed questionnaires, tabulate the numbers and reveal them only to Diefenbaker. They would never be made public. Only the outcome would be announced, not the actual votes. The results, he told Diefenbaker, should be interpreted as being advice from the executive, but not instructions that he necessarily should follow. Thus, Diefenbaker could accept the results or ignore them.

Camp hoped the questionnaire would accomplish two things: dispose of the Balcer ultimatum by giving the members of executive a chance to express their candid views on the leadership without provoking a public bloodbath; and give Diefenbaker, if the advice were negative, an opportunity to step down gracefully and at his own timing.

In Camp's view, the first question—on holding a leadership convention—would not carry; too many Conservatives were too nervous about going into a leadership campaign when the Liberals might suddenly call an election. The second question—confidence in the leader—was the crucial one, and it was the one that bothered Diefenbaker. "I think you'll get a vote of confidence," he told Diefenbaker. "I don't know how close it will be, but no one will know. This is for your guidance."[26]

At Diefenbaker's request, Camp added two more questions: Should the party create a policy advisory committee? and Should the party fully accept the new Canadian flag? Diefenbaker pronounced himself pleased with these additions, and, although he should have known better, Camp left the breakfast satisfied that he had secured Diefenbaker's agreement on the questionnaire.

When the executive assembled in closed session on the top floor of party headquarters, Camp, speaking first, welcomed the members and explained the questionnaire. "You're here to advise the national leader, and I think we can all get through this without further worsening our relationships one with the other, and I'm going to just ask you not to say things that will worsen relationships," he told them.[27]

After Balcer made a short, perfunctory, non-confrontational speech, Diefenbaker took over and spoke for nearly an hour and a half. He dredged up every favourable thing Balcer had said about him in the past, denounced everyone who had ever opposed him, starting in 1956, the year he won the leadership, and he lashed out at the "termites." He sent a chill through the room when he reminded the executive that Gladstone had won his last British election when he was 83. "You who have ambitions should not be other than hopeful," he told the meeting.

The leader's speech split the meeting down the middle. Camp had trouble maintaining order. The proceedings were interrupted briefly when someone discovered an eavesdropper—a reporter was hiding in the elevator shaft.

By this time, Diefenbaker had, as Camp put it, "cased the house." Emboldened by the support he detected, he looked at the questionnaire and said: "I won't accept it. Nope." His supporters argued that the second question (should the leader resign?) be excised. Camp and the senior members of executive withdrew to figure out what to do next. On their return, Eddie Goodman moved that the meeting proceed with the questionnaire. The session deteriorated into the sort of free-for-all that Camp had hoped to avoid. When Erik Nielsen, the MP for Yukon, delivered an impassioned defence of Diefenbaker, Joe Clark waded in. Speaking for young Tories, he demanded that the leader resign and a leadership convention be held.

Nielsen presented a procedural motion calling on the meeting to delete the second question. What this did was to force a standing vote on the issue of confidence in the leader. Those supporting the Chief would vote to delete the question; those opposing him would vote to retain it. Thus the executive members would be forced to do openly what Camp had hoped they would be able to do secretly via the questionnaire.

"Quite frankly, Dalton didn't have the whole meeting planned," MacDonald remembered. "He wasn't sure where he was going. And so, the morning ended in total confusion, with a lot of people being very critical of him."[28]

Matters got more confused in the afternoon as Camp tried to deal with Nielsen's motion. The meeting room on the top floor was in chaos as he called for the vote. "He really didn't know what to do in these circumstances," MacDonald said. "Dalton didn't like this sort of thing." In the confusion, the vote had to be counted three times. It was desperately close, with a margin of no more than two or three. It was probably 55 to 53 in favour of the motion to delete—in other words, in support of Diefenbaker. But some people thought it was 52–50, while others remembered 55–52 or 53–52. No one was sure.

Two things *were* clear, however. First, the motion had carried; question two would be deleted. Second, four people did not vote: the two "tellers" (the people who were counting the votes); British Columbian Dorothy Harrison Smith, the president of the Tory women's association, who was so torn between her personal loyalty to Diefenbaker and her personal reservations about his leadership that she asked for permission to abstain; and Camp himself. Camp said later that he felt it would be better if he, as national president, did not vote because he would have to work with both sides afterward. He would have voted only to break a tie and in that circumstance, he said, his vote would have been cast in support of the leader.[29]

He was not yet ready to take a public stand against the leader, an action that would have compromised his efforts to hold the party together. He believed—and it was a widely held view among Tories at the time—that the Liberals were angling for an opportunity to catch the Conservatives in the throes of changing leaders so that they could quickly call an election, in the expectation that they would achieve the majority government they had been so narrowly denied in 1963. Camp was not going to give the Grits that strategic advantage.

In his view, the four uncast votes would not have altered the outcome of the executive vote. Goodman, who had become increasingly upset with Diefenbaker, disagreed. He angrily challenged the vote, but was overruled by Camp. "We had them beat until Dalton ducked," he declared.[30] His view was shared by Finlay MacDonald and other disappointed Camp supporters.

The day after the executive meeting, Camp announced that question one—the call for a leadership convention—had been defeated. As promised, the figures were never divulged. "It's about the only secret in the Conservative party that's been kept, but it wasn't close," Camp said later. "Definitely against the convention."[31]

With his lease on the leadership extended, Diefenbaker went on national television to rail against his detractors, implying that he was victim of powerful, but unidentified, outside interests. His caucus continued to seethe. One Quebec MP, Rémi Paul, left the Conservatives to sit as an independent. Two months later, in April, Léon Balcer followed him, saying, "At first, I thought that Mr. Diefenbaker just didn't understand Quebec. Now, I'm convinced that he is genuinely against French Canada and that as a political expedient he is trying to whip up an English Canadian backlash for an election campaign."

Camp's relations with the leader were now damaged beyond repair: "I became increasingly uneasy about the leader of the Conservative party, and I formed this opinion that we could have no useful relationship, that he was incapable of what I considered to be an adult relationship."[32] His relationships with Bob Stanfield and Duff Roblin had always been based on complete candour, but candour was completely impossible with Diefenbaker. He decided his only course was to sweat out the next election, take the inevitable loss and hope that Diefenbaker's sense of history would lead him to do the right thing.

Denied a chance to catch the Tories between leaders, the Liberals waited until the fall of 1965 to call the election. A combination of their own ineptitude and a fragile unity among the Tories conspired to thwart Lester Pearson's second—and final—bid for a majority. By then, however, Camp's life had taken a new turn. He was ready to move out of the backroom and take his chances in electoral politics.

CHAPTER 13

The Ace of Spades

T HEY CALLED THEMSELVES THE "SPADES." They were Dalton
Camp's unofficial fan club and his personal political organization. A remarkable group of Toronto business and professional men,
they came together in 1965 when Camp ran for Parliament in the
Toronto riding of Eglinton, and they were at his side in every battle
over the next 10 years. They were united by personal devotion to
Camp and by a determination to advance his political ambitions.

Although their numbers waxed and waned over the years,
essentially there were a dozen of them: Camp himself; Norman
Atkins, his brother-in-law and partner in the advertising agency;
businessman Chad Bark; William Saunderson, an accountant and
investment counsellor who years later would become Ontario's
minister of economic development, trade and tourism; lawyer Roy
McMurtry, who became attorney general under William Davis and
later chief justice of Ontario; Paul Weed, who owned a collection
agency at the time; accountant Eric Ford; lawyers Pat Patterson,
Donald Guthrie and Brian Armstrong; Patrick Vernon, also a
lawyer and national party fundraiser; and investment dealer Ross
DeGeer, who would become executive director of the Ontario Tory
party and later the province's agent general in London.

They took their name from the playing card each man—there
were no female Spades—carried in his wallet. Camp was the ace of
spades. The others drew cards at random. Atkins, for example, was
the five of spades, Bark the six, Vernon the seven, Guthrie the nine.
In this private society of grown men, the playing cards were the symbol of belonging, of membership, of common causes, like a secret
handshake in a college fraternity. The activities of the Spades, and
even the group's existence, were never mentioned to outsiders.

The Spades met at irregular intervals, usually at the Albany
Club, the Conservative club on King Street East in downtown

Toronto, and usually when Camp wanted to try out ideas and enlist some help in his battles. Camp looked to them for advice, for example, when he was deciding whether to challenge John Diefenbaker in 1966, and again a few months later when he was considering his own bid for the leadership.

The Spades were the core of the organization that eventually brought about Diefenbaker's downfall, and they became the nucleus of Robert Stanfield's leadership campaign in 1967. They campaigned for Camp when he ran for Parliament again in the 1968 election. In 1971, they—with the exception of McMurtry, who supported his college football chum Bill Davis—came within 23 votes (out of 1,580 cast) of making Allan Lawrence leader of the Ontario Tories and premier of Ontario; when the convention was over they went to work for Davis, becoming the heart of the vaunted Big Blue Machine. Still following Camp's lead, they worked for Stanfield's Conservatives in the 1972 and 1974 federal elections; then, like Camp, they began to drift away. By the time Joe Clark won the national leadership in 1976, the Spades had scattered, gathering from time to time to celebrate Camp's birthday or the anniversaries of battles shared.

Each of the Spades had a career outside politics. They were gifted amateurs, skilled volunteers and the breed of believers who are the backbone of every serious political party. In their case, the bond was not a political party or ideology. They were in it because they believed in Dalton Camp. If he had chosen to run for the Rhinoceros party, they would have donned costumes and led his parade.

The Spades seem anachronistic today. Albeit chauvinistic, they were a reasonably accurate reflection of the politics of the time. Politics in those days was viewed as a game for white males, a whisky-and-cigars game, like football or prizefighting. There were almost no women in Parliament, and there was precious little pressure to elect any. There had never been a woman on the Supreme Court of Canada. No woman had ever been speaker of the House of Commons. No one in the all-male inner fabric of Canadian politics would have conceived of a woman as governor general. It was not so much that they would have objected, as it was that the notion simply would never have occurred to them. Women had defined roles in political organizations. They looked after phone banks in committee rooms, organized coffee parties for candidates, mailed out pamphlets and washed the dirty glasses in hospitality suites at political conventions.

Flora MacDonald, the one-time secretary from Cape Breton, was one of the few women who had achieved real influence and respect in the backrooms. But she was not one of the "boys." Camp, who was more enlightened about women in society than most males of his generation, never really put MacDonald on an equal status with the men he worked with. He sought her advice, valued her wisdom and relied on her support. But he still assumed she would type his speeches, and she did.

MacDonald was not a Spade. She could drink with the best of the men, but she was not part of their frat-house style of partying. She was not there the night the Spades and their friends gathered to celebrate Camp's birthday in a private room at the Ports of Call restaurant in Toronto. The Royal Bank of Canada at the time was running an advertising campaign inviting potential customers to direct their inquiries to "Mary at the Royal Bank." In addition to being a bank pitchwoman, "Mary" was an entertainer. The highlight (if that was what it was) of Camp's birthday occurred when "Mary" jumped out of a cake and landed, stark naked, in Camp's lap. Nothing if not quick-witted, he covered her with his tuxedo jacket and addressed his friends: "The Queen and I ..."

"The public tends to be cynical of those who are involved in politics," said Chad Bark, who kept his six of spades in his wallet for 30 years. "I'm going to tell you the commitment of the people who were involved with Dalton was total. There was no room for cynicism, and no room for what's best for 'me,' either. I wonder how often you run into that kind of devotion."[1]

Bill Saunderson, who came up with the playing card idea, recalled the first time he met Camp. It was in 1964, when, as national party president, he came to speak to a meeting of young

Conservatives in Toronto. "When I heard him," Saunderson said, "I thought, this is the most wonderful thing that's ever happened to the Conservative party. I think what he did was, he gave us all a hero, someone we could follow."[2]

Roy McMurtry credited Camp with inspiring him to pursue a career in politics. He was a young lawyer, in practice for seven years, when he first encountered Camp. He had never been to a political meeting and was not even sure he was a Conservative. One day in 1965, he heard Camp speak to a Kiwanis Club meeting in downtown Toronto. "I remember being tremendously impressed with him because he brought a civilized dimension to the federal political scene that we hadn't seen for awhile, because I always felt that Diefenbaker and Pearson brought out the worst in each other," McMurtry recalled. He was so impressed that he went up to Camp afterward to tell him that if he ever decided to run for office, McMurtry would like to work for him. "Dalton certainly evoked that sort of instantaneous enthusiasm," McMurtry said. A day or two later, he got a phone call from Camp saying he had decided to run in Eglinton, where McMurtry lived: "I ended up being very involved in the campaign. I basically ran the campaign team, and took a big chunk of the constituency where I lined up the canvassers, and did a lot of canvassing myself."[3]

Camp had been toying with the idea of running for Parliament even before the meeting of the national executive in February 1965—the meeting at which Léon Balcer had challenged Diefenbaker—had dashed his hopes of restoring a measure of unity and common purpose to the party. The timing seemed right. He was 45 years old, the father of five children and the owner of an advertising business that gave him ample income but no longer required a major investment of time.

To his mind, seeking electoral office was consistent with the choice he had made in 1963, when he had put aside his doubts and agreed to take over the Tory organization for the election that year, and with his decision in 1964 to seek the presidency of the party. In each case, he had been motivated by what he saw as the short-term need of the Conservative party to survive, and by its longer-term interest—to be a united, strong and viable alternative government. As he contemplated the prospect of an election in 1965, he feared the party, hemorrhaging from self-inflicted wounds, might be annihilated. He believed he had a continuing duty to try to save the Tories both from themselves and from the Liberals.

Camp hated the Liberals more than the average Tory did. Most Conservatives in Ottawa were so busy hating their leader or, alternatively, hating other Tories who hated the leader that they had scant passion to expend on the governing Liberals. Although many Conservatives tended to dismiss Lester Pearson as a benign bungler, Camp was barely rational on the subject. He saw the prime minister as a malignancy—as, at best, an incompetent presiding over a corrupt ministry with an appalling record of mismanagement. Ever since his post–London School of Economics conversion to Toryism, he had despised Liberals. He *really* despised the Liberals of Pearson, Walter Gordon and Keith Davey. "To me it was never a question of whether Pearson would be prime minister or Diefenbaker. The question would be whether or not Pearson got a majority, and I was prepared to do anything I could, personally and otherwise, to prevent that."[4]

As much as he loathed Liberals, he did not, however, loath Mitchell Sharp, the Liberal MP for Eglinton and minister of trade and commerce in Pearson's cabinet—and that, contrarily, was a factor in Camp's decision to run in Eglinton. He looked at three other ridings in Toronto. In addition, Bill Davis, then minister of education at Queen's Park, urged Camp to come out to his hometown of Brampton, west of Toronto, to run in Peel against Bruce Beer, a popular farmer who held the seat for the Liberals.

Camp's elitism showed. As he told historian Jack Granatstein: "I thought in a calculating way that if I had to lose to anybody, I'd hate like hell to lose to Bruce Beer, but I could lose to Mitchell Sharp.... I'm a better man than Bruce Beer for a job in the House of Commons, but I'd be prepared to submit to some arguments whether or not I'm a better man than Mitchell Sharp.... He has a lot to recommend him."[5]

Camp knew the chance of winning any seat in Toronto was nearly non-existent. The city was a hotbed of anti-Diefenbaker feeling.

Camp's strategy of not letting Diefenbaker campaign in Toronto in 1963 had succeeded to the extent that there were no riots or angry demonstrations against the leader in the city during that election. But the Tories also won no seats there. Of all the Toronto seats, though, Eglinton, in affluent North Toronto, was marginally less bleak than most. It had a Tory history, at least. Donald Fleming, Diefenbaker's finance minister, had held it until 1963; he beat Sharp in 1962, with Sharp taking the seat in 1963 when Fleming left politics. Although Sharp was turning into a formidable minister in Ottawa, he was not a natural politician; he never seemed at ease in the cut–and thrust of the all-candidate debates.

Running against Sharp had the added attraction of putting Camp squarely in the Toronto-centric lens of the national media, and it might enable the Tories to keep Sharp tied up at home, safely removed from the Liberals' national campaign.

The Conservative riding association president was Chad Bark, the young businessman who was trying to give the party a more modern image in Eglinton. Until then, it had been using a Loyal Orange hall for its meetings; Bark moved them to a more contemporary venue. He had heard about Camp and pursued him. He and Pat Vernon had lunch with Camp at the Carriage House in downtown Toronto, where they talked about philosophy and the state of the world, as well as domestic politics. By the end of the meal, they were convinced. And they sold Camp on their team approach. "My argument to Dalton was, look, we've got a group of guys here in their 30s and 40s who are really keen and who have party experience outside Eglinton as well as in Eglinton. I think it's fair to say that we didn't see the glamour of Mitchell Sharp the way some of the Liberals did. We pitched Dalton with great enthusiasm."[6]

As the campaign went on, his organization—they called themselves the Eglinton Mafia in that election, switching to the Spades name after it was over—found it had a candidate who was thoughtful and articulate and could handle Mitchell Sharp in debate, but who did not enjoy door-to-door canvassing and, by his own admission, was inferior to Sharp when it came to mainstreeting. "It was painful to see him go to a bus stop and shake hands with strangers," Flora MacDonald commented afterward. "Dalton is basically not a very public person and a lot of people don't understand that.... He would be the one to write the blueprint rather than to lead the charge."[7]

Despite Camp's deficiencies as a candidate, Chad Bark and the other Spades grew more impressed by the day. "I became very convinced that the guy would not only make a good candidate, but had the intellectual capacity to be prime minister," Bark said. "... I thought he was a gentleman. He was loyal. He was loyal to his party. He was loyal to his friends. [Subsequently] he was, I think, given a terribly rough ride by many people who seemed to enjoy doing it—and this angered me and it angered a lot of his friends. I guess nobody could do anything about it. He was just a decent, highly intelligent guy and would have made, in my opinion, a wonderful leader."[8]

Although Camp did not win that election, he had nothing to be ashamed of in losing to Sharp, who was appointed minister of finance the following month. He cut Sharp's margin to 1,942 votes from 8,231 in 1963, and he polled the highest percentage of popular vote of any Tory candidate in Toronto as the Tories were again shut out in the city. The votes came at a price: Camp reported expenses of $43,000, more than any other Conservative in the country.

On election night, November 8, 1965, while Diefenbaker was chortling with glee over Camp's loss, the defeated candidate was attending a victory party—Mitchell Sharp's. "I couldn't think, if you have to lose, of a more satisfactory loss than that," Camp said. "He was a good winner, and it was a good campaign."[9] Camp came out of the 1965 campaign with a new public profile as an electoral candidate amid raised expectations in the party that he would one day be a force to be reckoned with on the Tory front benches.

Because he was fully occupied in Eglinton, Camp had no role in the national campaign for the first time since he had worked for George Drew in 1953. The Tories' happy warrior, "Fast Eddie" Goodman, took over as campaign chairman, which had been Camp's role in the 1963 election. Despite his opposition to

Diefenbaker's leadership and his differences with him over nuclear weapons, Goodman managed to establish a satisfactory, if distant, working relationship with the Chief for the duration of the campaign. While Diefenbaker stumped the country railing against the Liberals over a variety of scandals large and small, real and imagined, Goodman kept the party machine going. "There was really a great atmosphere around headquarters, a great esprit de corps," he remembered. "I have never done anything which was more enjoyable than the 1965 election."[10]

Part of his enjoyment came from working with old friends, notably Flora MacDonald and Lowell Murray. They cobbled together an election platform that even contained a Tory science policy—which was stolen, although Diefenbaker was never let in on the secret, in its entirety from the British Labour party. MacDonald recalled being in Britain a couple of years before when Labour leader Harold Wilson had made what she thought was a brilliant speech on science policy. MacDonald located a copy of the speech and gave it to Goodman. "Eddie took it, and revised it a little bit, and we had it printed in the *Globe and Mail* as our science policy," MacDonald recounted, laughing at the memory. "And people said, 'Gee, they've got some great thinkers in the Conservative party.'"[11]

With the exception of James Johnston, whom Diefenbaker would soon appoint to be his new national director, all of the people in charge of the campaign were Tories who wanted nothing more than to see a change in the leadership.[12] The Conservatives would lose once more, they were sure; then Diefenbaker would be bound to resign, a new leader would be chosen and the party would rise again. Or so they thought.

This mindset was conducive to a certain amount of heavy drinking and black humour. With Davie Fulton, George Hees and some of Diefenbaker's other detractors running again, they set about to construct a hypothetical Tory cabinet composed entirely of members who had opposed the Chief's leadership. They scripted imaginary debates around the cabinet table. And they wrote some make-believe campaign slogans. Someone—MacDonald thought it was Brian Mulroney; Goodman said it was Johnston—came up with the unanimous winner: "Let's give the old bugger another chance."

This late-evening kibitzing produced one of the most enduring anecdotes in the party's history. Several versions have circulated over the years. This is Eddie Goodman's recollection:

> Lowell and Flora and I—and I don't know which one of us it was—decided that when we won, I, as national chairman, the architect of this great victory, would go on the air to accept the plaudits of the multitudes, and then after I would say to them, "Oh," I would say to everybody, "Ladies and gentlemen, this has all been a great hoax." And we'd link hands and jump off the top of the Chateau Laurier. But, you know, at that point the three of us had all had a fair amount to drink.

Somehow the story leaked out, because Goodman heard it back from members of Lester Pearson's staff a day or two later. On election night, Goodman and MacDonald got a call from Murray, who was at a local television station watching the returns come in from Atlantic Canada. The Tories were doing exceptionally well, and it looked as though they might even add a number of seats in Quebec. "Lowell," Goodman said, "says to me, 'I'm coming over there. Get ready to jump!'"[13]

The 1965 election results mirrored those in 1963. The Liberals again came tantalizingly close to a majority. They won two additional seats, to finish with 131—including the seats won by three newcomers in Quebec: Jean Marchand, Gérard Pelletier and Pierre Elliott Trudeau, the so-called "Three Wise Men." That left the Liberals two members shy of a majority. Diefenbaker managed to add three seats, ending with 98.

Goodman was euphoric. The Tories had again denied the Liberals a majority. But Camp did not share his pleasure: "I think he [Diefenbaker] kept the Conservative party alive in '63. I think he did a disservice in '65, because under any other leader we would have won in '65. There's no question in my mind about that."[14] Worse, Camp knew the outcome would simply fuel Diefenbaker's determination to hang on. The leader would see vindication in the results. There was no way he would go peacefully now. The Conservatives would either have to reconcile themselves to having him as their leader indefinitely, or they would have to find a way to remove him from office.

Camp knew which fork in the road he would take. The Ace of Spades would soon be calling on his friends again.

CHAPTER 14

Bearding the Chief

PEOPLE WHO KNEW BOTH Dalton Camp and John Diefenbaker would say in hindsight that the only surprising thing about their shootout was that it took them so long. They were too different, too driven and each ultimately too convinced of the rightness of his own course to be able to sleep indefinitely in the same political bed.

Alexander Ross, a brilliant magazine writer, captured their differences in a profile of Camp in *Maclean's* in February 1967, three months after the historic Conservative annual meeting that brought the leader down. "They never became friends," Ross wrote.

> They never could have become friends. They're too dissimilar. Camp is affable, creative, tolerant, contemporary, humorous, candid, sophisticated and heavily disposed toward seeing several sides to every question. Diefenbaker is not. Camp drives a Buick Riviera, likes wine at dinner and tries to understand Marshall McLuhan. Diefenbaker does not. Camp tries to learn from young people; Diefenbaker tries to instruct them. Camp prefers talking to individuals; Diefenbaker is at his best addressing crowds. Camp would have got along famously with John F. Kennedy. Diefenbaker emphatically did not. Camp's style is cool, controlled, and intellectual. Diefenbaker's is fiery, impassioned and evangelistic. Camp is a man of reason. Diefenbaker is a man with visions.

Although Sandy Ross did not note it, Camp and Diefenbaker did have one thing in common—and it served to drive them even further apart. It was ego. Toronto *Telegram* publisher John Bassett, no shrinking violet himself, observed after first meeting Camp: "I never thought I'd see a son of a bitch with an ego bigger than mine."[1] Bassett meant it as a compliment, and Camp took it that way.

After the general election of November 1965, Camp, in his capacity as national president of the Progressive Conservative party, went to Ottawa to pay his respects to his leader. He took with him a memorandum on the state of the party. Without specifically citing the leadership struggles that had tormented the party for several years, he identified a number of problems. Young Tories were angry and dismayed over the party's direction and future. Fundraising had been so unsuccessful in the 1963 and 1965 elections that the party was destitute; Camp himself was constantly badgered by the party's creditors. It had become increasingly difficult to recruit good candidates. It was hard to motivate the workers. There was a general lack of confidence in the party among average Canadians. "Any sensible man reading it," Camp said later, "would say, 'What this fellow's telling me is that I really ought to resign.' Because at the end of it, I said, 'Now, one thing you can be sure of is that the party still has for you a great deal of affection and loyalty and regard.'"[2]

Resigning was far from Diefenbaker's mind, however, although he did ask Camp what advice he would give him: "What shall we do now?" Camp replied cautiously. The election had been pretty divisive, he told the leader.

> I think you should, we should, become more positive as an opposition. All this business about lime pits [an organized crime scandal in Quebec that Diefenbaker had exploited in the 1965 election] and so on may be true, but it didn't do us any good. It isn't doing Parliament any good and it isn't doing politics any good. I think it would be greatly in your interest if you would offer some kind of olive branch.[3]

Camp had a specific olive branch in mind. At the time, the Pearson government was proposing to nominate as the new speaker of the House of Commons Lucien Lamoureux, a bilingual francophone Liberal MP from the eastern Ontario city of Cornwall. Lamoureux had been an excellent deputy speaker in the previous Parliament, and Camp thought this was not only an opportunity for the Tories to support his promotion but to go a step further and propose that he be designated as "permanent speaker"—an idea that had been discussed for a number of years as a way to insulate the chair from partisan pressures. Diefenbaker would not hear of it. "The French have too much," he snapped, cutting off discussion on that subject.

He had plenty to say on another topic that was preoccupying him that day: the inadequacies, real or imagined, of the people who might seek to succeed him as leader. He dismissed the aspirations of all of those who had served with him in Parliament, laughing aloud when he mentioned the name of Davie Fulton, his former justice minister. Then he startled Camp by adding: "No man can lead the House—the Conservative party of Canada—who hasn't had experience in the House of Commons." That, to Diefenbaker's mind, ruled out premiers Robert Stanfield of Nova Scotia, Duff Roblin of Manitoba and John Robarts of Ontario, each of whom had been mentioned as a possible leader at one time or another. By process of elimination, the Chief had established to his complete personal satisfaction that no one, other than John George Diefenbaker, was fit to lead the Tory party.

He had convinced himself that the election defeats of 1963 and 1965 had actually been great victories because the Liberals were stopped short of a majority. Camp could not accept that rationalization. It was time, he told other Tories, to stop celebrating defeats as though they were victories: "We'd had two successive 'victories' in a row and we're still in opposition.... We still had the government over a barrel, and we still had Mr. Diefenbaker as leader of the opposition, and this apparently was to be the established order of things in perpetuity."[4]

There were three power centres in the federal Progressive Conservative party. One was the party association, of which Camp had been president since 1964. The second was the leader's office. The third was the parliamentary caucus—the Tory MPs and senators—which remained overwhelmingly loyal to Diefenbaker. Camp knew the caucus would not turn against the leader. "A good number of people in the caucus were perfectly satisfied," Camp reflected.

> What difference did it make to them whether [they won or lost]? If they were in government, it was more tedium for them. If you're the average back-bencher, what's the difference between $18,000 a year in opposition and $18,000 in government? Except that it's more fun in opposition. You have nothing to explain. And in most of their cases, their leader was acceptable. They didn't have to apologize.[5]

Some MPs who supported Diefenbaker did so because they believed it would be dangerous politically to oppose him. This was particularly true of members from Saskatchewan and the other Prairie provinces who, like it or not, were prisoners of Diefenbaker's grassroots appeal in the West. Eloise Jones, a psychiatrist from Saskatoon, was elected in a by-election in 1964, but was so appalled by what she saw of Diefenbaker when she got to Ottawa that she refused to run again in the general election the next year. "She was absolutely convinced he was paranoid," Camp said. "She just couldn't stand it anymore."

With the leader unyielding and most of the caucus toeing the line behind him, the only vehicle available for Camp to challenge Diefenbaker was the annual meeting of the party association. Typical of Camp, he did not confront the leader directly with a resolution calling for his resignation. Instead, he decided to use his own bid for re-election for a second two-year term as party president as a surrogate for a confidence vote on the leadership. He would campaign on the issue of leadership review. People who voted for Camp in the secret ballot for president would be voting to change leaders; those who voted against him would be endorsing Diefenbaker's continued leadership. It was a battle he knew he would not be able to win in the caucus, but he felt there was a fighting chance that the sort of party regulars—constituency delegates and officials—who came from across Canada to annual meetings would support him. That, of course, was assuming Diefenbaker's supporters fielded a candidate against him. At the 1964 annual meeting, he had been elected president by acclamation. Camp's biggest concern was that he would again be unopposed—"Then we didn't know what we'd do."

The secret ballot used to elect the national president was central to Camp's strategy. If he had simply introduced a resolution expressing non-confidence in the leader, or calling for the convening of a leadership convention—or moved an amendment to the party constitution requiring that the leadership be reaffirmed at regular intervals—the vote would have been taken publicly, in a standing head count. Camp knew he would not be able to defeat Diefenbaker in a public vote. As had happened with the open vote on Léon Balcer's bid to unseat the leader at the national executive meeting in February 1965, party members would swallow their reservations rather than expose themselves to Diefenbaker's rage or retaliation. "This [secret ballot] is the only way to make brave men out of cowards," Camp observed.[6]

Three events in the early months of 1966 made him decide to strike. The first was the suicide of his close friend George Hogan. Camp and Hogan, a Toronto car dealer and Tory insider, had lunch together most Fridays at the elegant restaurant in One Benvenuto Place, an apartment complex in midtown Toronto. Although he had become an uncompromising critic of Diefenbaker's leadership, Hogan had run in the 1965 election in the riding of York West, where he was crushed by Robert Winters, Camp's nemesis from his days as a Liberal two decades earlier. Hogan was devastated by his defeat and depressed by business and personal problems. After the election, Camp travelled across the country with Hogan, as Hogan filed columns to the Toronto *Telegram* in which he painted a dire picture of the future, if any, of the federal Conservatives as long as Diefenbaker remained.

Camp was badly shaken by his friend's death. That night, he, Norman Atkins, John Robarts and John White, the provincial treasurer, went out drinking. They ended up drinking and talking until dawn in White's apartment, trying to understand their friend's death. "Hogan was a kind of rudder for me, a stabilizer," Camp said. "...I was always trying to hold Hogan back, and in the course of doing this I was restraining myself." With Hogan gone, Camp lost that sense of restraint. He felt the same awareness of the shortness of life—the "one-way run of life"—that he had experienced when his father died. "I realized you just didn't have forever," he said.[7]

The second event was the firing of Flora MacDonald. For all practical purposes, she had been running Tory headquarters for nearly 10 years. Although the axe was wielded by James Johnston, the economist and small-town newspaper publisher whom Diefenbaker had named national director, the dismissal bore the imprimatur of the Chief. Obsessed about loyalty, he had been suspicious of MacDonald for some time. He had heard rumours, passed to him by some of his faithful MPs, that MacDonald had been talking behind his back and that her allegiance was greater to Camp than it was to Diefenbaker himself. Even though he was the president of the party, Camp had not been consulted before the leader chose Johnston to be national director, and he had been warned that MacDonald's job would be in jeopardy if Johnston took over at headquarters. He had tried to head off the firing by sending a blunt warning in Diefenbaker's direction—"If Johnston came into the headquarters and Flora MacDonald went out, Johnston was dead."[8]

He also talked to Johnston himself, urging him to work out an arrangement with MacDonald whereby each would have clearly defined responsibilities. Camp then went off on a Caribbean holiday. He had been gone only two days when Johnston fired her.

A man who was as loyal to his friends as they were to him, Camp was incensed; he was angrier than some of his friends had ever seen him. He knew it was Diefenbaker's way of striking at him: "I took that as a declaration of war." His anger intensified when he returned to Canada and heard from a friend that Diefenbaker was spreading innuendo that it had been necessary to let MacDonald go because she was involved in a personal relationship with Camp. "When I heard this, I was absolutely enraged," Camp told historian Jack Granatstein.

The firing was a strategic error on Diefenbaker's part. He did not understand the affection that a great many caucus members, including a number of his own loyalists, felt for MacDonald. She was their friend at headquarters, their link to their constituency organizations, the person who gave help when they had problems in their ridings. Her dismissal caused an uproar in caucus, and it probably turned a few more waverers against the leader. Some of them went behind his back to throw a testimonial lunch for her.

The third event was a conference of young Progressive Conservatives at McMaster University in Hamilton, Ontario, in May. Camp was sitting in the back of the audience during a panel discussion on "The Press Looks at the Conservative Party." The journalists on the panel were brutal. Fraser Kelly, a young reporter for the Toronto *Telegram*, said things about Diefenbaker that caused even Camp to wince. But what shocked him more than Kelly's comments was the reaction of the audience: "In this roomful of young people, of Conservatives, sitting through a long attack on their leader, *no one budged!* Nobody protested the attacks, because nobody disagreed with them." The crowd laughed and applauded. "The tolerance of it was corrupting," he said. "To accept it, you had to be a cynic. And among the young people of a political party— that's the worst place for cynicism."[9]

Not willing to drift with events any longer or to continue to play peacemaker, as he had been doing since the 1962 election, Camp decided it was high time to force the issue. He had already prepared an opinion piece for the *Telegram* on "The Responsibility of Leadership." He asked the newspaper not to publish it. Instead, he reworked and expanded it and, a week later, on May 19, 1966, he delivered it to a closed dinner of about 120 ranking Conservatives at the Albany Club in Toronto. Delivered in private and never published anywhere, the Albany Club address was the defining speech of Camp's political career. He set out the democratic principles that he believed should apply in a political party, throwing down the gauntlet to Diefenbaker.

Camp knew Senator David Walker, a Diefenbaker loyalist, would be at the dinner. He watched with amusement—"Now don't leave, Senator," he said—as Walker slipped out to call the leader with the news that he was now being directly challenged by the party's national president. And Diefenbaker did not like Walker's news, even though Camp did not once mention the leader by name.[10]

"It seems to me there are limits to the power of political leadership and these should, from time to time, be examined and appraised," Camp said.

> Leaders are fond of reminding followers of their responsibilities and duties to leadership. And followers sometimes need reminding. What is seldom heard, however, is a statement on the responsibilities of the leader to those he leads. Leaders are fond of saying how arduous their

labour, how complex the circumstances and how unfair the press criticism, as though they had been called to their high office by some supreme power rather than by those they are addressing. . . .

[T]he leader should give at least as much loyalty to his followers as he demands from them. This is not a personal loyalty, but rather loyalty to the party, to its continuing strength, best interest and well-being. This must be shared by leader and followers alike, if unity and harmony are to be enjoyed by both. While it is natural that a leader will gather about him a number of like-minded men and women, if their like-mindedness is chiefly that of loyalty to the leader, then the party system ceases to function and politics becomes a matter of subservience rather than service, and of personality rather than purpose.

Although Camp's enemies would accuse him of being a Liberal, or worse, it was obvious to those who listened to him at the Albany Club that night, and those who would hear the speeches to follow in his leadership "pilgrimage," that in one sense at least he was a classic Conservative. He had a stubborn belief in institutions and their important place in society. Specifically, he believed that the institution of the political party was the bedrock of parliamentary democracy. When he challenged John Diefenbaker, he was doing it to defend the institution he valued most highly: the Progressive Conservative party.

Quoting Mackenzie King, Camp told his fellow Conservatives at the Albany Club that Canadian political parties, like the nation itself, must be built on a spirit of reconciliation. "Men who lead cannot demand adherence," Camp said. "They may only be given it, and this is the gift of those who are reconciled in some greater and more impersonal cause, which is the party's role and place in the nation. . . . In the relationship between the leader and the led, there is a mutuality of interest and, as well, a continuing common experience of discovery, learning and revelation. Where the leader does not know the limits to his power, he must be taught, and when he is indifferent to the interest of his party, he must be reminded."

It was not the sort of message that any political leader in Canada had ever been sent by a high official of his own party. Camp had deliberately not forwarded an advance text of his speech to

Diefenbaker because he knew the leader would interpret it as a direct and personal threat. He did, however, read the speech beforehand to Lowell Murray to get his sense of how the caucus would react to it; Murray lent his encouragement.

The core of the Albany Club speech lay in this paragraph:

> The party is not the embodiment of the leader, but rather the other way round; the leader is transient, the party permanent. The argument is made that to question at any time, or in any matter, the acts of leaders will invoke a grave question of non-confidence. This is an argument for sheep, not for men. Men are not required to act in perfect harmony and concert, or to dwell in docile agreement, in order to belong to political parties. Since silence is always taken for consent, why then should those who do not consent be silenced by the irrelevant question of non-confidence?

The limits of the powers of leadership cannot be precisely determined, he continued, but those powers are far short of absolute and less than arbitrary. Speaking of his decision to force the leadership issue, he said:

> This is not a role anyone wants. No one could want it less than I do.... It is not possible to satisfy everyone, but there must be some position taken so that some consensus may form, whether for or against, and the party can be spared this steady hemorrhaging of morale and interest and initiative.
>
> What I fear is the growth of misunderstanding, the gulf between caucus and party, between leader and followers, and the return to kitchen revolts and futile recrimination. Nothing could be more deadly to the party interest, not to speak of the national interest, than we continue to drift into a period of time when external forces ... will dictate internal realities.

Camp set out three steps he felt the party must take: choose a fresh leader and equip him or her with fresh policies before the next election; give potential leadership candidates forums to make their views known to party members; and hold a leadership convention no later than the spring of 1968.

The initial reaction of the Albany Club members to Camp's speech was subdued. It took a few minutes for many of them to realize that the speech, which might have sounded like a homily on the prerogatives of leaders and followers, was actually a call to arms. The Spades who were in the audience understood, of course, what Camp was doing, and some of them were worried—not by the fact that he was challenging Diefenbaker but by the risk he was running to his own political ambitions. Roy McMurtry was one of those. In a memorandum to Camp not long after the speech, Norman Atkins reported that McMurtry believed Camp should proceed with caution: "Roy feels there is a danger that you take the chance of destroying your own political future."

Another Spade, Chad Bark, remembered discussions with Camp about ways in which Diefenbaker might be persuaded to retire without a showdown at the party's next general meeting. "He said to me, 'You know, Chad, if I take the lead in this thing, my political career is over.' My answer—and I was never sure whether it should have been this—was, 'Look, Dalton, if it's the right thing to do, you've got to do it, regardless of the [consequences].'"[11]

Atkins, on the other hand, saw opportunities for Camp. In a memo to his brother-in-law, he said: "In my opinion, the public is ready for someone with a strong voice and with the determination to outline a program of national purpose, who is able to add a new style to the game of politics." He urged Camp to take the leadership of a reform movement—"Hopefully, this will also put you up there with the others mentioned [George Hees, Davie Fulton] to succeed the Chief, and then it becomes a better fight from there on in. In fact, you might even get a chance for a by-election. Who knows?"

If politics were as tidy as political scientists make them out to be, after Camp fired his opening shot at the Albany Club in May 1966, a measured six-month campaign would have ensued, leading to the annual meeting of the Progressive Conservative party in Ottawa in November. In fact, as practitioners know, more things in politics happen by accident than by design. Camp had made his speech, the word of his challenge to Diefenbaker slowly percolated through the party—and for the next few months nothing much happened.

Some advance planning had been done. Camp had made sure that the party's annual meeting would be held as late in the year as possible. There were two reasons for that. First, he wanted to allow time to build a campaign against Diefenbaker. Second, important party conferences were being held in some provinces—Nova Scotia, Manitoba, Ontario and Quebec—and he wanted the national meeting to come after them, in the hope that the provincial meetings would take up the leadership issue and give momentum to his campaign. He also had the foresight to write very early on to James Johnston to request 10 rooms at the Chateau Laurier Hotel for his key people for the week of the annual meeting in Ottawa. He realized that if he waited until after Johnston became aware of his campaign against the leader, the national director would do everything in his power to keep the Spades and other Camp organizers out of the hotel where the final battle would be fought.

But what campaign? Typical of Camp, his friends concluded— he was great at coming up with ideas, then leaving it to others to turn his ideas into reality. Having delivered his Albany Club speech, he repaired to Robertson's Point, where he stayed most of the summer, waiting to see what Diefenbaker's next move would be. Some of his key agents were active, however. Lowell Murray, who was working on Parliament Hill, monitored the mood in the Tory caucus and kept Camp briefed. After her firing, Flora MacDonald had taken a job at Queen's University in Kingston, Ontario. Before she left party headquarters, however, she packed up a valuable weapon—the list she had compiled of the names and addresses of all the Tory association presidents in the 265 federal ridings. She wrote to each of them, thanking them for their co-operation and saying she had enjoyed working with them over the years. She was pleasantly startled by the flood of complimentary and supportive mail she got in return.

MacDonald's list provided the base for Camp's national leadership-review campaign, and later for Robert Stanfield's leadership organization. She also worked the phones hard from Kingston, calling the friends and acquaintances she had made in a decade as everyone's contact and helper at headquarters. She worked the phones so hard that after the first month she found the RCMP at her door wanting to know what kind of covert activity she was engaged in that required her to run up such enormous phone bills.

In late spring, with Camp coaching from Robertson's Point, MacDonald and Murray went off to Prince Edward Island to see if they could help Walter Shaw win a third term as premier. They knew it was not going to be easy. The Liberals had a dynamic new leader in Alex Campbell, a 32-year-old lawyer and son of a former premier. Shaw was 78, although, as one of his cabinet ministers said by way of reassurance, "he's only senile for about 20 per cent of the time." MacDonald and Murray wondered about the acuity of the entire ministry when Shaw took them to a cabinet meeting. The Conservatives had been in office for seven years but no one had ever thought to make a record of their accomplishments. Shaw introduced his visitors to the cabinet and said he would go around the table, asking each minister to cite a few things he had done so that MacDonald could write them down and put them into an election pamphlet.

He started with his labour minister. "Now, Hubert," Shaw said, "Flora and Lowell are here, and they're going to help us with the election. And you've got to tell 'em what you have done as a minister since I appointed you minister of labour." Silence. "Hubert, in the name of God, have you done anything at all since I appointed you?" It went like that around the table, MacDonald remembered— "It was just a riot."[12]

The 1966 P.E.I. election would long be remembered in Atlantic Canada. There were 16 constituencies, each sending two members to the legislature in Charlottetown. One Tory candidate, however, died before election day, meaning the vote in that riding had to be deferred. The results on election night were a dead heat—15 Tories, 15 Liberals, with two to come in the deferred election in July. In the province-wide popular vote, the two parties were, as MacDonald recalled, just 14 votes apart.

Camp came over from the mainland for the deferred election. From a motel near the Charlottetown airport, he worked on issues and banged out speeches for the two Conservative candidates. Never had so much money been spent in pursuit of the votes of so few. MacDonald had already come up with what she thought was a killer campaign plank. In the 1965 federal election, John Diefenbaker promised that a Tory government would raise the old age pension from $75 a month to $100. That promise helped Tories win all four P.E.I. federal seats, but they lost the election. When the P.E.I. election came along, the provincial Liberals promised that *they* would top up the pension to $100. The Conservatives were outraged. "We said, there's no way the Liberals can steal this issue from us," MacDonald remembered. "We own it as a national party. So we talked to Shaw, and persuaded him to announce exactly what we were going to do, knowing that eventually it would all be taken over by Ottawa. But for the interim, we would have to pay this much. I worked the math all out. There were about 10,000 old age pensioners in Prince Edward Island, so $25 would be $250,000." That did not seem like too much to invest to retain power.

It was not until MacDonald woke up the next morning that she realized the error in her calculation. The $250,000 was for one month only, not for a year. It was too late to do anything. The cabinet had agreed and the announcement had gone out. Soon, the cheque-writing machines were operating at capacity—the Tories made sure that the first wave of cheques went to Souris, where the deferred election was being fought. So many cheques were cashed in such a short space of time that the bank there ran out of money.

The road crews were out in force, of course. "We had also promised to pave so many miles of highway—I mean, what else are you going to do in Prince Edward Island but pave roads?" MacDonald said with a laugh. "I remember Dalton and I driving down to Souris, and there were little signposts everywhere saying, 'I'm a potato patch, please don't pave me.'"[13]

In the end, the incumbents' access to the public purse could not overcome the Liberals' deep campaign pockets. They had more to spend on "treating" voters—by means of judiciously distributed sums of cash—than the Tories had. The Liberals won both seats in the deferred election. Alex Campbell became premier, a post he would hold for the next 12 years. The Tory strategists left the island, feeling they had been out-hustled and grumbling about being out-bribed. Camp returned to Robertson's Point to think about Diefenbaker and the future of the Conservative party.

His attitude still seemed to be that he had planted a seed and he would sit at the cottage and watch the plant flower—or not. In September, he went to Montreal, where he spoke to a group of Young Progressive Conservatives, repeating some of the things he had said at the Albany Club. Lionel Jenks, an eccentric Tory activist in Montreal, stood up and challenged Camp: "What are you going to do about this? I mean, you've taken this position, now what are you going to do?"

It was an indication of the lack of strategic planning on Camp's part that he replied, "Well, there's my position, and I'm just going to put it forward." Not satisfied, Jenks persisted, "Well, are you going to travel around the country?" Camp surprised himself with his reply—"Yes"—to much applause. "And I was committed to a pilgrimage," he said. "I had no plans as to what I was going to do. I [thought it] was going to evolve, but I didn't have it half well thought out."[14]

Once he was committed, his campaign kicked into gear with impressive speed. At the instigation of one of his Spades, Chad Bark, Camp was invited to address the Junior Board of Trade in Toronto, whose president happened to be another Spade, Ross DeGeer. The morning he was to address that group, he talked to his unhappy wife. The bad news, he told her, was he was going to spend the next two months campaigning for leadership review. The good news was he was going to lose and be home again with her before long. "I'm going to do it," he told Linda. "You can be sure of one thing: we're going to lose, but we're going to lose with honour, and then I'm going to be home, I promise you that. You get your husband back; I'll have done the right thing. We can win by losing."[15]

Camp's promise secured Linda's acquiescence, if not her whole-hearted assent. It is possible he actually believed at this point, in mid-September, that he was going to lose. He had been following the manoeuvring of the Diefenbaker forces. He knew they were determined to field a candidate against him, which came as a relief because it meant the annual meeting would be able to register a clear verdict: for Diefenbaker or against him. He had lain awake nights worrying about what would happen if Diefenbaker simply said, "All right," announced he could support the principle of leadership reappraisal, and carried on. "But I got the impression that this was a challenge to him and he would fight it on that basis," Camp reflected. "It wasn't like him to out-think you. He would only try and out-fight you."[16]

He knew the leader's supporters had tried and failed to enlist Mike Starr, a popular Ontario MP who had been Diefenbaker's minister of labour, and Roger Regimbal, an MP from Quebec. He had been aware for some time that many Diefenbaker supporters favoured Arthur Maloney, a brilliant courtroom lawyer and former MP from Toronto. Maloney had a number of strengths: he was well liked by Tories on both sides of the leadership issue; he had avoided being labelled as either a Diefenbaker supporter or an enemy; and he was a conciliator who could honestly campaign by saying, as he did, that a vote for him was not a vote for John Diefenbaker— rather, it was a vote to let Arthur Maloney take care of the problem and resolve it in a peaceful, amicable way without a bloodbath. Conservatives who knew Maloney could reassure themselves that, yes, he just might be the man who could persuade Diefenbaker to resign of his own volition. He would make it easier for all of them.

Maloney's candidacy would cause a crisis of conscience for two of Camp's important supporters, Brian Mulroney and Roy McMurtry. McMurtry was particularly close to Maloney. He regarded him as his mentor in the law, almost as an older brother. McMurtry remembered talking to his wife about what he should do. "What the hell am I going to do?" he asked. "Arthur's such a close friend, and what Dalton did is right. It's very important, and Arthur's wrong on this one." In the end, McMurtry wrote a letter to Maloney in which he described his dilemma and his decision to support Camp. Later, he discovered that Mulroney had written a nearly identical letter.[17]

McMurtry and Mulroney consulted when they got to Ottawa a few days before the annual meeting opened. They agreed they should go to Maloney and see if he would have a drink with them. McMurtry phoned him. "Come up and see me late Saturday night, but not before midnight," Maloney said. "I'll get these people cleared out of my suite. We'll have a drink at midnight." They went up at midnight, only to find some Diefenbaker loyalists still in the hospitality suite. Maloney displayed the style that made him so popular as he told the loyalists not to be upset about the interlopers from the Camp campaign—"Brian and Roy, they're going to pay a price. When I win the presidency on Tuesday, they're going to come up here looking for a drink, and you know what I'm going to say to them? They're going to have to stand in the washroom, out in the can, for 10 minutes, and do their penance before I pour them a drink—and then we're going to put this party back together again."[18]

If the Albany Club speech was the opening shot, the speech to the Toronto Junior Board of Trade on September 20, 1966, was the declaration of war. The timing was important. Mr. Justice Wishart Spence of the Supreme Court of Canada was about to bring down the report of his inquiry into the Munsinger sex and security scandal. Camp knew the report was likely to be highly critical of the way Diefenbaker, when he was prime minister, had handled allegations that two of his ministers had been involved with Gerda Munsinger, an East German prostitute and possible Cold War–era spy. Camp wanted to declare war *before* Spence produced his report, lest he seem to be taking advantage of Diefenbaker when he was under attack from another quarter.[19]

Just as the timing of the Junior Board of Trade meeting suited Camp's purpose, so did the group itself. Unlike the Albany Club, it was not an exclusively Tory group, and it was a public forum. Camp was amused afterward. Most of the businessmen at the dinner, he thought, did not quite grasp what he was talking about. The press, however, understood very well. "CAMP CHALLENGES DIEF," read the huge front-page headline in the Toronto *Telegram*. The *Globe and Mail* also ran the story at the top of page one, albeit in smaller type: "Camp Challenges Diefenbaker's PC Leadership." Inside, the *Globe* ran a partial text of Camp's remarks—which had the effect of getting his words out to Conservatives across the country.

The speech itself was a minor reworking of his Albany Club address in May. He made all the main points he had made then and added a few wrinkles. "It is assumed by some that leaders have a responsibility to win elections, or at least to command a good proportion of public support, and the matter ends there," he said.

> If this were true, then the party system is a deadly waste of time and enterprise, and we would do better to recruit our leaders through popularity contests or by public opinion polls. But, of course, we do not: leaders are chosen by their parties, through the admittedly imperfect system of the convention, a process which produces a willing leader and a party willing to follow him. It is not, as every politician must know, a lifetime contract. Further, it is based on a certain set of assumptions which are to be proven or disproven, but which are in any event not enduring.

He looked ahead, saying the nation needed a new agenda:

> We cannot begin to prepare such an agenda so long as our political parties are huddled about obsolescent political platforms, debating the past, divided on their leadership and leaving their future to the fate of accident. We need to reform our political party system. We ought, as well, to reform Parliament....
>
> It is time to speak, and time to act. As someone said, procrastination, putting things off, is the art of keeping up with yesterday. In all the unfinished business of the nation, nothing is more necessary than that we resume the art of politics, for that is the art of keeping up with the challenges of tomorrow.

The Junior Board of Trade speech, and the wide publicity it received, galvanized Conservatives across the country. Led by Winnipeg MP Gordon Churchill, Diefenbaker's loyalists rushed into the breach. "Churchill Demands Camp's Resignation as President of Tory Party," headlined the *Globe and Mail*. In fact, now that he was into his reappraisal campaign, Camp thought about surrendering his party position. The temperature of the leadership battle might be lowered if he took the office of the national president off the front line. It would let him speak his own mind as an individual member of the party, rather than as an elected officer. And it might free him, if the opportunity arose, to seek the leadership himself. He rejected that course, however. If the Tories wanted to fire him by electing someone else to be president, so be it. But he was not going to make it easy for them. When he talked to friends about it, he would cite Lord Beaverbrook's injunction: "Never resign over a matter of principle. Get fired!" "So I thought," Camp said, "'By God, I'll get fired, but I'll espouse a principle.'"[20]

Diefenbaker flew to Toronto two days later to deliver a previously scheduled speech at the Albany Club. Would he, reporters asked, be meeting Camp while he was in town? "I thought he had decamped," the Chief replied. Would he be offering his resignation at the annual meeting in November? "Ha. Ha. Ha," Diefenbaker said, adding for good measure a final, emphatic, "Ha!"[21]

Camp's speech to the Junior Board of Trade not only energized the Diefenbaker forces, it excited younger Tories who were prepared to throw themselves into the battle on Camp's side. One was David MacDonald, a young United Church minister and freshman MP from Prince Edward Island, who had already run afoul of the leader. MacDonald had been elected for the first time in November 1965; he had never been to a Conservative convention, and he was astonished by the civil war he found raging in the Tory caucus in Ottawa. He had also been appalled by the way Diefenbaker had tried to use the Munsinger affair to embarrass the Pearson government and derail the business of the House of Commons. MacDonald said as much in an interview with the *Toronto Star* and found his criticism of the leader splashed on the front page. "Diefenbaker went bananas," MacDonald recalled. "I was called into the office. He was sitting behind his desk 'Oh, you were one I thought I could always count on, then you *stabbed me in the back!*' At one point when Dief is going at me hammer and tongs and saying, 'If we'd won, you'd have been in my cabinet,' the door opens and in walks Olive with her cane. For a brief moment I said to myself, 'I'm going to be caned by Olive.' In the end, I said I was sorry, but from then on, I knew what we were dealing with."[22]

When MacDonald read Camp's Junior Board of Trade speech, a light went on. "Until that moment, I barely knew Dalton," he remembered. "I was really impressed by the approach he was taking: no person is bigger than the party and if the party needs to make a decision about leadership, that's the decision of the party and not any one person, including the leader." He phoned Camp: "Mr. Camp you don't know me. I'm a new MP, but I have just read your speech and you are absolutely right. I couldn't agree with you more. I've watched for almost a year. This Tory caucus is a shambles. We are going absolutely nowhere. This old man is isolated and won't do anything about it. I don't know what your plans are, but if there's anything I can do to help…" He heard a soft chuckle down the phone line. "As a matter of fact there is," Camp replied. "A few of us are getting together in a motel in Kingston. Would you like to join us?"[23]

Six people spent the weekend in Kingston planning strategy: Camp, Norman Atkins, Flora MacDonald, Lowell Murray, Paul Weed and David MacDonald (no relation to Flora or Finlay MacDonald). They divided up the tasks. Atkins would be the campaign manager; he would organize Camp's pilgrimage across the country and command the troops at the annual meeting. Flora MacDonald would be the contact with delegates across the country. From his base in the office of Senator Wallace McCutcheon, Lowell Murray would monitor the Tory caucus, only about one-quarter of which was supporting Camp. David MacDonald, who had just turned 30, was assigned to organize youth groups, and he spent the next several weeks travelling the country, meeting groups of young Tories and making speeches here and there.[24]

The organization grew quickly. Camp's great friend, Halifax broadcaster Finlay MacDonald, looked after Nova Scotia. Richard Hatfield, then a Tory MLA but soon to be party leader and premier, sold the Camp message in New Brunswick. Nathan Nurgitz, later a senator, then a judge, and Sterling Lyon, later to be premier, marshalled the forces in Manitoba. One of the Spades, Don Guthrie, was put in charge of Ontario and assigned to be the liaison with John Robarts. The premier had deliberately avoided taking any public position in the federal leadership dispute. But Camp knew he was sympathetic, and he also knew he would need a gesture from Robarts at the appropriate time if he was going to capture the lion's share of Ontario's large delegation. Another Spade, Pat Patterson, who was Camp's personal lawyer, raised the money for the reappraisal campaign. He collected about $7,500, most of it in donations of $100 or less from individuals. Camp had a few thousand dollars set aside from money he had made writing newspaper and magazine articles, and his advertising agency picked up the airfares as he and Atkins took their pilgrimage across the country.

The brothers-in-law spent a frenzied six weeks on the road: Toronto to Quebec to Winnipeg to Calgary to Vancouver. Edmonton to Ottawa to Toronto to Halifax to St. John's. And so on. They made a point of hitting every province at least once, even venturing into Saskatchewan, Diefenbaker's lair. "Going to Regina was a great success because I survived it," Camp recalled. "Going to Newfoundland was a success because I got their understanding and support."[25] Along the way, they picked up key allies: Malcolm Wickson in Vancouver, Andrew Snaddon in Edmonton, Janis Johnson in Winnipeg, John Carter in Newfoundland.

Camp followed the advice he gave to all of his supporters: on no account should they criticize the leader personally during their speeches and meetings with delegates. "He reinforced that to all of us who were making speeches: we should never, ever attack the old man," David MacDonald said. The issue was party democracy, and it was essential that everyone stay on message. And they did. Most of them followed Camp's example of never even mentioning Diefenbaker's name.

There were some bumps along the road. Camp's ally, Nate Nurgitz, was defeated for the presidency of the Young Progressive Conservatives in Manitoba. In Alberta, however, the new Tory leader, Peter Lougheed, came out for leadership reappraisal, and the Quebec wing of the party, after a bit of nifty footwork by Camp's supporters, passed a motion of support—they had the vote taken while most of the delegates supporting Diefenbaker were at the airport welcoming the leader. In Nova Scotia, Finlay MacDonald, at the urging of Bob Stanfield, agreed to stand for election as president of the provincial party—only to be blindsided by Diefenbaker, James Johnston and their Nova Scotia supporters. Stanfield was embarrassed by MacDonald's defeat and annoyed by this federal incursion into his political patch. The incident helped to draw the premier out as an open, if low-key, Camp supporter. In Ontario, Eddie Goodman worked frantically to arrange that a resolution endorsing the principle of leadership review would be presented and passed at the annual meeting of the provincial party. That would have been a huge psychological boost for the Camp forces, but at the last minute Robarts backed out. Camp was shaken. The blow was soon softened, however, when Elmer Bell, a power broker in the Ontario party, publicly endorsed the reappraisal campaign.

Emotionally, Camp did not weather the vicissitudes of the campaign too well. He was gloomy at times, irritable at others. "He would sometimes interpret quite innocent remarks and gestures with a darker meaning, which is what I suppose happens when you get into that sort of situation that he was in," Lowell Murray remembered. "He had his moods—these are in my notes from the time—that went up and down. He was quite encouraged at one point, and then rather down."[26]

Halfway through his pilgrimage, Camp delivered a major speech to the Empire Club in Toronto, and it was clear that his belief in the institution of the political party and, specifically, the Progressive Conservative party was, if anything, growing even stronger. His message was getting sharper as he talked eloquently about accountability:

> Any public man ought to be accountable, first to his conscience, and, of course, he must be accountable to his country, but in the course of his duty, he must accept his responsibility to his party. He should never be its slave, nor should he ever be its master. In all the complexity of his responsibilities, some priority must be given to the sensibilities of his party. This is a responsibility of his leadership, and in that responsibility there must be the assumption that the party has a right

to bestow confidence in him, or to withdraw it. The party must have the right to warn, advise or encourage. Otherwise, the party cannot be what it ought to be, which is a public instrument of the national will. It cannot be merely the private convenience of a national leader....

All I have said in speaking, not for myself, but for the thousands of members of my own party and certainly countless others, is that the Conservative party, whose importance to Canada surely no one would deny, has a responsibility to itself to decide for itself its future course.

He turned to the two-edged campaign Diefenbaker had mounted. The leader himself was insisting he had the right and intention to continue to lead the party until he decided otherwise. Meanwhile, his supporters were spreading a softer message: the Chief knows the hour to go is approaching; he really is planning to retire this time; just do not push him; let him choose his moment to depart in dignity and with honour. Camp had been hearing that refrain for years, and he did not buy it any longer. Why, he asked, should the party not be told in candour what the future holds? "If the leader intends to continue, then surely he will submit the decision to the judgment of his party, and allow them, freely and democratically, to express their wishes," he said. "If he intends to stand aside, as his closest supporters are saying, why do they have this intelligence when the party does not? The interests of the party are paramount, and they cannot be served by silence, secrecy or strategy."

Camp had no clear sense of what to expect when the annual meeting began in Ottawa. Publicly, he conveyed confidence; privately, he was still pessimistic. He thought he might be able to keep his promise to his wife: lose the battle with Diefenbaker, leave the presidency and come home to his family. He knew he had the better organization and, he believed, the better cause. But Diefenbaker still enjoyed tremendous loyalty among grassroots Tories. He had led them out of the political wilderness. He had beaten the despised Grits. He had taken a party of also-rans, electoral afterthoughts in many parts of the country, and made them the government. He had done it before, and he could do it again. Or so they believed.

This loyalty was especially intense among caucus members. Camp was exposed to it personally during the annual meeting.

Stanley Korchinski, a backbencher from northern Saskatchewan, came late one night to the suite Camp was sharing with Roy McMurtry. Korchinski had been drinking, but the anguish was written on his face. He started to cry. "What are you going to do for me?" he asked Camp. "John Diefenbaker picked me up off the street and I'm making $18,000 a year. I've never seen so much money in my life. Now what are you going to do, because you just ruined me!"[27]

The spirits of Camp's supporters were buoyed when they got to Ottawa—and they soared when they won a major tactical victory on the Sunday night before the annual meeting opened. James Johnston had sent a Diefenbaker-endorsed agenda for the meeting to the national executive for approval. It provided for the leader to address the meeting on Monday night. Delegates would then be presented with a motion expressing confidence in the leader, which they would be asked to decide in an open, standing vote. The secret-ballot election of officers, including the national president, would take place on Wednesday. Under Diefenbaker's agenda, the leader might be confirmed on Monday night and Camp re-elected on Wednesday—meaning nothing would have changed.

Camp decided to attack these arrangements. He asked the national executive to revise the timetable. Diefenbaker would still speak on Monday night. The election of officers would be moved ahead to Tuesday, with debate on resolutions—including the vote of confidence or non-confidence in the leader—to take place on Wednesday. This would give him time, if he won on Tuesday, to introduce a leadership-review resolution on Wednesday.

Diefenbaker's partisans and Camp's supporters fought a pitched battle at the executive meeting. When the dust settled, Camp had won by a surprisingly large margin, 80–41. As important as the margin were the votes of the three premiers who belonged to the national executive. Stanfield was there in person, and he voted with Camp. Robarts and Roblin sent their proxies, also cast for Camp.

The leader was now on the defensive. It would take a vintage Diefenbaker performance on Monday night to reverse the momentum. No one who was there that traumatic Monday night would ever forget it, though many undoubtedly wished they could. An evening of high drama, it started on a note of great excitement. The ballroom in the Chateau Laurier was packed two hours ahead of time and the overflow watched the proceedings on monitors in the corridors outside. The Camp organization pulled off a small coup early in the evening. They had installed an audio feed from the ballroom to their operations centre in a suite upstairs. They could hear everything that was going on and time their moves according. At the crucial moment that Monday night—with Camp at the podium, calling the meeting to order, welcoming delegates and reporting on his stewardship (and being booed by some in the audience)—Don Guthrie took Robarts down in a freight elevator and guided him to the ballroom. Robarts made a dramatic entrance, walking to the platform and pausing at the podium to shake Camp's hand before taking his seat on the stage. It was taken as a signal that Ontario was supporting Camp; most of the province's delegates fell in line behind their powerful premier.

The audience was overwhelmingly hostile to Diefenbaker—hostile and rude. Camp supporters who had packed the front six rows would not stand when Diefenbaker entered the hotel ballroom, even though Camp motioned them from the stage to rise. The leader was heckled, jeered and drowned out. At one point, he snapped at the crowd: "Is this a Conservative meeting?" "Yes, yes!" they shouted back.

It was a speech in which Diefenbaker could have called for reconciliation, reassured his critics and reinforced the will of his loyalists. But instead of being positive, he went for the negative, excoriating his enemies, principally the party president. He quoted words Camp had said and written over the years to argue that he had turned from friend to foe without cause. The news photographers captured a memorable shot of Diefenbaker as he wheeled and pointed his index finger at Camp, challenging him to explain his betrayal. Camp was expressionless. "I was determined that I would keep my own cool, and I wouldn't back away from him," Camp said later. "So I spent all my time really looking at Diefenbaker and whenever he looked at me, I smiled." Stanfield, who was seated next to Camp on the platform, looked as though he wanted to shrink through a crack in the floor. Robarts managed to appear bored. Whatever magic Diefenbaker had had in the past deserted him that night. Camp was shocked. "You always assume that your opposition will do its best," he said. "I was always astounded to see them do their worst."[28]

Toronto *Telegram* publisher John Bassett, who was a real back-stage power in the Conservative party in those days, was astounded, too. He went straight to his hotel room and dictated an editorial for the next day's paper. "The Diefenbaker Years of the Conservative Party are over," the editorial began. "They ended here tonight when the former prime minister's appeal for continued support fell on deaf ears and was greeted time and again with boos and jeers."

Patrick Nowlan, a young MP from Nova Scotia and son of the late George Nowlan, spoke for many delegates when he said, "It's not often you can feel a page of history turning, but we all felt it that night."[29] The Diefenbaker legend, or what was left of it, had been destroyed. Even his partisans could see him for what he had become: an old man cornered by his enemies who could, and would, fight on, but who could no longer rouse his troops or inspire them with any sense of common cause or shared vision. He was his own worst enemy, and he hurt his own cause more than Dalton Camp ever could.

It was sad. It was profoundly distressing to many of Diefenbaker's most committed followers. Because they could not bring themselves to blame their hero, they turned on Camp and his supporters. It got ugly in the corridors of the Chateau Laurier that Monday night, and it did not get much better in the remaining days of the annual meeting. Booze had always been a potent ingredient in politics. Most politicians in the 1950s and 1960s routinely drank more than they should have. In the good times, a bottle of Scotch or a pitcher of martinis contributed to the fun and the shared experience of political campaigns—the jokes exchanged in the wee hours, the confidences revealed and the memories forged. In the bad times, alcohol brought out the worst in unhappy men.

"I'd never been to a national meeting before," David MacDonald recalled. "It was electric. The level of viciousness was astonishing. The Horner brothers (Alberta MPs Jack and

Hugh Horner) threatened to knock my teeth down my throat."[30] Jack Horner did take a swing at Roy McMurtry, which was a mistake. The old football player punched him out. Another MP, a Diefenbaker supporter, slugged a student whom he heard calling Diefenbaker "the old S.O.B." Someone, no one was quite sure who, punched Brian Mulroney, bloodying his nose.

Camp and his wife had brought their eldest child, Gail, then 21 and a student at Queen's University, to Ottawa for the annual meeting. She watched the proceedings with amazement and observed as delegates came to the Camp hospitality suite to drink, smoke, rehash the activities of that day and plot those of the next. "I thought it was intoxicating, scary, because it was so polarized," she said. She recalled how a group of elderly women supporting Diefenbaker had mistaken the bald-headed James Johnston for her bald-headed father and started smacking the hapless national director with their umbrellas.[31]

It was a mark of Camp's detachment from his children that he did not take the trouble to explain to them, the younger ones at least, what the uproar with Diefenbaker was all about. Gail's younger sisters, Connie, 14, and Cherie, 11, watched on television from their home in Toronto. "Cherie and I followed it, but without any help from our parents to understand what was going on," Connie said. "What I remember is that picture of my father on the stage, head down, with Diefenbaker looking at him. To a child, that was a devastating picture. It looks like your father is in trouble or something, and I didn't know how to interpret that. My father didn't bother explaining. I don't know why. I didn't know what was going on in his head, that he didn't think he should [explain]. We were all interested, we'd read the stories."[32]

Camp himself was appalled by the strategy of Diefenbaker's supporters and disgusted by their behaviour. "I have to say that if I'd been on the other side and [been] national director, I'd have beat those fellows two to one," he said after the dust had settled. "There were so many ways to win that thing, so many arguments to be made. They just never made them. They just had their yahoos around. They were drunk, obscene, and they offended people."[33]

In hindsight, the leadership issue was effectively decided on the first night of the meeting. Diefenbaker had done himself in. The next day, Tuesday, was when delegates would, by secret ballot, elect their president and the other national officers. The two candidates for president addressed the delegates. Camp struggled. He had been up all night following Diefenbaker's Monday evening performance. He was exhausted, perhaps hungover. He knew he wanted to avoid polarizing the party any more than it already was, but other than that he had no idea what he wanted to say in his speech. By his own admission, he made one of his worst speeches ever. Arthur Maloney, by comparison, sparkled. He made a great speech that included the line that everyone who attended the 1966 annual meeting would remember for years: "When John Diefenbaker, former PM of Canada, leader of Her Majesty's Loyal Opposition, when he walks into a room, Arthur Maloney stands up."[34]

The vote when it came—Camp 564, Maloney 502—was closer than anyone had expected. Maloney's speech, and perhaps a measure of guilt felt by some delegates over the meeting's uncompromising treatment of Diefenbaker the night before, had swung a number of hesitating Tories to the leader's cause. But Camp had been re-elected. Flora MacDonald, who had been asked by Camp to put her name forward, was elected national secretary. Other Camp backers filled the principal positions, leaving him firmly in control of the party machine.

The extent of that control was evident the next day, Wednesday, as Camp, Elmer Bell, Eddie Goodman and other supporters shifted the agenda to win passage of a motion calling for the holding of a leadership convention. The traditional motion of confidence in the leader, along with other items from the party's resolutions committee, was scheduled to be voted on in the afternoon, following discussion of amendments proposed by the constitutional committee. As the morning session was about to begin, however, Goodman, who was to chair the session, got word from Parliament Hill that Diefenbaker was preparing to descend on the Chateau Laurier, determined to rally the delegates to his cause. After a quick consultation with Camp and Bell, Goodman called the session to order and announced a change in the order of business: the report of the resolutions committee would be considered first and that of the constitutional committee later.

He recognized Bell, who moved that the motion of confidence in the leader be taken by secret ballot. That passed on a standing vote. Drawn by the sound of bagpipes, Diefenbaker delegates were already pouring out of the room to prepare a welcome for the leader when he arrived at the hotel as Goodman recognized Ben Cunningham, a Kingston, Ontario, lawyer and Camp ally, to introduce an amendment to the standard confidence motion.

The amendment had caused some anxious moments. Ever the creator but never the implementer, Camp had not given much thought to the wording of the amendment. Flora MacDonald remembered the late-hour session the night before at which the subject had been discussed over several rounds of drinks. "There was argument, discussion, people going off in all sorts of directions with their thinking," she said. "Somebody came up with a resolution—we all said, 'Oh sure, that kind of thing will be all right'—but nobody wrote it down." Next morning, no one could remember what had been agreed. "The next day, when we got to that, there was pandemonium—what was it we were putting forward?"[35] Luckily, Cunningham had had the wit to scribble some words on the back of an envelope. When Goodman called on him, Cunningham pulled out the envelope.

The main resolution moved: "That this party expresses its confidence in its leader, the Rt. Hon. John G. Diefenbaker." Cunningham, however, amended it to read: "That this party expresses its support of the Rt. Hon. John G. Diefenbaker, its national leader, and acknowledges its wholehearted appreciation of his universally recognized services to the party; and in view of the current situation in the party directs the national executive, after consultation with the national leader, to call a leadership convention at a suitable time before January 1, 1968."

Amid the din of bagpipes, shouts and cheers marking Diefenbaker's arrival in the hotel lobby, Goodman cut off debate after 40 minutes. Delegates, he declared, would vote on both the confidence motion and its amendment, but the results of the main motion would be announced only if the amendment were defeated. That didn't happen. By secret ballot, the Tories voted—563 to 186—to thank their leader and hold a convention to replace him. Camp's vote had held from the day before; Diefenbaker's had evaporated as his supporters gave up the struggle.[36]

The battle was over. Camp had won, Diefenbaker had lost. But at what cost? What about the party? Whatever happened to the vision? Camp had embarked on his crusade vowing to democratize, renew and rebuild the Conservative party. Instead, it seemed more divided than ever. As they headed to their homes across the country, many Tories, including some Camp supporters, feared that their party had lost as badly as its leader had. In his account of the 1966 annual meeting, a book entitled *The Night of the Knives*, Robert Coates, a Nova Scotia MP and Diefenbaker loyalist, wrote, "The division between the Diefenbaker forces and the Camp forces became a schism. The Progressive Conservative Party divided, with a real danger it would never unite again."[37] From the other side of the battlefield, David MacDonald recognized the same danger. Thirty-six years later, he commented, "It got so personal between those with or against Dief that I think a real level of anger and distrust still exists in some quarters to this day."[38]

David Camp, Dalton's eldest son, worried about the lasting effect on his father. "The continuing reaction against Dalton from the Diefenbaker wing of the party was so hostile that it drove him inward," he said. "He became an outsider, an onlooker, instead of an insider and participant in politics."[39] The reaction was stronger than anything Camp had anticipated. And it proved more enduring than anyone could have predicted, surviving even the departure and death of Diefenbaker. Camp had always been a contrarian and a loner, even in his own party. Soon he would discover that to many Tories he was now a pariah.

CHAPTER 15

Richard

P EOPLE—NOT POWER OR POSITION—are the real glue of politics.
Ask any politician what he or she loves best about the game, and
they will say it is the people they meet, the friendships they form
and the adventures they share. Sometimes, these bonds extend across
party lines. Most often, however, they link people who have fought
for the same causes, the same political party or the same candidates.

Dalton Camp had a way of drawing people to him, of instilling
them with some of his own intellectual curiosity, of turning them
into devoted workers and dear friends. Those who were closest
to him, almost without exception, were people who had worked
with him in Conservative battles: in campaigns for Hugh John
Flemming, Robert Stanfield, Duff Roblin or Bill Davis at the
provincial level, or George Drew, John Diefenbaker or Stanfield
in federal politics. They included members of the Spades, the
group in Toronto that was the organizational nerve centre of most
of his campaigns from 1965 on, and of his "Maritime Mafia"—
Finlay MacDonald (who was so close to Camp that people said
they might as well be brothers), Flora MacDonald, Lowell Murray
and a few others whose loyalty to Camp had been forged in the
dark years when the Tories had no power, no money and few
prospects in Atlantic Canada. There were other like-minded
Conservatives on the fringes of the Camp inner circle. Nate
Nurgitz in Manitoba was one; Joe Clark was another; and so, at
one time, was Brian Mulroney.

Like Camp, they could all fit more or less comfortably within
the rubric of Red Tory, with the exception, perhaps, of Mulroney.
Although he might, by stretching the definition a bit, have been
classified as a Red Tory in his early years in politics, he had strayed
from the fold by the time he came close enough to smell the scent
of power.

There was one other person who occupied a very special place in Camp's life: Richard Bennett Hatfield. Hatfield worked with Camp in most of his battles in the late 1950s and the 1960s, including the leadership review fight in 1966. He was, in turn, helped by Camp to become a member of the New Brunswick legislature in 1961, leader of the provincial Tory party (on his second try) in 1969, and in 1970 premier of the province—a post he held for a record 17 years. Hatfield (he was named after Canada's eleventh prime minister, the Tory R.B. Bennett) was the third son of Heber Hatfield, a Conservative MP and potato merchant from Hartland, New Brunswick, who established the country's first potato chip plant after the Second World War. Hatfield Potato Chips, with its stylized top hat logo, was a Maritimes institution until the family sold the business to Humpty Dumpty in 1965.

A graduate of Acadia University and Dalhousie University law school, Richard tried his hand at criminal law, abandoning it after his first and only court case. He was called on to defend a young boy accused of stealing a heart-shaped box of chocolates from a candy store in Truro, Nova Scotia. The evidence indicated the lad had taken the chocolates to give his mother as a Valentine's Day present because he had no money for a gift. Somehow, Hatfield managed to lose the case, badly. The judge convicted the boy and sent him off to an institution. Devastated, Hatfield concluded that once was enough. "I decided then that the law was not for me," he said.[1]

He was already more interested in politics than law anyway. As a university student in Nova Scotia, Hatfield—like Mulroney—became involved in the campaigns that Camp was running for Stanfield. Following the election of the Diefenbaker government in 1957, Hatfield went to Ottawa as executive assistant to Gordon Churchill, one of the new cabinet ministers. He was recommended for the job by Churchill's secretary, who had once been, or so the story went, the mistress of Hatfield's father, Heber, in his years as an MP in Ottawa. Richard, however, hated Ottawa, as he had hated it when his father was in Parliament, and after nine months he packed it in, returning to New Brunswick to be vice-president of sales for the family's potato chip company. When Hugh John Flemming resigned his provincial seat to go into federal politics, Hatfield won the by-election and entered the legislature in 1961.

He was a regular visitor to Camp's cottage at Robertson's Point by then. As the years went by, Hatfield passed increasing amounts of time there or, after 1978, at Camp's hilltop home, Northwood, outside Jemseg. The Camps regarded him as an honorary member of the family; a ground-floor bedroom at Northwood was known simply as "Richard's room." He would arrive uninvited and unannounced, disappear into the kitchen and emerge hours later with some culinary curiosity. Often it was soup of some sort. On one occasion, he came with a salmon and a slab of pine and declared that he was going to cook the fish over an open fire the way, he claimed, the Indians used to do it. He spent most of the day labouring over the coals, finally summoning his hosts to sample the finished product—a charred piece of something that might once have been fish.

Before he became premier, he would drive his own car from Fredericton, a 40-minute trip along the Saint John River on the old Trans-Canada Highway. His chauffeur drove him during his years in office. After he and his government self-destructed, being wiped out in the election of 1987, Hatfield would often come by bus—"a humbling journey," Camp said, "but one in which he found some quiet satisfaction, especially when recognized by fellow passengers. 'They were all very friendly,' he once said, 'but they all voted against me.'"[2]

Various things conspired to draw the two men together. Both Carleton County boys, they shared a love of New Brunswick, the Tory party, vodka martinis, the ideas of Marshall McLuhan and the politics of John. F. Kennedy. "I think I can become the Kennedy of New Brunswick, maybe even the Maritimes," Hatfield once told a Radio-Canada reporter.[3] He was delighted when Camp advised him to wear black turtleneck sweaters on television in the 1970 election campaign. "Great visual stuff," Camp told him.

The Saint John *Telegraph Journal* dubbed him Canada's first mod premier after that election, and Hatfield loved that, too. He was flamboyant and eccentric. He drove a black Mercury Cougar and later a New Brunswick-built, gull-winged Bricklin sports car; he listened to Led Zeppelin and had seen the rock musical *Hair* on Broadway. He collected dolls and had a trampoline in his living room. "He had even read *The Strawberry Statement*, a book about the U.S. student rebellion of the sixties," wrote his biographers Michel Cormier and Achille Michaud. "People in Fredericton began to speculate about the bachelor premier's love life, much as Canadians had speculated about Pierre Trudeau's amours."[4]

Hatfield was gay. If he managed to stay in the closet at home in New Brunswick, he did not when he vacationed in Europe or North Africa or when he headed to New York, Boston, Montreal or Toronto to check out the action on weekends. Columnist Allan Fotheringham described Hatfield as the only Canadian politician who was on the guest list for author Truman Capote's parties in New York. Bandleader Peter Duchin first met Hatfield when he was playing at a fancy party at the Waldorf Astoria Hotel in Manhattan. They started talking about salmon fishing, a Duchin passion. Shortly thereafter, he was invited to join Hatfield for a few days at a fishing camp on the Restigouche River. Duchin arrived laden with all the latest fishing gear, only to discover that his host was not a fisherman at all. Hatfield's "equipment" consisted of a few books, several bottles of Scotch, an old raincoat and a pair of sneakers.

"He earned the 'Disco Dick' image by throwing himself into the night life of whatever city he happened to be in," said his friend Lowell Murray. "But he came back from his travels laden with gossip, anecdote and hard information. He knew bankers and businessmen, journalists, hotel porters and clerks, politicians of all stripes and nationalities, artists and diplomats. He traded information with them, adding to his repertoire but also to his understanding."[5]

Camp was unperturbed by, perhaps uncomprehending of, his friend's sexual orientation. He simply ignored it; if the subject came up in conversation, he talked about something else. Camp had a way of blocking out unpleasant facts or information that was hurtful to someone he cared about. He blocked out Hatfield's homosexuality in the same way that, as a newspaper columnist, he would sometimes block out the failings of his friend Brian Mulroney's government. He did not want to hear about them; therefore they did not exist. He loved the Hatfield he knew; he would not acknowledge that there was a Hatfield he did not know.

His blind spot showed in the way he managed to ignore contrary evidence in defending Hatfield when a patronage and fundraising scandal shook his government in the late 1970s, and when the premier himself was accused of possessing marijuana after a small quantity of the weed was found in his luggage during a royal tour of New Brunswick in 1984. Five days after Hatfield's acquittal on the marijuana charge, the Southam News Service distributed a story claiming that the police in New Brunswick had statements from two former university students alleging that Hatfield had offered them marijuana and cocaine at his home in Fredericton.

Camp was vacationing in Antigua when the story broke. He was deluged with calls from the press, Hatfield's friends and the premier's office. Fearing his friend was the victim of a media lynching bee, Camp cut short his holiday to return home. As a newspaper columnist, he should have stayed out of the fray. But Camp's loyalty to Hatfield was far stronger than any journalistic principle. He went on the CBC to confront the accusers, starting with host Barbara Frum and Southam's Nick Hills on *The Journal*. He denounced Hills as a "retailer of gossip." Later, Camp would concede he had gone too far. "It was a rancorous confrontation in which I appeared relentlessly hostile and angry," he wrote. "Unhappily, I do not believe Barbara and I spoke again."[6]

Camp, the journalist, never hesitated when his politician friend called out for help. "There were nights here when Richard Hatfield would arrive in a heap and say, 'I need your help,'" recalled his second daughter, Connie Camp, who was also a journalist. "And my father would take him off, and I'd hear him scolding Richard, and typing up a rescue speech for him.... I thought there was a conflict, but I thought that because he was a columnist that it was okay.... He still was independent to me, really, in the best way."[7]

By the time of Camp's confrontation with Frum—in 1985— Hatfield had been premier for 15 years. He was wearing out his welcome among the public. His prospects of re-election looked increasingly bleak. Even some of his supporters were beginning to say—as others had said of John Diefenbaker from the 1962 federal election on—that it was time he stepped down. But where Camp had clearly seen the need for Diefenbaker to depart, he could not see the same need in Hatfield's case, although it could certainly be argued that Hatfield was doing the New Brunswick party more harm than Diefenbaker had done the national party.

"Richard Hatfield was not a perfect being, as perfection would be rated by apocryphal mothers and the lesser children of the fourth estate," Camp said following his friend's death. "Still, he was a saint compared to most of his detractors. That was enough for me. As one who was raised to despise hypocrisy and humbug only slightly less than cruelty, the hounding of Hatfield reeked of all three. Richard was cruel to no one; and he could detect humbug at the instant of its utterance, and spot a hypocrite across a crowded room. He himself was terribly vulnerable, which made him both compassionate and private; he was a person about whom no one could say that he or she knew nearly all there was to know."[8]

Camp made no apology for any inconsistency in his attitudes toward Diefenbaker and Hatfield. Diefenbaker had never been a friend, they had nothing in common, and they had come to despise each other. Hatfield was "like a brother who had grown up, moved away, had a career of his own, and came to visit." They shared the same reformist approach to politics, and both were men of considerable political courage. Although he was the leader of a party whose strength rested in English-speaking New Brunswick, Hatfield championed French language rights. He made New Brunswick the country's only officially bilingual province—and he was rewarded with a Tory breakthrough in the Liberals' Acadian stronghold in northern New Brunswick. He was more than a partisan politician. As opposition leader in the late 1960s, he made a point of understanding the subtleties of the then Liberal government's "Equal Opportunities Program"—a massive overhaul of the province's tax, education, social services and municipal systems to benefit the poorest, mainly Acadian, regions—and as premier in the 1970s, he consolidated and implemented the program. He campaigned alongside Liberal Prime Minister Pierre Trudeau for the patriation of the Canadian Constitution and the entrenchment of the Charter of Rights and Freedom. In his last days in office, he worked for acceptance of the Meech Lake constitutional accord.

In 1976, when he left his wife and took off for Portugal with a younger woman, Camp tried his hand at writing a thinly veiled autobiographical novel, which he called *Some Political People*. Camp cast himself as Caleb Shaw, a minister in the cabinet of Henry Fox Heustes, the new premier of a small province. Like Hatfield, Heustes was single, a bit of a dandy and he took his mother as his date to official functions. Caleb Shaw battled the demands of liquor agents and government contractors, just as Hatfield's ministers did. He struggled to find the line between patronage—which in Camp's eyes was good and necessary and, as in the case of his own advertising business, something to be embraced—and corruption—which was clearly bad and needed to be stamped out. Camp never found a publisher for the novel, perhaps because it fell far short of the real-life drama of Richard Hatfield's years in power.

To Camp, Hatfield was "the most contemporary politician in the country." Because he was fun to be with, even his friends tended to forget that he was "a dedicated public man for whom the practice of government was serious business. He cared about governing, about people, and he cared profoundly about New Brunswick. He was palpably human. He also had a profound sense of compassion and of justice."[9]

He also cared profoundly about his friends and his friends' families. Whenever he visited the Camps in Toronto or in New Brunswick, "Uncle Richard" would come with shopping bags filled with gifts for the children, keeping the younger ones squealing with delight. At one stage, when he was trying to quit smoking, he took up origami, the Japanese art of folding paper into decorative shapes. He would entertain friends' children for hours as he patiently taught them how to turn sheets of coloured paper into the fantastical shapes of flowers, birds and animals.

He loved to have a good time with friends, even at seemingly incongruous times. Flora MacDonald had a vivid memory of one such occasion. Nova Scotia MP George Nowlan, Camp's great pal in the Tory caucus—and the man whom the caucus would have made interim leader if the early coup attempts against Diefenbaker had succeeded—had died of heart disease in hospital in Ottawa, shortly after being re-elected in the 1963 election. His friends suspected the real cause of death was whisky withdrawal when the hospital cut off the supply of Scotch to Nowlan, a man accustomed to consuming a bottle a day.

MacDonald, Camp, Hatfield and Finlay MacDonald met at the airport in Halifax to drive together to the funeral in Wolfville, Nowlan's hometown. As they got underway, they realized none of them had brought any liquor, and they agreed it would be an affront to Nowlan's memory to pay their last respects without a proper drink or two. Worse, no one had thought to bring the permit that was required to buy liquor in Nova Scotia in those days.

When the four friends got to Kentville, they stopped at a liquor store. They waited until Finlay MacDonald spotted a young woman heading toward the store. "He was out of the car in a flash, approached her, before long had his arm around her and, like a happy twosome, they entered the store," Flora MacDonald remembered. The woman obligingly agreed to use her permit to buy a bottle for the quartet of mourners. A bottle of gin in hand, they proceeded to Wolfville, where they checked into a hotel. "We refreshed ourselves liberally before lunch, after which we proceeded to the Baptist Church for the funeral service," Flora MacDonald said. "We were all on our best behaviour, with two well-grounded Baptists, Dalton and Richard, to guide us through the service. All went well until the minister read the opening lines of the first hymn:

> Sunset and evening star,
> And one clear call for me
> And may there be *no moaning at the bar*,
> When I put out to sea.

All four collapsed in gales of laughter in the church. "George would have loved it!" she said.[10]

In October 1982, Richard Hatfield won his fourth consecutive election, and it was his greatest victory: the Tories took 39 of the 58 seats in the legislature. He was 51 years old and had already been premier for 12 hectic and productive years. Soon, or so his political friends and opponents assumed, he would want to move on: to the bench or the federal House or perhaps the Senate. It did not happen. He hung on, increasingly mired in the muck of scandal, refusing to quit and unable to recover the respect and popularity he had enjoyed for so many years. He knew he had stayed too long; he admitted as much to friends. Realizing he was doomed, he waited, stretching his fourth term until it could be stretched no longer. When he finally called the election in October 1987, it was five years and one day after the last one—and the result was complete devastation for the Conservatives, with the Liberals winning all 58 seats.

The one person he always trusted to give him straight advice, the person to whom he often turned when he was in trouble, was Dalton Camp. If Camp had done him the favour of telling him it was time to go, Hatfield might well have taken the advice. But Camp would not tell him. He maintained a curiously detached attitude. "I liked Richard as a friend, and didn't give a damn whether he was premier or what he was," Camp said by way of explanation. "... It was always clear to me that Richard hung on so long because he really couldn't imagine himself doing anything else. And I also sensed that he had been enormously successful, and done a lot of good things.... It seemed to me that he had a perfect right to sail the ship over the falls. He didn't owe anything to anybody."[11]

If Camp felt any regret that the provincial party he had helped to revive 35 years earlier with the election of Hugh John Flemming in 1952 had now been eliminated from the legislature, he did not let it show. And he certainly did not blame his friend Hatfield.

Hatfield seemed like a lost soul after his ship went over the falls. He had no idea what he wanted to do with himself. In earlier years, when people had asked him what he would do when he was no longer premier, he would say that was like asking what he would do after his death. He tried writing his memoirs. Brian Mulroney appointed him to the Senate in September 1990, but his health was failing. Within months, he was diagnosed with an inoperable brain tumour. He was just 60 years old when he died in April 1991 at the Elizabeth Bruyère Palliative Care Unit in Ottawa with his friends Dalton Camp, Finlay MacDonald and Nancy Southam at his side. In his final days, his friends had kept a vigil in his hospital room where they had a bar set up. The dying patient joined in as they drank vodka martinis, reminisced and talked politics and people. It was the way Richard Hatfield wanted to go.

CHAPTER 16

Ambition Denied

THE CONSERVATIVE ANNUAL MEETING of November 1966 made Dalton Camp a national figure. He had been a prominent player in the national party for more than a decade, but it was not until he embarked on what he called his "pilgrimage" for leadership reappraisal that he broke through to the consciousness of the general public. Almost overnight, or so it seemed to him, he became the focal point of heated debate—at the family dinner table, in the workplace and on radio talk shows.

Politics abhors a vacuum as much as nature itself does, and the Tory party was in a vacuum—"a long twilight period," as Camp described it—six months following the November meeting. There would be a leadership convention by the fall of 1967, but meanwhile nothing much was happening. Who would the candidates be? The two most ambitious caucus members, yesterday's men George Hees and Davie Fulton, were stumping the country, exciting no one. Would one of the premiers—John Robarts of Ontario, Duff Roblin of Manitoba or Bob Stanfield of Nova Scotia—make the jump? Would John Diefenbaker run to replace himself, or would he, at long last, fade into history?

And what about Camp, the party's new celebrity? He controlled the party machinery through the national executive. He knew everyone of influence in the party. He had demonstrated in his battle with Diefenbaker that he could fight and win. He commanded a personal organization that was ready and more than willing to help him to achieve the leadership. He was progressive, a reformer, a modern man for the new age ushered in by Centennial Year and Expo '67. He connected with young people. He had ideas, and he was certainly bright enough for the job.

Camp felt the pressure. Although he was never consumed by lust for political power, he nevertheless was interested in the leadership.

He believed he could do the job as well or better than most. He had at least toyed with the idea on two earlier occasions. The first time was in 1965 when he decided to step out of the backroom to challenge Mitchell Sharp in Eglinton. He took on Sharp, the key economic minister in the Liberal cabinet, in the knowledge and expectation that if he upset him, he would be on a track that could lead to the cabinet, to Stornoway, the home of the opposition leader, and perhaps to 24 Sussex Drive, the residence of the prime minister.

The second time was during his leadership-reappraisal campaign in 1966. He talked about the leadership with some other members of the Spades, including Chad Bark and Roy McMurtry, who worried that his fight with Diefenbaker could only damage his chances of succeeding him. The subject of his putative candidacy came up from time to time as he took his "pilgrimage" across the country that fall. Although he offered no encouragement to the party members or journalists who quizzed him, insiders read the language of his speeches, and they were suspicious. "The speeches were not those of a party president simply to cheer up the troops," Lowell Murray said. "The speeches were trying to give some vision of the future. They were speeches of a leadership candidate. I could recognize those, having written a few of them myself."[1]

During the leadership-review campaign, Camp had promised his wife Linda that he would get out of the political wars and come home to her and the children. The November meeting had no sooner ended, however, than he found himself breaking that promise. In the aftermath of the dramatic votes to re-elect Camp as party president and to hold a leadership convention, Diefenbaker's most devout followers in the caucus circulated a document pledging loyalty to the leader; they demanded that all Tory MPs sign it. Seventy-one of the 96 signed. The next week, the loyalists used their majority to remove five of the dissenters, all Camp supporters, as caucus representatives on the party's national executive.

Camp was livid. He interpreted the caucus move as evidence that Diefenbaker had no intention of going quietly. He felt he was trapped and could not resign until the battle was finally resolved. "I thought if that's the way the game is going to be played, there was only one person who could stand up to him in the party," Camp said, "and I'm afraid it was I."[2] Camp felt he was double-crossing his wife; she felt that, too, and she wept when he told her the fight was not yet over.

Diefenbaker went on the offensive, calling for an immediate leadership convention—one that would be held before his opponents could get organized. He also proposed that the only people entitled to vote be delegates elected by constituency associations—thereby excluding the "automatics" (the party establishment and appointed at-large delegates, who tended to be anti-Diefenbaker). In January, Camp called a meeting of the party's principal officers—the executive committee of the national executive. The executive committee, which Camp controlled, agreed to appoint his choice, Eddie Goodman, as chairman of the convention planning committee. It then rejected both of Diefenbaker's demands. The convention would be held in the fall (early September dates, at Toronto's Maple Leaf Gardens, were chosen later) and the automatics would be welcome, as always.

By turning the convention organization over to Goodman, Camp was able to avoid the tedious, detailed work of planning what would be Canada's first big American-style political convention. The move also allowed him to get out of Diefenbaker's sights while he assessed his own leadership prospects.

Some of the people close to him knew something was afoot. Lowell Murray picked up on it. "I would be talking to various people, friends of Dalton's, and it was clear that to his most loyal friends and supporters Dalton had sent out word: 'Keep your powder dry.'"[3] Camp asked Flora MacDonald to decline Goodman's request that she serve as secretary of the leadership convention. "Don't get into anything," he said, "We're going to need you when this whole effort comes forward." She did as he asked.[4]

Camp had not made any commitment to seek the leadership, and he was far from sure in his own mind that he wanted to run, but he was putting contingency plans in place, just in case. He had also been taking French lessons—he told people they were intended merely to assist him, as party president, to communicate better with

Tories in Quebec. Some of his friends reckoned that if he persisted with the lessons he *might* one day be as proficient as Bob Stanfield—which is to say his French had some distance to go.

The more Camp surveyed the field of potential leadership candidates, the more depressed he became. Eddie Goodman was an enthusiastic supporter of his old pal Hees—"Heesie," as he called him—who had been Diefenbaker's trade minister. Camp had a low opinion of Hees, whom he regarded as a buffoon. Hees, he would say, "has the body of Adonis and the brain of a gnat." (The jibe eventually made its way to Diefenbaker, the master of the putdown, who quipped that Camp himself had quite the opposite problem.)

The other early front-runner was Davie Fulton, who had been Diefenbaker's justice minister. Fulton had left Ottawa to make an ill-fated venture into provincial politics in British Columbia before returning to Parliament in the 1965 election. As much as he hated Diefenbaker, Fulton could not bring himself to support Camp in the leadership review, lest he offend Diefenbaker supporters, whose votes he would need at the leadership convention. Although three people Camp respected—Lowell Murray, Joe Clark and Brian Mulroney—were all working in Fulton's campaign, he lacked respect for their candidate. Fulton himself understood why. "I think he may have mistrusted my judgment in the clutch," he said.[5]

That, as Camp saw it, left three premiers as viable candidates: Robarts, Roblin and Stanfield. He canvassed all of them. Robarts was no fool. He appreciated that it was a better thing by far to be premier in Ontario than to be opposition leader in Ottawa. When anyone asked, he would say he had no ambition to be prime minister. He had a very good life in Toronto. He did not want to live in Ottawa. He did not want to run for the leadership. He would not run. Period. Many Tories, and most journalists, did not believe Robarts; how could anyone, they asked themselves, resist the siren call of the national stage? Camp believed Robarts. He had talked to him many times. When he said no, he meant no.

Camp thought it highly unlikely that Stanfield would run. Stanfield shared his belief in the importance of the party as a national institution, but he had no particular desire to move to federal politics—he told reporters he would rather take up ski jumping. He had been premier, with Camp's help, since 1956; he had grown even more popular than his beloved Liberal predecessor, Angus L. Macdonald; and he was well aware that he could probably keep winning in Nova Scotia until he died (and, given the Maritimes creative electoral practices, probably for one election thereafter). He was due to call an election in 1967 (it came on May 30), and he could not leave before the vote, or for a decent interval, perhaps a year or two, afterward. Finally, Stanfield would not move unless he were convinced the Nova Scotia party and government would be in good hands. The only person whom Stanfield, and Camp, thought capable of taking over was the finance minister, G.I. "Ike" Smith. And Smith had a heart condition and wanted to get out of public life.

That left Duff Roblin. He was Camp's last hope. Camp at that time was working on two assumptions, both of which would prove incorrect. He assumed that only one premier would run. And he assumed that if a premier did become a candidate, Diefenbaker would not run. His big concern was that if none of the premiers ran, Diefenbaker would run, and he might well be re-elected.

In that situation, Camp convinced himself, he would have to be a candidate himself in order to complete the job he had started with his speech at the Albany Club in May 1966. "Some of our own people began to talk about it [a Camp candidacy], so as they began to talk about it, I began to think about it," Camp said. "But I couldn't tell you how serious it was...except as we went closer and closer to the convention itself, I became more and more annoyed and more and more concerned, because I was convinced that if Roblin, Stanfield and Robarts had all been hit by a truck on the same day, Diefenbaker would have won that convention."[6]

Camp had been close to Roblin in earlier years. He had helped him to become premier of Manitoba and had worked in his re-election campaigns. Roblin had rewarded him by giving the provincial tourism account to his advertising agency. In more recent times, however, they had grown apart. Camp had been disappointed by Roblin's failure to support his leadership-review campaign. Roblin had suffered from the Fulton Syndrome: he knew Diefenbaker had to go and he agreed with what Camp was doing, but he would not associate himself publicly with the party president lest he alienate Diefenbaker partisans. At the annual meeting in November, Stanfield had been quietly but firmly supportive; Robarts had made a very public gesture of support when he deliberately arrived late for the opening session, walked to the platform and shook Camp's hand while the assembled Tories watched; but Roblin had been invisible.

Accompanied by his brother-in-law and campaign organizer, Norman Atkins, Camp went to Winnipeg to see Roblin, at the invitation of the premier's advisers. While Atkins waited at the International Inn, Camp was taken to see Roblin. He assumed they would meet in his office at the legislature or perhaps at his home. Instead, to avoid the press, he was driven to the suburban Winnipeg home of a member of Roblin's inner circle, Wally Fox-Decent. The premier was waiting in the living room. "It was like a spy story," Camp recalled. "It was all very sub-rosa—secret—and I didn't like it very much." While Roblin's retinue withdrew to the kitchen, he and Camp had a long, frank talk. Camp told Roblin that if he entered the race, he would do whatever he could to support him, including resign as national president, "so I wouldn't be a bone in anybody's throat."

They talked about Diefenbaker. Camp said his position would be impossible if Roblin sought or received Diefenbaker's support: "While I wouldn't oppose him, there was no way I could support him openly." When Roblin said he would want Diefenbaker's support, Camp replied he would never get it. "Well, you know," Roblin said, "I need help with regard to strategy, speeches and so on." Camp said although he no longer wanted to assume that role, he would do what he could and would not let Roblin down. He tried to set a deadline, saying if he did not declare his candidacy by the end of June, later extended to July 10, "he'd be a hostage to fortune—anything can happen—and all bets are off."

He warned the Manitoba premier that if he decided not to run, Camp himself would be a candidate. "I can't just sit here and wait and see this thing fall apart," he told Roblin. "We [the Camp organization] are going to be a presence at the convention. We're going to be a presence in the form of one candidate or another."[7]

Leaving Roblin to wrestle with his dilemma—which did he need more: Diefenbaker's blessing or Camp's strategic advice and organizational muscle?—Camp returned to the International Inn for dinner and some verbal fencing with hovering reporters. He got a message that Roblin wanted to see him again. This time, he was taken to the home of Sterling Lyon, Manitoba's attorney general and a staunch Camp supporter. Roblin wanted to talk about organization and whom he should get to be his campaign chairman. "I made it absolutely clear to them that I wasn't going to be anyone's speech writer, or underground organizer, and I meant that at the time," Camp said.

Then Roblin asked him whether he had seen that day's newspaper and, when Camp said he had not, Roblin told him not to look at it. When he went to the kitchen to get a drink, however, Camp found the Winnipeg *Tribune* with a front-page story that quoted sources close to the premier as saying Roblin was embarrassed by Camp's visit and was very uneasy that he was in town. Camp knew instantly where the leak had come from—it was a member of Roblin's inner circle who had supported Diefenbaker in November. "I thought it was dirty pool, and I rather felt I'd been taken," Camp said. The leak backfired: it sent Camp away angry, and it made Diefenbaker suspicious of Roblin's true agenda.

Camp started to reconsider his opinion of Roblin. He questioned Roblin's judgment in asking him to come to Winnipeg, then exposing him to the embarrassment of the *Tribune* story. He knew the premier's hand was behind the leak because Charles Lynch of Southam News, having interviewed Roblin, reported the premier's unease over Camp's visit. Camp began to wonder whether Roblin had what it took to be a national leader if he could not attract more savvy advisers. "If I had made up my mind about anything," Camp recalled, "it was that no one was going to have it both ways. Whatever relationship there was with me had to be out in the open."[8]

In the end, Roblin blew his chance to be leader. For fear of being labelled the Camp candidate, he delayed entering the race until after Stanfield had become a candidate, with Camp's support. His organization was woeful—a group of well-meaning Manitoba Tories who had no connections to the party power brokers in Toronto and Ottawa and who did not have the faintest idea of how to run a national political campaign. They misread Diefenbaker completely: he never had any intention of endorsing Roblin, and in the end he joined the field against him. And they failed to understand the importance of the candidates' policy speeches at the start of the convention; Roblin was ill prepared, and he fell flat. In baseball parlance, the Roblin team were sandlotters trying to compete in the big leagues.

When Camp got back to Toronto, he told the Spades that he proposed to support Roblin. But they were unimpressed by the man, indifferent to his ambition and still peeved that he had not supported them in November. Some of them might have gone to Fulton in preference to Roblin. But clearly, the Spades had in mind a candidate they liked far better: Dalton Camp.

The prospect of a Camp candidacy heightened as the weeks passed and as none of the premiers stepped forward. Diefenbaker was keeping his options open, and Camp's fear that the Chief might manage to succeed himself grew. He was ready to give up on Roblin. He and Atkins had a shadow organization in place, and in June they assembled their key supporters for a planning meeting in Toronto. "We had an organization that was prepared to go in any direction and we had various contingencies, various reactions, based on various candidates," Camp said. Their planning extended to the timing of his announcement and the issues of whether he should resign as president and whether he should couple his resignation to the announcement of his leadership candidacy.[9]

Meanwhile, the Stanfield government had been re-elected easily in the provincial election of May 30. Camp went to Halifax to see if Stanfield was still adamant about not running—and he seemed to be. Pressed by Camp, Finlay MacDonald and Senator Grattan O'Leary, he held to his position that he could not walk out on the people of Nova Scotia unless Ike Smith was prepared to step in as interim premier. The finance minister was still unyielding.

After a long session at Stanfield's home, however, Smith

relented. Stanfield said that, on the understanding that Smith would stay, he was prepared to be a candidate. Smith and Camp talked outside after the meeting. Smith said Stanfield was making a mistake; he could not win if he went to Ottawa and the Tories would lose Nova Scotia without him.[10] "You should run," Smith told Camp. "I want you to know that. I want you to know that if anything happens to [Stanfield's candidacy] and you want to run, I will support you."[11]

Camp went back to his room at the Lord Nelson Hotel to phone the members of his organization with the news that Stanfield would run. He asked Flora MacDonald to drop everything in Kingston and fly to Halifax to make plans for the campaign. He was still in bed the next morning, however, when Stanfield called to say he had changed his mind. He was facing a budget crisis, he had a drunken minister he needed to fire and there were other reasons why he could not leave. Norman Atkins phoned Flora MacDonald to tell her of Stanfield's change of heart. Forget about going to Halifax, he told her. Go to New Brunswick, to Camp's cottage at Robertson's Point. "This has cleared the way for Dalton," he told her.[12]

Besides Camp, Atkins and Flora MacDonald, the group that met at Robertson's Point that weekend included Richard Hatfield, then an opposition MLA in New Brunswick; two Tory MPs from Prince Edward Island, David MacDonald and Heath Macquarrie; New Brunswick MP Gordon Fairweather; and Paul Weed, one of the Spades from Toronto, who also had a cottage in New Brunswick.

Atkins had already prepared a battle plan—a chart setting out Camp's leadership campaign from the day he declared his candidacy to the end of the convention in Toronto in September. There were going to be so many candidates in the field, Camp believed, that no one would have a majority of the delegates locked up before the convention. His would be a short, dramatic campaign, orchestrated to peak at the convention. As Flora MacDonald recalled, the group spent two days going over the plans—"what would be done, when he would travel and where he would go. We were really rolling."

Camp, she felt, was ready and eager now that he had made his decision to run: "I think he had convinced himself, after having been in the presidency, and gone across the country, and had all sorts of barbs thrown at him, and all these things because of the leadership review, that he really understood the party and the country and that he would make a pretty good candidate," she said.[13]

The meeting wound up on Sunday night. It was agreed Camp would make his announcement on the coming Tuesday. His preferred venue was a studio at Finlay MacDonald's television station in Halifax. Because the phones at Robertson's Point in those days were party lines and were usually busy, Flora MacDonald was dispatched to Jemseg, the nearest village, to phone Finlay MacDonald with their plans. "I finally got through to Finlay, to tell him that we needed this help from him," she said, "and he said, 'My God, I've been trying to figure out how to get in touch with you people all weekend, to let you know that Stanfield has changed his mind.'"

Flora MacDonald had to tell the group at the cottage that not only was Stanfield going to be a candidate after all, but also that he wanted Camp to come to Halifax post haste to draft his announcement speech. Most of the group was dumbfounded. Linda Camp was enraged over the way she felt her husband had been jerked around. She stormed out of the cottage and was not seen again for three hours. Camp withdrew into himself. He disappeared into one of the rooms in the cottage, apparently battling what he called his "Black Dog," the bouts of depression that he, like his idol Winston Churchill, suffered periodically. For 48 hours, he said almost nothing.

David MacDonald had a puzzling conversation with Camp when he asked the young MP to go for a walk with him. "It was a long walk," MacDonald said, "and it was a funny conversation because he was curious to know my reaction about Stanfield running. I thought that was kind of strange, given that Dalton was the chief architect of persuading Stanfield to run. He asked if I was comfortable with Stanfield. Would I be quite keen? And I said 'yeah.' He had so many questions like, 'You don't have any second thoughts?'"[14]

Having made up his mind to be a candidate, and having persuaded himself that his candidacy was necessary to preserve the process of reform he had initiated, Camp found it extremely difficult to shift gears, to go back to being a guru to another politician. He knew he would probably never have another opportunity to be a national leader and conceivably prime minister.

"Dalton had suffered a really big blow emotionally," David MacDonald remembered.

> He had convinced himself that he should do this, and could do it, and could win. But now, Bob Stanfield having announced his candidacy, that totally ended that dream, that possibility. This was his one shot at running for the leadership of the party, and virtually overnight it had been swept away by somebody he admired as much as anybody. It's interesting because it was pivotal to a whole bunch of things that happened for the rest of Dalton's life. [But] Dalton was pretty careful never to say, "Dammit, I should have done it."[15]

At Camp's funeral in March 2002, Norman Atkins observed to MacDonald: "You know, we came awful close in 1967. It would have been very different. Where would we be today if Dalton had run?"

That is a question Camp's friends asked themselves often over the years. "If Dalton was here today, and if he'd be totally candid with us, he would say the biggest disappointment in his life was not having run for the leadership," said David MacDonald. "Whether he believed he could have won it, and would have won the election, there are a whole bunch of what ifs, but…"

"What would the '70s have been like with Camp and [Pierre] Trudeau?" asked Andrew Stark, a university professor who worked with Camp in the Prime Minister's Office in Ottawa in the 1980s. "It would have been an unbelievable political dialogue."[16]

Camp and Trudeau had at least three things in common: they were intellectual, they had charisma and they were essentially loners. "He might have been a bit like Trudeau, an intellectual who required long periods of solitude," said Lowell Murray. "They don't always make the best politicians. It is sometimes quite difficult for them, because their periods of solitude conflict with the imperatives of Question Period, and media demands, and colleagues' demands."[17]

Columnist Allan Fotheringham was intrigued by the notion of Trudeau and Camp leading the two big parties. "It would have been fun for me," he said. "It would have been wonderful. It would have been like Lincoln and Douglas: duck soup for a columnist."[18]

Could Camp have won the leadership? Most of the people who were close to him in those days think not. "I think there was still too much anger in the party," said David MacDonald. "Even those who welcomed the fact that he had forced the issue and forced Diefenbaker into a convention—there likely weren't enough of them who at the end of the day would have voted for him. He was regarded as a hatchet man."[19] Murray agreed: "He would have put up a good campaign, but it would have been Anybody But Camp. That's what would have killed him."[20]

Hugh Segal, who worked with Camp in advertising and politics, said he believes Stanfield's decision to be a candidate after all was spurred, in part, by the knowledge that Camp was poised to enter the race, which, he feared, would cause further damage to the already fractured party. In Segal's view the events of the fateful summer of 1967 changed Camp forever:

> It's one thing to run for leader. Win or lose, there is some clarity there, delivered by the voters. It's quite another to think you should have been prime minister, without ever actually having tested those waters. My sense always was that both his greatness as an analyst, writer, strategist and creative person and to some extent his bitterness was driven by how he reacted to that seminal event. I always felt sad about him. I always felt that other things that entered his life, whether they were romantic interests or fixations on large houses in obscure places, were all about compensating for not having had that seminal experience.[21]

Camp did not go to Halifax to help Stanfield prepare the announcement he made on July 19. He stayed at Robertson's Point, where he wrote a speech that Flora MacDonald dictated over the telephone to Finlay MacDonald's secretary in Halifax. Hurt and perhaps disillusioned, he told the others at the cottage: "I have done my bit. I have written the announcement speech. Now I am going to stay here quietly at Robertson's Point for the rest of the summer. Good luck to you all."[22]

That resolution lasted only a week before Flora MacDonald

persuaded Camp to join her in Halifax to talk some sense into rival groups of campaign workers. As would happen shortly in the Roblin campaign—Roblin finally declared two weeks after Stanfield— local Stanfield supporters thought they knew how to run a national leadership campaign. MacDonald and Camp disabused them of that notion, and when the dust settled, Stanfield had the national organization that would carry him to victory in September. A campaign had already been plotted in meticulous detail in anticipation that Camp himself would be the candidate. All he and Atkins had to do was to change the name at the top of the chart from Dalton Camp to Robert Stanfield. Camp agreed to direct the campaign, with Atkins running the crucial convention organization, but at Stanfield's insistence Camp was to remain invisible. Like Fulton and Roblin, Stanfield worried that overt association with Camp would alienate the Diefenbaker wing of the party. It was the first of several wedges in their relationship.

Camp returned to Robertson's Point; a private phone line was run in—he would remember the summer of 1967 almost as fondly for his private phone as for Stanfield's victory—and he directed the campaign from the cottage. Although unseen by delegates and the press, he was completely involved in the leadership campaign, despite his earlier assertion to Roblin that he was no longer prepared to play speech writer and strategist. As the convention approached, he went to Toronto to prep Stanfield for the weeklong ordeal at a farm north of the city owned by lawyer Donald Guthrie, one of the Spades. Sitting in armchairs on the lawn, the two men discussed the opportunities and pitfalls of convention week.

The Stanfield campaign was in dire shape at that point. Stanfield had travelled 27,000 miles since July 19, but he was not going anywhere. He underwhelmed most of the delegates he met. "I wonder why anybody comes to see me at all," he told a group of Tories in Montreal. Finlay MacDonald, who accompanied Stanfield across the country, ducking out of sight when the campaign entered Diefenbaker territory in Saskatchewan, admitted things were not going well. "Our campaign left a lot to be desired," he said. "The wheels fell off as we tried to roll."[23]

Listening to MacDonald's reports, Camp was concerned that the campaign was bombing. The consensus among reporters covering the candidates was that Stanfield was in fourth place—behind Roblin, Fulton and Hees—entering convention week. It was clear, however, as Camp had anticipated earlier in the summer when he was plotting his own campaign, that no candidate was even close to having a majority of the delegates locked up. The leadership would be won, or lost, at the convention.

Three things saved Stanfield. The first was Atkins's convention-week organization. With seven subcommittees reporting to him (reception, demonstrations, advertising, press, intra-organization communications, delegates and floor management and scrutineers), Atkins had by far the most professional operation at the convention—and it was built around the team he and Camp had assembled over the years. Every move Stanfield would make was meticulously planned and timed. Nothing was left to chance.

The second thing that saved Stanfield was superior strategy. For example, delegates supporting the other candidates trickled into Toronto as the week went on. Camp, Atkins and Flora MacDonald, who was responsible for delegates, made sure their committed supporters got to Toronto well ahead of time.[24] Reporters sniffing around the Royal York Hotel found that just about every delegate they interviewed was a Stanfield delegate. When uncommitted delegates arrived, they were taken aback, and impressed, by the apparent strength of the Stanfield forces. Stanfield appeared to be surging ahead.

As Camp talked to Stanfield on the lawn at Don Guthrie's farm, he stressed the crucial third thing: the importance of making a favourable first impression on delegates. That would be when the candidates delivered their policy speeches on the opening evening of the convention. While Duff Roblin spoke in generalities from a few notes scratched on a piece of paper, Stanfield had a text crafted for him by Camp.

It was a speech designed to position Stanfield where Camp had deduced most Tories wanted their next leader to be—to the reform side of the party: advocating responsible economic and foreign policies; in favour of broadening the base of the party; concerned about those Canadians who were not sharing in the prosperity of the country; and committed to the advancement of both French and English language rights. The language issue was important because in the weeks leading up to the convention, the Tories had held a "thinkers' conference," chaired by William Davis, later the premier of Ontario, at Montmorency Falls in Quebec. The conference passed a resolution with this simple and seemingly innocuous observation: "Canada is composed of two founding peoples (*deux nations*) with historical rights who have been joined by people from many lands." It was the translation of "*deux nations*" back into English, not as "two founding peoples" but as "two nations" that caused the controversy. It gave Diefenbaker a pretext for presenting himself as the champion of "one Canada," whatever that meant.

Stanfield handled the controversy deftly. English Canadians, he said, in French, "must accept...that French-speaking Canadians have the right to enjoy their cultural and linguistic distinctiveness. This right was clearly accepted by the founding fathers as a basic principle of Confederation, and it is our responsibility to see that it is given meaningful expression." He rejected the notion of "special status" for Quebec, if the term meant that some Canadians would enjoy rights and/or privileges not enjoyed by other Canadians. "But I do not believe that this is what the people of Quebec mean."

It was the only good speech of the evening, and it was an impressive start for the premier of Nova Scotia. After listening to the speeches, Toronto *Telegram* publisher John Bassett dumped his first choice, his old friend George Hees, and gave his editorial blessing to Stanfield. The *Telegram* also played into the Camp–Atkins–Flora MacDonald campaign strategy by conducting a post-speeches straw poll of delegates. It showed an apparent upswing in support for Stanfield. Some of it was real, but much of it was due to the strategy of getting delegates to Toronto early. Claude Ryan, editor of Montreal's small but influential daily *Le Devoir* was also impressed by the Nova Scotia premier. "The election of Mr. Stanfield would be the logical continuation of the spirit of renovation," he wrote.[25]

The next day, Stanfield was to appear at a press luncheon at the convention, and Camp used the occasion to dispel the notion that Stanfield was nothing more than a dull, dour man whose idea of a ripping good read was a Jane Austen novel. He wrote a humorous speech for him. "Ladies and gentlemen," Stanfield began, "this is the moment you have been waiting for. Up until now, some of you have tended to regard me as a low-key candidate—devoid of passion and reluctant to take a strong position on the many matters which confront us as Canadians. Some of you have gone so far as to label me a pragmatist. This is a vicious and ugly rumour deliberately circulated by certain members of the press simply because they have tried in vain to get answers to their questions."

He announced that as soon as he was sworn in as prime minister, "There will be established a new department, to be known as Canadian News Relations, hereinafter referred to as the CNR. The CNR will be a government information centre dedicated to the proposition that no news is good news and that suppression is the better part of valour." It was not side-splittingly funny, but it served Camp's purpose. It added a touch of lightness and warmth to Stanfield's austere image. That night, Stanfield took over the Canadian Room of the Royal York and threw a huge party for 2,000 delegates and others attracted by the free drinks and the down-home music of Don Messer and his Islanders. It was the biggest, wildest party of the week and it established a perception, however improbable, of Stanfield as a fun-loving guy.

Although Camp was seen infrequently during the convention—he worked out of the Westbury Hotel rather than the Royal York, which was the main convention hotel—his hand was felt everywhere. He wrote Stanfield's speech to the full convention later in the week, and he charted the strategy Stanfield was to follow when Diefenbaker, after addressing the convention as the retiring leader, turned around and entered the race—to save the party, he said, from the "two nations" heresy.

It took seven frenzied hours and five tense ballots, but Robert Stanfield, after leading from the first ballot, finally won the Conservative leadership on Saturday, September 9, 1967. He was helped, ironically, by Diefenbaker, whose candidacy grievously damaged Roblin's chances by denying the Manitoba premier the early-ballot strength that he needed to stay close to Stanfield. He was also helped by his and Camp's friends on Davie Fulton's team— notably Lowell Murray, Joe Clark and Brian Mulroney—who, by pre-arrangement, swung most of their delegates to Stanfield when Fulton withdrew after the fourth ballot.

When he took the podium to be hailed as the new leader, Stanfield tried to start the process of healing his wounded party. Turning to Diefenbaker, he said, "I appreciate very much the size of the shoes I am now to try to fill." For the benefit of the reform wing and the people who had helped him to the leadership, he added, "Personally, I'm determined to get along with that fellow Camp."

It was not much, just a small gesture of reconciliation, but it had larger implications than Stanfield could ever have foreseen. Diefenbaker was enraged by the line about Camp, which, he told a friend, was "a deliberate slap" at him by the new leader. His relations with Stanfield were strained and they worsened as the months passed. He appeared in the House of Commons for the daily Question Period, leaving as soon as it ended. He boycotted caucus meetings. When Stanfield won a seat in a by-election, Diefenbaker refused to escort him down the aisle of the chamber, as was customary; he stayed away from the House that day. Soon the two men were barely on speaking terms. Diefenbaker made it clear he wished for Stanfield's failure. As it became obvious that Stanfield, in an effort to mollify Diefenbaker, was keeping Camp at a distance, the old leader took a *Telegram* cartoon of Camp slinking away from Ottawa and gleefully put it on prominent display in his outer office.[26]

For his part, Camp was badly wounded by Stanfield's line. He had served the Conservative party for 15 years. He had been Stanfield's friend for almost as long. When he first met him, Stanfield had been almost the antithesis of a successful politician; he was awkward, diffident and self-effacing. Camp had helped him become premier, winning four consecutive provincial elections. He had led the fight to democratize the party, to establish the principle of leadership review, and, in the process, he had driven Diefenbaker from office. He had given up his own chance to be leader when he had thrown his support behind Stanfield. Finally, he had directed the campaign that gave Stanfield the leadership. And the best the new leader could say to the thousands of Tories who packed Maple Leaf Gardens that night was that he would try to get along "with that fellow Camp."

Stanfield's desire to keep Camp at arm's length was understandable. The Diefenbaker rump of the party made his life as leader miserable. The wounds opened by the leadership-reappraisal campaign did not heal. Camp paid a heavy price for doing what he believed to be right. He could never be leader. He would never have a chance of being prime minister. He had been made an outcast in his own party.

Stanfield felt bad about the way he had shunned Camp, and his regret deepened over the years. Thirteen years later, in 1980, when 75 friends gathered at the Albany Club in Toronto to help Camp celebrate his sixtieth birthday, Stanfield, by now retired from the leadership, finally tried to make amends. He was close to tears when he said of Camp:

> He is one of the few Canadians who have taken courageous positions in politics and not merely in print. It is one thing to urge a bold line upon other people; it's something else to put your life on the line in support of a position. Dalton Camp has paid a high price for having the courage of his convictions, for having the courage to support positions that he believed were right and finding himself—as well he knew he would be, I'm sure—in the eye of the storm as a result of that.

Looking directly at Camp, Stanfield ended: "I hope that after these years of helping others, after all these years of speaking your mind bluntly and courageously, I hope that after all these years you have no bitterness in your heart toward any of us personally and no bitterness in your heart toward the anguish which I'm sure you have suffered."[27]

The 1967 leadership convention was a watershed for Camp. Never again would he be as active in, or as committed to, the game of politics. There was one final favour, however, that he would perform for Bob Stanfield. In April 1968, the Liberals

Dalton's first summer.
With his mother,
Aurilla, in New
Brunswick in 1921.
(PROVINCIAL ARCHIVES OF NEW
BRUNSWICK)

A family gathering. Dalton's father, Harold, is in the dark suit in the second
row. Aurilla is at the right end of the same row with Dalton on her knee.
(FAMILY PHOTO)

A brand new officer. Poor eyesight notwithstanding, Dalton is promoted to lieutenant in the Canadian Army toward the end of the Second World War. (FAMILY PHOTO)

Ready to party. Finlay and Ann MacDonald join their best pals, Linda Camp and Dalton, on vacation in the Bahamas in 1958. (FAMILY PHOTO)

The politician and his guru. Duff Roblin takes Dalton fishing in
Northern Manitoba in 1960, two years after Camp helped him become
premier. (N.B. Archives)

Confronting his enemies. John Diefenbaker wheels and points at Dalton
Camp (second from right) at the historic Tory annual meeting in 1966.
Robert Stanfield is on the extreme right. The bald man to the left of
Camp is Diefenbaker ally James Johnston, the party's national director.
(Toronto Telegram)

The first Camp family. Dalton and Linda with their five children, about 1965. The eldest, Gail and David, are at the back, with Michael beside his mother and Connie (left) and Cherie in front.
(N.B. Archives)

The Red Tory. At times Dalton made conventional Conservatives uneasy, in part because of scenes like this. A critic of the United States war in Vietnam, he joins Tommy Douglas and other protesters (including a few Maoists) at an antiwar demonstration in Confederation Square in Ottawa in the late 1960s. (CP)

A great mistake. Brian Mulroney jokes with Dalton on the day in 1986 that Camp agreed to work in the Prime Minister's Office—a decision he soon came to bitterly regret. The inscription is to his son David. (FAMILY PHOTO)

For David from Dad (right): This is on the day the bargain was struck. The rest is history. Merry Christmas! Dad 25/12/86

A member of the family. New Brunswick's longtime premier Richard Hatfield (third from left) spent so much time with the Camps that a bedroom at Northwood was permanently reserved for his use. Here he is at Robertson's Point with Dalton and, among others, Dalton's son Michael (at left) and daughter Cherie (holding child). (FAMILY PHOTO)

Three amigos. Dalton evoked intense loyalty,
even love, among his friends and supporters. Two
of the closest were his pal Finlay MacDonald
(left) and his brother-in-law and business partner,
Norman Atkins. Together, as MacDonald put it,
they did some "serious damage to the grape."

A New Year's child.
Dalton was 57 years
old when his second
wife, Wendy, gave
birth to Christopher
on January 1, 1978.
Christopher is 18 in
this 1996 photo.

Football fans. Although their marriage had collapsed years earlier, Wendy and Dalton attend a 1997 football game together at Acadia University, which their son, Christopher, attended before switching to Queen's University. (FAMILY PHOTO)

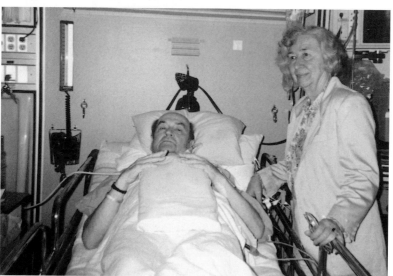

A new heart. Dalton received the heart of a 19-year-old woman in 1993. Here, with his first wife, Linda, he recovers in intensive care at the Ottawa Heart Institute. (FAMILY PHOTO)

A new man. His health restored, Dalton lived for nearly nine highly productive years following his heart transplant. He walked regularly, watched his diet, kept his weight down—and did some of the best writing of his life. (FAMILY PHOTO)

changed leaders, electing their own charismatic loner, Pierre Elliott Trudeau, to replace Lester Pearson. Camp had a sinking feeling as he watched that convention. Trudeau, he knew, or at least suspected, would make it very difficult—perhaps impossible—for Stanfield to win the next election. He was asked by the president of the Conservative association in Toronto's Don Valley riding, Anne Austin, if he would let his name stand for the Tory nomination.[28]

Camp was of two minds. He had lost just about all of his interest in being in Parliament, and he knew the chances were slim of winning the new riding in the teeth of Trudeaumania. On the other hand, part of Don Valley had been carved out of Eglinton, the riding where he had battled Mitchell Sharp in 1965, and Camp still had the Spades as the core of a powerful organization there. He also felt that having gotten Stanfield into the leadership, it was the least he could do to stand with him in what seemed destined to be a painful election.

Camp went off to Antigua to think about running. When Trudeau called the election for June, Norm Atkins and Roy McMurtry flew down to talk it over with him. In the end, he decided to run, came back and mounted a spirited campaign against neophyte Liberal Robert Kaplan. Camp knew he could not win—and he did not. He lost by nearly 5,000 votes to Kaplan, a much less impressive opponent than Sharp had been. The Liberals finally won a majority, and the Tories took 25 fewer seats under Stanfield than they had taken with Diefenbaker as their leader in 1965.

Four days after the election, Camp wrote an article for the Toronto *Telegram* in which he declared Trudeau to be the first Canadian leader to master the media. "The mastery was complete," he wrote. "Trudeau converted television confrontation with newsmen into fan-club interviews. One had the impression that, once the interview was over, he would be asked for his autograph."[29]

Diefenbaker was delighted by the results, especially the defeats of Camp, Roblin and others he regarded as his enemies. He was beaming when he went on national television, almost chortling as he declared, "The Conservative party has suffered a calamitous disaster."[30]

Camp, however, did not regard his defeat as a personal disaster. He was relieved. He was supporting five children, who were attending university or private schools. "We had a lifestyle based on my occupation," he said in an interview years later on VisionTV. "If I were elected to Parliament, I would have been a member of the opposition. Now figure it out. I mean it would have been tragic.... It wasn't a life I treasured."[31]

His children sensed that, too. "When he lost in 1968, all of us kids felt awful for him," said Connie, the middle daughter. "We felt sorry for him, and we couldn't even manage a smile. And the thing that was so surprising, the thing I could never figure out, is why he was so happy. He really seemed genuinely relieved, and it wasn't that he was acting. It was genuine relief."[32]

Norman Atkins understood better than most people did the reasons for his brother-in-law's relief. A sense of obligation to the party had led to him to mount the leadership-review campaign. Obligation to Stanfield had caused him to agree to run his leadership campaign at a time when, as he had told Roblin, he wanted to get out of that kind of involvement. And obligation both to Stanfield and to the party had made him agree to run in the 1968 election. "But once he did that, he didn't feel that he owed the party, or Stanfield, the same commitment any longer," Atkins said.[33]

Camp was his own man again. He called an executive meeting and resigned as party president. After nearly two decades of service to his party—as an innovative publicist, strategist, speech writer, guru to leaders (federal and provincial), party president, reformer and inspirational mentor to a new generation of Tories, he needed a breather. He had known the exhilaration of victory and the bitter taste of defeat. With a sense of relief approaching joy, he turned his attention and talent to the role he loved best, and for which he would, in the end, be best remembered: observing, writing and commenting on political happenings in Canada and the world. He felt liberated.

PART 3
_____

THE WRITER

CHAPTER 17

Not a Conventional Father

DALTON CAMP'S FAVOURITE SONG was "My Way," sung by Frank Sinatra. Camp was a true individualist and nonconformist, and the lyrics captured the essence of his spirit, style and determination to be true to himself, to go it alone if necessary—regardless of what anyone else thought.

> I've lived a life that's full.
> I've traveled each and ev'ry highway;
> But more, much more than this,
> I did it my way....

> To think I did all that;
> And may I say—not in a shy way,
> "No, oh no not me, I did it my way."
> For what is a man, what has he got?
> If not himself, then he has naught.
> To say the things he truly feels;
> And not the words of one who kneels.
> The record shows I took the blows—
> And did it my way!

Camp lived those lyrics. He did it his way—whether it was standing by John Diefenbaker through 1965, or taking him down the following year, or putting aside his leadership ambition in favour of his friend Robert Stanfield in 1967, or running for Parliament in 1968 in an election he knew he would surely lose. And he did it his way again when he abruptly resigned as national president of the Tory party, without even alerting his closest ally, Norman Atkins—"He knew I'd try to talk him out of it."[1]

Camp would continue to do it his way as he shifted his focus from political guru to political commentator. He had been dabbling in journalism since his days in university. He was never a reporter; the process of collecting, assembling, digesting and regurgitating facts bored him. He preferred to stand above the crowd and write commentary. Although he had an astonishingly broad network of friends and informants, he seldom conducted interviews or delved into public documents. His forte was opinion and interpretation rather than the unearthing of fresh information. He started writing a weekly "Inside Politics" column for the Toronto *Telegram* in 1966 while he was still party president, moving later to the *Toronto Star*, *Toronto Sun* and back to the *Star*. In later years, his column caused as much discomfiture among Tories as among their political opponents.

If Camp did it his way in politics and in journalism, he was no different in his personal life. His children all have slightly different perspectives on him, but they agree on one thing: he was not a conventional father. Part of this was due to the distractions of business and politics. Camp devoted so much time to building his advertising agency and to political activity that he was home only on unpredictable and infrequent occasions while his children were growing up—although, when he was there, his personality filled the house. He once added up the hours and days that politics had taken him away from his family during the hectic decade of 1960s. The total came to two years.

Linda raised the children, nursed them when they were sick and tended to their schooling, leaving Camp free to spend endless hours with other men who liked to drink Scotch, smoke cigars and stay up late talking politics. For 20 years, she cooked two dinners each night: one for the family and one for Dalton when he happened to be in town. "He was not a father that came home every night and sat with the kids, never," Linda said. "He always listened to them, I'm sure, in a civilized way. He never was mean to any of them. I was the sergeant major."[2]

Camp made a great deal of money in the advertising business, and spent it. He always flew first class, stayed in the best hotels (Four Seasons or equivalent), vacationed at luxurious resorts (usually Curtain Bluff on the south coast of Antigua) and drove an expensive car like a Jaguar or Buick Riviera. Through his personal holding company, Travel Direction Limited, he owned two cottages at Robertson's Point, New Brunswick. His advertising agency, Camp Associates, rented a luxury apartment in downtown Ottawa for Camp and other executives to use on visits to the capital. Camp stayed there for just one night. There was no room service, he discovered, no one from whom to order a chilled martini, so he moved to a hotel and never set foot in the apartment again.[3] Yet despite his expensive tastes, he and Linda and their family lived unpretentiously in Toronto—in a modest suburban house on Nipigon Avenue in Willowdale in the northern reaches of Toronto. Later, they moved closer in, to a much larger house—five bedrooms, library, family room and three fireplaces—on Daneswood Road in the Lawrence Park district of the city. His children knew they were not poor, but they were raised to believe they were not rich, either.

They had five children. Gail, the eldest, was born in 1945 while Camp was still in the army, and she accompanied her parents to New York when her father was a student at the Columbia University Graduate School of Journalism, then to England when he studied political science at the London School of Economics. A graduate of Queen's University in Kingston, Ontario, she is a producer in television (The Nature of Things and The Sacred Balance, both for David Suzuki) and film (a partner in Stormy Nights Productions, which makes films about the arts). Gail is married to John McIntyre, a creative director whom Norm Atkins hired at the Camp Associates advertising agency; after Camp and Atkins sold out, McIntyre became one of the principals in the successor agency. Reflecting on the success of Atkins, his brother-in-law, and McIntyre, his son-in-law, Camp was moved to comment: "Nepotism works."

Gail was an only child for five years and was enjoying her special status when her mother gave birth to four more children in the space of seven years. David, born in 1950, was a journalist, but after a tour of duty with the Saint John Telegraph Journal in the Parliamentary Press Gallery in Ottawa, he switched careers. He went to Cambridge University in England to study law and, on his return, moved to Vancouver to join a large law firm—and to insulate himself as best he could from the influence of his famous father.

"Nothing grows under the shadow of an oak tree," David said. "I didn't always want to be known as the son of Dalton Camp, and had I lived in Toronto, I would have gone into every room with people thinking, 'There's the son of Dalton Camp.' I come out to Vancouver and nobody knows. That was important to me. I liked to visit my father, but to be around him for a long time was hard, because it was clear I could never have a relationship of equality with him. I would always sense, always feel, my own inadequacies around him."[4]

The next child, Connie, born in 1952, was a bundle of insecurities when she was young. She remembered a time when she was suspended from Bishop Strachan School, a private girl's school in Toronto, for going to a restaurant off campus for lunch while wearing her school uniform. Both of her parents were away at the time, and Connie was in a state of dread for four days until their return. She was sure she was in terrible trouble; she feared her father would cancel a trip he had promised she could take to Europe. "I told him my story—this is how little I knew him—and he just cracked up. He thought that it was funny that I would be suspended for going out to eat. And he put me at ease, and told me about his own career in school. He wasn't the best-behaved student. So I thought I'd really pleased him."[5]

David gave Connie a nickname that stuck. He called her "Boris" because she flirted with Marxism, travelled in Eastern Europe while still in her teens, then attended Antioch College, a small arts school in Ohio, where she took Marxist studies, among other subjects. She became a journalist, working on newspapers in New Brunswick, Ontario and Vermont.

The fourth child (and third daughter), Cheryl, known as Cherie (or "Choo" to her siblings), was born in 1954 and is the only one with no direct connection to journalism. A drama graduate from Queen's, she is an actor, singer and songwriter. With her husband, composer John Welsman, a five-time Gemini Award winner, she started a jazz band, Cherie Camp and Friends, which played the club circuit for a number of years; her proud father loved nothing better than to catch her performances whenever he was in a city where she was appearing. She has sung backup on recordings by such artists as Rita MacNeil, Dan Hill and Jane Siberry, worked on film soundtracks and been both a singer and an announcer on television commercials. Pretty and seemingly self-possessed as a youngster, she was likened by her father to "some remarkable plant—growing, blooming, perpetually drawing love and affection and returning it."[6]

In Linda Camp's opinion, her youngest child, Michael, was the most like his father, especially in his sense of humour, his independent spirit, his need for solitude and his love for New Brunswick. He is the only one of the children who lives in the province. Born in 1957, Michael became a newspaper reporter, then joined CBC radio, where he has been a reporter, producer, news editor and on-air host of the morning show at the Fredericton station.

If Camp had been a more conventional father, he would have been fit to be tied when Michael managed to get thrown out of schools on both coasts. As a grade 10 student at Kings College School in Nova Scotia, he was a passenger in a car with two other boys and their dates when it went off the road and slammed at high speed into an earthen dike. Miraculously, no one was seriously hurt, but the youth who had been driving was drunk. The boys were asked to leave Kings the next day. From there, Michael went to Brentwood College School, a coed boarding school on Vancouver Island. A month from the end of grade 12, he and his girlfriend were expelled after his housemaster caught them in bed together. The school's headmaster phoned Camp to tell him Michael was being sent home. "What did he do?" his father asked, fearing drugs or perhaps something even worse. "He was found in bed, naked, with a fellow student," the headmaster replied. "Oh, thank God," Camp said.[7]

Camp's sixth child, Christopher Camp, was born to his companion Wendy Cameron at 12:52 a.m. on January 1, 1978, in Fredericton—as luck would have it, the first baby born in New Brunswick in 1978. When she awoke in the morning, Wendy was startled to discover a stranger in her hospital room. "There was this man in a shiny three-piece suit," she remembered. "He said,

'Congratulations! You had the first baby born in New Brunswick. You have tons of Gerber baby food and diapers and stuff waiting for you downstairs—and we're going to take your picture.' And I said, 'No. Take the next one.' We didn't need all that stuff, and I didn't need the notoriety.... Christopher's a love child. We decided to have him. It was a concrete decision between the two of us."[8]

Their relationship drove a wedge between Camp and his first five children—an estrangement that lasted for years. Camp and Cameron subsequently married, in 1984. They separated in 1988. Although it was a bitter split, they never completed their divorce proceedings, and they were still legally married when Camp died in 2002. In his final years of his life, he struggled to meet Wendy's financial demands. Camp also covered the cost of putting Christopher through Queen's and the London School of Economics. (After his father's death, Christopher finished at the LSE, placing third in his class, then decided to stay in England to study international commercial law.)

Growing up, the children of the first family knew their father was somebody important, maybe even famous, because they had heard their friends' parents talking about him. But they were not entirely sure why he was so celebrated. Camp seldom talked to the children about what he did during his prolonged absences. "It was very strange," said Cherie. "He would talk about [politics] if I brought it up. But it had to come from me. I think he felt that it wasn't really what I was interested in. I wasn't a confidante of his; he didn't tell me a whole lot of things."[9]

Camp always wanted to know whether his children were happy, and he was interested in what they were thinking. But he was much less interested in what they were actually *doing*. He sent them all to private schools and he paid their tuition and other bills without the slightest complaint. But he was never entirely sure what school any one of his children was attending at any given time. And he did not have the faintest idea what grade they were in.

Cherie adored her father, and he was proud of her when she broke the family mould to become a professional singer. But as far as she was aware, he never knew where she was going to university. "He never asked me what university I went to, or what I was studying. It sounds awful, but he didn't ask," she said. "I'm not sure I ever did tell him."[10]

"I think he knew the schools we were in," said Connie, the middle daughter, "but I'm sure he couldn't say what grade. He wouldn't have been able to say how old we were."[11]

He was certainly not the sort of parent who attended functions at their children's schools. David, the eldest son, played on the football team at Trinity College School in Port Hope, Ontario. His father came to only one game in those years. Later, when David played on the rugby team at the University of Toronto, his father came to one game, watched David score, and left.

"He was away a lot. And when he came home, he wasn't interested in our report cards," Connie said. "He assumed that we'd all do well, and if we didn't, that our mother would look after it. He wasn't interested in conventional things. He really did want to have fun, and that's how we saw him: a man who wandered into our lives a few times in the summer, and threw us around the water, and told us stories."[12]

Every now and again, however, he would reveal that he had been paying more attention to his children's lives than they thought he had. David felt his father was intuitively sensitive to other people. "He always knew what was going on around him," he said. "You'd think he wasn't paying any attention to you at all, and then he would take you aside and say something that made you feel he saw into your life, so easily and so far. He saw you more clearly than you saw yourself."[13]

The children thought their unconventional father was wonderful. "I loved having that kind of father," Connie remembered. "We'd had the conventional mother, and I think maybe it was sort of unfair, because my father left all the difficult things to my mother. Not that either of them cared much about discipline."[14]

Gail, the eldest, saw more of their father when she was growing up in the late 1940s and 1950s than her younger siblings did in the 1960s, when Camp was knee-deep in Tory politics. "I thought he was magical," Gail said. "I thought he kind of did everything. It was hard to describe—kids just gravitated to him like a magnet, kids and dogs. He was really playful, and really fun, and he'd roll on the floor. My earliest memories of him are in England, reading. We used to read together all the time. He'd do all the parts, and he could do all the voices, or be the villain. We had all kinds of books that we knew by heart. I know the entire Christopher Robin series."[15]

Camp's playfulness extended to the exchange of gifts at Christmas. He always made a big ceremony of the opening of presents, a process that could go on for hours. "My father loved secrets and subterfuge, and he loved Christmas," Cherie said. "He could make a bottle of LePage's glue seem an exciting and cherished gift—just what he always wanted." One Christmas, when she was 12 years old, Cherie was the object, or victim, of her father's playfulness. "A couple of hours had passed and I had not received a single present," she remembered. "My father made a big deal of this, turning occasionally to my mother to ask, 'Isn't there anything here for Cherie? Oh well...' It was a monumental struggle for me to maintain composure. I was determined not to cry. His plan was to make me suffer a little, perhaps to heighten the joy, before he gave me the thing he knew I had always quietly wished for, but never in a million years thought I could actually have."

Finally, when the rest of the gifts had been distributed, Camp discovered an envelope for Cherie buried in the braches of the tree and passed it casually to her. The enclosed card read, "You have a..." above a hand-drawn picture that looked like a four-year-old's rendering of a horse. Cherie had to read the card four times before the gift registered. "I had wished for a horse on every birthday candle, star, anything that could possibly be wished on, and, after that Christmas, I was at a loss," she said. "I don't think I ever wished for another thing—just intangibles like health and happiness, and possibly good marks."[16]

By the time Michael, the fifth child, came along in 1957, his father's attention was elsewhere. That was the year John Diefenbaker was elected prime minister, the year after Robert Stanfield had become premier of Nova Scotia and the year before

Duff Roblin would become premier of Manitoba. For the next decade, through the federal leadership convention of 1967, Camp's life was consumed by Tory politics. Michael grew up not expecting a great deal of attention from either parent. Something of a loner, like his father, Michael seemed content to be ignored. "They weren't the kind of parents who showed up on visitors' day," he said. "I didn't expect them to, or really want them to. I was also a solitary kind of person, happy to have my own life."[17] According to his brother David, "Michael has his own private interests, which he pursues very intently. He never wanted to get into any kind of situation where he felt like he was carrying a torch that had been passed to him by Dad. It's not an easy thing to carry."[18]

A conventional father who had important thoughts to impart to his 18-year-old son before sending him off to school in Europe would probably have sat the lad down for a man-to-man talk. But when David Camp went off to Switzerland in 1968 for his final year of high school at Neuchatel Junior College, his father could not bring himself to discuss personal matters face to face. It was reminiscent of the time, 25 years earlier, when he had struggled to find the courage to ask George Atkins for permission to marry his daughter Linda. Rather than talk to David, he wrote him a letter—"so we will not need to have a conversation, which is not always satisfactory"—with instructions that he not open it until he was aboard the ship that would take him to Europe. Filling five typed pages, it was a remarkable letter.

"The first son is a special person to a father, who will watch him grow and look for his own reflection and likenesses," Camp wrote. "Therefore, when I say that I see in you a good deal of myself, it could be that all fathers do, and probably all fathers are right. It is the same seed, after all." But he wanted David to be a better version of himself:

> I do not want you to run away from things you do not like, or condemn things you do not understand. Whatever you do, wherever you go, you will find it largely that way. God knows the world needs people who will ask questions, resist authoritarianism, challenge mythology,

but a hell of a lot of protest is really self-pity, a form of ducking the issue. If you know it to be wrong, don't pretend it isn't, and if you don't know it to be wrong, don't pretend, either. I'm talking about vulgarity, cruelty, selfishness and plain bad manners.

He told his son to retain his personal pride and respect, and to take care of himself:

You've got a healthy animal body. It has always had a certain amount of discipline, which you have imposed on it. Don't let it impose on you.... Smoke, and you become a walking ashtray. Booze, and your liver sucks in alcohol and squeezes out acid. Gorge, and you become a walking stomach, all gut and tissue. If I had to do it all over again, I would never put anything through my lungs other than air. I took [smoking] up in the army, out of desperate boredom, repressed by the lack of women or any other sort of action. My experience with liquor is perhaps better—I started very slowly, found my level of tolerance, never drank alone, never denied that I enjoyed it and have always been confident I could handle it. But it's a judgment call—one you have to make yourself....

I have never tried whores. Pride. A woman had to be clean, to begin with, and non-professional. Why pay for a knothole? Why kid about sex? I suspect you have imposed yourself on a few girls; transient with you, traumatic for them, unless they are compulsive—and who needs that? Just don't kid yourself about it. Permissiveness and the emancipation of girls and the sexual revolution—hip, hip, hooray. But little girls are scarred for life, or little boys find themselves at the altar ahead of their time (how now, free spirit?), or there is sex without love, which is body without soul, heat without light, knowledge without understanding, all unspeakably dreary.

The qualities he had admired most among the young men of his age, Camp said, were courage and cool:

People do not carry signs saying, "I'm Brave," but you know them soon enough. The Kennedy definition—"grace under pressure"—sums it up. What it really means is not the guts of a guy who suddenly gets up and machine-guns 20 Huns and takes the trench for the Allies and General Haig, but a guy who gets up every morning, faces the sun, washes his face and teeth and sails into life. So that at night he has nothing to hide from, no fears to take under his blanket with him.

When Connie, the next oldest child and the one Camp thought was "timid and afraid," went off to school in Switzerland a year later, he also wrote down his thoughts for her— "at least they will be easier read than said." But the father-daughter letter was quite unlike the father-son letter to David. There was no mention of smoking, booze or sex:

> I am thinking what sort of advice I can give you, because a father, as you know, has been a boy but has never been a girl, and the advice he is inclined to give a girl is the result of having been a boy, which is not very satisfactory because it mostly begins with "Don't" and "Be careful" and other protective adjurations, which are well meant but not very helpful.
>
> Anyway, you will be reasonably careful and you won't try speed or hang out the windows of moving trains. But you will take time to look at things; really see things so that when you shut your eyes, they are still there. And explore people, who can be like mirrors to yourself— find out what they think and feel and patiently develop that special awareness you have of other people, which sometimes makes you uncomfortable. . . .
>
> Look people in the eye—find the eye colour of everyone you encounter—and be candid, direct and honest with yourself. . . . Maybe you are not like I am, but I have found that people can be disarmed by simple candour, especially people who are themselves desperately playing a part as something they are not.

However unconventional he may have seemed to his children as they were growing up, Camp felt paternal pride at how well they turned out. Gail, a film and television producer. David, a lawyer specializing in aboriginal issues. Connie, a journalist. Cherie, a singer, songwriter and actor. Michael, a broadcaster. And Christopher, a student of international law. Camp made sure they all had a good education. He taught them to love language, to care about the world and to chart their own course in life. After that, he left them free to do it their own way. And they did, without trading on the Camp name.

CHAPTER 18

The Writer

T HE YEAR 1968 WAS A YEAR of upheaval and change around the world. In Vietnam, it was the year of the massive Tet offensive, when 70,000 North Vietnamese soldiers launched what proved to be one of the greatest campaigns in military history, dooming American hopes of victory or even peace with dignity. In Czechoslovakia, the euphoria of the "Prague Spring" gave way to the reality of Soviet tanks as Moscow moved to crush the attempt by the new Czech leader, Alexander Dubcek, to reconcile Marxism with personal liberty—"socialism with a human face," they called it. Riots by workers and students paralyzed France and nearly top-pled Charles de Gaulle (he would resign as president of the Fifth Republic the following year). In the United States, 1968 brought the assassinations of Martin Luther King and Robert Kennedy, bloody riots in the black ghettos of major cities, and waves of anti-Vietnam protest that pushed Lyndon Johnson from the White House and sparked violent protests at the Democratic party con-vention in Chicago.

Even Canada—peaceful, tranquil Canada—felt the winds of change. A new separatist party, the Parti Québécois, was born in Quebec under the leadership of a charismatic former Liberal, René Lévesque. In Ottawa, the governing Liberal party, a determinedly risk-averse party in normal times, rolled the dice and bet its future on an exciting stranger, Pierre Elliott Trudeau. Trudeau promptly did what no Liberal had done since Louis St. Laurent in 1953—he led his party to a majority government as he engaged the imagina-tions of Canadians, especially the young.

For Dalton Camp, 1968 was also a pivotal year, a year of reflec-tion, renewal and change. Resigning as national president of the Tory party, he chose a new career path. No longer would he be an adman and politician who dabbled in journalism; henceforth, he would be first and foremost a writer and commentator. Queen's University eased his transition by awarding him a Skelton Clark Fellowship for the 1968–69 academic year. For Camp, it was the equivalent of a sabbatical; he spent most of his year on campus at Queen's—reading, thinking about great issues, meeting students and writing the manuscript that would be published in 1970 as *Gentlemen, Players and Politicians*. He would eventually publish four books, but *GPP* was his best by far. A brilliantly crafted account of his early experiences in politics (ending with the election of the Diefenbaker government in 1957), it may be, as his friend British Columbia judge Nancy Morrison described it, "the finest political book ever written in this country."[1]

He also set about getting his body in shape that year. In the Toronto advertising world, he said, "I got into the martini culture.... It wasn't a myth about advertising, people did drink a lot of martinis. It was a rite, a ritual thing. I got quite attached to that lifestyle for a long time." Ironically, it was Pierre Trudeau and his example of physical fitness that finally prodded Camp into doing something about his own flabby, hard-drinking, heavy-smoking self. "Trudeau only impressed me in one way," he told oral history archivist Janet Toole in a 1998 interview for the New Brunswick Provincial Archives. "He was an inspiration to me, probably helped save my life." Trudeau was a year older than Camp, but he was in splendid condition, while Camp could feel himself beginning to fall apart.

"Too much self-indulgence," he said, "too many bad habits: smoking, drinking, late hours, the tension.... I began to treat it as a badge of honour, when it was not that at all. But after he became prime minister, I started seriously to look after myself, to turn my life around." He stopped smoking, for a while at least. He cut back on his alcohol intake, even to the point of declining when people offered him a drink. And he started running—"I thought, 'That son of a bitch is not going to grow young while I grow old. I'll keep up with him.' I admired him for his discipline."[2]

When he was not running to keep up with Trudeau—and Camp managed to knock off 25 pounds in 1968—he worked on his writing. One way he did it was by keeping a daily journal. Before his eldest son, David, left Canada at the end of the summer of 1968 to spend a year at school in Switzerland, he and his father agreed to take the time each day to type a page or half-page of news and thoughts. "So much of writing a journal is like running up and down a hill; it trains the mind in concentration, sharpens the vocabulary, tests the capacity for expression—and, of course, imposes a discipline on the writer," Camp wrote. He was not shy about his own talent: "I write better than most, having, I suppose, a superior vocabulary, a remarkable, and dangerous, talent for imitation of styles, and a sense of irony, humour and satire."[3]

Once a week, roughly, each would mail his pages off to the other. Dalton's journal offers a fascinating glimpse of a middle-aged man in transition in terms of career, interests, lifestyle and perception of the world around him. He wrote about visiting his mother, David's grandmother, Aurilla Camp, at her home in Woodstock, New Brunswick:

> Poor Mother. The world continues to conspire against her: the grocer overcharges, people steal her flowers, loot her garden. Animals burrow under the house, children break windows with batted balls, the stores in Woodstock do not have what she wants, doctors cannot be trusted. But she carries on, always in command, always right, always afraid, always certain that nothing can be done. I do not know where this strain comes from in the family. Or is it old age? God knows, but I hope the gene has passed my children by.... She will fight progress all the way, throw herself under the wheels, sabotage the works, in order to prove her pessimism well founded.[4]

Camp tried to reassure his 18-year-old son, who found himself going bald, like his father:

> What to say to a son who fears he will be maimed by a father's inheritance? Possibly only that everything works out for the best—including hair. During my hair-fetish period, I recall that it seemed to me that the most beautiful belles might be beyond my grasp. Now, whenever I return to alumni meetings of one kind or another and see the once-beautiful belles, I recognize the psychological disadvantages of a standard "good looks" à la Hollywood. The poor things are today faded, dumpy, lined—and just as dumb as ever, but no longer able to coast on

their physical assets. My [Linda] puts them all in the shade, in the figure, form, conversation and class department. When I think how I
might have married Rosemary Snade, the Queen of the Campus, 1940!
God is good.[5]

He told David about his nervousness about spending $94,000 for
a house in Lawrence Park in Toronto:

> I despise mortgages and having to pause, even for that small second,
> when I want to enjoy something and ask myself: "But can I afford it?"
> Now I shall have to. The trail goes back to my childhood, of course.
> My father's death—suddenly we were poor and in debt and thrown
> upon the world. And there are two decades of poverty, a despairing sur-
> render to life, and only DKC [Dalton] manages to claw his way back;
> the rest of the family remains behind, lost in limbo, with their past and
> their dreams. Now a home on which the taxes are higher than my
> salary when I first came to Toronto and went to work at J. Walter
> Thompson.[6]

Recounting a debate he had with Lester Pearson at Queen's, he
described his impressions of the former prime minister (and demonstrated that old animosities do not fade away):

> Pearson is 72 and shows it, although I detect beneath that bland exte-
> rior a streak of petulance, vanity and a sort of spoiled-child
> disposition. And he is a man who had surprisingly little to offer, other
> than extraordinary luck and a diplomatic charm, and he was a failure
> as a statesman.... But the Liberal establishment now wants to paper
> over his record, gild him with white paint and raise him to a pedestal
> in history.[7]

Camp, a sports fan, told David how he felt when the Soviets
clobbered Canada in hockey:

> I sometimes become enraged by Canadian apathy and mediocrity.
> Hockey players are pitiful anyway, spending their learning and enrich-
> ing years scrambling about on ice rinks, plotting empty, brutish lives
> for themselves. As baseball dies of old age and boredom, hockey will be
> next.[8]

And he reminisced about the long days and short nights of his
years in politics:

I go [to the hotel] by taxi, enter the lobby to the sound of the night bellman vacuuming the rugs—how many times have I heard that sound in the early hours of the morning? The desk clerk looks at me with his blank, colourless face peering over the grill. At night, the lobby smells of dust, rancid air and stale smoke, and the night staff are like zombies, lurking behind their cages or bent over the humming vacuum cleaner, and I have never heard them speak.[9]

Although Camp prized his 1968–69 journal—he talked of keeping it in a safety deposit box—he made no effort to have it published. It was not his only unpublished work. He tried his hand at short stories, giving some of them as gifts to Linda when they lived in London during his year at the London School of Economics. On the title page of one of them, "See Venice and Die," he wrote a note that would have been appropriate for his other short stories as well: "The beginning is deadly—too slow—character identification is vague."

He wrote poetry and made an attempt at a stage play. Although he refused to read fiction, maintaining it was a waste of time, he wanted to prove that he could write it, and he made a stab at two or three different novels. He completed—or nearly completed—one of them, a novel that was a curious and confusing amalgam of a passionate love affair and petty political manoeuvring. His friend Finlay MacDonald read it and advised him not to give up his day job.

What Camp could do—and did superbly in *Gentlemen, Players and Politicians*—was write about real politics: the sort of politics he had lived, observed, breathed and played for years. As a hockey player, Wayne Gretzky had a genius for being able to see the whole ice, to anticipate how the action was going to unfold before it happened. Camp did not play hockey, but he did play bridge—he played it extremely well—and he brought similar skills to his political analysis. He could see and understand the entire competition as it played out before him; he usually knew what was going to happen next, and why—sometimes before the players themselves knew.

In *GPP*, he combined that perspective and intuition with some beautiful writing to create a book that is a joy to read. Although most of the characters he portrays are dead and gone, and the battles they fought are largely forgotten, GPP remains fresh; its insights into the political game are as relevant today as they were when Camp wrote the book at Queen's in 1968–69.

Some of the scenes are memorable. The first page of the book presents this remarkable word picture of Liberal Prime Minister Mackenzie King near the end of his long career:

A pale, colourless, little man, clad in the aura of indestructibility, moves slowly down the centre aisle, his inscrutable, featureless face as familiar as a worn five-cent piece, like an animated icon whose eyes emit refracted glints of secret pleasures, cynicism, and wisdom.... Then he has gone, retired to the vaulted, hidden labyrinth of power, the big room seems emptier and darker, as though he had come and taken away the essence of the day.

There was this description of polling day in rural Nova Scotia:

On election day clouds of dust hung over the country roads as the cars of competing political parties hustled from house to house, hauling out their vote, bargaining, bartering, and buying the poor and recalcitrant. These men, consumed by their partisan pride and fervour, compulsively rendered meaningless the fundamental purpose of their restless energy, which was to maintain a party system by allowing the free choice of free men as to who should govern them.[10]

And this assessment of the political process:

[P]olitics is a wasteland of aborted intentions and rusting, failed enterprise. It is a grand design, fashioned by amateurs and novices, as well as by experienced professionals. In its circuitry is the complex imprint of many minds and judgments, and a good deal of caprice and luck. Somehow men are drawn to working on it with love, hate, and tireless fascination and, if they are wise, they come to see it as a life process of trial and error, triumph and defeat, elation and despair, and faith and experience, and it is unwise not to recognize its ongoing, epic personality.[11]

While he was writing Gentlemen, Players and Politicians, Camp became interested in television as a serious sideline. He had done TV work in the past, but it was mainly as an interviewee, a panelist in political discussions, or—as in the case of the tumultuous Democratic convention in Chicago—an interviewer. In November 1968, producer Warner Troyer invited Camp to become co-host and program consultant on the CTV network's flagship public affairs program, *W-FIVE*. Camp accepted with misgivings. "I am afraid the present format has already had its time," he wrote. "It lacks depth and constantly courts frivolity and titillation; more important, it lacks personality.... I am left to ask myself why they want me, and what they expect I will bring to their program. God knows."[12]

He enjoyed his experience and his colleagues at CTV. *W-FIVE* did well, garnering more favourable reviews than its competition, *The Way It Is*, on CBC. Camp's doubts deepened, however: "It is strange, all of this; I have the feeling that CTV has very high hopes for me in television and I have no idea whether they are right, what it is based on, or how I am doing. It is a morosely subjective experience." His insight into the nature of television is as valid today as it was when he wrote it in 1968: "My own secret view...is that the medium runs too fast over too shallow shoals for me to survive in it. It is not really a medium for words, but for images; not for depth, but for lightning."[13]

Camp's ability to keep many balls in the air was never more evident than it was that year at Queen's. He was writing a book, as well as magazine articles and book reviews, commuting to Toronto to co-host the weekly television program, mentoring students, making speeches, travelling to Ottawa from time to time (he advised Robert Stanfield on personnel for the opposition leader's office) and helping out occasionally in his advertising agency. (Camp Associates lost the Manitoba government tourism account after Camp refused to commit himself to direct the next election campaign for the provincial Tories, but he pitched in to save the Nova Scotia account.) Meanwhile, he was also writing his newspaper column.

Camp had become a regular columnist for the Toronto *Telegram* in 1966; prior to that, he had written sporadically for the *Tely*, essentially as a spokesman for the Conservative party. Following the suicide of his friend George Hogan, the *Telegram* invited Camp to take Hogan's place as a once-a-week political columnist. Camp accepted and—with the exception of a two-and-a-half year hiatus while he worked in the Prime Minister's Office in the 1980s and a few other brief interruptions—he would be a newspaper columnist for the rest of his life. He knew his place in the panoply of *Tely* writers, and his Monday columns for that paper in the 1960s bore little resemblance to the graceful pieces he would write in later years for the *Star*. Anthony Westell, writing in the *Star* in 1969, was not impressed by Camp's work in the *Tely*, describing it, not inaccurately, as "a newspaper column of sour and spiteful comment." Camp made no apologies: "When I was writing for *The Telegram*, much of the stuff I wrote was supportive of my party and meant to be so. It had been [publisher John] Bassett's purpose to open his pages to unbridled partisan comment, from identifiable partisans—Liberal, NDP, or Tory. For me, it was like writing years ago for the *Liberal Review*."[14]

His first weekly column for the *Telegram*, written while he was still national president of the Tory party, was a savage assault on the Liberal justice minister of the day, Lucien Cardin, for making an issue of John Diefenbaker's handling of the Munsinger sex-and-security scandal when he had been prime minister. Camp questioned Cardin's sanity before thundering: "Now that the decent customs and traditions of politics have been violated, the copy book stained, the reputations of men cast in doubt, their families terrorized, and the confidence of Canadians in their government damaged beyond repair, who will set all these wrongs right?"[15]

Camp might have mentioned, but did not, that Cardin had blurted out Gerda Munsinger's name (initially, he called her "Monsignor") in the House of Commons only after he had been goaded beyond endurance over an unrelated security case by Diefenbaker, who, as Camp well knew, had a nasty penchant for baiting French Canadian ministers.

His progression from polemicist to analyst was a slow one. "He evolved as a writer and as a wordsmith," observed *Star* publisher John Honderich. "His early [*Star*] columns were all right, but he had not in any way developed into the magician with words that he became. One of the great delights to me was always his writing ability. He raised the level. He had a real signature style toward the end."[16]

His daughter Connie, also a journalist, thought it was her father's life experience as much as his writing ability that raised the level of his work. "He had credentials. He had experience outside newspapers, and he knew what he was writing about," she said. She noted a significant difference between her father and most other journalists. "After those years in politics, he knew the country, which I'm not sure every journalist does. He was proud of that," she continued. "And he cared about history, and I think that often he found journalists in general to be people who didn't know their country and didn't know history beyond a few years back."[17]

Camp may have been peddling the official party line in his years with the *Telegram*, but he did not lose his Red Tory instincts. When the Trudeau government proclaimed the War Measures Act in October 1970, contending that it needed extraordinary powers to deal with the FLQ crisis in Quebec, Camp was one of the few commentators—the *Globe and Mail*'s George Bain, whom Camp admired greatly, was another—to call the prime minister to account. "How long?" he asked. "In the rhetoric of the moment, we will keep the troops in Montreal, the politicians under guard, the enemy in jail, and the country in a paroxysm of patriotism until hell freezes over, or until the 'apprehended insurrection' has been fully apprehended. But it is rhetoric and not resolve. I hope the prime minister realizes how fragile this present state of mind really is...."[18]

When Bassett decided to fold his money-losing newspaper in 1971, Camp looked around for another outlet. Friends urged him to go the *Globe*. In light of what he would evolve into as a columnist—the commonsense voice of moderate conservatism—the centre-right *Globe* would have been a more natural home than the *Star*, which flaunted its liberal and Liberal convictions. But the *Globe* was not interested—"Dalton Camp will never write for the *Globe and Mail*," an editor said when approached by a friend on

Camp's behalf. That suited Camp, or so he maintained—"I found a number of those with high titles at the *Globe* to be pompous bores and full of themselves." He was, however, invited to have lunch with the newspaper's publisher. After lunch, Camp thanked the publisher, whom he did not name, for spending so much time with "the humble president of an advertising agency." Placing a hand on his guest's shoulder, the publisher confided, "Mr. Camp, all newspaper publishers are whores."[19] It was an observation that Camp, no lover of the corporate elite, could endorse.

At the suggestion of Val Sears, a veteran *Star* writer, Camp met with Martin Goodman, the paper's managing editor, who agreed to take his column on the condition that he increase its frequency to twice a week. He told Camp, wisely, that he would never establish himself as a columnist if he wrote only once a week.

He began his first career (of three) at the *Star* in November 1971 with a column about things he had observed during a weekend in Belfast. "The violence and tension that permeate this city and its half-million population defy either rational or precise description. Once exposed to it, even for a day or so, one comes to accept it, in a curiously passive way, as a continuing, observable aberration of human behaviour. Each day brings its measure of violence, the casualties reported, like the numbing recapitulation of traffic accidents, in the media."[20]

It was a deceptively calm beginning to what was, at times, a difficult relationship. Camp was constantly irritated by the way the newspaper "covered its ankles" by running a disclaimer with his column identifying him as a former president of the Conservative party and, later, as a former senior adviser to the Mulroney government. Although he could often be moody and difficult, his editors did not always handle him well or give him the respect he thought he deserved.

The relationship snapped when, in the last days of the 1980 election campaign, Camp's antipathy toward Trudeau collided with the *Star's* editorial commitment to support the return of the former prime minister and the defeat of his Tory usurper, Joe Clark. Camp wrote a very tough—but not unfair—column in which he took

Liberal campaign organizers to task for their strategy of keeping Trudeau out of the sight of the public and the press (the strategy, which would become known as "low-bridging the leader," was extremely effective). He called the Liberal campaign "one of the most cynical, manipulative, and wantonly irresponsible in our history." Trudeau, he added, was running "what is presumably his last campaign as though he were a frightened Richard Nixon."[21]

That was too much for the liberal *Star*. It spiked the column. Camp and an editor had (uncivil) words. He quit and switched immediately to the tabloid *Toronto Sun*, which hailed his arrival by gleefully publishing "The Column the *Star* Would Not Run."

The *Sun*, which prided itself on its lunch-pail readership, was further to the right than the *Star* was to the left, making it an even less comfortable fit for Camp's Red Tory views. Although Camp wrote for the *Sun* for three years, his columns never achieved the influence they were beginning to have in the *Star*; the *Sun* was simply the wrong vehicle for anything approximating intelligent political discourse.

Camp left the *Sun* after another of its writers wrote a column that attacked Red Tories, dismissed Camp as being senile and claimed he was feeding at the public trough. Although *Sun* publisher Douglas Creighton acknowledged that the attack had gone too far, Camp packed up his column and went back to the *Star*, which hired him to write three columns a week (later reduced to two) and gave him a written assurance that, henceforth, editors would not make changes in his copy without prior consultation.

He wrote for the *Star* until the fall of 1986, when he accepted Brian Mulroney's offer of a job in Ottawa as a senior deputy minister; although he was on the payroll of the Privy Council Office, he worked in the Prime Minister's Office as policy adviser to Mulroney. After he left the government's employ in 1989, he returned to the *Star* and stayed there until his death in 2002, interrupting his service only long enough to have a heart transplant in 1993. He eventually managed to persuade the *Star* to drop the disclaimer he so resented.

He became the most popular columnist at the largest newspaper in the country, and through the *Star* syndicate, his column was picked up by newspapers from Nova Scotia to British Columbia. His column had influence. Everyone in Ottawa who cared about politics followed Dalton Camp. Liberal Prime Minister Jean Chrétien started reading him in the mid-1980s and quickly became a regular reader and an admirer. "He was a man of ideas. And he was not an ideologue," Chrétien said. "...He was a gentleman.... He was a great, great Canadian. I was a secret fan."[22]

He and Denise Morrison, the editorial board assistant who was his principal contact at the *Star*, became good friends. Because Camp would not use a computer, she made sure his column was legible when it arrived by facsimile machine and, when it was not, she retyped it or took it down over the phone. She loved every word he ever wrote. On one visit to the newspaper, Camp forgot the Harvard baseball cap he had been wearing. "I used to wear it when I typed his columns," Morrison said. "I just liked the way it smelled, because it reminded me of him. I wouldn't say I was in love with him; because of the age difference [of nearly 40 years], it would have been silly. But I simply adored him, and he adored me."

Morrison was also in charge of the letters to the editor, and Camp, she said, drew more mail than any other *Star* columnist; most of it was complimentary.[23]

Celebrity, however, has its limits in the Canadian newspaper business, especially at the *Star*, which was always regarded as more of an "editors' paper" than a "writers' paper" (such as the *Globe*). The *Star* treated Camp reasonably well financially—by the end he had slowly worked his pay up to $1,050 for each of two columns per week, or a little better than $100,000 a year. That was more than any other *Star* freelance columnist was paid, though it was less than some high profile, if less accomplished, columnists were making at other publications in town. And when he travelled to political events, he, unlike *Star* staff writers, was expected to pay his own way.

Some of his friends felt the *Star* did not do enough to promote Camp among readers or to acknowledge his importance to the paper. He felt like a stranger whenever he visited the newspaper's offices at One Yonge Street in Toronto. On one occasion, Denise Morrison took him on a tour of the newsroom. Camp was pleased, and the staff seemed genuinely delighted to have a chance to meet the man they had been reading in their own pages for so many years—or had been listening to on CBC Radio's *Morningside* program with fellow panelists Eric Kierans and Stephen Lewis. Camp and Morrison developed a tradition of having a Christmas lunch each year; they would go to a good restaurant, drink good wine and talk for hours—but it was Camp, not the *Star*, who picked up the tab.

The columns he wrote over the years for the *Telegram*, *Sun* and *Star* total roughly two and a half million words. His magazine articles, book reviews and books would add something close to one million more words, bringing the output of a prolific writing career to well over three million words—the equivalent of 30-plus full-length books.

It is an imposing legacy. Daily journalism tends to be highly perishable, its best-before date about 10 minutes after the paper lands on a subscriber's doorstep. Most of Camp's columns fall into this category; they ceased to be of interest once the issue or event that prompted them faded from the public ken. But some of his writing has stood the test of time because of his perception, insight and grace with the English language. He also knew how to turn a phrase, to come up with a memorable observation or a stinging putdown.

As often as not as the years passed, some of his most trenchant lines were aimed at his old friends on the political right. On the "Neanderthal wing" in the Tory caucus: "You cannot argue with stupidity, someone said, you can only pity it. And one can only pity the mental squalor of those few Tories in Parliament who shouted down a motion moved by the NDP member from Regina East to mark the death of John Lennon, gunned down outside his New York office building."[24]

On the influence of corporate interests and corporate money on the political process: "Among the fruits of this bitter harvest were the emergence of George W. Bush and Stockwell Day, each grown from the same sour soil of a virtual democracy, nourished by voracious self-interest and an idiot's simplistic ideology."[25]

On Joe Clark's (successful) 1979 election campaign strategy: "Had slavery been an issue, the Tories would have fudged it."[26]

Ouch!

CHAPTER 19

Stopping Spadina

A N ELECTION WAS COMING; everyone knew that when William Grenville Davis, the newly installed premier of Ontario, rose in the legislature on June 3, 1971, to deliver the most important speech of his political career. It was the speech in which he would attempt to chart a new direction, to put his own imprint on the provincial government and to give the Conservative party the momentum it would need to extend its unbroken skein of 28 years in power in Canada's biggest and richest province.

As Davis began to speak—"Mr. Speaker: I should like to inform the House of the government's decision in the matter of the William R. Allen (Spadina) Expressway"—a small, bald man listened intently, virtually unnoticed, in a seat in the Speaker's Gallery. Dalton Camp was the author of that seminal speech—a speech in which Davis would override the wishes of Toronto's municipal politicians and of many members of his own caucus, risk the ire of tens of thousands of suburban commuters, and incur the rage of the Toronto *Star* by announcing that the government, his government, had decided to stop the construction of the Spadina Expressway.

For Camp, the Spadina speech was one of the two most important he had ever written—the other being his own Albany Club speech in May 1966 when he launched his campaign to review the federal leadership of John Diefenbaker. Like the Albany Club speech, the Spadina speech was gracefully written and balanced.

"We are fully aware," Davis read, "that our decision will represent not a judgment upon the past, but a decision upon which policies for the future will be built.... We must make a decision as to whether we are trying to build a transportation system to serve the automobile, or one which will best serve people."

In the past, there would have been no doubt about that decision.

For nearly three decades, successive Tory governments had paid obeisance to the automobile, building highways to service commerce and commuters with scant regard for the degradation that unbridled highway construction wreaked on the quality of life in the province's cities. Debate over the Spadina Expressway had raged for several years between the city people who lived and played in the central part of Toronto and the suburban people who wanted to drive through (or over) those neighbourhoods to reach their jobs downtown. The expressway was already under construction in 1971. If continued, it would have destroyed parks and ravines and cut into the heart of the University of Toronto—but that had seemed to Spadina's proponents to be a small price to pay for the convenience of a fast trip downtown.

The key paragraph in the text that Camp wrote encapsulated this issue. "If we are building a transportation system to serve the automobile, the Spadina Expressway would be a good place to start," Davis said. "But if we are building a transportation system to serve people, the Spadina Expressway is a good place to stop. It is our determination to opt for the latter."

It was just three sentences, but they had more impact than three dozen speeches or conferences of urban planners could have had. They sent the signal Camp wanted Davis to put before the people of Ontario: this was a new government, with new approaches, new priorities and a new attitude.

A case can be made that the Spadina decision did more for Davis and the Ontario Tories than it did for the people of Toronto and environs. True, the expressway was stopped in its tracks. But the speech also promised to help commuters get out of their cars with a new emphasis on, and new provincial funding for, mass transit. The Davis government's execution failed to live up to the promise. The era of major subway construction in Toronto ground to a halt on Davis's watch. Traffic congestion worsened dramatically; three decades after the fact, frustrated commuters from the bedroom suburbs still cursed the decision to stop the Spadina. Transportation and traffic congestion, of course, were not Camp's concern when he wrote the speech in June 1971. His sole concern was to position Davis and the party for the election that would follow in the fall—and the Spadina speech did that very nicely.

I ronically, it was a speech that Davis nearly did not get an opportunity to deliver. After being the heir apparent to John Robarts for the better part of a decade, he came perilously close to blowing the coronation. If just 23 delegates—out of 1,580 voting on the frantic final ballot at the Tory leadership convention in February 1971—had gone the other way, the premier of Ontario would have been Allan Lawrence, not Bill Davis.

To understand what almost went wrong, it is necessary to go back to the period following the 1968 federal election and the unhappy situation in which Camp's friends, the Spades, found themselves. The Spades were disheartened by the election of Pierre Trudeau's majority Liberal government in June 1968. They had worked hard to elect Camp in Don Valley riding in that election, and were discouraged when he lost, badly. They shared his sense of grievance when Robert Stanfield distanced himself from Camp in a futile attempt to assuage the Diefenbaker rump of the national party. And they were distressed by what they interpreted as Camp's loss of interest in politics—and in them—as he turned his focus to writing during his 1968–69 fellowship at Queen's University. Camp understood their unhappiness. "I have turned away from my old friends, the Spades," he wrote in his journal on November 14, 1968. "I am using Queen's as an excuse to duck responsibility."

In 1970, however, the Spades were re-energized when it became apparent that Robarts, premier since 1961 and the most powerful Conservative in the land, was preparing to retire from public life. There would be a race, a leadership convention, a candidate to work for and a campaign to be plotted and executed. The Spades were ready to return to action.

They met at Don Guthrie's house in Toronto to survey the field of probable candidates. Roy McMurtry was strongly in favour of his old friend Davis, who doubled as minister of education and minister of university affairs in the Robarts cabinet. Camp told the meeting he, too, felt committed to Davis, because of Davis's support during the 1966 leadership review battle. He had known and liked Davis for 10 years, since they worked together on Robert Macaulay's campaign for the Ontario leadership in 1961; Davis managed that campaign, while Camp handled the advertising and promotion, advised on strategy and helped Macaulay stay within his $75,000 budget by running his mailings to delegates through the postage meter at his ad agency.[1] Among the Spades, Guthrie alone favoured Lawrence, the minister of Northern affairs, whom he had known since university. The rest seemed inclined to follow Camp's lead.

The Davis people, however, rebuffed the Spades' overture, in effect telling them, "Thanks, but we don't need you." There were a couple of reasons. The first was that, while the Spades were eager to enter the fray, Davis himself was unwilling to make even the slightest move until Robarts had publicly announced his decision to retire. "What you have to understand is, Davis's interest in anything had an overlay of procrastination. He turned procrastination into a goddamned science," said his long-time aide Clare Westcott.[2] The other reason was never spelled out, but it did not need to be. "It was because of the Diefenbaker thing," Roy McMurtry said. Some of Davis's handlers were as nervous as Duff Roblin's handlers had been at the time of the 1967 federal leadership campaign that any overt association with Camp would alienate former supporters of John Diefenbaker, of whom there were still many in rural Ontario. "These [Davis] people, quite understandably, said, 'Bill Davis is going to have a coronation for the leadership,'" McMurtry remembered. "So their attitude was, 'Why be associated with the Camp team?'"[3]

McMurtry was irritated by the attitude of the Davis group, but he supported his friend anyway; suffering from serious back trouble that laid him up for three months, he ended up playing a peripheral role in the campaign. The other Spades—like horseplayers who are miserable if they do not have a horse to back in any race that is being run—had no desire to sit out the leadership campaign. If they could not have the candidate they wanted, they would go for a candidate who wanted them. So they cast their lot with Lawrence. Norman Atkins ran his campaign, and Camp provided the strategy and the speeches, replicating the modern, high-powered organization they had assembled for Stanfield in 1967.

They came within a political eyelash of pulling it off. With a better campaign, Davis might have won on the first ballot. As it was, he had to battle through four ballots before he finally defeated Lawrence by 812 votes to 768. "The irony of it was, the fallout of the Diefenbaker battle nearly cost Bill Davis the leadership," McMurtry said.

One of the canniest politicians of his time, Davis did not make the same mistake twice. After the convention, McMurtry called him and said, "You'd better get the Lawrence people. You're going to need them.... We'd better get them on side."[4] Davis agreed. With McMurtry acting as the connector between the two organizations, they set up a meeting at the National Club in Toronto and invited five or six key players from each team. (Camp himself did not attend that meeting.) At first, they barely spoke to one another. Davis, however, made a strong speech. "He hit all the right chords," Atkins recalled. "He started out by saying the convention was over but the campaign was just beginning. And he took it from there."[5] Afterward, Davis, McMurtry and Atkins went out for a late-night drink. Davis and Atkins hit it off. The leader asked him to run the election campaign and offered key positions to other Lawrence workers. "They were pros," Davis remembered. "Norman was on side within 10 minutes of being asked."[6]

As it happened, Atkins had an organizational plan ready to go—one that he and Malcolm Wickson, the national director of the party, had decided to put together after the loss of the 1968 federal election. The first opportunity to try it out was in Ontario, and it worked brilliantly as the Tories won 78 of the 117 legislature seats in the October 1971 election. It was the birth of what journalist Claire Hoy would dub "The Big Blue Machine"—and it would produce four consecutive election wins for the Davis government. Atkins and Davis grew as close as Camp and Stanfield had been in happier times; each became the other's biggest fan.

The Big Blue Machine was Atkins's baby. Giving priority to his journalism, Camp did not involve himself in the organization, although he did occasionally join Atkins and the others at their Tuesday morning breakfast meetings at the Park Plaza Hotel, just up the street from Queen's Park. His involvement in the 1971 campaign was primarily through a one-on-one relationship with Davis. He developed strategy. He helped the premier work his way through some thorny issues, including perennial questions involving the organization and funding of the province's Catholic separate school system, which Roberts had cheerfully left on his successor's plate. And Camp advised Davis both on the Spadina decision itself and on ways to sell that decision to the caucus and to the people of Ontario.

David Camp, Dalton's eldest son and a university student at the time, remembered his father coming home one night with a file on the Spadina Expressway controversy. He asked his son what he thought Bill Davis should do. "I don't think I was of very much help to him, because I didn't know very much about it," David said. "He had something else to do that night, and he handed me the file, and said, 'Why don't you take a look at this, and tell me what you think?' And I was busy, or I wasn't diligent, or I didn't realize it was urgent, and I put it aside. He came down to my room and grabbed the file back later that night." Camp got up early the next morning and started typing at 6:30; by the time David crawled out of bed at eight o'clock, his father was heading out the door, the finished speech in hand. "What impressed me," David said, "was that he was able to get up at 6:30 in the morning, take the file, settle in front of the typewriter, and write a six-, eight-, ten-page speech, which was so important to Davis and his prospect for re-election, which was so beautifully written and which so impressed the media." David added with a laugh, "It's as though he'd spent a week at a seminar with city planners, or with Jane Jacobs or someone like that."[7]

Camp was never what in baseball would be described as an everyday player on the Davis team. He was more of a designated hitter, brought in from time to time over the years to provide strategic advice on specific issues—such as the battle over plans, eventually aborted, to build a second major Toronto airport near Pickering, east of the city; to help with policy—including the line

Davis would take at the 1971 Victoria constitutional conference; and to plot the selling of the Davis government's messages to the news media. "He was a comfort to be with," Davis said. "He didn't get excited and all the rest of it; he was a very stable person. And, of course, I think he enjoyed the relationship, too. I think he enjoyed it partially because it ultimately worked."[8]

Camp undertook two ambitious projects. The first was the Ontario Royal Commission on Book Publishing, of which Camp was one of three commissioners—the others being author/lawyer Richard Rohmer, who was the chairman, and Marsh Jeanneret, of the University of Toronto Press. The royal commission was actually established just before the transition from Robarts to Davis; it continued its work under the new premier and brought in its final report at the end of 1972.

It was created in response to one of the periodic crises that afflict the beleaguered Canadian book publishing business—McClelland and Stewart, the flagship of the Canadian industry, was either going broke or about to be sold to Americans (no one was quite sure which). Then, about a year into the commission's mandate, Davis became concerned by police reports that organized criminal elements from the United States were moving in on the wholesaling of magazines and paperback books in Ontario. He asked the royal commission to look into that issue, too.

The commission brought out the cultural nationalist in Camp. "The problems of publishing in this country are economic ones, but the importance of publishing in the life of Canada is cultural before it is anything else," the commission stated in its final report. "...[T]he Canadian book publishing industry simply makes too small a contribution to the gross national product for economic considerations to earn it any priority over many other fields of enterprise. But from the cultural standpoint, the fact that book publishing is the indispensable interface between Canadian authors and those who read their books places it squarely in the centre of our stage."[9]

Economic considerations, however, blunted the impact of the commission's 70 detailed recommendations; the government was not prepared to throw more money at the book business. In response to the commission's work, however, the Davis government did move to make it more difficult for American publishers to take over Canadian firms by setting up a procedure that required Canadian publishing houses to jump through several hoops before they could sell out to foreigners. And the commission's examination of magazine and paperback distribution resulted in legislation that blocked the mob's attempt to take over in Canada.

Camp's other project was to chair a three-member committee— the Commission on the Legislature, known as the Camp Commission—to examine the operations of the Ontario legislature, and especially the role of private members. With his fellow commissioners, Liberal Farquhar Oliver and New Democrat Douglas Fisher, Camp produced five reports that served as a blueprint for far-reaching reforms that would make the legislative branch independent of the cabinet and the entrenched bureaucracy. Taken together, the recommendations recognized that the job of an MLA was no longer a part-time occupation, as it had continued to be regarded long after Ontario had ceased to be an agricultural economy with short legislative sittings arranged around the planting and harvesting seasons.

The commission addressed members' salaries and benefits, the need for every member to have a secretary or personal assistant, funding for caucus research offices, the independence of the speaker of the legislature, establishment of a legislative internship program, and the financing of political parties and campaigns. Camp, the consummate strategist, was not content simply to make recommendations and leave it to the government to decide whether to accept, reject or ignore them. So rather than bring in one final report— which the government might shelve—he hit on the strategy of issuing multiple reports. "We'll produce not one, but five separate reports," he told the commission's executive secretary, Robert Fleming. "We'll only release a second report after the government acts on the first, and so on."

In the end, virtually all of the commission's principal recommendations were adopted—to Camp's great delight. When it issued its fourth report in early 1974, Camp declared: "The government has already acted on 95 per cent of the recommendations we've made—that's a pretty good batting average."

The work he did for Davis in the early years of his 14-year run as premier would have repercussions that Camp could never have anticipated. A dozen years later, in 1986—just two years after his landslide federal election—Brian Mulroney found himself floundering, his political honeymoon over. His government had lost whatever sense of direction it initially had. His ministers were making dumb mistakes. Nothing was working. The public was thoroughly disenchanted. The Tories slipped behind the Liberals in the polls in the summer of 1986, and they would soon find themselves trailing the New Democrats as well.[10]

Mulroney did not have to call a general election for at least another two years, but the trend was obviously going in the wrong direction. He needed help, and he needed it fast. Enter Bill Davis. Remembering the assistance Camp had given him on the Spadina Expressway and other issues, Davis recommended that Mulroney hire Camp, telling the prime minister, "Dalton would be a great asset in terms of helping to think through [strategy] or develop policy positions.[11]

Mulroney made the phone call to Camp, who agreed to join the Prime Minister's Office in Ottawa. It was, he told friends afterward, one of the greatest mistakes of his life.

CHAPTER 20

The Skunkworks

F<small>OR A MAN WHO WANTED</small> to devote himself to his writing, Dalton Camp found it uncommonly difficult to disentangle himself from political obligations. In addition to delivering two columns a week to the *Toronto Star*, by mid-1972 Camp was finishing up with the Ontario Royal Commission on Book Publishing and starting to work on his Commission on the Legislature when he began to feel pressure to return to the aid of the party in Ottawa.

The years between 1968 and 1972 had not gone well for Pierre Trudeau and the Liberal government. Trudeaumania had withered in the cold reality of governing. The government wasted its majority by undertaking too many schemes and seeing too few of them through to implementation. The list of its uncompleted initiatives included legislation to curtail the foreign takeover of Canadian companies; a new Competition Act; overhaul of family allowances; political spending legislation; a new deal for Canada's native peoples; assistance for middle-class Canadians to obtain home mortgages; and more money for urban renewal. Worse, inflation seemed out of control, unemployment was rising at an alarming rate and the government deficit had climbed to $2 billion in fiscal 1972–73. If ever a government was ripe for the plucking, it was the Trudeau government in 1972. The polls reflected the public's disenchantment. In March, undecided voters reached 43 per cent in the Gallup Poll; by June, Liberal support had slumped to 39 per cent, 6.5 percentage points below their vote in the June 1968 election. The Liberals had planned to call a spring election. Knowing they would be lucky to get a minority government, and perhaps not that, they put the election off, waited past the four-year mark and hoped the political climate would improve enough for an election in the fall.

Much of the problem was Trudeau himself. Having raised the public's expectations to an unrealistic level in 1968, he found he could not deliver. He failed, in the words of Dalhousie University political scientist J. Murray Beck, "to satisfy the demands of rational exponents of Trudeauism for a new kind of politics."[1]

Camp was not surprised. He had been convinced since Trudeau first burst onto the political scene that he was more flash than substance, more dilettante than deep thinker. He agreed with the assessment that Robert Stanfield made the day before Trudeau, his back to the wall, finally called the election in the fall of 1972:

> In 1968, Mr. Trudeau was accepted as the new spirit, above politics in the ordinary sense of the term. Now the people have seen him as prime minister for over four years. Some have seen him as a playboy who takes too many holidays. A great many doubt whether there is any warmth in his concern.... I think he has difficulty in listening to people, difficulty in spending enough time with his caucus, keeping in touch with them and, through them, with the people of the country.... I have the impression Mr. Trudeau is pretty largely making the main decisions himself and relying mainly for advice on people he chooses. I don't think he suffers fools gladly. I don't want to sound patronizing to the Canadian people when I say this, but the prime minister has to be prepared to listen and to understand all kinds of people.[2]

The public's disillusion with Trudeau did not—as Stanfield and Camp both knew—mean the country was ready to elect a Tory government. But it did mean that the Conservatives had a fighting chance, a chance that had seemed extremely remote in the dark weeks and months following the 1968 election. As the party's national director, Malcolm Wickson, had reported to the party executive in 1970, the Tories suffered from a diminishing electoral base: it was elderly and rural in an age when the electorate was becoming younger and more urban. Camp understood perfectly; he had been arguing for years that the party's greatest need was to attract young people and city dwellers, and he had advanced that proposition throughout his leadership-review campaign in 1966.

There was no doubt in 1972 that the party needed Camp, the modern Tory, with his appreciation of the party's priorities, his sense of the country as a whole and his ability to excite and engage young people. Stanfield knew it—and so did Camp. The problem was, relations between the two men were still severely strained. Camp was hurt and angry at the way Stanfield had pushed him away after the leadership convention in 1967 and had kept him at arm's length in the hope of mollifying the Diefenbaker wing of the party. And Stanfield, still struggling to instill a sense of common purpose in his fragile caucus, knew Camp remained a lightning rod for former Diefenbaker supporters, some of whom regarded Dalton Camp as a far more insidious enemy than Pierre Trudeau.

Despite these strains, the two men were close friends. They had been through political wars together since the 1953 Nova Scotia election. They had the same approach to public service. They understood each other completely, and each sparked off the other intellectually. Connie Camp, Dalton's middle daughter, remembered an evening—"one of the most exciting nights of my life"—when Stanfield and Richard Hatfield, the premier of New Brunswick, came to dinner with her father. For two hours or more Stanfield and Camp debated issues from foreign policy to abortion to capital punishment. Every now and again, Hatfield, no slouch himself in the brains department, would try to break in, but he could not keep up with the other two as ideas tumbled over ideas. "It was breathtaking," Connie said.[3]

It was a foregone conclusion that, if Stanfield asked, Camp would agree to help in the 1972 election. Friendship, loyalty and a sense of obligation dictated as much. What is more, there seemed to be a real chance to defeat Trudeau and make Stanfield prime minister. But if Stanfield wanted Camp's assistance, he would have to ask him; Camp's pride demanded that.

With their mutual friend Finlay MacDonald brokering the arrangements, the two men met secretly at the Chateau Laurier Hotel in Ottawa; it was further testimony to the lasting bitterness of the 1966 Diefenbaker battle that Stanfield felt it would be too risky to have Camp come to Stornoway, the residence of the opposition leader—someone might see him and word might get back to the troublemakers in the caucus. While Camp and Stanfield talked, Bill Grogan, the leader's senior assistant and speech writer, waited in the next room. He remembered it was a long wait before

Camp joined him and they worked out arrangements for the election campaign.

The nerve centre for the Tory campaign was the Westbury Hotel on Yonge Street in Toronto. Grogan and Camp set up shop in a suite there. Borrowing a line from cartoonist Al Capp, they christened it the "Skunkworks." (Other Tories called it the "Sausage Factory.") All pronouncements made in the national campaign had to pass through the Skunkworks. Camp wrote what was known as the "vision speech"—the speech in which Stanfield described the kind of Canada he wanted to see. He delivered it twice—in Kingston, Ontario, where Flora MacDonald was running for the Tories, and later in Victoria—and the Skunkworks worked elements of it into other speeches during the campaign. Grogan and Camp took policy ideas generated by Tom Symons, the founding president of Trent University, who travelled with the leader as his policy adviser, and kneaded them, diced them, sliced them, cubed them and mixed them with background data from the party's research office in Ottawa to create "modules"—two- and three-paragraph chunks of policy that could be dropped into Stanfield's speeches as required. They soon had a menu of about 20 modules from which they would select a few for use each day.

This content control was important. "You'd work very hard on the language to get committed what you wanted to commit—and to make damned sure you hadn't committed what you didn't want to commit, and to get these both in French and English," Grogan said.[4]

Grogan was the manager of the Skunkworks; Camp came and went, doing his best to stay invisible lest his involvement become known and cause Stanfield further anxiety. He would usually drop by twice a day, review the material that had come in from the research office and the leader's aircraft, figure out which issues would play the best that day and sometimes write a new lead for the standard speech or some new bridges to connect the modules. The finished product would then be sent by facsimile machine to the leader's staff on the road.

There was a third person in the Skunkworks in both the 1972

and 1974 campaigns. Her name was Wendy Smallian. Born Wendy Cameron, the daughter of a doctor in Ottawa, she was 26 years old at the time of the 1972 election and was married to Bob Smallian, a businessman in the capital. She would soon become a very important person in the life of Dalton Camp, a man who was then exactly twice her age.

Wendy was the Skunkworks' liaison with the research office in Ottawa, where her opposite number and contact, coincidentally, was Maureen McTeer, who in 1973 would marry a rookie MP and Camp protégé, Joe Clark. Grogan or Camp would notice that Statistics Canada was about to issue a report on the cost of living. Wendy would round up the report and assemble background information, which Grogan and Camp, the counter-puncher, would forge into a hammer for Stanfield to use to batter the government at his next stop on the campaign trail.

"Wendy had a lot of smarts," Grogan recalled. "She had a good memory. She would say, 'Back in such and such, we did something on that.'" He was impressed with her in other ways—she was gorgeous. "It would have been impossible for any 'civilized' male to avoid being at least somewhat enchanted by Wendy," Grogan remembered. "She was quite a 'looker' in those days: slender, with shoulder-length dark hair and sparkling eyes to go along with a very pleasant personality. And she was extremely bright.... She was an eclectic soul. She was what I always wanted to be: a 'dippy'—a disciplined hippie."[5] Romantic as well as eclectic, Wendy loved the *Great Gatsby* movie with Robert Redford and Mia Farrow, Emmylou Harris singing "Boulder to Birmingham" and Neil Diamond's music composed for *Jonathan Livingston Seagull*.

The election on October 30, 1972, was a heart-stopper, the closest federal election in Canadian history. When the counting and recounting were finished, Trudeau clung to the barest of minority governments, with 109 seats to Stanfield's 107. David Lewis and the New Democrats—who had waged a vigorous and effective campaign against government handouts to corporations—held the balance of power with 31 seats. The outcome sent two messages: there would be another election before long, and Dalton Camp would be back for it. Having helped Stanfield reach the very brink of power, there was no way he could abandon him now. He would be back in the Skunkworks for the July 1974 election.

Politics, at least in the 1960s and 1970s, was not an occupation that placed any significant premium on sobriety or marital fidelity. By the norms of the day, Camp was not a lush; he drank a lot, but he knew his limit. Nor was he a conspicuous womanizer in the fashion, say, of his close friend Finlay MacDonald. But he liked women. And women, attracted by his intelligence, his wit and his celebrity, liked Camp—*very* much. (Many years later, Camp, although still nominally a Conservative, went to Halifax to speak at a fundraising event for his friend Alexa McDonough, then leader of the federal NDP. He was a great hit, so much so that, as he confided later with some amusement, he received *three* proposals of marriage.)

Camp's close friends suspected—or a bit more than suspected—that he had a few romantic adventures over the years. But Camp was such a private person that no one, not even Norman Atkins, would ask him about love interests, and Camp would never tell. There was one woman, however, who very nearly turned his life upside down. Her name was Carol Jewers and she was the daughter of a seaman in Halifax. Camp first met Carol, small, blond, attractive and 31 years old, in February 1969 when she interviewed him for CBC Radio in Halifax, where she was working at the time. It was a friendly, flattering interview—"maybe too much so," Camp wrote in his journal. Afterward, he invited her for coffee and a chat. "She has ambitions for the Great World of Broadcasting in the Big Leagues," he wrote. "Somehow, I seem to create the impression in people that I have some magic powers to advise and direct—a sort of occupational guidance touchstone."[6]

Not long after, Jewers found her way to Toronto, where she fetched up at the Camp Associates advertising agency; she did a number of jobs there, including looking after some of the agency's United States accounts. At some point, she and Camp became lovers. He was living at the family home with Linda and their younger children on Daneswood Road in Toronto; Carol had an apartment to which she gave Camp a key. The relationship was rocky. She was in love; he was married; she was inclined to drink too much; he felt guilty about the relationship and thought he should bring it to an end. In early June 1974, Camp went to Jewers's apartment, let himself in with his key and found her on the floor. She had been dead for some time. Initially, he thought she had killed herself because of her unhappiness with him or with the state of their relationship. He feared he was responsible. Later, however, the coroner concluded that death was the result of an accidental overdose of pills and liquor.

Camp was distraught—so much so that he went home to Linda and told her what had happened. If he expected sympathy, he did not get any. His "Black Dog"—a spell of depression—returned.

Pierre Trudeau's minority Liberal government survived longer than anyone had expected. It lasted 18 months—until the Liberals judged the moment propitious to regain a majority; until the New Democrats concluded that their credibility would be ruined if they propped up the Liberals any longer; and until the Conservatives, finding themselves trapped, decided their prospects would only worsen the longer an election was delayed.

In retrospect, the Tories could only have won if a second election had taken place hard on the heels of the first, while they still enjoyed some momentum, while antipathy to Trudeau still hung over the land and while the public was prepared to consider Bob Stanfield as a reasonable prime ministerial alternative. Timing is everything in politics, and the Liberals controlled the clock. The longer they could stave off an election, the more time they had to reinvent themselves and to rehabilitate Trudeau's image. They managed to move just far enough to the left, and to introduce just enough progressive measures, to keep the NDP on side. The Conservatives were in an impossible position. Inflation was out of control in Canada, as it had been in the United States, and there was no way the Liberals would do anything about it beyond creating a toothless Food Prices Review Board; as long as they needed NDP support, they would not move on the crucial wage side of the inflation equation. The Tories had positioned themselves as the alternative government. As such, they believed they had no option but to present an anti-inflation policy to the country. That policy called for the imposition of a 90-day wage and price freeze (to break the inflation psychology) followed by 18 months to two years of comprehensive wage and price controls. That gave the Liberals the issue they needed to regain their majority.

Camp was far more active than outsiders realized during the minority government period. He wrote speeches for Stanfield, for which he was paid a fee. He advised the leader on strategy throughout 1973 and into the early months of 1974. Although he was consulted on the wage-price freeze, the economy was not his strong suit, and his reservations did not carry the same weight as the arguments mounted by the principal advocate of controls, James Gillies, a former university dean who had been elected in Toronto Don Valley in 1972 and on whom Stanfield had come to rely for advice on economic issues. When prominent economists whom the Tories consulted agreed with Gillies, and when controls seemed to be having an anti-inflationary effect in the United States, Stanfield decided to embrace the controversial policy.[7]

Camp's objections were tactical. He believed, as he had throughout his years as a political strategist, that an opposition party wins by identifying problems that the public is concerned about, by making those problems into election issues and by laying the blame squarely at the doorstep of the government. An opposition party loses if it proposes solutions to problems—solutions that the government can and will attack. In 1974, the problem was inflation—it was running at over 10 per cent annually—but the Tory solution, rather than inflation itself, became the election issue. Keith Davey, who was running the Liberal campaign, was overjoyed. "Instead of talking about the problem of inflation and making it their issue, they offered their solution," he said. "Any solution they offered would have been a critical strategic mistake, but this one took the form of a highly contentious wage and price freeze. Pierre Elliott Trudeau had a field day with his 'Zap! You're frozen!'—a phrase he used repeatedly. Everywhere he went, he warned Canadians of what the freeze would do to aspiring wage earners and struggling small businessmen."[8]

Camp, said Grogan, "was always concerned about what the Grits would do. And it was exactly what they did do: the 'Zap! You're frozen!' thing. Dalton, the counter-puncher, intuitively knew what they would do with it. But he felt there was nowhere to go once that policy decision had been made."[9]

Camp bore some of the responsibility for the decision to force the Liberals into an election call. The centrepiece of the musical show at the annual dinner of the Parliamentary Press Gallery that spring had been a double bed—occupied by Trudeau (as played by journalist Peter Desbarats) and David Lewis (acted by Grogan)—as the gallery made mock of the Liberal-NDP relationship. That show grated on the already exposed nerves of NDP MPs, an increasing number of whom were agitating to dump the Liberals and take their chances on the hustings. Ed Broadbent, then the caucus chairman, was having trouble holding back his impatient members. A grapevine between the NDP and Tory leaders' offices ran through their caucus research offices. "What people in our research office were hearing from the NDP research office was that Broadbent was now in the role of lion tamer," Grogan said. "He'd bloody near got a chair and a pistol. It was really getting to them."

Grogan asked Les Horswell in the Conservative research office to make inquiries of NDP researchers to see if Broadbent would be interested in exploring a deal to defeat the government when John Turner, the finance minister, brought down his budget in May. The reply came back through the grapevine: perhaps Grogan would like to drop by Broadbent's office for a chat. Before he did anything, Grogan called Camp in Toronto for advice. "I've just got a feeling these guys are getting really antsy," he told Camp. "I know Broadbent. I like him as a person. If you make a deal with him, you can count on it. What do you think?" Camp said, "Go for it. Things aren't going to get any better the longer this goes on." Grogan then went to Stanfield and told him Camp thought it was worth pursuing an agreement with Broadbent. Stanfield was hesitant. "He said,

'Ah, no, well, whatever you think, Bill. It's not going to happen. Won't happen,'" Grogan recalled. "I said, 'Is it any problem for you if I do this?' and he said, 'No, no. Fine.'"

The negotiations almost became unstuck before they began. As Grogan was entering Broadbent's Centre Block office on Parliament Hill, he spotted CBC correspondent Ron Collister coming around a corner. "Collister looks and his ears go up and his nose is sniffing," Grogan remembered with a laugh. He went ahead with his meeting with Broadbent, and they struck a tentative deal, subject to the approval of their respective leaders and caucuses. When the budget came down, the NDP would move a straightforward sub-amendment to the main Tory amendment. The sub-amendment would not call for the nationalization of the Canadian Pacific Railway or any other detritus of NDP dogma that would antagonize Tory backbenchers. The Tories would then vote for the sub-amendment, and the government would fall.

That agreed, Grogan went in search of Collister to persuade him not to file a story about his negotiations with Broadbent. Collister was agreeable; he was more interested that spring in securing a Tory nomination than he was in breaking a story on the national news.[10]

Grogan reported to Stanfield, who told him to call Camp again. "Well, tell Stanfield I'm for it," Camp said. "I'll give him a call myself." Grogan then called Malcolm Wickson, the Tories' national campaign chairman, who supported the decision but said he was growing disturbed by some signs in the party's polling that suggested that, although Canadians wanted action against inflation, they were not sure Stanfield was strong enough to make a controls program work. But, Wickson concluded, "I think we should do it. Let's get this bloody thing over with."[11]

It was over in eight days. Turner brought down his budget, the NDP moved its non-contentious sub-amendment, and the Tories voted with the New Democrats. The Liberal government fell, Parliament was dissolved and an election was called for July 8, 1974.

The Skunkworks reopened at the Westbury Hotel in Toronto. It operated just as it had in 1972, with one significant difference. This time there was very definitely something going on between Dalton

Camp and researcher Wendy Smallian. "It shouted out to you," Grogan said.

Camp was reeling from the death of Carol Jewers, Wendy was going through a painful divorce from Bob Smallian—and as Tory insider Hugh Segal, who had formerly dated Wendy himself, put it, "I think you go into that hothouse of being locked up in a hotel during a campaign, generating stuff every day, and…"[12]

As the wife of the most senior person in the Conservative campaign group, Linda Camp took it upon herself to organize dinners and other social activities for the workers who were holed up at the Westbury. She made a point of including Wendy, whom she knew was going through a divorce. "I thought, she's a young girl and we should include her in our dinners," Linda said. She suspected Wendy was having an affair with someone in the Tory campaign—"that was pretty obvious to me; I thought she needed a father"—but Linda had no idea that someone was her husband. "That's how it happened," Linda continued. "There's no sense saying it any other way: it was extremely devastating for me. It was unbelievably devastating…. I just thought it was probably a question of time [before the affair ended], but it wasn't."[13]

Hugh Segal thought Camp and Wendy Cameron—she reverted to her maiden name following her divorce—were a good match. "She was an extremely thoughtful, very bright, energetic and attractive person," he said. "She would have had a sense of discovery about Dalton and a cheerleading kind of thing. For men in their mid-fifties, that's probably not unattractive. And because she worked in the policy area, the research area, she had, I think, an appreciation of just how bright he was, how capable he was and how much of a craftsman he was. Quite aside from any other normal human attractions, that would have been pretty compelling."[14]

The 1974 election unfolded as Camp had feared it would. The Liberals exploited the Tories' wage and price freeze promise mercilessly, many voters started having new doubts about Stanfield and the business community grew increasingly skittish about the possibility of another minority government. The result did not surprise Camp: a majority for the Liberals and a cruel setback for the Tories.

On election night, workers in the Conservative national campaign gathered for a last dinner at the Westbury Hotel. It was a magical night, as Grogan remembered it. As the meal went on, he watched Camp and Wendy sitting together, their fingers touching, and felt moved to write a love song for them. He got his baritone ukulele and sang the bluesy song as they sipped liqueurs and cognac. He called it "Last Night Blues," and it went like this:

Cocktails, waiter, something for my friend
To help her mind believe tonight won't end...
Mine's a double, make it bittersweet
To toast our last night out, who knows when next we'll meet?
I'd like a tip of sirloin, waiter, make mine rare,
Just like I feel while she's still sitting there.
You know that time is something that nobody can control,
And it's our last night out to feed each other's souls...

We'll have some sparkling wine to make the evening gay,
Just like her sparkling eyes I'll miss when she's away.
Now, please don't let a teardrop cross your mind...
Just be happy about the "us" we leave behind.

And now just one more dance; we'll ask for something slow,
Though empty tables say, "It's time to go"...
We'll have one more glass of warm by candlelight
To toast our last night out while your fingers hold mine tight...
It's been a last night out that will last beyond tonight.

Camp and Wendy went their separate ways after that night. Before long, however, Camp called to ask whether she would like to win an election for a change. He invited her to help him in the November 1974 election in New Brunswick, where his friend Richard Hatfield was seeking a second term. "I'd love to," she replied. It was a hard election for her, however. Her father, an obstetrician in Ottawa, had been seriously ill, and he died during the campaign. She flew home to bury him, then returned to New Brunswick. She and Camp stayed at Robertson's Point. They went for long walks on the beach at Grand Lake; they talked for hours by the fire. If they were not in love before, they were by the end of the

New Brunswick election (which Hatfield won). They would be together for the next 14 years.

They lived a nomadic existence for the first few years, dividing their time between Robertson's Point and a rented apartment on the Rideau Canal in Ottawa. They went to Toronto often, usually staying at the Four Seasons Hotel. It took awhile for Camp's friends and family to realize that he was in a new relationship. "When I found out, you could have blown me over, because I had no idea," said Camp's brother-in-law and partner, Norman Atkins.

Flora MacDonald, however, was less surprised. She had had a sense for quite some time that Camp's marriage to Linda was falling apart. "I can remember going to visit them, and having supper with them, and I didn't like the feeling," she said. "There was a sense of tension in the air that I didn't want to be part of." MacDonald always found Camp to be at his happiest when he was down in the Maritimes, on his own.[15]

Jackie Webster, a Fredericton-based journalist, was a close friend and confidante to Camp for most of his life. He and Linda married too young, she believed. "Linda was from New York. He saw her as exotic, foreign," Webster said. "The contrast between the two of them was so dramatic it's amazing they stayed together as long as they did."[16]

Cherie Camp, Dalton's youngest daughter, was dumbfounded to learn that her father was living with a woman who was younger than her sister Gail. "He wrote me a letter, telling me that he'd fallen in love with someone," Cherie said. "It was a total shock to me—a complete, utter shock. I almost passed out.... He said that he'd fallen in love for the first time, which I thought was very interesting. I don't think that was true.... It was like an announcement, that he was sharing this great joy. I think he just felt we should all be happy for him."[17]

David, the eldest son, was visiting Robertson's Point when his father called him over from the next cottage, saying there was someone he wanted him to meet. "It was obviously a matter of importance, and I guessed from something he said later that I didn't treat the occasion with much seriousness, as I kind of said 'Hi' and turned to talk to him, or greeted her very perfunctorily and went out.... I didn't mean to be rude; I took no interest in her or in meeting her."[18]

The Camps were a tough family for any outsider to break into. All the children were close—even when they were scattered across the continent, they kept in touch—and they were fiercely protective of their mother, whom they all saw as the wronged party, despite Wendy's efforts to win their understanding. In a revealing letter to David in June 1975, Wendy struggled to explain how she and his father had happened to find each other. She had been coming out of a failed marriage, feeling hurt, vulnerable, withdrawn and very much alone, she wrote. Although she still believed in love, she had decided it was not going to happen. The Dalton Camp she came to know was warm and gentle, with a respect for life and a strong sense of himself and his own worth. And he was troubled:

> He was very sad and for some strange reason I wanted to see him happy. I cared and I hadn't cared for a long time. It became very important to me to see him laugh. And then one weekend he went away, back to Toronto to tape a show, and it was black cloud time. It was as if the sunshine had been taken away and I knew I was in love with him. I thought about that for a whole long time, about all the reasons why it wasn't right for me to love him. What gives me the right to love a man twice my age and my experience who has a wife and five children he also loves?...[B]ut if I am to be honest with you, I have to tell you I could not help it then and I cannot help it now.

Wendy probably never had a fighting chance to win the children over. They did not like her looks, they did not share their father's high estimation of her intellect and they did not appreciate the way she spent Dalton's money much more extravagantly than Linda ever had. In later years, Camp would blame the failure of his relationship with Wendy in part on the refusal or inability of his children to accept her into the family.

David, however, took a different view. He said that in retrospect he blamed himself for not doing enough to defend his mother's interests when he first learned of his father's new relationship. "I didn't see it as something that would be so destructive, and damaging to my mother, or something that would upset the whole family order," he said. "I thought it was something that would pass; I didn't conceive for a moment that it would result in a second family.... [But] I wasn't going to find fault with him, and by being prepared to accept her being around, I had access to him in a way that I hadn't had before."[19]

A reporter for the *Telegraph Journal* in Saint John at the time, David was posted to the press gallery in Ottawa, where he rented an apartment in the same building as his father and Wendy. Despite his initial discomfort in Wendy's presence, he had to admit that she made Dalton come to life and sparkle with wit and intelligence. David's apartment was on a higher floor, and from time to time he would come down for a drink or a meal, some talk and a few laughs. "He was very outgoing and youthful during that phase of his life; he was very lively," David recalled. "The relationship with her was very stimulating for him, and he had a lot of fun. She was a great audience for him. I think she had this hold on him because she so clearly loved him and admired him, and she thought he was a huge entertaining personality."[20]

They had a playful, loving relationship that belied the 26-year difference in their ages. They left witty messages for each other on the refrigerator door. They made up pet names. He called her "Pi" or "Piesie" (for "Sweetie Pie") or H.L. (short for "Hamburger Lady"—a name he gave her because of her ability to whip up burgers on the spot for unexpected guests or for Camp's golden retriever dog, Whiskey). She called him "Varlet"—a name that Camp appropriated for the storyteller in his 1979 book *Points of Departure*. She was warm, creative and full of laughter. He was charming and seductive. "He was just a great ongoing tour de force in those days," David said. "... When he was 'on,' he was very witty, mocking, theatrical and eloquent, and he was 'on' a lot when Wendy was around."

One day in 1976, the two lovers decided to run away. They got on a plane and flew to Europe, where they drifted like vagabonds around the continent, inspecting historical sites and enjoying each other. Camp kept a journal for part of that period. "There is my darling: my seeing-eye, explorer, lover, companion, child of dreams—soft, tactile, surprised, so painfully like another, so unlike anyone else," he wrote on May 29, 1976. "We fly together, dine together (mostly the same things) and are silent together—and we sleep together, a subtle warmth passing between us. She is impulsive, profligate, diffident—I struggle to cope—and still endearingly close.... I am torn by her youth, her beauty, the subtle folds of her body, the chemistry and all that magic voodoo of her self."

Camp, the hardnosed adman and political strategist, was utterly disarmed, besotted with Wendy Cameron. "I am tempted to say that I love her, goddammit, and it is as simple as that. But it is not so simple as that. Ours has been a long and lovely apprenticeship; somewhere there is a harder test. When I see her in the morning, on the pillow, or at night, in the mirror of my mind when we go to bed, I only know that I want her to be mine—and to be what I dream. A lot to ask of a girl from the Ottawa Valley."[21]

Eventually, Camp and Cameron settled in the Algarve, that region of southern Portugal that had been a Moorish kingdom in medieval times. There Camp rested, read, ran five miles a day ("He was in incredible shape," Wendy said) and set to work on an autobiographical novel about passionate love and grubby politics. As a novel, *Some Political People* did not work. But as a demonstration of Camp's writing style, it worked quite well, especially when he wrote, in the third person, about the woman he loved:

> That she was so clearly, simply, strikingly beautiful was surely a reason for his loving her. He was proud of it, even though he sometimes feared it, and was, as often, perversely jealous of it....
>
> If he had any fantasies, they were not about romantic love, or girls who looked like film stars. He had known a long, widely esteemed, civilized marriage and he had survived one brief, traumatic affair.... [H]e walked wide of preying women who had been liberated by the pill, menopause or booze, looking for fixes for their fading hopes and sagging egos. Promiscuity appalled him; of all the sexual mores of the contemporary society, he understood least the one-night stand.
>
> He watched the girl emerge from the surf, drenched and laughing, white teeth shining, eyes bright with joy, beads of salt water standing

on her skin, sparkling in the sun, small-breasted in the fashion of the day, a long-waisted body curving to full hips, tapering to long, lean, clean-shaven legs. She ran to him.[22]

Camp apparently never finished *Some Political People*, although he did sound out potential publishers; they gave him scant encouragement. Following his death, a draft of the novel was found in the basement of his home, along with fragments of one or two other attempts at novels and some bits of stage plays or screenplays. Camp had obviously discovered what countless writers had found before him: it is a far harder thing to write fiction than non-fiction. He had a sure eye for describing a scene, but a tin ear for dialogue and no command of plot and story development. His characters looked real; they talked a lot in stilted sentences, but nothing interesting ever seemed to happen to them.

In 1977, Camp and Cameron returned to Canada, where two noteworthy developments occurred. They started to build their dream house, Northwood, perched in isolated splendour atop a hill a few kilometres from the family cottages at Robertson's Point, New Brunswick. And Wendy got pregnant.

CHAPTER 21

Northwood

WENDY CAMP LIKED TO SAY that she had given Dalton two lives. The first was in the early years of their love, when she brought him joy, happiness and the inspiration to make that period one of the most creative in his long life. The second was when she made the arrangements that led to the 1993 heart transplant, which not only snatched him from the very brink of death, but also gave him nearly nine additional and productive years.

The first of those two lives seemed almost idyllic, as the couple returned from Europe and prepared to make their home in rural New Brunswick, in what Camp's friend Finlay MacDonald would later describe as a "brick mansion on a hill with rifle slits for windows." They had given serious thought to buying a villa and remaining in Portugal, where Dalton would write to his heart's content and they would surely live happily ever after. But there were practical obstacles, as Camp had discovered. It was one thing to talk about writing a novel and quite another thing to actually pull it off. It was also no mean feat, week after week, to write a column of political commentary for the *Toronto Star* and other Canadian newspapers from the Algarve, which, beautiful though it was, was not a station on the Canadian information highway. It was a struggle, Camp found, to write for Canadians when he was out of contact with events in Canada. And although Portugal was a grand escape and a marvelous indulgence, it did not offer in the longer term an intellectually stimulating life for a fifty-plus-year-old Canadian with interests, friends, children and other obligations back home.

Instead of a villa in Portugal, they would build the finest home in Queen's County, New Brunswick—a nest for her and a retreat for him. Northwood is the sort of home that only the people who built it can truly appreciate. Located on 70 acres on a back road between the hamlets of Cambridge Narrows and Jemseg, it took nearly two years to construct. The land, which Camp had had his eye on for a number of years, cost $30,000 and the building $300,000 or so more, with landscaping, furnishing and decorating adding undetermined amounts on top of that. About five years after they moved in, Wendy decided to get rid of the comfortable curved sofas and the huge coffee table, around which Camp and his political friends had passed wonderful evenings debating the issues of the day. She hired Giovanni Mowinckel, the interior designer who would later, controversially, redo 24 Sussex Drive for Mila and Brian Mulroney. Out went the comfortable furniture; in came loveseats, an elegant glass and brass coffee table, Ming-style lamps and lacquered reproductions of Chinese opium chests. The pretentious décor looked as out of place in rural New Brunswick as an igloo in the tropics. By the time all the bills were in, Camp had probably spent $500,000—and, by some estimates, somewhat more.[1]

Camp grumbled a bit. He complained when he was handed an unexpected invoice for $16,500 for brickwork. He whined when the roofers wanted $11,086.76: "I am building Northwood the same way Hugh John Flemming built Beechwood—on overdraft."[2] For all that, Camp was both pleased and proud. He loved New Brunswick, especially the Saint John River Valley, and he was delighted that Northwood would give him the solitude he sought for his writing. He was pleased with the handsome two-storey house he saw rising before him: the beautiful fireplace that opened into both the living and dining rooms with "V" and "HL" (for Varlet and Hamburger Lady) in brass letters on the dining room side; the light-filled solarium; the writing loft overlooking the living room; and the spacious apartment built into the house for his mother and his handicapped younger brother, Red.[3] And he was proud of the care with which Wendy had planned every detail of this spectacular home for the two of them and their unborn child, on whom they had bestowed the prenatal name of "El Cid."

Wendy's pregnancy raised a painful issue for Camp—breaking the news to Linda Camp. They had not told her anything when they took off for Europe. "I thought he was going to Europe to get away, and then I found out that she had gone with him. And she had the great time of her life," Linda said, a trace of bitterness in her voice a quarter-century later.[4] Ever since her husband had left her, Linda had been able to tell herself that one day he would return. For four years, she avoided encounters with him and Wendy by staying away from Robertson's Point until, as she reassured herself, he would come back to her.

Unaware in the summer of 1977 that Wendy was pregnant, she talked to her children about what she would say to their father when he returned. One morning, she announced, "I know what I'll say when he comes in the door. I'll say, 'Hi, Ulysses. How was your voyage?'"[5] Camp did come back, briefly. He sat her down and told her Wendy was pregnant and he intended to stay with her. Linda was desperately hurt. "All of us were called on to help her, [but] most of the burden fell on my sisters Gail and Cherie," said their elder son, David. "We all had terrible, heartbreaking moments with her. She loved him, and her sense of self derived from him: she was very identified with him, she had five children with him, she'd been through very significant political events with him, and she wasn't by her very nature prepared for this kind of thing to happen. She often mentioned her own father, and the importance he attached to the quality of loyalty, and she felt very betrayed."[6]

Her brother, Norman Atkins, torn between family loyalty and hero worship of Dalton Camp, defended his friend. "Your father has never had a promiscuous private life," he would tell Camp's children. "He's never chased women, and now he's got this relationship with Wendy.... This is a relationship that he cares about and, unlike other men, he's not prepared to lie about it and be hypocritical about it.... Many men carry on these adulterous relationships in secret, and they lie about it, and there's all kinds of hypocrisy. Your father is not like that."[7]

But loyal to their mother and uncomfortable with Wendy, the five children of the first marriage saw even less of their father than they had when they were growing up and he was off fighting the political wars. It was not until years later, after Wendy and Dalton had separated, bitterly, that they would begin to reconnect with their father.

For Camp, the decision to adopt the life of a country squire had a certain logic. He had retired from the advertising business, in which he had made a great deal of money. Except for his continuing interest in the career of his friend Richard Hatfield in New Brunswick, Camp's active involvement in politics slowed to a crawl with the retirement of Bob Stanfield from the national Tory leadership in 1976. New Brunswick was his first love. It was where he wanted to live. He found it a simple thing to shuttle from Fredericton to Toronto, Ottawa or other cities to speak on university campuses, appear on television, write his column and keep in touch with friends in politics. He was pleased when he was appointed to the board of governors of his alma mater, the University of New Brunswick. Perhaps it was the contrarian in him, but he was only too happy to escape from what passed for high society in Toronto, with its cloying atmosphere in which money and family connections seemed to him to count for more than intelligence and human worth. Northwood gave him the peace and the detachment he craved.

For Wendy, the logic was less apparent. As the daughter of a prominent doctor in Ottawa, she was a city girl with city tastes. She relished the sort of bright lights that Camp was only too happy to turn his back on. And she really loved to shop. From Northwood, however, anything more ambitious than a quart of milk or a loaf of bread called for a 40-minute drive into Fredericton—which was not exactly Fifth Avenue or Rodeo Drive or even Bloor Street. When their son Christopher reached school age, Wendy wanted him in French immersion. That meant two trips to Fredericton, five days a week, along a two-lane stretch of the old Trans-Canada Highway, which was notorious for its heavy truck traffic.

Wendy, however, did more than just agree to live in rural New Brunswick. She embraced the life enthusiastically. She was with the man she loved. She threw herself into his world. Some of the best-known people in Canadian public life passed through their home in those years. There were lobster dinners with champagne and the blueberry pies she loved to bake. Every January, a crowd would gather to watch the Super Bowl on Camp's big-screen television.

Hatfield, who cared nothing about sports, would wander in and out. "What sport is it?" he would ask. "Who's playing? Who's winning? Which ones are they?" Hatfield would look at Wendy, who did not know, either. Then he would drift back to the kitchen, leaving Camp and his pals to their guy fantasies.

Most important, of course, Wendy was going to have Camp's child. She immersed herself in decorating, preparing the bassinet and scouring stores for designer baby clothes. A month before the birth, she wrote a note that both expressed her joy and indicated the strain that her pregnancy had put on their relationship. "Dalton: My man, my love," she wrote. "...I love you. I hope you know it, remember it and, at the risk of sounding trite, cherish it. It is as hard for me right now, and has been, as it is for you. But things will be back to normal soon enough and we'll have one more [the baby] to enjoy this love between us."[8]

Whatever he may have thought about becoming a father for the sixth time at the age of 57, Camp shared Wendy's excitement over the impending birth, to the extent of sitting in on every consultation she had with her doctor. When Christopher Jonathan Kingsley Camp, eight pounds, eight ounces, was born at 12:52 a.m. on January 1, 1978, Camp was in the delivery room—capped, gowned and masked. "I find the experience awesome," he wrote in his journal that day. "I am fully involved in this vision of immortality, in the discovery of my own strength, in an astonishing gathering of wonder and tenderness devoid of sentimentality and myth."

On the way home from the hospital, Camp's Honda was struck broadside by a Ford Thunderbird driven by a man who was slightly under the influence of strong drink. "We were lucky," Camp reported. "I have a sore rib cage and W. was shaken up by it all, understandably. As for Christopher, it was a rude introduction to the outside world."[9]

Northwood was finally finished a few months after Christopher's birth, and Camp settled comfortably into the routine of rural life with his young partner and their infant son. A devoted father, he lavished more affection on Christopher than he had on his older children. One of his oldest friends, Jackie Webster, remembered having lunch with Camp at the Lord Beaverbrook Hotel in Fredericton one day when Christopher was a baby. "Wendy came in with this child," Webster recalled. "She was in town for some shopping—she was big on shopping. So she put the child on the table and said, 'Oh, Dalton, he needs to be changed. Go change him.' And Dalton got up and went off and changed him. I thought this was a good thing. I'm sure he never changed the other children. I think he was closer to this last child."[10] Although Camp could never remember his older children's birthdays, Christopher's were mini-festivals with fireworks, entertainment and many, many presents.

As Easter 1978 approached, he wrote to David to invite him and his girlfriend to visit Northwood that summer. He had been keeping fit, Camp reported, by chasing squirrels—"Score: Squirrels 89, DKC 0." He had not had a drink of hard liquor in two weeks, compensating, however, by laying in a supply of cheap red wine from Portugal. "I am—and may this not seem immodest—a wiser, kinder, saner man," he wrote.

Perhaps so, but he was clearly worried about the deterioration in his relations with the children of his first family. "I have not made peace with my children," he admitted. "Michael drove down a few weeks ago, bringing his hang-ups and diffidence and an unexpected belligerence and intolerance. And we quarrelled and said harsh things, in a quite painful confrontation.... I am not free of problems of a personal kind and...I am not yet certain about who or what I am but I am done with playing at being God."[11]

Other strains, too, gradually made life at Northwood seem less idyllic as time passed. On the positive side, Camp was at or near his creative peak in those initial years with Wendy. His newspaper column was becoming a "must read" in the political community in Canada as, over time, his writing became less predictably partisan and more even-handed. It was almost as though Stanfield's departure had liberated him. While Camp could never bring himself to be overly critical of Stanfield, he did not feel the same compunction when it came to his successor, Joe Clark. Camp also published two books in those years—*Points of Departure*, his take on the 1979 federal election that produced the short-lived Clark government, and *An Eclectic Eel*, a collection of his better columns. Not least, his early Northwood period saw the birth of "Kierans, Camp and Lewis," the spectacularly successful weekly political panel on CBC radio.

On the negative side of the ledger, as a man approaching 60, he felt the stress of living in virtual isolation with an infant who, however delightful, demanded more attention than he was accustomed to giving to children. A man who had always prided himself on being an ethical person, he felt guilty about his alienation from his older children. He was living with a woman who no longer seemed to him to be quite as beautiful, quite as talented, or quite as amusing as she had seemed in the first blush of love. Her conversation did not sparkle as much as he thought it had. He started to worry about the amount of money they were going through. As someone accustomed to living life his own way, he began to feel trapped.

Camp's periods of depression—his "Black Dog"—became more frequent. In September 1980, he wrote a savage review of a book, *Discipline of Power*, written by *Globe and Mail* reporter Jeffrey Simpson about the Clark government. "The failure of *Discipline of Power* lies in its flawed style, which leads a reader to the conclusion that it was too hurriedly written or that the author had considerable difficulty in his first attempt to break out of journalism into literature. Perhaps it was something of both," Camp wrote. "But he appears not to have heard of Charles Lamb's advice to aspiring writers: 'Kill your darlings!' Trying, for instance, to grasp the meaning of a Simpson simile is like trying to carry water in a sieve...." And so on in the same vein.[12]

It was a hurtful review, and it was made doubly hurtful by the fact that it was written for, and was published in, Simpson's own newspaper, the *Globe*. Although Wendy also thought Simpson's book was poorly written, she believed Camp should not have written the review. He was in the grip of a "Black Dog" at the time and, vexed by a critical review Simpson had written of his *Points of Departure*, Camp set out to even the score. "He had the capacity to be quite cruel in his writing," Wendy said. "When he didn't like somebody, he could do that."[13] Although *Discipline of Power* went on to win the Governor General's award for non-fiction that year—which testifies to the influence (nil) of most book reviewers—it took two years for Simpson's anger over the review to subside. During that time he did not speak to Camp, nor would he shake his hand if they happened to meet.

Camp would say later that he had six good years with Wendy.[14] He did not specify which six years they were, but assuming they were in the early part of their relationship, the good years would have been over by 1980 or shortly thereafter—after the birth of Christopher but before Camp and Cameron decided to get married. Christopher was nearly seven years old when his parents were wed at Timothy Eaton Memorial Church in Toronto in December 1984. Arranged by their mutual friend Hugh Segal, it was a small wedding; the guests repaired afterward to the Four Seasons Hotel for a reception.

None of Camp's five older children was present. They had not been invited; nor, for that matter, had they been informed of their father's wedding plans. "I don't even know what year they got married, and I wasn't invited," David Camp said.[15]

Years later, Camp told his first family that he had made a mistake when he married Wendy—a "terrible mistake," he said to Linda. After 10 years together, their isolated life in rural New Brunswick was beginning to drive them apart more than it drew them closer. The decision to marry may have been a bid to recapture some of the old magic. Camp was also anxious to protect Christopher as he was growing up from any stigma arising from his parents' unwed status. For her part, Wendy still loved Camp and she may well have thought that formalizing their relationship would help keep them together.

But she, too, would come to realize that the marriage had been a mistake. Being married seemed to make their relationship more difficult—and it drove another wedge between Camp's two families. "We weren't very good at marriage," Wendy admitted. "We were much better living together."[16]

Life at Northwood was becoming increasingly stressful. Wendy was bored. Aside from assisting Camp from time to time to gather material, there were few employment prospects for her in Queen's County. She was worried that Christopher, with no friends his own age to play with, was becoming a lonely little boy. Then, in the summer of 1986, Brian Mulroney called and offered what seemed to her, at least, to be a lifeline.

CHAPTER 22

Kierans, Camp and Lewis

VISITORS TO PARLIAMENT HILL in the 1980s and early 1990s were sometimes puzzled by the number of people they would see—politicians, staffers and journalists—sitting in their cars between 9:00 and 9:30 on Tuesday mornings listening to the radio before they went in to work. What they were listening to was a unique, and uniquely successful, political panel on Peter Gzowski's *Morningside* program on CBC. Known to its fans as "KCL"—short for its participants: Kierans (Eric), Camp (Dalton) and Lewis (Stephen)—it was unlike any other political panel on radio or television, then or now. There was no shouting, no diatribes, no partisan posturing and no pompous banalities. The three panelists demonstrated that intelligent discourse and informed opinion, vigorously expressed, do have a place on the airwaves of the nation. KCL managed to be civil without ever being boring.

If Camp made his journalistic reputation as a newspaper columnist, that weekly radio panel—at its peak, it reached one million Canadians every Tuesday—gave him much of his loyal following. Whenever he travelled in Canada, he would meet people, many of whom had never read his column, who wanted to talk about something they had heard discussed on "Kierans, Camp and Lewis." The show became fixed in public consciousness. Years after the panel went off the air, Camp and the others encountered admirers who told them how much they were still enjoying KCL every week.

The panel's origins dated to the birth in 1982 of *Morningside*, the three-hour morning show that made Gzowski, the host, a national institution. Gzowski and his producers had the idea that a political panel would work as one of their regular features. They wanted panelists who represented differing points of view but who were not apologists for any party. The chemistry among them would be almost as important as the issues they discussed. They needed to be good listeners—and wit would be a decided asset.

When the panel made its debut, the participants were Camp, Doris Anderson, then president of the National Action Committee on the Status of Women, and Roy Romanow, who would later be the NDP premier of Saskatchewan. It did not work. It was virtually humourless. "The panel wasn't a failure; there just wasn't any chemistry," said Talin Vartanian, the CBC producer in charge of that segment of *Morningside*. "They never took the gloves off and were overly polite."[1]

After three months, *Morningside* tried again. Camp was kept on, while Anderson and Romanow were replaced by Kierans and Lewis. All three members of the reconstituted panel had been political players and, as Camp put it, "usually, we knew what we were talking about."[2] Kierans, the Liberal, had been a minister (along with René Lévesque) in the cabinet of Jean Lesage during Quebec's Quiet Revolution and later in Pierre Trudeau's federal cabinet. An economist, he had also been president of the Montreal Stock Exchange. Lewis, the son of one-time federal NDP leader David Lewis, had himself been leader of the provincial NDP in Ontario. One of the most articulate public figures of his day, Lewis would soon be named Canadian ambassador to the United Nations.

In Camp, *Morningside* had a player who had been through the political wars; he had brought democracy to the Conservative party with his leadership-review campaign in 1966, and he had since made a considerable name for himself as a writer and commentator. Although his principal client was the *Toronto Star*, his column found its way into most parts of the country. At one time or another, it appeared in newspapers in Charlottetown, Halifax, New Glasgow (N.S.), Saint John, Montreal, Ottawa, Edmonton, Lethbridge and Vancouver. He was believed to be the most widely read political analyst in the country.

The CBC paid Kierans, Camp and Lewis each a rock-bottom $150 a week. They made their debut on January 4, 1983, with a discussion of economic issues and the 75-cent Canadian dollar. One minute into the segment, Vartanian lifted her thumb behind the glass window of the control booth; Gzowski in the studio answered with a raised thumb of his own. The panel was an immediate success, and within a few months the CBC noticed a Tuesday morning bulge in its radio ratings.

The three panelists were seldom in the same studio. Kierans was usually in Halifax, where he lived at the time. Lewis was generally in Toronto, unless he was travelling somewhere else. Camp also travelled a great deal, but as often as not he was in Fredericton. As his heart began to fail in the early 1990s, the *Morningside* ritual became something of an ordeal.

Rising early, he would drive 40 minutes into the CBC studio in Fredericton. His eyesight, which had never been good, was deteriorating, and his second son, Michael, a CBC producer in Fredericton, worried about him being on the road alone. When he got to the CBC, Camp would struggle, short of breath, to walk from his car to the studio. "I would get Dad into his chair for the panel," Michael said. "They didn't know on the other end how bad it was, but I knew on my end that it was very bad. He didn't want to stop doing it, but if you listen to the recordings of any of those panels, he was breathless. He was really having trouble; just walking into the studio and sitting down, he'd need a few minutes to recover his composure."[3]

Preparations followed the same pattern each week. On Monday, the producer would call the panelists, starting with Kierans, with ideas for Tuesday's panel. Lewis would get the next call, with Camp last—"He was difficult to reach and didn't like being pre-interviewed," Vartanian said. Of the three, only Kierans prepared meticulously. One Tuesday, Camp happened to be in Halifax and did the show from the same studio as Kierans. "He was shocked that Eric Kierans came to the show with notes that he would read from," said Camp's daughter Connie. "My father thought when they had a conversation, it was all coming off the top."[4] Neither Camp nor Lewis relied on notes, although both made sure they had a few good lines ready for use when an opportunity presented itself. The panel would begin immediately after the 9:00 a.m. (Atlantic) newscast; it was taped for airing in later time zones. Although it was supposed to run for 22 minutes, until 9:30, Gzowski would let it creep past the half hour if sparks were flying.

Camp gave much of the credit for the success of KCL to Gzowski, who died not long before Camp. "There was wit without cynicism, chagrin without petulance, and sorrow without bathos, but most of all there was a thoroughly predictable decency," Camp wrote. "One felt comfortable in the presence of a rational, reasonable, responsible adult; the demeanour was not an act but an art."[5]

KCL, Gzowski once said, was notable for its "courtliness and civility. Even the most ardent disagreements were marked by the respect they had for the other person's view." Camp agreed with that. The three panelists, he noted, were not intimates, and though they disagreed often, each respected the others' opinions. "*Morningside*'s listeners enjoyed KCL for the civil tongue the panel kept in its head, or cheek, which effectively demonstrated what most Canadians believe, which is that politics can be argued with sincerity and passion but without heat and still shed light on the subject."[6]

Over the years, subjects covered the full range of political discourse, from whatever issue was preoccupying the country in any given week to the election of new leaders and changes of government, to such social issues as smoking and the right to die, to the appointment of additional senators to force through the Goods and Services Tax. One week they debated a tongue-in-cheek proposal for a referendum on the proposition that the national capital be moved to Winnipeg. Kierans said he liked the idea. So did Camp, although he expressed mock concern about what could possibly be done with Ottawa if the government moved out.

The GST debate was interesting because all three panelists agreed that then prime minister Brian Mulroney was justified in packing the Senate to end Liberal stalling on the GST bill. It was not surprising that Camp, the Tory, would agree. But Lewis, a bitter opponent of the GST and an advocate of abolishing the Senate, also agreed—on the ground that the unelected upper house had no right blocking a tax measure, good or bad, once it had been passed by the Commons. Kierans agreed, too, for the same reason.

In September 1984, as MPs approached a free vote on capital punishment, KCL also took up the topic. Kierans wrestled with his conscience on air, finally coming down in favour of retaining the death penalty for the murder of police officers and prison guards. Lewis, an abolitionist, rejected the idea of any exceptions. Camp took the broadest view. He noted that Florida was trying to build more jails to accommodate all the people it had on death row. That not only suggested capital punishment was no deterrent to murder, it also raised questions about the condition of society when most of the death-row inmates were black and poor. Should society, he wondered, be taking the lives of people who are victims of racial discrimination and of commercial violence sanctioned by society? "I have gone through it so many times in my mind," he said, "but I've always come back to the fact that I really don't want to live in a society which is capable of perpetrating vengeance."

In Camp's view, KCL worked "because none of us felt obligated to present a designated political view. Each said pretty well what he thought. The candour proved infectious. We were not obliged to be role-players, to provide controversy for its own sake, or to feign outrage, injury, or piety. It was not *Crossfire* but *Morningside*."[7]

Powerful figures in the political parties were not as sanguine as KCL's panelists about their lack of partisan orthodoxy. New Democrats complained about the dearth of socialist fervour in Lewis. Camp, in particular, made Mulroney nervous; his chief of staff, Hugh Segal, called regularly to demand transcripts so that he could tell "The Boss" what the panelists were saying about him. "I knew we were a success," Kierans reported, "when I got a call one day from Peter [Gzowski] to tell me that Senator Keith Davey had been on the phone demanding that I be taken off the panel, because I was no Liberal."[8]

"Kierans, Camp and Lewis" had a long life for a radio feature. It ran from January 1983 to September 1984, when Lewis was named ambassador to the UN. He was replaced on the panel by Dave Barrett, the former NDP premier of British Columbia; the chemistry was not the same but the panel limped along until September 1986, when Camp went to work in the Prime Minister's Office. It was discontinued at that time, but was revived in September 1989 after Camp left the PMO and Lewis completed his term at the UN. The panel then continued until March 1993, when it was cancelled.

A number of factors conspired to bring about KCL's demise. Pressure from political power brokers would have been part of it. More important, KCL was no longer politically correct: three aging white males, no matter how astute and entertaining, were deemed to be inappropriate in an era when the political system had expanded to five parliamentary parties, all of which wanted to court youth, women and visible minorities. Finally, there was the CBC's peculiar programming philosophy, which the corporation demon-strated time and again in radio and television: if it is not broken, break it so that it can be fixed—or not.

On the other hand, no broadcaster other than the CBC would have conceived of a show like "Kierans, Camp and Lewis," put it on air and let it run for the better part of a decade. KCL had a very good run. Its three players helped to raise the level of political dis-course. They made politics interesting and relevant to tens of thousands of Canadians who had not previously taken the time or had the opportunity to involve themselves in the world of political ideas. It was a sad commentary that, when KCL went off the air, there were no new players in the wings to take their place.

CHAPTER 23

The Ottawa Debacle

I N AUGUST 1986, DALTON AND WENDY CAMP travelled to Nova Scotia to spend a weekend with their good friends Finlay MacDonald, Norman Atkins (Camp's brother-in-law by his first marriage) and his wife, Anna Ruth, at MacDonald's rented summer home in Chester, Nova Scotia. Atkins had been appointed the previous month to the Senate of Canada, where he joined MacDonald, who had been named two years before that. On the first evening of their visit, the Prime Minister's Office called, asking if Camp was available to speak to Brian Mulroney.

He had had little contact with Mulroney—perhaps a half-dozen fleeting phone calls—in the three years since Mulroney had won the Conservative leadership from Joe Clark. Camp liked it that way. "Being removed from any direct role in politics had proved a tonic to my spirits," Camp recalled. "I had found better things to do and enjoyed the luxury of deciding what to do next, whether it was journalism, writing, or spending the better part of my time in Portugal. I wrote about politics much as a critic writes about theatre; I could watch from a distance an election campaign and not give a damn who won."[1]

After an exchange of pleasantries, Mulroney asked Camp to consider moving to Ottawa as a top-level adviser to the government, with the rank of senior deputy minister, the highest rank in the public service, a car, a driver and a salary in the $120,000-plus range. Camp told him he was happy in New Brunswick with his young wife and eight-year-old son. Mulroney said he understood, but asked Camp to think about the proposition. The Prime Minister was going on a trip out of the country; they would talk on his return.

After fixing himself a martini, Camp polled the group. MacDonald was enthusiastically in favour of accepting Mulroney's offer. He was delighted at the thought of having his best friend close to him in Ottawa. More than that, MacDonald understood the enormity of the political problems that had enmeshed the Tory government just two years after its landslide victory. Most of the public's antipathy was directed at Mulroney personally—"Lyin' Brian," they called him, and "Brian Baloney." If anyone could rehabilitate Mulroney's image, improve his media coverage and reverse the party's slide, it was Camp, MacDonald believed.

Wendy was even more enthusiastic. Mulroney's offer was a chance to escape from rural New Brunswick. The romance had leached out of Northwood for her. She was tired of driving to and from Fredericton for Christopher's school. She had lost interest in chauffeuring his friends back and forth whenever he wanted someone to play with. She longed to return to Ottawa, her home town, to her friends and family, to the shopping and other attractions of city life, to the political buzz of the capital and to an interesting job in the workforce. "When I came to Ottawa, I had a sort of psychic change," she said, many years later. She took a real estate course, renewed old friendships and started walking her son to school.[2]

Norman Atkins, who had run the Tory election campaign in 1984 and would run the next one in November 1988, was not enthusiastic—he knew government was no place for Camp. "[Atkins] also knew the Prime Minister," Camp said. "'Mulroney has a very unique management style,' he would say—and he also knew me: he suspected, rightly, that my temperament and disposition, and my impatience with detail, would make life in the civil service in Ottawa difficult for me."[3] Despite these misgivings, Atkins gave his brother-in-law cautious encouragement, if only because he knew Mulroney needed help and the task of getting the government re-elected would be easier if Camp were working on the inside. Anna Ruth Atkins, however, was flatly opposed. "Why give up a good life for that?" she asked.

So, when he asked her later, was Camp's daughter Connie. "I thought it was a terrible idea," she said. "It was too much for my father to take on at his age, when he seemed to be becoming frail. The person who wanted it most of all was Wendy, because she wanted to get back to Ottawa.... I was in tears."[4]

Camp himself had many reservations. He disliked Ottawa as a place to live. He had made up his mind after serving in the Canadian Army during the Second World War that he wanted no part of bureaucracy ever again. He loathed meetings—and meetings are the lifeblood of government. "A man's worth is often measured by the number of committees where his presence is required," he reflected. The capital, he knew, was no place for the restless or for those who are not obsessed by the intricacies of policy or the minutiae of politics—"those who are believed to be impetuous are thought dangerous, those whom the prudently sensible will avoid."[5] Finally, he had well-founded reservations about Mulroney and, especially, about the cronies who served him and fought among themselves for influence.

He knew Mulroney too well. He had known the future prime minister since he was a student in Nova Scotia and Camp had sent Mulroney, a good Catholic boy, out in the 1960 provincial election to charm the nuns and priests on Cape Breton and to spread the message among Catholic voters that the Liberal party under its leader Henry Hicks, a Protestant, had become a vehicle for religious intolerance.

Camp, too, had felt the Mulroney charm. He liked Mulroney better than Joe Clark, but he trusted him less. And he was acutely uncomfortable with the Mulroney style. In a 1989 interview with author John Sawatsky, Camp described going into a bar during the Tory general meeting in Winnipeg in early 1983, when Mulroney was trying to topple Clark from the leadership: "Brian and Mila were there, and Brian was wearing a multicoloured sweater, a cashmere, and I said, 'That's a nice-looking sweater, Brian.' And he said, 'I'll see that you get one.' I just thought, that guy's got a lot of things he has to learn.... If I had said, 'I like your wife,' he would have said, 'She's yours,' or 'I'll get you one just like her.'"[6]

The anti-Clark campaign at that Winnipeg meeting—after which Clark resigned his leadership—was one of the Tory party's low points. Lavishly funded Mulroney agents flew in planeloads of "instant" Tories from Quebec to cast votes in favour of a leadership convention. Camp was especially unimpressed by the tactics of former Newfoundland premier Frank Moores, who operated a high-pressure "boiler shop" for Mulroney just down the hall from Camp's hotel room. "You were up to your knees in sleaze," Camp said. "You could just smell it, and sense it and feel it."[7]

Following the Winnipeg meeting, Camp wrote to his son David about his uneasiness about having to choose between Clark, who was running to succeed himself, and Mulroney at the leadership convention to be held in June 1983. Mulroney, he acknowledged, had come a long way from Baie Comeau, his hometown in Quebec. "But I fear his shallowness, the lack of any sort of reflective nature but much pizzazz and persona," he wrote.[8]

In the end, Camp decided to accept Mulroney's offer to go to Ottawa. He may have hoped that moving to Ottawa would make Wendy happier and revive his flagging marriage. Loyalty to his party and its leader also inclined him to accept. Child of the manse that he was, he was a prisoner of his sense of duty. "I have this old-fashioned belief that when the Prime Minister asks you to do something, you don't turn him down," he told Connie.[9]

His fellow *Morningside* panelists professed to be scandalized. "It's shadow, not substance," Eric Kierans said. "Mr. Camp will be there to tell them how to manoeuvre." "The era of the witch doctor is back," snorted Dave Barrett, who had replaced Stephen Lewis on the panel. "And he can blow smoke and rub sticks together and come up with advice, but it's too late.... It would have been a helluva lot cheaper to buy a Ouija board. That's what Mackenzie King used."[10]

Camp's first day on the job was probably his best day. Mulroney took him out to lunch, escorting him ostentatiously in a cavalcade of cars to the Chateau Laurier, barely a hundred yards away. "He made sure everybody saw them," David Camp remembered. "He was making a statement. It was a good lunch, and Dalton felt that they were off to a good start. It just didn't continue."[11]

It could not have continued—and that was partly Mulroney's fault and partly Camp's. Mulroney had the option of installing Camp as a senior policy adviser in the Prime Minister's Office and, although some noses would have been out of joint, the arrangement could have worked. Instead, too smart by half, he created a new public service position and put him on the staff of the Privy Council Office. That enabled him to pay Camp a higher salary as a senior deputy minister than he would have received in the PMO. It meant he could be assigned a car and driver. It meant the PCO, not the PMO, had to carry Camp's salary and perks on its budget. Yet Camp's office was physically located in the PMO, and he reported not to the clerk of the Privy Council but to the Prime Minister.

The appointment created a precedent by politicizing the PCO. Never before had a senior political player been parachuted into a top position in the PCO. Careerists in the civil service were scandalized. "It is a devastating blow for Paul Tellier, the clerk of the Privy Council," Stevie Cameron wrote in the *Globe and Mail*, "because it makes it clear that he is merely the Prime Minister's deputy minister for administration while Mr. Camp takes over his traditional role as the deputy minister for policy. Mr. Camp has also said himself he will be 'the go-between for the ministers, their departments and the Prime Minister.'"[12]

Tellier, however, was no defenceless victim. A lawyer from Montreal who became a public service manager, Tellier was as tough as they came—a quality he demonstrated after he left Ottawa to take over and turn around Canadian National Railways and later Bombardier Inc., the troubled maker of aircraft and recreational vehicles. Another man whom Mulroney wanted to appoint as a deputy minister at around the same time recalled how Tellier, without expressing a single negative thought, effectively killed the appointment—by sitting on the file, by discovering complications where none existed and by declaring insoluble problems that he could have resolved with a single phone call, had he been so inclined. In the end, the prospective deputy minister gave up waiting and withdrew his name.[13]

Tellier was the top guerrilla in the jungle warfare of the bureaucracy, whereas Camp, for all his experience in political battles, was a neophyte. "Dalton was always alive to the possibility that the bureaucracy was doing things for its own reasons that might not be serving the broader aims of the government," said Andrew Stark, who was Camp's assistant in Ottawa and went on to become a professor of strategic management and political science at the University of Toronto. "He thought bureaucrats had their own games and concerns and often threw sand in the gears."[14]

Flora MacDonald, by now a minister in Mulroney's government, had urged him to bring in Camp. She had been thrilled when she thought Camp was going to be the Prime Minister's chief political adviser, and she was flabbergasted when Mulroney made him a civil servant. "I don't think Dalton ever felt the least bit at home there," she said. "He just wasn't accepted. Any time I saw him, he was not himself. Some of us never quite knew what he was supposed to be doing, and I'm not sure he knew what he was supposed to be doing. In cabinet meetings, he would sit there like a person who wasn't there, and didn't take part in anything."[15]

Camp's position allowed him to attend all meetings of the powerful inner cabinet as well as the full cabinet. Seated in the second row, behind the minister of defence, he surreptitiously took notes, ostensibly so that he could brief others in the Prime Minister's Office about the ministers' deliberations. Under the arcane rules of cabinet government, only the clerk of the Privy Council was supposed to take notes. Others suspected that Camp was simply trying to irritate Tellier—"We never really got along," Camp acknowledged[16]—and, if that was his intent, he succeeded. Tellier complained repeatedly to Mulroney. The Prime Minister, however, was not about to order the man who was widely regarded as his political mentor to leave his notebook at home.

Finlay MacDonald sadly agreed with Flora MacDonald's assessment. "It was the wrong place for him," he told the *Globe and Mail's* Hugh Winsor. "...He could talk political philosophy and talk it beautifully. That was his forte. But knowledge of government was not his field at all.... That was Mulroney's mistake. That sure as hell wasn't a decision made by anybody who knew what the hell they were doing. They weren't taking advantage of Dalton's talents."

Camp found that he had no influence on the bureaucracy and far less than he had hoped on the Prime Minister. He and Mulroney never managed to sort out their relationship in a satisfactory way.

The Prime Minister was delighted with his coup in persuading Camp to join him in Ottawa, but he had no clear idea what he wanted him to do once he got there. It was not even clear who was supposed to knock on whose door. Formerly Camp's protégé, Mulroney was now his boss. Camp had seniority and greater political experience, but he was not prime minister. "That was one of those status issues that often became problematic for Dalton," said Hugh Segal, who became Mulroney's chief of staff a few years after Camp had left Ottawa. "He said to me afterwards he probably should have gone down the hall and knocked on the Prime Minister's door, because he was the prime minister. But at the time his view was: 'I'm here, I'm here to help, he knows where I am, and if he needs me, he'll call.' But when you are a political aide, whether you are one of immense standing and experience, which he clearly was, or a young whippersnapper, the bottom line is you are always a supplicant to the duly elected leader, who in the end has to make fundamental decisions and carries the can."[17]

Knocking on the door only worked to a point. "He's accessible but unapproachable," Camp recalled with a laugh shortly after he left Ottawa. "Access is not the problem. Audience is. Getting his ear is another thing.... If he thinks that someone has come to see him to talk about something he doesn't want to talk about, they will never get a word in. He will just take over the discussion. He'll get them nodding and smiling and agreeing with him, and the next thing you know, you're out of the room and have forgotten what you went in for."[18]

Mulroney had surrounded himself with people who had been his loyal supporters for years—led by Fred Doucet, a buddy from his St. Francis Xavier University days, who had been Mulroney's chief of staff in opposition and was a senior adviser during his first term in office. The loyalists energetically promoted their own agendas, most of them far to the right of the positions that Camp felt the Prime Minister should take to regain the goodwill of mainstream voters. But Mulroney, as Camp discovered, was no lump of clay in the hands of his staff. He had his own agenda for the government—free trade being the most prominent component—and that made him,

Camp commented, "the only prime minister since [Mackenzie] King that had a real honest-to-God agenda."[19]

Mulroney's agenda included national reconciliation, which meant rapprochement with Quebec and constitutional renewal—which led to the Meech Lake and Charlottetown accords—as well as raising Canada's status in NATO and the world, repairing relations with Washington and, on the economic side, establishing a program of fiscal responsibility.

Some of it worked and some, such as deficit reduction and the Meech Lake and Charlottetown agreements, did not. Camp wrote two throne speeches for the government in his two and a half years in the PMO-PCO. He organized Mulroney's agenda, giving a nudge to items he thought should have priority while holding back others that he felt would not contribute to moving the government to firmer political ground before the next election.

Camp could rightly claim to have made a difference on three major issues. One was the decision in 1988—stubbornly resisted by veterans' groups and a number of cabinet ministers—to pay financial compensation, and to officially acknowledge the injustice done, to 20,881 Japanese Canadians who had been removed from their homes and had their homes and businesses confiscated by the government during the Second World War.

The second issue was one especially close to Camp's heart: the creation of the Atlantic Canada Opportunities Agency. Ever since his days as a student Liberal, he had believed that the Atlantic provinces would never prosper or be able to preserve their way of life unless they received special help from the central government that would be above and beyond the equalization payments by which the rich provinces subsidize the poor ones. ACOA, he was sure, would address those needs. Almost single-handedly, he pushed the government into approving the agency. He put it in the Speech from the Throne and he fought off the regional ministers who wanted to control ACOA—and the dispensing of its funds. In the end, however, Camp felt let down—and betrayed by Mulroney—as ACOA turned into just another pork barrel, like so many patronage-driven regional-development agencies before it.

The third issue—the creation of a national park on South Moresby in British Columbia's Queen Charlotte Islands—was Camp's greatest achievement. More than anyone else in the government, he was the one who made it happen. His role was documented by environmental activist Elizabeth May in her 1990 book *Paradise Won: The Struggle for South Moresby*.[20] The battle to save South Moresby from logging had been going on for 14 years; it was one of the epic environmental struggles of the 1970s and 1980s. May, who was working at the time as an adviser to Environment Minister Tom McMillan, was desperately trying to get Mulroney involved personally in her campaign to persuade a recalcitrant Social Credit government headed by Premier William VanderZalm to agree to the creation of a national park on South Moresby.[21]

In desperation, May approached John Fraser, a Tory MP from Vancouver who was then Speaker of the House of Commons. He advised her to seek out his friend Camp. "I was speechless," May wrote in her book. "Dalton Camp, the legend, the power-broker, the man who, in terms of political geology, is a mountain who watches grains of prime ministerial sand blow away. He's not someone you actually meet."

With great trepidation, May called Camp's office and made an appointment. She put on her best suit and armed herself with a background file. "Camp was affable, cordial, and far less intimidating than people with half his clout," she wrote. "His eyes twinkled, and his face betrayed a nearly constant sense of humour. . . . He smiled, and gestured to a chair in front of his desk. 'Sit down and tell us what all this is about.' I liked him immediately." Camp listened intently, then asked, "What would you say were the potential downsides of getting the Prime Minister involved?" May did not answer that question. Instead, she enumerated the advantages of getting him involved. "You couldn't write a movie script with more drama," she told Camp. "I mean, it's better than the last scene in *The Natural* or *The Verdict* or *High Noon*. The Prime Minister can ride in and stop the logging and save South Moresby." She sketched some ways Ottawa could revise its offer to make it more acceptable to the province. "Well, you've sold me," Camp said.

He went to Mulroney, who had been reluctant to press the South Moresby issue with VanderZalm lest he jeopardize British Columbia's support for the Meech Lake Accord. But Camp persuaded him that the political advantages of aligning himself with environmentalists and native groups far outweighed the risks of antagonizing the premier or the lumber companies. He sold the doubters in the cabinet and pushed the plan past reluctant senior bureaucrats. "It took someone with Camp's clout and savvy at the centre to get it done," said Lowell Murray.[22] Pat Carney, a senior minister from B.C., got it right when she told Mulroney at the signing ceremony in Victoria: "Announcements about ice-breakers are a one-day wonder. But this matters. This is important. It is an achievement that will last, and it is something for which future generations will thank you."[23]

Camp did not fare as well on other issues. He campaigned actively to have the government implement a promise to establish a national child-care program. But the finance department did not like the cost projections and other ministries worried about the implications for federal-provincial relations. Mulroney would not lend his weight to the program, and child care disappeared from the agenda when he called the 1988 election. Camp believed the Prime Minister had let him down, and he felt the same way on the government's controversial decision to award a huge maintenance contract for Canada's new fighter aircraft to a company in Montreal rather than to the one in Winnipeg that had submitted the better bid.

Senior bureaucrats lobbied strenuously in support of Montreal—partly because the bidder there was Canadian owned while the Winnipeg company was a subsidiary of a British firm, and partly because they were anxious to reinforce Montreal's aerospace industry. But Camp, the political realist, was not convinced. Quebec always loomed large in the minds of Ottawa bureaucrats, he knew. And, although he understood Mulroney's desire to award the contract to Montreal—Quebec had become an important political base for the Tories—he feared the damage to the party's credibility in the West would be greater than the benefit in Quebec if Winnipeg were rejected. He allowed himself to be persuaded to go along with

Montreal, however, and he was angered afterward when he discovered that he and others in the government had been fed misleading information that suggested the Montreal bid was virtually identical to the Winnipeg bid—which it was not. The contract went to Montreal. Politically, it was the wrong decision and, as Camp had anticipated, the Conservatives paid a heavy price in Western Canada. The CF-18 maintenance contract became a flashpoint; it reinforced Western alienation, helped to destroy the Tories as a viable entity west of the Lakehead and contributed significantly to the rise of the Reform party (later the Canadian Alliance). If Camp had had the clout he thought he would have when he agreed to go to Ottawa, the CF-18 fiasco might never have happened.

Perhaps Camp's biggest challenge was to tone down Mulroney's rhetoric. He tried to get him to ease off on the hyperbole, to drop his excessive use of the first-person pronoun and to abandon his irritating habit of larding his speeches with quotations, often pointless, from other people. He tried to convince the Prime Minister that leaders do not quote others; they say important things in interesting ways, and other speakers quote *them*. Camp called himself "the 'I' doctor," and at one point, while vacationing in Florida, he wrote a speech for Mulroney without a single first-person pronoun in it. He sent it off to the Prime Minister. When he got back, he found the word "I" had been inserted in almost every line. He asked Mulroney's speechwriter L. Ian MacDonald what had happened. "I didn't do that," MacDonald said. "Mulroney did that."[24]

Camp tried to tell the Prime Minister, and anyone else who would listen, that his speeches were appalling. "They were wooden, hollow and empty," he said. "Trite. Awful. Just terrible. And hyperbolic, too. And full of bullshit. And self-serving. A speech should be self-serving. That's the reason for making it. But to have it audibly self-serving is another matter."[25]

There was no way Camp could change Mulroney. The best he could hope was to calm him down until the election was over, to moderate his speaking style and remind him he did not need to go into overdrive every time he met a group of three or more people.

Winning the election, of course, was the principal reason for

Camp's presence in Ottawa. He was part of the central group, attending the daily planning meetings and helping to develop a tightly focused strategy on issues. He was influential, more influential in the campaign than he had been in the government. Atkins, the organization man, concentrated on what he did best: running the election machine.

Free trade was the only significant issue as the 1988 election began—the Tories were committed to implementing the free trade agreement with the United States that Mulroney had signed with President Ronald Reagan, while the Liberals, under John Turner, were fighting it tooth and nail. Among the Canadian public, however, opposition to free trade was greater than support for it, and Camp knew the Tories could not win unless they could shift the issue. That is what they did. Using polling data from researcher Allan Gregg and a massive advertising campaign—financed in large measure by the big business interests—the Conservatives attacked Turner. It was what Gregg called the "bomb the bridge" strategy— the bridge being the link between opposition to free trade and intention to vote Liberal. As Gregg reported, the link was Turner's credibility. If the Tories could destroy his credibility as a prospective prime minister, swing voters would turn on the Liberals and move to the Conservatives, despite free trade and despite their dislike of Mulroney and his government.

The Tories did not have to make Canadians love Mulroney; all they had to do was make them frightened of Turner. It was a classic Camp counter-puncher strategy—find the opponent's weakness and attack it relentlessly. It was not pretty, but it worked brilliantly. Although their majority was sharply reduced, the Tories managed to win 169 of the 295 seats—a solid victory scratched out against what had seemed to be oppressive odds.

Camp may have been the only Conservative in Ottawa who did not celebrate Mulroney's second majority. His life was in a shambles. He was miserable in his work and wished he had never taken the job. He felt Mulroney had not been there for him when he needed him. For his part, Mulroney was losing patience with his prickly adviser. Hugh Segal, who was friendly with both men, remembered talking to Camp about his estrangement from the Prime Minister. Some of Camp's views, Segal said, "became problematic for Brian, and he wasn't quite there at his beck and call as a staffer should be. I think Dalton's perspective was, 'Look, at a time when I wasn't all that well, I pulled myself up from a pretty comfortable lifestyle, gave up a column and various other important sources [of income] to go work in Ottawa—and I'm isolated; I'm not invited to staff meetings in the morning, and I'm not invited to sessions at 24 [Sussex Drive], and I'm not part of the inner circle. So why the fuck am I here?' I think you could probably make a case that they're both right, but I think that was the source of it, essentially."[26]

"We had a very difficult relationship," Camp acknowledged. "He's different than I am. He's a great believer in bullshit, and I'm not. I'm too old for that."[27] As his frustrations grew, his bouts of depression became more frequent and prolonged. Wendy Camp would arrive home to find her husband sitting alone in the dark, not wanting to talk to anyone. "Then he'd go away someplace, and it [the depression] would be gone," she said.[28]

His health deteriorated. The man who a decade earlier was in the habit of running several kilometres every day, stopped exercising and started eating and drinking too much. He put on weight, and Segal was worried: "You know, when a guy's breathing is audible when you're sitting at a table just eating and drinking, that caused me concern."[29] At one point, his doctor told him that if he did not stop drinking and smoking—immediately—he would die.

He began to lose interest in his wife and son, preferring after-work drinks with Finlay MacDonald to going home to his family. "At an earlier stage of his life, he would have been prepared to make a bigger effort," his son David said. "He would have been more accepting of the compromises and frustrations that went with [the PMO job]. It wouldn't have been as strenuous and exhausting, as it was at this stage in his life, with his health deteriorating and with his relationship with Wendy deteriorating. I think he was pretty troubled by then."[30]

David's sister Connie got an early sense of trouble in their father's marriage. Dalton, Wendy and Christopher, along with Camp's government driver, Willie Jobin, had gone home to New Brunswick to spend Christmas at Northwood. When Connie dropped in to see her father, she found him reading alone in the solarium. In another room, she found Wendy, Christopher and the driver laughing, playing and having a great time. "There was such a difference between the two scenes, I could tell there was something [going on]," she said. To Connie's eyes, the happy couple seemed to be Wendy and Willie, not Wendy and Dalton. "Something had happened.... I thought it was really obvious.... My father seemed to be not at all interested in what was happening. We had dinner, and it was the most uncomfortable dinner."[31]

Before long, rumours began to spread in Ottawa about trouble in the Camp marriage. Jackie Webster, Camp's old friend and a journalist in New Brunswick, heard the same rumours in Fredericton. As Camp told it to David, to Webster and to other friends, a person he knew in Ottawa—he did not say who it was—came to him to say he felt he should know that his wife was having an affair with his driver. It was October 1988, six weeks before the general election. He went home and confronted Wendy, who, Camp said, admitted it was true. Jackie Webster asked what he did then. "He said, 'I packed my bag and I left the house and I never spent a night in the house since.' He went to the Chateau [Laurier]."[32] He subsequently moved to an apartment hotel. (In separate interviews with the author, both Wendy Camp, who became a real estate agent in Ottawa, and Willie Jobin, who went on to chauffeur cabinet ministers, denied they had an affair. Camp petitioned for divorce in 1990, but the suit languished and the couple remained legally married, although profoundly separated, at the time of his death.)

When Camp talked, as he did from time to time, about the breakdown of his second marriage, he never blamed Wendy. "He told me he had been hired for a role that didn't exist," Jackie Webster said. "It was frustrating all the time. He gained a lot of weight and was drinking too much. He knew he was poor company. And he said Wendy had tired of him.... He was very nice about it. He said, 'I don't blame her. I've never blamed her.'"[33]

The election won and his marriage lost, Camp could not wait to get out of Ottawa. As word of his intention to leave spread, sympathetic friends tried to look after him. A Senate seat was suggested. Camp was not interested; he had no desire to have anything to do with the capital. He was offered, and declined, an appointment as Canadian consul general in Boston. Early in 1989, he wrote a brief note of resignation to Mulroney and packed up his files and possessions.

There were no parties, no flowery tributes and no public expressions of gratitude or regret when Dalton Camp quit Ottawa. He slipped away so quietly that some people who thought they knew him were unaware that he had gone. He went back to the one place he wanted to be—to New Brunswick and his beloved Northwood, there to live the life he wanted—by himself.

CHAPTER 24

A New Heart

DALTON CAMP SUFFERED from a variety of health problems during his life. As a schoolboy in California, he had been sent to bed for most of a year with a severe infection and nearly lost both big toes. He was born with 20 per cent vision in his right eye, a handicap that prevented him from enlisting in the air force and almost kept him out of the army in the Second World War. His eyesight was a constant concern as he grew older. He loved reading and he lived to write, and he feared that if his eyes betrayed him he would not be able to do either. He was never able to find glasses that he felt were adequate. In 1982, he had surgery for a detached retina; despite the operation, he continued to experience blurred vision from time to time.

Toward the end of his life, his hearing began to fail and his eyesight became so bad that, in the judgment of his children, he was a menace on the highway—not that they could persuade him to give up driving. He was too stubborn. His son Michael, who lived in New Brunswick, did what he could to persuade his father that he and the rest of society would be safer if he gave up his licence. "I was the hammer and he resented it," Michael said. But he understood his father's resentment—"Taking away someone's driver's licence is like revoking his citizenship—and that's how he felt—especially here in rural New Brunswick."[1]

His heart trouble, which began in the 1980s, had much to do with the pressures of his work, and, especially, with his personal lifestyle. He had joined the martini circuit when he was in advertising in Toronto, and in his years in politics he sat up far too late smoking and drinking far too much on far too many nights. That he never seemed to get drunk had more to do with his tolerance for alcohol than with restraint in consumption. Hugh Segal remembered family dinners at Northwood with Camp and Wendy in those years. "We'd have two or three martinis, then split two or three bottles of wine, when there's just four of you at the table. Then we'd have a Cognac or two afterwards." Segal would feel hung over for days, but Camp would be up in the morning, typing cheerfully away.[2]

In 1984, Camp was hospitalized for 11 days with a virus that proved to be unexpectedly serious. The virus apparently attacked and weakened his heart muscle. It was months before he regained his former strength. By the time he accepted Brian Mulroney's offer to become a senior deputy minister in Ottawa in 1986, he was already suffering from a heart condition. His breathing had become laboured, and he seemed to his children to be growing prematurely frail.

Going to Ottawa was the worst thing he could have done for his health. The frustrations of the job and the stress at home, combined with the too-ready availability of old drinking buddies like Finlay MacDonald, led him into a cycle of heavy drinking and excessive eating that often left him gasping for breath with the slightest exertion. He went to see Dr. Goodman Cohen at the Ottawa Heart Institute, who told him he was in very bad shape. "I run with a fast crowd," Camp quipped. "Well, you won't run very much longer," Cohen told him.[3] When Andy Stark, his assistant in the Prime Minister's Office, had lunch with his boss, Camp would routinely down a couple of martinis before the meal. One day, after being frightened by Cohen's warning, Camp went cold turkey. He would not drink a drop. Stark was impressed by Camp's inner strength in abruptly giving up liquor, which had been so central to his lifestyle for so many years. His abstinence did not last, however.

By the time Camp returned to New Brunswick in 1989, he was in bad shape, although he resumed his pre-Ottawa routine at Northwood as best he could. He found the Tuesday morning trek into Fredericton for "Kierans, Camp and Lewis" an increasing struggle. Some weeks he would drive himself; other times his son Michael would drive him; in bad weather he would occasionally stay over Monday night in a hotel in Fredericton.

Camp was excited when St. Thomas University in Fredericton awarded him an honorary doctorate, but he was also worried—not about his speech, but about whether he would able to walk into the main building to the platform. "He gave a beautiful speech, but he was more preoccupied with those steps," his daughter Connie recalled. "He didn't want people to know. I don't think anyone had any idea how hard it was for him."[4]

Connie, his second daughter, moved into Northwood to be with her father during this time. "He was in very bad shape," she recalled. Despite his doctor's orders, she found him sneaking cigarettes from time to time. On days when he had a column to write, Connie would fix his breakfast, and for a long period she had to bring it to his bedroom because he was unable to manage the stairs to the kitchen. A column that in the past would have taken him a few hours to write was taking all day. "He wasn't really looking after his health. And then he had a couple of bad episodes—one that could have killed him," Connie said.[5]

Anna Ruth Atkins, the wife of Camp's former brother-in-law, Norman Atkins, probably saved his life. Camp's customary response when he found he could not breathe was to slip away and hide where people could not see him. Anna Ruth saw him acting strangely one summer day, realized what was happening and got him to hospital in Fredericton. The cardiologist told the family Camp was suffering from cardiomyopathy, a disease of the heart, that had brought on congestive heart failure—a condition caused by the inability of the heart to pump enough blood to the lungs and other tissues.

"He had a really flabby, useless heart," Connie remembered. "He couldn't get a breath.... The cardiologist just basically said he was dying. She essentially told my sisters to grow up and face it: 'Your father's dying.' He was only about 70. She called him an old man."[6] They put Camp on a special diet, and his daughters tried to make him eat healthy food. Although he had some relatively good days to offset his bad ones, his condition continued to deteriorate.

The crisis came at Christmas 1992. With Connie ill in Toronto, Camp's estranged wife Wendy and their son Christopher came from Ottawa to spend the holidays at Northwood. Wendy was shocked when she saw how sick he was. So was Norman Atkins when he dropped by Northwood on his way to Halifax for Christmas. They found Camp alone, in bed and barely able to breath. "Wendy and I literally thought he might not make it through the night," Atkins remembered.[7] "He was scared," Wendy said. "He knew exactly what was happening."[8]

Wendy was not prepared to accept the Fredericton physician's verdict that Camp was dying. Her gynecologist father had died of heart disease in 1974. The doctor who had performed emergency bypass surgery on him following an earlier heart attack was Wilbert Keon, the director of the Ottawa Heart Institute and Canada's leading transplant surgeon. He was also a Conservative senator—a colleague and friend of Atkins. Wendy was determined to try Keon. "Dalton always said, 'You have the gall of a canal horse,'" she said. "I'm like that with certain things: something's wrong, I fix it."[9]

She made the call: "Dr. Keon, I need your help. Dalton's very ill." Keon replied: "Why don't you get him up here? I'll do everything I can." The next challenge was to persuade Camp that it was worth pursuing the seemingly remote possibility of a heart transplant. It was arranged that Camp would call Keon at a pre-arranged time. "Why don't you come up and let us take a look at you?" Keon suggested. Camp agreed. He flew to Ottawa the following week for a battery of tests. His heart was operating at about one-fifth of its normal function. The Heart Institute panel that evaluated him found, however, that he was in surprisingly good health in other respects.

"All those years of boozing had apparently kept his arteries in a beautifully clear condition," said his son Michael. "It's hard on your heart, but great for your arteries, I guess."[10] Keon said the healthy condition of his other organs pointed to a virus or some kind of autoimmune reaction, rather than lifestyle, as the principal culprit—"The reality is, the booze in moderation is good for the heart, too."[11]

Despite his age—he was 72 at the time (January 1993)—he qualified for consideration for a transplant. Keon cautioned Camp and his family, however. He had been diagnosed with terminal heart failure. There was no guarantee that a suitable heart would be found and no assurance at all that he would live long enough to undergo the surgery. Experience, Keon said, showed that more than 50 per cent of patients over the age of 50 who suffered from terminal heart failure would die within a year; in fact, the mortality rate was likely closer to what the doctors euphemistically called "universal attrition." Keon gave Camp "probably two or three months, but he could have fibrillated and died any minute. The problem is, when the heart gets that bad, they frequently die of terminal arrhythmia. It just dilates and quivers."[12]

With those sobering thoughts echoing in his head, Camp was sent home to New Brunswick with instructions to return by April 1 —to wait for a heart.

For Camp, the most disagreeable aspect of the whole transplant saga was not the anxiety of waiting for a new heart or even the physical pain and discomfort associated with the surgery. It was being "pole-axed," as Camp put it, by his own newspaper, the *Toronto Star*. During his convalescence, the *Star* published a front-page story headlined, "Heart Transplant: Who's First in Line to Live?" The story quoted "one Canadian heart surgeon, who did not want to be named," as claiming that Camp's transplant had been "the ultimate in Tory patronage"—the implication being that Camp had been permitted to jump the queue for a new heart because he had been a prominent Conservative and his surgeon was a Conservative senator.

There were several things wrong with the story. The surgeon "who did not want to be named" was, in fact, the brother of an editor at the *Star*, and the information he passed to her was low-grade water-cooler gossip that he had picked up at his hospital. Responsible newspapers do not run one-source stories in which the sole source refuses to be named. They do not publish allegations affecting the reputations of individuals without identifying the accuser to the accused (Keon and Camp). They give accused persons a full and fair opportunity to respond. And they get their facts straight. The *Star* story failed each of these tests.

Keon, who had heard allegations of this sort before with prominent patients, dismissed the story as "silliness" and the *Star* as "the rag press." Camp, on the other hand, was outraged. He worried about the effect the story would have on the family of the young woman whose heart he had received. He did, however, manage to get off a couple of good lines. "If the *Toronto Star* were my doctor, I'd be dead—and you can quote me," he told the *Star*. To the *Globe and Mail*, he commented: "The lesson is that you can get bit by your own dog."

The *Star* back-peddled, publishing a brief apology on page two in which it admitted it had no evidence of patronage. The paper's ombudsman reviewed the dispute and concluded the story had been unfair. Not mollified, Camp wrote a column in which he called the unnamed doctor "a liar and a coward" and said he would sue for defamation if he knew who he was. Newspapers tend to get defensive when criticized, and the *Star* was no exception. It circled its wagons and refused to publish the column except as a letter to the editor. Camp angrily quit as a columnist—a breach that lasted for several months until the *Star*'s then editorial page editor, Haroon Siddiqui, a sensitive man and a fine journalist who admired Camp's work, talked him into coming back. As an inducement, he offered to eliminate the tag line on his column that identified him as a former Conservative official—long a source of irritation to Camp, who felt he had left partisan politics in his past. *Star* publisher John Honderich admitted the newspaper had goofed: "I believe now it was totally above board. I believe that [the Keon-Camp version] is exactly what happened."[13]

On April 1, 1993, Camp checked into the fourth floor of the Chateau Laurier Hotel in Ottawa. Known as the Chateau's Gold, or Concierge, Floor, the fourth floor offers tranquility, privacy and attentive service from the long-time chief concierge Thom Ouellette and his staff. Camp would spend the next several months there—his nights in room 466 and his days in the Gold Floor lounge—as he waited for his heart and, afterward, when he was recovering from his surgery. Recognizing it had a very special guest, the hotel gave him a rate of $80 a night for a luxury room that would have cost anyone else three times as much.

During the day, he held court from a comfortable chair in the corner of the lounge. Wearing a jogging suit, baseball cap and slippers, he watched baseball games on television and received a who's who of Canadian politics, government and journalism. Peter Gzowski was in Ottawa one day following the operation, and he sent a note to Camp on the Gold Floor: "Dalton, I understand you just got a new heart. May I have the old one?"

Camp spent six weeks on that floor waiting for word about a heart. He knew it was macabre, but he could not help himself: every night he listened to the sound of bikers roaring past the Chateau Laurier, through the Bytown Market and along the Rideau Canal, waiting for the noise of a crash. "A biker going off the road—they were potential donors," he said. "It's an awful way to think. [But] you can't stop it.... You feel it all the time that really what I'm doing is waiting for someone to die."[14]

He knew the odds were stacked against him. There were five transplant centres in Canada—in Edmonton, London, Ottawa, Toronto and Montreal—each with long waiting lists for replacement organs. A computer in Toronto kept track of the patient information in each case—tissue typing, blood groups, the size of the organ required, the white cell cross-match and other details. If a heart became available, the computer would search for a match in the five centres. The recipient who was most compatible with the donor heart would get the transplant, subject to categories of urgency. For example, all things being equal, a patient who was being kept alive with an artificial heart would be given priority over someone like Camp whose condition was not yet that dire.

Camp's situation, however, turned out to be unique. A young woman, 19-year-old Natalie Young, died during dental surgery in Ottawa. Frantic efforts to revive her at the Montfort Hospital in the capital proved futile. Her parents agreed to donate her organs to save the lives of others.[15] Young's heart, however, had been badly bruised when it was massaged by doctors during the resuscitation attempt. The computer could not identify a suitable recipient in Edmonton, London, Toronto or Montreal. Either there was no patient-donor match, or the surgeons in those centres did not feel the damaged heart would withstand the stress of being transported well enough to permit a successful transplant. The computer kicked out just one name: Dalton Camp in Ottawa. If the heart had not gone to Camp, it would have gone to no one. Wilbert Keon knew the bruised heart was a risk, but he calculated the donor was young, her heart was healthy enough to recover, and the chances of another heart turning up in time to save Camp's life were slim, so the risk was worth taking. But because of the risk, he elected to perform the surgery himself.

The call went out to the Chateau Laurier at 8:30 that evening, May 14. Catherine Fetherstonhaugh, the concierge on duty on the Gold Floor, took the call. She rang Camp's room but there was no answer. Not knowing whether he was in the bath, watching television with the volume turned up, or too ill to reach the phone, she walked down the hall, knocked and in six memorable words announced: "Mr. Camp, your heart is ready."

In fact, he had been watching a baseball game, San Francisco Giants versus Cincinnati Reds, with his first wife, Linda, and had not heard the telephone. Camp was barely able to get up from the bed he was lying on. He struggled into a clean shirt while Linda helped him with his shoes. She got him to the elevator, then half-carried him across the wide hotel lobby, calling to the desk clerks to get them a taxi. She manoeuvred him into the cab, only to find that the driver, newly arrived in Ottawa, had never heard of the Ottawa Heart Institute and did not know how to get to the Ottawa Civic Hospital, to which the institute was attached. They got lost. Eventually, however, they got there and Camp was rushed off to be prepared for surgery.

Wilbert Keon always took the time before surgery to talk to his patients about their lives and their concerns. He found Camp fascinating as they talked that night about Camp's adventures with John Diefenbaker and his friendship with Frank Mankiewicz dating to their days together at Columbia University. Camp was particularly interested in Keon's motivation in coming back to Canada rather than staying in the United States, where he could have achieved greater fame and fortune as a premier transplant surgeon.

As Camp lay on a gurney, waiting to be wheeled to the operating room, his son Michael phoned from New Brunswick. "Well, best

A NEW HEART

of luck," Michael said. "Close your eyes and think of England."[16] Camp chuckled as they wheeled him away. The surgery started at 4:00 a.m. on May 15, 1993. "His heart was terrible," Keon remembered. When the surgeons opened Camp up and put him on a heart-lung machine, Keon exclaimed to one of the other surgeons: "Jesus, this guy really is a Tory! He's got this big blue heart." As he told Camp later, his new heart "was nice and red, and now I said, 'You've got a Liberal heart.'" The surgeon and his patient both laughed at that.[17]

When Camp emerged from the anesthetic, he asked the first nurse he saw what day it was. Told it was Sunday, he made a request: "Would you mind getting me a *New York Times*?" He wanted, he explained, to catch up on the sports pages.

At 72 years of age, Camp was the oldest person to that time to receive a new heart in Canada. Since then, there have been successful transplants with patients in their 80s. According to Keon, age is not a huge factor. "It's quite remarkable," he said. "Thirty years ago, they thought no one over 55 could survive heart surgery. Indeed in Britain, you couldn't get an aortic valve replacement if you were over 65. Now, people aged 95 have aortic valve replacements, and they leave hospital in four or five days." Camp lived for eight years and 10 months following his heart transplant. "And had he not had a stroke, he might have gone on for a very long time," Keon said.[18]

Camp was still in considerable pain when his son David visited him in his room at the Heart Institute. David had been working for Kim Campbell in her campaign to succeed Brian Mulroney as leader of the Conservative party. The convention was fast approaching, and David brought a draft of Campbell's convention speech for his father's opinion.

Camp flipped through the speech, rolled his eyes and tossed it on the floor. "David," he demanded, "what are you trying to do? Kill me?" As one of a committee of authors who had been struggling for a month to come up with a speech that would enable Campbell, the front-runner, to strike just the right note before delegates voted,

David could no longer judge whether the draft was good or bad. "If she gives that speech she'll lose," his father assured him.

"What's wrong with it?"

"Everything," Camp replied. "The opening is awful. She'll lose everyone in the hall, and then the convention." Grimacing with pain, he thought for a moment, then burst out in an irritated voice: "Why not say, 'Tonight I want to talk to you about winning. I want to talk to you about winning the war against the deficit. About winning the battle for jobs. About winning the trust of Canadians. About winning the next election. To do all of that, we need a different kind of leadership, one that understands the yearning of Canadians for real change in our politics and our politicians.'"[19]

David scribbled down his father's words. The speech was rewritten incorporating Camp's opening. David took it to Campbell, who read through it in her hotel suite and seemed thoroughly unimpressed. "She read it in a monotone and looked very disappointed at the end, and said something derisive like, 'So that's it?' or 'Well, it's too late to do anything about it,'" David recalled.[20]

Campbell delivered that speech to the convention, and she won the leadership, unaware that the crucial opening portion of her winning speech had been dictated by a 72-year-old man in a hospital bed who had just survived a heart transplant.

CHAPTER 25

A New Man

W HEN DALTON CAMP returned home to New Brunswick in the early summer of 1993 following his heart transplant, he was a changed man. The most noticeable change was physical. He was almost back to his old self—vigorous and active. He went on long walks with his dogs, black Labrador retrievers named Shadow and Spencer (after Winston Spencer Churchill). He resumed a full load of column writing, public speaking and television appearances.

Every week, he drove into Fredericton to meet close friends at lunches of the Tuesday Club (which, despite its name, gathered on Wednesdays) in a private dining room at the Lord Beaverbrook Hotel. Those friends—Jackie Webster, Barry and Janet Toole, Dan Skaling, Donna Leggatt, Harry Bagley, Tim Andrew, John Baxter, Gordon Gregory and a few others—formed the core of an informal support group for Camp for the remainder of his life, accompanying him on his rambling around the Maritime provinces, travelling to college football games at Acadia, Yale and West Point, talking politics, reminiscing, and lending a hand whenever he needed it. After their long Tuesday Club lunches, they would often regroup around a table in a back corner of DJ Purdy's, the bar in the Sheraton Hotel. That corner became Camp's favourite watering hole and he was there so often, and with so many friends, that the hotel named it "Camp's Corner" and placed a plaque to that effect on the wall. Many nights, Camp could be found seated in his favourite cracked-leather armchair in his corner, drinking Italian red wine and talking intensely to his friends about the latest political events, literature, New Brunswick, sports or just about anything else.

Technically, Camp was limited to one glass of wine per week—at least, that was the instruction from the doctors at the Ottawa Heart Institute. Never one to let technicalities intrude, Camp drank what he felt like drinking, when he felt like it. He did not, however, resume his former late-night carousing, and he took somewhat more care with his diet, keeping his weight down and watching what he ate to the extent of not accepting dinner invitations until he had checked out the menu.

Oh, how he enjoyed his new lease on life! For the first time in years, he woke up in the mornings feeling healthy. "I decided, now I have a chance to learn all the things I don't know," he said. "I've gotten into the classics, into Homer, all this stuff, a lot of areas of inquiry that I never had time for. Suddenly, all this vista of time opened up. It's a gift."[1]

His youngest daughter, Cherie, remembered how happy her father seemed. "My dad really wanted to be alive," she said. "He was just so grateful, and excited.... I don't think he really expected to survive—and he was leaping with joy that he did. He recovered really well. He was just thrilled."[2]

Although the anti-rejection drugs he had to take following the transplant could make him irritable at times, he resumed his life almost as though nothing had happened. Most of his family and friends found him a little more reflective, philosophical and open-minded than he had been. He was more cheerful and more tolerant of the shortcomings of others.

"He suddenly realized he had grandchildren," Cherie said. His eldest daughter, Gail McIntyre, had given birth to her children about the same time that her father and Wendy had Christopher. "He just didn't want to know," Cherie recalled. "He'd say, 'I hate being a grandfather.' He didn't like the idea at all. He didn't want to be old."[3] After his heart transplant, however, as he came to realize how short and fragile life really is, his attitude changed dramatically. "I think he really started to take a lot of pleasure in us, and our kids," Cherie said. "That's what changed for me. I really enjoyed those last 10 years with him. And he was much more easygoing, and wanted to spend time with us. He was much more of a pleasure to be with."[4]

Camp's eldest granddaughter, Emma McIntyre, saw her grandfather often during her years as a student at the University of King's College in Halifax: "Oftentimes, he'd call me up to say, 'I'm taking you out to a dinner.' And he wouldn't be more specific. He wouldn't say who it was for, or what it was."[5] One night she found herself at the head table with Joe Clark and his daughter Catherine at a dinner for an elderly Conservative whom she did not know. He turned out to be Robert Stanfield.

Her grandfather was fun. Sometimes, they would go out for drinks and laughs. Other times, they would set off by car in search of garage sales and back country auctions. "I knew him completely apart from his life in the political sphere," Emma said. "In fact, it didn't really register with me until I was in university and people said they'd read his name in a poli-sci textbook. I knew him as sort of a reclusive writer, with mismatched socks and jogging pants and hoser hats." He became her friend more than her grandfather.

Emma remembered a Christmas dinner with Camp, her then boyfriend and other family members. They had barely taken their seats when Camp, feigning disapproval, demanded of the thoroughly intimidated boyfriend, "So what are your intentions with my granddaughter? Are you going to marry her? Kids these days just mess around." The entire table went silent, as Camp, enjoying himself immensely, said, "Ah, for the Fifth Amendment." Camp would tell Emma he expected to have the power of approval, or disapproval, over any man she was serious about. "I'd tell him that he was the only man for me, and he'd tell me that I made his day. We had a very joking relationship like that."[6]

Emma also established a close relationship with Christopher Camp, who was her uncle even though they were the same age. She found Christopher more serious than his father and much more withdrawn. "A lot of that can be attributed to the fact that he didn't feel comfortable with our family," Emma said. "I think this is part of the reason why Dalton and I became rather close; because I was close to Christopher, I was sort of a go-between for our families. I was a way for him to feel that he was involved with us."

Ever since his father's death, Camp had had a sense that life was, as he put it, a "one-way run." That sense reasserted itself following his transplant. He was determined not to waste a single day.

And he was doubly determined to run his life his own way and to speak his mind when and where he chose.

No other journalist would have taken on author Stevie Cameron the way he did when her best-selling book *On the Take: Crime, Corruption and Greed in the Mulroney Years* was published in 1994. Camp hated the book. He despised the very *idea* of anyone writing a book like that. He believed leaders should be judged by their policies, not their personalities. More important, Brian Mulroney was his friend, just as Richard Hatfield had been—and just as he had not wanted to hear about Hatfield's homosexuality, he did not want to hear about Mulroney's extravagances. He refused to believe a single word in Cameron's book. He condemned it in his column. And he debated it on national television. The only thing he did not do was *read* the book. "Critics of my criticisms of Cameron's book complain I have not read it," Camp wrote in the *Toronto Star*. "Fair enough. But my position on the book is the same as my attitude toward that well-known Bedouin delicacy comprised of sheep's eyeballs smothered in buzzard gravy. I have never cared for it even though, truth to tell, not so much as a spoonful has ever passed my lips."[7]

No other commentator would have taken on the federal (Liberal) government's deficit-slashing spree in quite the way Camp did a few days after that *On the Take* column. The targeting of social programs made him feel like a stranger in his own country—or his country a stranger to him:

> One of these days, you wake up in the morning, look out the window and find the country gone. You might think it's a hard thing to do—to lose a country—but busy minds have been working on it.
>
> Some might be inclined to say it's preposterous. How could you lose a country the size of this one? You could lose Luxembourg or mislay Burkina Faso but surely this would be a helluva hard place to lose, most of it rock and much of it frozen; where would you hide it?
>
> Easy. We could hide it from ourselves. People do that all the time with the car keys, the family pliers, a borrowed book. Why not Canada?
>
> Well, you might say, Canada is a great country, envied and admired

all over the world. Which is more than you can say for your car keys. And, of course, that's true. So far as it goes, I'd have to say today's Canada doesn't look all that familiar to me. If it weren't for Peter Gzowski and a couple of others, Canada could be anywhere, or nowhere. It could be the northern branch office of the World Bank at the corner of King and Bay.

Or a neo-conservative think tank on the windswept corner where Pennsylvania Avenue joins Laurier.

It shouldn't be called Canada anymore anyway. I've been reading my morning paper, looking for a new and more suitable name. The name that comes to mind is Dontneedit; the capital of Dontneedit is Cantaffordit. I am writing this from my hotel room in Cantaffordit, formerly Ottawa, from whence I can see the Parliament of Dontneedit, all of whose members are now redundant, except for the minister of finance, who is in transition.

The movers and shakers here all agree the country's problems have become insurmountable and nothing can be done except do nothing. It is generally agreed in the media and in other opinion circles, that doing nothing becomes us and can be a positive experience as well as serving to earn respect of the international banking community, the Business Council on National Issues, the Citizens' Coalition and Jesse Helms, everyone's designated neo.

The two major political parties—Reform and Liberal—are in general agreement that doing nothing is the best policy; the major difference between them is only the proper rate of speed at which to do nothing. (Those who flat disagree with doing nothing have the choice of joining the separatist party.)

Visitors trying to discover what happened to Canada will find a few clues, he continued:

It is a widely held view that Canada has become more than Canadians deserve, and in today's competitive marketplace only the leanest and meanest can survive with adequate survivor benefits such as stock options, termination bonuses, drive-by consultant fees and paid-up pensions. This can only mean major benefits once enjoyed by average Canadians must be taxed back, including old age pensions, Canada Pensions and family allowances.... I seem to have become a man without a country, living in exile. Confusing it is, because I haven't left Canada but it appears to have left me.[8]

The sense that the country had left him ran through much of Camp's writing in the period after 1993. He did not subscribe to the argument of many of his readers that he had moved to the left, that the life-altering experience of receiving a new heart had made him a loony Liberal, if not a raving socialist. He believed he was upholding the values he had always believed in—social justice, compassion for the less fortunate, the protection of old age pensions and universal medicare, a friendly but wary relationship with the United States, Canadian cultural sovereignty, distrust of corporate Canada, pro-choice on abortion, bilingualism, abolition of capital punishment, minority rights, generosity to the have-not regions of Canada, gender equality, preservation of the CBC and a willingness to pay higher taxes, if necessary, to fund essential public services.

Perhaps, with those views, Camp had never been a true Conservative. But he had been consistent throughout his adult life. What really happened in the years after his heart transplant was that he felt a new sense of urgency. He began to articulate his long-held views more frequently and single-mindedly, more forcefully and more eloquently as he saw the Canadian political centre sliding downhill (as he would have it) into a slough of right-wing rhetoric, greed and indifference to the desperate needs of the most vulnerable members of society. Some of his heightened appreciation for the social safety net and public health insurance was undoubtedly the product of his advancing age and the medical crisis he had recently survived. But most of his political philosophy dated to the days when he studied with Harold Laski at the London School of Economics. "I'm a Red Tory in the same sense, at the risk of being presumptuous, that Winston Churchill was a Red Tory," he told interviewer Pamela Wallin in November 1995. "I'm in favour of people, and I'm in favour of trying to alleviate the problems people have, and I think that's one of the functions of government, and I just don't want to see us abandon that role."

He despised the Mike Harris Conservative government in Ontario because of the way it turned the middle class against the weak and the poor and made them the victims of the so-called

Common Sense Revolution. He was dismayed at what he saw happening to conservatism. "It's become fragmented and corrupted—it's being corrupted," he said to interviewer James Cullingham on VisionTV. "It's been taken over by the money-changers, people who think good conservatism is according to the tax rate, that conservatism is really an appendage of the business ethic, and its sole purpose is to help people make a profit. That kind of monetary or fiscal conservatism has corrupted the meaning of conservatism."

He loathed Preston Manning's Reform party—which, after a fast facelift, became the Canadian Alliance—and held it accountable for the destruction of the spirit and meaning of representative democracy. What was left, he argued, was a Parliament of right-wing politicians, all singing from the same song-sheet. "Call it Manningitis—a disease of politics where everyone talks and no one listens," he wrote. "It produces a false euphoria in its victims who, having spoken out, imagine they have been heard. But that is precisely the sickness: The newspapers are listening to their business-section readers, and the politicians are listening to them."[9]

He took great delight in eviscerating Manning's hapless successor, Stockwell Day. Day stood for everything Camp believed was wrong and dangerous in politics. He was a true ideologue, and Camp had a deep distrust of ideologues of the right or left. One of Camp's bedrock convictions was a belief in institutions—in Parliament and in the political party system. He saw Day and the Alliance as menaces that were intent on undermining the role of Parliament and fragmenting the party system. He was appalled by the way Day allowed his religious beliefs—he was a creationist, a biblical literalist who believed that the Earth was created only 6,000 years ago, that Adam and Eve were real people, that humans and dinosaurs roamed the Earth at the same time, and that creationism should be taught in schools—to influence his politics. Finally, he thought Day was not bright enough to be a political leader.

Week after week, Camp attacked and ridiculed him:

- "Stockwell Day…exuded youthfulness, virility and a strikingly simple mind combined with a naiveté many columnists found endearing."[10]
- "It is not the courage of his convictions that strikes one, but the convenience of them."[11]
- "We are now getting a somewhat better look at Stockwell Day. Save for the gullible, there are no surprises. The Reform Alliance leader is a twister, a wobbler, a primitive."[12]
- "I am anxious to declare my interest here, in the most noble tradition of chain gang journalism. I am a Stockwell Day supporter. In my opinion, Day is a gift to Canadian politics, conservatism and the suspension of disbelief. He offers confirmation that anyone can do politics; anyone can get hired on as finance minister in Alberta, and that skateboarding improves the mind."[13]
- "Under a Day government—how bizarre the thought—public broadcasting would be terminated. And public education would be challenged as never before. Private schooling and religious education would be considered equally valuable assets to the community, and equally state supported, which, of course, encourages fragmentation of the system along with greater isolation and alienation for Canada's children….

  "A Day government (to test your credulity) would create deep, profound divisions in the country, resulting in a nation of bitterness and rancour, by national referenda on abortion and capital punishment; it would Americanize and politicize the manner of appointing judges to the Supreme Court. And as a bonus payment for the redneck vote, the Reform Alliance would extinguish the right of status Indians on reserves not to pay sales and other taxes."[14]

Almost alone among political commentators, Camp admitted to an abiding admiration for the pragmatic Jean Chrétien—"the best politician currently in practice in this country"—and a distaste for his putative successor, Paul Martin: "Martin has had a soft life, even for a politician. He may be the only man in the Liberal caucus who owns an offshore tax haven and, further, who has had the finance portfolio at the softest time in Canadian history. Still, what I like about the Finance Minister is that he has made it all look hard."[15]

His contempt for media baron Conrad Black—"Lord Almost," as Camp called him—knew no bounds. Black had several strikes against him on Camp's scorecard. He was an irksomely visible, self-indulgently verbose symbol of a corporate establishment for which Camp had scant regard. For all his love of Winston Churchill and his reverence for parliamentary democracy, Camp was much more American than British in his thinking; he was amused, and a bit offended, by Black's shameless pursuit of a seat in the House of Lords. To Camp's disgust, Black embraced, as though revealed wisdom, the shallowest kind of reactionary cant. And he published a newspaper, the *National Post*, that Camp did not care for. Or, as he described the *Post* in his *Star* column in 1999: "We discover now there is a market in Canada for a publication glorifying snobbery, relishing titillation, cloying vulgarity, voyeurism and celebrating the mindless prattle of political columnists mysteriously employed by the London *Daily Telegraph*. These manifestations and representations of an anal stage in chronic arrest do sell. It is formulaic, produced under the direction of veteran British public school boys who graduated as suppressed, guilt-ridden post-adolescents and have not moved on. Pity."[16]

Another princeling of corporate Canada for whom Camp had no affection was Fredrik Eaton, of the department store family. He thought Eaton, who had been Canada's high commissioner in London, was an empty suit who had treated Eaton's workers badly and, although a Tory, had wrong-headedly backed the Canadian Alliance, to the detriment of the Conservative party. Maybe worse, Eaton was a duck hunter and Camp had no love for people who found sport in killing birds and animals.

One night, a friend invited Camp to accompany her to a pre-convocation dinner at the University of New Brunswick, of which Eaton was chancellor at that time. Dalton had had a couple of glasses of wine when he spotted Fred Eaton and headed for him. Too late to intervene, his date hurried to catch up. Eaton, she noticed, had a bandage wrapped around his hand. "Dalton in a kind of cheery way says, 'Oh, hello, Fred,'" she remembered. "And then he says, 'Such a shame to see you've injured your hand.' Dalton continues to inquire—I mean his voice is just dripping poison— 'Oh, how could this have happened?' Fred is just oblivious. He was out there hunting, and something happened with a shotgun and he injured his hand. At which point Dalton raises his glass, turns around to me and says, 'Here's one for the ducks.' And then I took him by the arm, and dragged him away. It was so well done. Dalton knew I got exactly what he was saying—and it was so venomous. I just loved him for it."[17]

To argue that Camp did not make an abrupt left turn after his heart transplant is not to suggest he never changed his mind. Sitting on the deck at Finlay MacDonald's summer home in Chester, Nova Scotia, one summer afternoon, he confessed to Bob Stanfield that he had changed his view on a central issue for the Tories: regionalism. Camp, like other Conservatives, had tried diligently for years to promote a party approach that emphasized the rights of the regions against the power of the central government and that advocated a more decentralized federation. That approach was designed partly to attract support in Quebec and partly to assuage the angst of voters in the outlying regions of the country who believed the country was controlled by uncaring Central Canadians. It was why the Tories ended up with such clumsy policies as Joe Clark's "community of communities"—the meaning of which was never clear to anyone. As he grew older, Camp found himself drawn increasingly in the opposite direction, toward Pierre Trudeau's concept of a federation based on a strong central government in which parliamentarians, rather than provincial politicians, would uphold the interests of the regions. "I think [regionalism] was probably a mistake," he told Stanfield. "If I had to do it over again, I'd like to think I wouldn't do it." The "community of communities," and variations on that theme, had "fundamentally detracted and blinded Canadians from what they were and what they had," he conceded to his friend, New Brunswick oral historian Janet Toole.[18]

As an "arch regionalist" from the Maritimes, Camp found it easy to understand Quebec—"I was always on their side." As he told filmmaker Terence Macartney-Filgate in 1999, "What we should have done, what everybody should have done, is to talk about the country more." He almost envied the Liberals for having a spokesman like Trudeau—"There was about him, that sort of scent of an authority, a strong man who would put Quebec in its place. He dined out on that. We [Tories] haven't really had anybody who came along and talked simply and clearly to tell us how to put the country first."[19]

Camp also did an about-face on the issue of ownership of the news media. In 1972 he had gone so far as to testify before the New Brunswick Supreme Court on behalf of the Irving newspaper monopoly in New Brunswick; the Irvings owned all of the English-language newspapers in the province and, with the help of Camp's testimony, they managed to convince the court that, although they had a monopoly, it was not contrary to the public interest. In those days, Camp was absolutely convinced that the state had no place in the newsrooms of the nation. "As to the eventuality of one man owning all the papers in Canada," he wrote to one Irving publisher, "[my answer] would be to the effect that provided the publishers were professionally competent and personally honourable, I would not worry about it."[20]

He took an equally strong, non-interventionist line when he appeared before Senator Keith Davey's Special Senate Committee on the Mass Media in 1970. "If men are allowed to own more than one newspaper, they must be allowed to own them wherever they wish to acquire them." And this: "Good newspapers are those published and edited by competent and well-motivated journalists—and such men are just as likely to be found working for a group or chain of newspapers as in independently owned newspapers. In fact, such talent may be more likely to appear in the larger companies, where the opportunities are more varied."[21]

In later years, Camp abandoned that position entirely. "Davey turned out to be right. I turned out to be wrong," he told Macartney-Filgate. "It [independent media] is gone now. It can't be recovered. There's an absolute requirement for newspapers to economize by becoming larger, by becoming acquisitive, by writing one column for 10 papers rather than having 10 papers with 10 columnists."[22]

There were two principal reasons for Camp's change of stance on media ownership. The first was the emergence of Conrad Black and his Hollinger media group as the dominant newspaper owner in Canada. At one point, Black owned 58 of the country's 104 daily newspapers. Camp felt that was too much power for one person, especially a man like Black. He had no use for the right-wing agenda that Black promoted through his newspapers. He despised the owner's contemptuous attitude toward journalists—"an owner, by the way, who has been heard to say that one of the great myths of newspapering is that journalists are essential to producing a newspaper." Nor did Camp like Black's lieutenant, David Radler, who "once boasted that Hollinger's contribution to journalism was the three-person newsroom, 'and two of them sell ads.'"[23] The ownership picture changed, but the concentration problem simply got worse when Black sold most of his holdings to Winnipeg's Israel Asper, whose CanWest Global already owned the Global television network. Asper proved to be every bit as right wing and even more interventionist than Black.

The second reason was Camp's own experiences as a columnist. Having quit the *Toronto Sun* once and the *Toronto Star* twice over what he regarded as matters of principle, he understood the dilemma that all Canadian writers and editors—young or old, stars or journeymen—ultimately face: not enough outlets and too many of them controlled by too few owners.

If he had any doubt on that score, he had only to reflect on the treatment he and his friends received at the Saint John *Telegraph Journal*. "The *TJ*" was, of course, an Irving paper. And because it was an Irving paper, the bottom line was the only line. In the words of New Brunswick NDP leader Elizabeth Weir, working for the Irving newspapers was equivalent to "modern-day serfdom." The Irvings had no objection in theory to putting out an interesting, even exciting, paper—as long as interest and excitement did not get in the way of profit. There was another problem for journalists who worked for the Irvings, as Camp, the chain's one-time defender, discovered: with their many business interests, from forest products to mining to natural gas distribution, the family put a premium on maintaining close and cordial relations with whomever was in power in Fredericton. "The *TJ* was just an organ of the provincial government," said Camp's friend Donna Leggatt.[24] A complaint from the press secretary to the premier of the province weighed far more heavily on the Irving scales than a bushel of National Newspaper Awards ever would.

Every now and again, however, the Irvings hired editors who actually wanted to make a difference and, for a while, the owners would let them try. One who tried—hard—was Philip Lee, the young editor of the *Telegraph Journal*. In the fall of 1997, Lee had the bright idea of retaining Dalton Camp as a freelance columnist. The *TJ* was already buying Camp's Sunday and Wednesday national political columns from the *Toronto Star* and paying a pittance for them. Lee wanted Camp to write about New Brunswick politics once a week, in Monday's paper. The idea was to run the column on page A3, the principal display page in the front section. If the column was especially interesting or provocative—or if it was a slow news day—it might run on page one. It took a bit of budgetary legerdemain, but Lee was able to bundle the New Brunswick column with the two *Star* columns and get all three for $450 a week. It was an astronomical amount for the purse-pinching Irvings, but they agreed to pay.

"We got into trouble right off the bat," said Deb Nobes, who was Lee's managing editor. "He was a Tory and not identified as a Tory in his columns. He was writing about everything. He's a wonderful writer and a star columnist so we would occasionally put him on the front page. I would get a call from the premier's office, saying, 'Why are you running him on the front page? He's a columnist.' We ran him on A3 regularly, but when he was really good we put him on page one. When it's a Monday paper, after a weekend, you often don't have a lot to put on the front page. So you go with the best stuff you have. Occasionally, it was Dalton's column."[25]

Phil Lee received a call from the director of communications in the office of Camille Thériault, a Liberal who was premier for a year between Liberal Frank McKenna and Conservative Bernard Lord. "He called to complain we didn't have a Liberal columnist to balance Dalton, and he was a partisan, and we were running him on the front page when it was not news," Lee said. "We told him it was our decision what we run on the front page. I said, 'I'm surprised I'm talking to you about this.'"[26]

That was not the end of the matter, however. Someone in the Thériault cabinet placed a call to the Irvings. According to scuttle-butt in the *TJ* newsroom, the minister who made the call was Alan Graham, the deputy premier. Graham was also the minister of natu-ral resources and energy, which made him the minister responsible for distribution of natural gas in New Brunswick—rights the Irvings were bidding for at the time.

Lee was summoned to meet J.D. and J.K. Irving in the spring of 1998. In a family where many of the males go by their initials, J.K. was a son of the late patriarch, K.C. Irving. J.D. was the son of J.K. (and grandson of K.C.). J.K. and J.D. were known as the "lumber guys"—that is, they ran the Irving forest products inter-ests—and the way the family had organized its businesses, the lumber guys looked after the *TJ* and its since-closed sister paper, the *Times Globe*.[27]

J.D. and J.K. told Philip Lee they were going to replace him as editor. "There were no reasons given," Lee remembered. "They said, 'We've made this decision and we want you to do something else in the company. We don't want you to leave.' I said I needed to think over my options and that's the way it was left." A few days later, he was summoned again. This time, the lumber guys wanted to talk about editorial content, including Dalton Camp's column. "They said they weren't happy with the way the paper was going," Lee said. "I think the words J.D. used were, he wanted a paper that was 'spicy' but not 'hot.' I had a hard time deciding what that meant. They talked about Dalton and the fact we were running his column on front page and he was a Tory—I guess that was hot, not spicy."[28]

The two Irvings told Lee that he could keep the title of editor, but he would report to a new person, an editorial director who would oversee the content of both the *Telegraph Journal* and the *Times Globe*. The person they had in mind was a political insider, Howie Trainor, who, as director of Communications New Brunswick, was the chief spin doctor for the provincial Liberal government.

The Liberals were in trouble, and they knew it. Within a year, the Thériault government would be ousted by Lord's Conservatives. "The Liberals were worried," said Deb Nobes, the young managing editor. "They were calling me. They were bitching about headlines, complaining about stories and editorials. They were worried about losing ground politically. We were writing about the Liberals' health care consultations, the [natural gas] pipeline hearings. Suddenly, there was a lot of scrutiny of what we were doing and saying. Dalton was wrapped up in this."[29]

Lee told J.D. and J.K. Irving that replacing him with the government's official apologist was the wrong move and terrible optics—"They said, 'Okay, we don't care. We want to do this.'"[30]

They did it. Bernard Lord, then opposition leader, raised a hue and cry in the legislature, and Nobes fought to get stories about the controversy prominently displayed in the paper. Meanwhile, the Irvings proposed that Lee write a biography of their family and its businesses. He declined but stayed on as a writer at the *TJ* for a year. Ironically, on the day of the announcement that he was being replaced by Trainor, there was a second announcement: the *Telegraph Journal* had been nominated for seven Atlantic Journalism Awards—and the paper had already won a National Newspaper Award for local reporting under Lee and Nobes.

Nobes resigned as managing editor and took a job with the CBC in Fredericton. Lee went on to become head of the journalism program at St. Thomas University, also in Fredericton, where he hoped one day to establish the Dalton K. Camp Centre of Journalism. Camp's friend Jackie Webster was fired as a *TJ* columnist, replaced by Elsie Wayne, the Tory MP for Saint John, whose ghost-written column was made available to the newspaper free of charge.

When Lee was removed as editor, Camp wrote a memorable column. "He wrote all about Philip being canned," Nobes remembered. "It was sort of, 'I dare you not to run this.' They ran it."[31] But they pushed his column back inside the paper, to the op-ed page. His days as a New Brunswick political columnist for the *TJ* were clearly over.

Lee and Nobes grew close to Camp in the wake of their shared experiences at the *Telegraph Journal*. "Some older men can be creepy, but he wasn't at all that way," Nobes recalled. "I don't think he had a sexist bone in his body. He never made me feel like a 'little woman.'" The three spent long evenings at Camp's Corner in the Sheraton, eating, drinking and talking about some of the subjects that were burdening Camp. He wanted to write about his life but found himself struggling to write honestly about himself and his family. One night, he talked about the Second World War and his desire to revisit the families of friends who had not come back. "Dalton was a more active thinker than most people take him for," Lee said. "He was one of the strong voices against the war on terrorism. He was talking that night that Canada should not have been sending troops over to fight in the Second World War. His pacifism was deep."[32]

Camp moderated his views on other subjects as the years passed. One was the legalization of marijuana. When his children were young, he had worried about drug use—which is why he had been so relieved to learn that his son Michael had been thrown out of boarding school in British Columbia for having sex with his girlfriend, not for using illegal drugs. Camp never had any personal interest in recreational drugs, other than alcohol, but he tended to believe that the government should stay out of the business of protecting people from themselves. "He felt the law was to protect you from someone else," Michael said. "Laws that are designed to make you a better person or take your choices away from you, he thought were a disaster."[33]

As time passed, he became a public advocate for the decriminalization of marijuana. With some delight, he reviewed arguments that had been made against pot over the years—it causes an increase in crime, leads to addiction, insanity and sexual promiscuity, diminishes the ability to resist homosexual advances and even (this being an old chestnut from the McCarthy era in the United States) makes people more susceptible to communist propaganda. His real objection, however, was that pot laws did not work: "Chasing and jailing people possessing or trafficking in marijuana has become an international sport for politicians, who create laws, and for the police who must enforce them. It has become an expensive and losing game.... Why are we doing this to ourselves? The result is widespread public contempt for the law—whatever it is—as well as a shining example of political cowardice. We should demythologize and legalize the stuff. And tell our politicians to get off the pot."[34]

He was delighted when Tory leader Joe Clark did just that. "To put it succinctly, Clark is driving his critics nuts," Camp wrote. "It was unsettling, to say the least, when he came out in favour of the decriminalization of marijuana. But his critics went berserk seeing the Progressive Conservative leader riding in the lead car in a Gay Pride parade in Calgary. For the Real Men who profess to be running the Real Right campaign, Clark's performance of late risks losing the homophobe vote, and could encourage children to visit opium dens. Also, it is timely to note that Clark is opposed to capital punishment and in favour of women having control of their own bodies. What Clark is saying—and what the Real Right is hearing—is that he is a Progressive Conservative."[35]

Camp also mellowed—although that was not a word he would have used about himself—toward Brian Mulroney. He had been angry, bitter and ill when he left Ottawa in 1989. Some of his criticisms of Mulroney had been unduly derisive. Back in New Brunswick, his perspective slowly returned. "Mulroney was a very compelling figure and he had great qualities," he told Terence Macartney-Filgate for a documentary that never made it to air. "He had a disposition a lot like Diefenbaker's. When he was angry, he was very angry. He said things he didn't mean." And yet Mulroney, as Camp had observed, would sit patiently for hours in cabinet listening to arguments he had heard before, some of them stupid; he treated his caucus with great respect and established a thoroughly professional relationship with the public service.

In an article for *Maclean's* in 1997, he ranked Mulroney as the sixth best prime minister in Canadian history (behind Sir John A. Macdonald, Mackenzie King, Sir Robert Borden, Sir Wilfrid Laurier and Lester Pearson—and two places ahead of Pierre Trudeau). He put John Diefenbaker twelfth, just behind Joe Clark. While he may have thought more kindly of Mulroney as time passed, if anything his opinion of Diefenbaker sharpened. "John Diefenbaker squandered, in one term, the largest mandate in Canada's history," he wrote in the same article. "He was, I think, the most unlikely and least competent prime minister since Mackenzie Bowell. He drove his colleagues to despair and drink. His friendships were rooted in sycophancy and his enemies were the product of an insatiable appetite for envy."[36]

He thought it was time for Canadians to reappraise the Mulroney years. "Blaming Brian has been our national crutch, our free flight from reality," he wrote in 1999. "It has become cover for inept government, negligent policy, and reckless partisanship. So long as politicians can exploit the Mulroney syndrome, accountability becomes elusive while responsibility takes a holiday."[37]

Even so, he could never come to terms with Mulroney's fascination with the trappings of power that surrounded presidents of the United States—and he could not resist twitting him about his ego. "He called me at the 2000 millennium," Camp said. "He said, 'Dalt, I just want you to know they're making all these lists. I've made up a list of the 10 greatest political minds in the twentieth century.' I said, 'You did?' 'Yeah, and I just want you to know, Dalt, you and I are both on it.'"[38]

Some of Camp's former fellow soldiers in the political wars drifted away from him. Graham Scott, a Toronto lawyer who had worked with Camp in the leadership-review campaign of 1966 and later was chief of staff to Stanfield, said he stopped reading his column. "I didn't deliberately turn it off," he said. "I drifted away. It wasn't any one thing; it was a series of things. Dalton had become so bitter and so full of himself that I couldn't enjoy it anymore.... I've got happy memories, and I want to leave them that way." To Scott, among others, Camp went too far when he turned against his old Tory comrades in favour of new friends in the Liberal and New Democratic parties. "He shouldn't always be totally at odds with his own party," Scott said. "He shouldn't be using his own situation to constantly shoot down his own party and his own friends, and that's what I felt he was doing at the end."[39]

Hugh Segal, who was one of the partners who bought the Camp Associates agency from Camp and Norman Atkins in 1986 and later was chief of staff to Mulroney, believed Camp "wasted large parts of his life being bitter. When the Harris government was elected [in Ontario]...he was sort of shooting the horses in the stable; he wouldn't even let them on the track for a week before they were dismissed as being bad. He had no obligation at that point in his life to be fairer to the Tories or anybody else, but certainly he had a journalistic obligation to at least wait a month before he came to any final judgments."[40]

Segal ran against Clark for the Tory leadership in 1998 following the departure of Jean Charest for provincial politics in Quebec. He was hurt by the way Camp first encouraged his candidacy, then dumped him in favour of Clark. The issue was capital punishment. Clark was an abolitionist; Segal favoured retaining the death penalty in extreme cases. It came up when Segal held a press conference in Fredericton and Camp showed up as a member of the media. He asked the candidate about capital punishment. "I'm saying to myself, 'What?' Dalton and I have had these discussions 6,000 times," Segal recalled. "I said, 'Mr. Camp, my view is that in the event of aggravated cruelty or mass murder, where the defendant is found to be both sane and guilty, the jury should have the option of recommending capital punishment. That's my view, period, full stop. It's always been my view.'"

"Well, do you see this as destroying your credentials as a Red Tory?" Camp asked. Segal was irked. "He proceeded to write a whole bunch of vitiating columns about me and how I was untrustworthy and all the rest," Segal said. "But after the press conference we went and sat in the bar, he and I with Dan Skaling and others. We laughed and giggled about the whole thing. He had become almost two personalities, the public personality—the journalist, very sincere, very determined—and then the friend, and he was having some trouble rationalizing both."[41]

If some of his old friends felt alienated, there were new friends who delighted in being close to Camp. One was Elizabeth Weir, the NDP leader in New Brunswick, who admired the "spare lean prose that he wrote so compellingly and cogently.... He enjoyed good food. He loved good wine. I would take him every now and again to NDP dinners, which would knock the socks off the Tories. My party supporters quite enjoyed it. It was the Tories that became unhinged at times." Under pressure to jump to federal politics, Weir turned to Camp for advice. "It was a solace to have someone say, 'Nah, you're doing the right thing. We need you here.'" She took his advice and stayed in the legislature.[42]

Another was Alexa McDonough, then federal leader of the NDP. "Without being patronizing, he championed me and Elizabeth Weir," McDonough said. "He had a great respect for women activists or women underdog activists. He was very transparent about it." Before the 1997 federal election, she feared the NDP might be facing extinction. She asked Camp for his advice. "He said to relax and to remember there is a reason why a dog doesn't chase after every car. I got him to decipher it. He said, 'You New Democrats make the mistake of thinking you have to champion every issue, but if you do that, you can't possibly get your target and catch up to where you want to be.'" McDonough thought about Camp's words many times—"It's exactly what we do to ourselves."[43]

Camp had a rare ability to attract young people. He liked their intellectual energy, he valued their conversation and he helped them with their careers when he could. One was Sandra Estey, a young widow, in whom Camp had a keen, if unrequited, romantic interest. He called her "Winnie Churchill" because she shared his interest in the wartime British prime minister. They would drink Rob Roys late at night and talk about literature, about his unhappiness when he was working for Mulroney in Ottawa and about his reasons for leaving Wendy. On occasion, Sandra would go to Northwood to cook dinner for Camp—he was going through a vegetarian phase at the time—and afterward he would insist on driving her home. "Sandra was terrified," said her aunt, Jackie Webster. "His eyes would bother him. He'd see other cars coming and stop his own car right in the middle of the road."[44]

Jamie Irving was another of the young people who gathered around Camp in the last years of his life. "He had a big head," Jamie said, admiringly. He followed Camp's career advice, graduated from Columbia's Graduate School of Journalism and became publisher of the *Kings County Record*, an Irving-owned weekly based in Sussex in the Bible belt of New Brunswick. "Dalton told me to find out how many Bibles they sold in Sussex last year. Then find out how many *Playboys* they sold—and put it on the front page," Jamie said, laughing happily at the memory.[45]

Another was Amy Cameron, a member of the reporting team that had won a National Newspaper Award for the *Telegraph Journal* in Philip Lee's days as editor. "When I first met him, Camp seemed unapproachable," Cameron wrote in a *Maclean's* obituary of her friend. "...[H]e was a Player. He knew prime ministers and premiers, award-winning writers and the who's who of business. More intimidating, he knew their secrets.... [H]e swept me into a conversation and, within minutes, I wanted to tell him everything. He had that effect. He read the papers voraciously and knew which stories we younger reporters worked on. He put us at ease and made us feel like part of an elite gang."[46]

The closest of his young friends was Donna Leggatt, the woman who became the last great love of his life. Camp met Donna through his Tuesday Club friend, Dan Skaling, an older man whom Leggatt was dating. Skaling and Camp had been pals since the days when Tory Richard Hatfield was premier of New Brunswick; Skaling was his deputy minister of tourism and Camp's agency held the contract for the province's tourism advertising. After the fall of the Hatfield government, Skaling went to Ottawa to work for one of Mulroney's ministers and Donna Leggatt was working for another. She first met Camp when he returned to New Brunswick in 1989 following his tour of duty in the Prime Minister's Office, but did not get to know him well until after his 1993 heart transplant. By this time she was running a consulting business in Fredericton and Dan Skaling had a similar business of his own.

Donna was in her late 20s at the time and Camp was taken with her. He liked her curiosity, her feisty spirit and her eagerness to listen, to absorb and to learn. She was an empty vessel into which he could pour the knowledge and experience of a lifetime in business, politics and journalism. He urged her to stretch her mind by returning to university for post-graduate work, and she did. Although he thought she should go to the London School of Economics, she settled for Carleton University in Ottawa and began to divide her time between the capital and Fredericton.

She was enthralled and somewhat awed to be a friend and confidante of the legendary Dalton Camp. "Like [Franklin] Roosevelt, he loved conversation; he loved when it sparkled and he loved when it drifted; and he even loved when it got confrontational," Leggatt recalled. "...He would try me on women's issues, he would try me on New Brunswick issues, Atlantic issues, trying to draw me out.... We had great conversations in restaurants. He warmed up to a number of authors I had been reading. He wanted to get the book, to read the text. He wanted to know: What did they mean? What was that about? It was a fascinating friendship, a fascinating coming together of two people and generations."[47]

Camp was lonely. He had been more badly hurt than he thought when his marriage broke up. "He got all kinds of understanding and support from me," Leggatt said. "I think it takes a lot for a person like Dalton Camp to trust and to reveal. Dalton trusted me—and he had lots of reason to trust me. He was a man who ran away from things, I think, for a lot of his life. He found that I was someone who ran away from things, too. You're running to find something. You're running to settle. You're running to be comfortable. You're running to find someone who understands."[48]

At first, they were a threesome—Dan, Donna and Dalton. Despite Donna's obvious affection for Camp, Skaling, who had children by a previous marriage, asked her to marry him. Not knowing what to do, she shared her misgivings with Camp. What would he advise her to do? Whatever his personal feelings for Donna, he was more anxious about her future and her financial security. Skaling's consulting business was doing well; it seemed as though he would be able to provide Donna with a comfortable life. Knowing this, Camp became an advocate for his old friend. "Dan's a great guy," he told

Donna. "He's been a loyal friend, and you know him well, and I think you should trust him. I think you could marry him. It would be a happy union."[49]

Skaling was grateful to Camp for his support, and the three of them grew even closer. The date had already been set for the wedding when Skaling's business suffered a grievous blow. Through no fault of his own, he was stiffed by a large client. He told Donna what had happened. She had some investments from money that her father had set aside for her and, using those, she helped to put Dan's business back in order. "She was having great reservations about marrying him," Jackie Webster said. "Her grandmother, who was in her 80s, was saying, 'Go ahead, marry him. If it doesn't work out, you can dump him.' The Saturday before the wedding, she was panicking, saying 'I don't know how to get out of it. I've made a big mistake.' She was really scared. Then she said, 'Well, I can maybe comfort myself by the fact I am going to Florence on my honeymoon.'"[50]

As Camp told it later, Donna blamed him for encouraging the marriage. He, in turn, worried that her financial independence had been compromised. "Dalton told me never, never, never to do that again," Donna said. "He got very cool to Dan." Skaling stopped coming to the Tuesday Club. According to David Camp, "It really led my dad to feel responsible for her, and feel care and concern for her, and feel some guilt about her, and to try to make up to her for what had happened."[51]

The threesome of Dan, Donna and Dalton became a twosome—Donna and Dalton. Camp and Leggatt would have dinner together at the Sheraton Hotel in Fredericton; Dan Skaling might show up for dessert and coffee. Leggatt and Camp were almost inseparable. "Dalton was very curious about the older man–younger woman thing," Donna said. With Skaling often away on business, Leggatt and Camp started a small company. It seemed a bit goofy. They called the company Fireside Chats, and its only purpose was to arrange interesting dinners with interesting people. "In a world full of people busy making money, it was our own form of anarchy in a little tiny community," Leggatt said. "He loved it. He thought it was grand. It was fun. We had very nice letterhead and very nice Christmas cards."[52]

One summer, they travelled to Prince Edward Island to visit singer Catherine McKinnon and her actor husband Don Harron. They drove to Wolfville, Nova Scotia, to check out the archives at Acadia University, one of Camp's old schools. He was excited to discover his father's academic transcript, and he and Donna sat in a coffee shop poring over his father's marks. As his eyesight grew progressively worse, Donna would drive him on his excursions and ferry him between Northwood and Fredericton. "My wife is on loan to this man," Skaling told friends, as his relationship with Camp grew more strained. It would not be restored until Camp was in his final illness.

Camp was an extremely complex man, and his relationship with Donna Leggatt was more complicated than most. He was clearly in love with her in the last years of his life. When he visited Toronto, he would talk to Denise Morrison, his friend and confidante at the *Star*, about his love for a married woman and how much it troubled him that he could not always see her when he wanted to, because of her husband.

Donna preferred the word "trust" to "love" to define their relationship; she trusted Camp and he trusted her. But, she added, "He was easy to love. The relationship I had with him will shape me for a long time."[53]

The heart, as Camp's oldest son David observed, is also a complex thing—"I think she loved him, but she might also have still loved Dan."[54]

She was the only woman Camp invited to the Clam Shack, a cabin overlooking Passamaquoddy Bay at Chamcook near St. Andrews, where he liked to go to write in early summer. His secret refuge, the Clam Shack was owned by his friend Jim Ross, a Fredericton developer and restaurateur and (briefly) a senator, who put in a fax line for Camp, along with a satellite dish so he could watch news and sports on television. Even people who thought they knew Camp well were not aware of the existence of the Clam Shack. He did not give out the phone number. Donna Leggatt, however, spent nearly six weeks there in the first summer that he rented the place and shorter periods in subsequent years. When he had a car accident near the Clam Shack the summer before his death, Donna Leggatt was the one person he asked to come to his assistance.

When Camp died, he left an unusual will. His estate, if any, was to be divided between his two wives, Linda and Wendy, but only after a special bequest was paid to a legatee who was not named in the will. It turned out to be Donna Leggatt. The amount was $50,000 and, while Camp probably intended it as reimbursement for the money invested unexpectedly in her husband's business, she has said she will donate any money she receives to an environmental group she and Camp both admired.

There is an old saying in New Brunswick: I came into the world with nothing, and I still have most of it left. The saying fit Dalton Camp like a glove. Raised in straitened circumstances in Woodstock, New Brunswick, following the death of his famous father, he died with virtually nothing left of the wealth he had amassed in his younger days. People would sometimes ask him why, in his 80s, he was still grinding out two columns a week, writing magazine articles and book reviews, and appearing frequently on television. The answer was as simple as it was sad: he kept working because he needed the money. The "fuck-you money"—the funds from the advertising business that he had counted on to finance his independent lifestyle—was long gone. "I used to be rich once," he told Sandra Estey.[55]

He was an odd combination of parsimony and profligacy. For the most part, he lived unostentatiously. The children of his first marriage were raised in comfort but not luxury; they all went to good schools, but they were expected to work in the summers and they knew they would be on their own financially when they finished their education. When David decided to give up journalism, he went to England to study law at Cambridge University. He ran out of money during his last year and wrote to his father asking for a loan. Camp sent him $6,000 on the understanding it would be repaid. After he started practising law in Vancouver, he flew to Toronto, met his father in a bar and wrote out four post-dated cheques for $1,500.

Camp's own lifestyle toward the end was the antithesis of ostentatious; in his trademark baggy sweats, sneakers and ratty ball cap, he looked more like a refugee from a rummage sale than a celebrated political commentator. Money, or the lack of it, did not affect his enjoyment of life.

Yet he treated himself to first-class air travel, the best hotels and the priciest vacation resorts. He never stinted when it came to entertaining his friends. He had spent so much money on Northwood, his elegant home on the hill in New Brunswick, that he could not afford to maintain it as he got older. The family found Christopher's old room filled with dead flies and ladybugs. Camp had dealt with that problem by closing the door and not using the room. In the solarium, the wood around the bottom of the window frame had rotted away, allowing the window to slide down and leave a six-inch gap at the top for rain and snow to come in. Camp ignored it. The roof over the garage and the apartment where Camp's mother and brother had lived started to leak. Water poured in, causing the apartment ceiling to collapse and the hardwood floor to buckle. He had the roof patched but left the ceiling and floor unfixed, and closed the door.

Although he earned roughly $150,000 a year from his writing, broadcasting and public speaking, about half of that went straight out the door in alimony for two wives and tuition and living costs in England for Christopher. What was left had to cover taxes, the costs of operating one house and two cottages, business and personal travel, food, entertainment, red wine and an occasional new baseball cap.

His undoing did not come in the first part of his working life when he was with Linda; he had ample income to finance their lifestyle in those days. Nor did it come in the third part, after he returned alone to New Brunswick from Ottawa; his needs and personal expenses were modest by then. His undoing came in the middle part, in the 14 years he was with Wendy. In addition to pumping far too much money into Northwood, they lived high on the hog, travelled extensively and went blithely through more money than he was bringing in. Although he received about $1.2 million from the sale of Camp Associates, he was not always a prescient investor; when he died, his retirement income fund was mostly made up of Nortel shares, by then relatively worthless.

Most of his friends blamed Wendy, who loved to shop in the most expensive stores, for his financial woes. That was not entirely fair. Camp himself was a willing accomplice in a conspicuously costly lifestyle. He wanted the best for his second family and for himself. He conditioned Christopher to expect a more lavish existence than his first five children had experienced. When Wendy decided she needed something, she bought it. When Christopher wanted something, he was indulged. That was the way the family lived. And it suited Camp, who had always said he never wanted to be in the position of having to ask himself if he could afford something he particularly wanted.

The day of reckoning came when he and Wendy separated. He had already made a settlement with Linda and was paying her $2,000 a month in alimony. In her settlement, Wendy got a house in Ottawa, $2,000 a month in support for herself and $600 for Christopher. In addition, she was earning about $2,000 a month in real estate commissions.

But Wendy was chronically short of money, and the bitterness and bickering that had plagued their relationship since he left her intensified following his heart transplant in 1993. In letters the following year, she talked about the time she had taken away from her real estate job to be with him when he was so sick with his heart condition. That, she wrote, had reduced her income and contributed to her worsening financial plight. "Chris and I do not have even enough money for food," she wrote in October 1994. "We are really struggling and I just don't know what we are going to do. Chris needs things for school like a warm jacket, books, sweaters and there is absolutely no money. Why are you doing this to us who did so much for you? What reason could there be for so much cruelty?"[56]

Eight days later, she wrote again to tell Camp that her financial condition had worsened to the point that she would have to sell her house and file for personal bankruptcy—which she did in 1995. "If you are going to be extraordinarily angry or retaliate against me, if I am to be punished any further, please let me know now so there are no more surprises.... I have loved you in the past. I love you now and will always love you even though that love is very complicated."[57]

The financial pressure on Camp increased as Christopher reached university age. An excellent student, he entered Acadia, which pleased Camp immensely, but switched later to Queen's in Kingston, Ontario, partly to be closer to his mother. Camp provided his son with substantial sums in those years. At one point, he gave Christopher a cheque for $13,000 to get through his year at Queen's, telling him not to come back for more money. As Camp later told his son David and close friends in New Brunswick, Christopher called a month or so later to say he had lost the money and could not pay his tuition. His father was furious, but sent more money. Christopher then wrote his father a letter giving an account of what had happened and sent the letter to New Brunswick by courier. Camp collected the envelope but could not bring himself to open it.[58] He told Donna Leggatt that Wendy's response had been, "Everyone's entitled to one mistake." Camp, Donna recalled, "just said, 'Yeah, okay,' and he never looked at the letter." Some of his friends, however, suspected that Christopher had secretly given the money to his mother and that Camp, suspecting the same thing, did not want to read his son's version.

"Despite that experience," David Camp said, "he continued to give him fairly significant amounts of money. I think he liked Christopher; I think he felt guilty about Christopher. I think he led Christopher into a certain lifestyle."[59]

Camp was not a man to complain about money problems. He was too private and too proud for that. His children, however, could sense how serious those problems had become toward the end of his life. "He kept talking about how much stress he was under," Cherie Camp remembered. "I think really he was chasing his tail. He was tired, he wanted to get a book finished, the wolf was at the door and Christopher was asking for money for the LSE. I think he always wanted to get Christopher back, and it was just a big mess."[60]

It got messier after Camp suffered a major stroke about one month before he died. He was recovering in hospital when he received a letter from Wendy Camp's lawyer demanding money for his client. Then Christopher wanted $40,000 to finish at the LSE; his half-brother David, an executor of the estate, had to tell him there was not enough money in the estate—and might not be enough unless they could sell Northwood. Then there was the issue of Christopher's unpaid students loans from Queen's. They came to $23,000—and Camp had signed as guarantor.

Some of the bitterness came out following a memorial service for Camp in Fredericton. Wendy and Christopher were worried that the first family ("their big family," as she put it) was painting an unduly bleak picture of his finances. They believed he had left more money than they were being told about, and that they ("our little family") were entitled to a fair share. "You should know that he really was hard on my mom," Christopher told David. "He'd come home, having had too much to drink, and he would treat her as if she was pathetic and pitiful." Wendy wanted to know just how much money was in the estate. "Not much," David told her. "You don't know what I have been through for the past decade," she said, walking away.[61]

However sorely money problems plagued Camp's last years, there were happy times to offset the stress. There was a reconciliation of sorts with his first wife, Linda. Although she lived in Toronto and he at Northwood, they became friends once more. He would see her if he was in Toronto, sometimes staying over at her house. They spent Christmases again with their children. In the summer, both took up residence at Robertson's Point. She had her cottage and he had his, but she would often cook dinner for him.

Tributes came his way. There were honorary degrees from three

Atlantic universities—St. Thomas, Acadia and the University of New Brunswick; in addition, he was made an honorary fellow of Ryerson Polytechnic Institute, as it was then. In February 1994— nine months after his heart transplant—he was back in Ottawa to be made an Officer of the Order of Canada. Personal and political friends gathered to pay tribute at an "Evening with Dalton" at the Chateau Laurier. Norman Atkins organized the celebration for his former brother-in-law. Both wives were there and all six of his children. His old friend Frank Mankiewicz came from Washington and was bemused to discover that the once mighty Conservative party that Camp had championed for so many years had been reduced in the 1993 election to just two MPs—Jean Charest, the leader, and Saint John's Elsie Wayne, the follower. Camp's heart surgeon Wilbert Keon was one of the speakers, but the star of the evening, most people agreed, was Camp's son David from Vancouver.

"I don't want to be morbid," he said, "or hit a wrong note on this happy occasion, but a year ago, as my father's health steadily deteriorated, I often asked myself, what was I going to say at his funeral? Tonight, as I look at him in his newfound good health, I ask myself: what's he going to say at mine?"

In the fall of 2000, Camp's friends gathered again—this time in his hometown of Woodstock, to celebrate his eightieth birthday and to raise money for the Dalton Camp Canadiana Centre at the Fisher Library. It was a glittering evening. Jean Chrétien, Brian Mulroney and Joe Clark sent their respects. Premier Bernard Lord praised Camp's tolerance and compassion. His son Michael twitted his refusal to write on a computer. "In a back alley in Toronto, there's a fixit guy," he said. "He's the last guy in Canada who repairs manual typewriters. And Dad is his last customer."

Elizabeth Weir, the provincial NDP leader, recalled how she had first met Camp in 1987 when she was summoned to lunch with him and then premier Richard Hatfield. "Through the years, Dalton Camp has worked not to tear down the ability and responsibility of government to make a difference, but to enhance it," she said. "He is what government should be: informed, articulate and guided by what it feels is best for citizens, not consumed by the narrow cynical view that seeks to win only by forcing others to lose. His compassion, decency and generosity of spirit are evident in his columns and political commentary."

Stephen Lewis said he had never met Camp prior to joining him on "Kierans, Camp and Lewis" on CBC Radio's *Morningside*. Praising his "excruciatingly rational mind," Lewis, a New Democrat, said Camp "was the intellectual glue that held our conversations together."

> I developed this subterranean, begrudging, baffling and intolerable admiration for Dalton Camp. God, the man was good. He had that gently meandering quality where the argument would gradually but irresistibly take shape. And right at the crucial moment, there'd be that disarming, throaty laugh and then, with an intellectual curlicue here and an historical anecdote there, he'd strike home. And I'd be sitting at my microphone thinking, he's wrong, he's dead wrong, I can't let him get away with that antediluvian gobbledygook, but I couldn't get the words out. I had suffered an ornate linguistic seduction. Or even worse, he'd be right. Which was ridiculous—the guy was a Tory. And I'd be left thinking, where are my convictions when I need them the most?

When Camp got his chance to speak, he reminisced about his summers in Woodstock's Sucker Flat. He fished in the river for eels, stole corn that he cooked and ate, and, at the age of seven, ran a minor scam at the Baird Company, makers of patent medicines, where his maternal grandfather was the chief chemist. The company collected a refundable deposit of two cents on every bottle of medicine it sold; Camp would steal bottles from the plant and return them for the deposit. It was a tidy little business, until he got caught.

Although he wrote for the *Toronto Star*, he said, he did not read the newspaper because he could not get it in New Brunswick. That was not necessarily a bad thing. "What I like about the *Star* is the *Star* lets me say what I want to say," he said. "Not reading the *Star*, I don't know what they are saying, so I'm not troubled if I am saying one thing and they are saying another. That's what you call freedom of speech."

Finally, he could not resist a dig at Mulroney. The former prime minister, he said, had called him to inquire, "'Dalt, what's this about Woodstock? I just heard about it. I'm on my way to Peru. I'm calling from the canyons of Manhattan. I suppose they're going to name a building after you? When they do, just make sure they leave room on the plaque for both of us.' I said, 'Well, Brian, I think it's the reformatory.'"

That got a very big laugh.

CHAPTER 26

Camp's Corner

FOR THE FIRST SEVEN YEARS after his heart transplant, Dalton Camp was robust and filled with energy—the picture of health for a man in his 70s, especially one who had come so close to death. One day when he was in Toronto, however, his vision suddenly became blurred and for quite a while he could not focus. He consulted a specialist, who could find nothing wrong with his eyes. His vision returned to normal, or as close to normal as it could be for a man who had had trouble with his eyesight since birth. Putting the incident out of his mind, he went on about his business.

In hindsight, however, it seemed clear that what Camp experienced that day in Toronto was not merely a problem with his eyes, but a small stroke or something akin to a stroke. It probably affected his hearing, too; his family noticed they had to speak more loudly to him. It was apparently the first in a series of stroke-like episodes that would lead to his death two years later, in March 2002.

There was another episode in the early summer of 2001 in which he could have been seriously injured. He was at the Clam Shack, his writing retreat at Chamcook on Passamaquoddy Bay, when he decided to drive into nearby St. Andrews for supplies. He drove up the driveway, got confused and turned the wrong way on the road, away from St. Andrews. Totally lost, he came to a dead end. He drove off the road and into the muddy excavation for a new building. When he tried to get out of the car, he fell into the mud, dropping his cell phone in the process. Somehow he managed to retrieve the phone and pushed the redial button. His call for help was answered in Woodstock, New Brunswick, more than 100 kilometres away, by Gordon Porter, a friend to whom he had been talking earlier. Realizing Camp was in trouble, Porter phoned Jim Ross, Camp's next-door neighbour at Chamcook and owner of the Clam Shack.

Meanwhile, Camp's close friend Donna Leggatt was frantic. Having flown from Ottawa to Fredericton that day, she had tried to find Camp to suggest that she drive down to the Clam Shack and join him for dinner. There was no answer at the Clam Shack or at Northwood. "After a while I began to worry," she said. "I said, that's not like him. He's somewhere. He'd let me know where he is." Checking her voice mail in Ottawa, she found a message from Jim Ross telling her what had happened and one from Camp asking her to come to him. Leaving her husband at home in Fredericton, she hurried to the Clam Shack.[1]

Camp seemed to be all right following that incident, which he was inclined to dismiss as just another problem with his troublesome eyes. In November, however, he crashed into the back of a farm tractor while driving along a rural road near his home. He simply didn't see the tractor. His elderly Jeep Cherokee was demolished, and Camp was taken to hospital in nearby Oromocto with severe cuts and bruises. Too battered to be able to type, he scratched out his *Star* columns in longhand. "He never really regained his composure after that," said his son Michael, who was finally able to persuade his father to stop driving and let his Tuesday Club friends chauffeur him around.[2]

Camp's children, especially his middle daughter Connie, would blame themselves for not recognizing that these episodes were the result of something much more serious than deteriorating eyesight. In fact, it would not have made any difference. After he died, an autopsy revealed he had been suffering from amyloid angiopathy, a buildup of brittle protein in the lining of the tiny blood vessels in the brain. The protein is the same one that causes Alzheimer's disease, Camp's doctor told Connie, adding there is no known treatment for the condition. Physicians were unable to diagnose amyloid angiopathy clinically; it would not have been detected with a blood test or any of the other tests he had to undergo regularly in connection with his heart. The protein deposits caused Camp's eye problems and memory loss, and eventually they plugged the blood vessels in his brain, triggering stroke-like spasms. The condition had been developing for many years, the doctors said, and, if he had lived, he would have shown symptoms of dementia within about two years.[3]

Camp recuperated at Northwood following his tangle with the tractor. He went to Toronto for Christmas with Linda, their daughters and grandchildren; he seemed frail to them. Back in New Brunswick in January, he checked into the Sheraton Hotel in Fredericton to work on his memoirs. He had been there for six weeks when, on February 13, 2002, he went for dinner at the home of his old Fredericton friends, Janet and Barry Toole, just off the campus of the University of New Brunswick. They knew something was wrong. He could not see well enough to dictate his column over the phone to the *Toronto Star*. When Barry took him back to the Sheraton, he had to hold his hands on Camp's shoulders to steady him as he went down the steps. Next morning, Camp suffered a major attack. He had gone downstairs at the hotel for breakfast before catching a flight to Ottawa. One of the restaurant staff summoned Ian Hurst, the hotel's general manager, to say that Camp seemed unwell. He was leaning forward, staring into space. When Hurst wished him good morning, Camp was unable to respond. "Is that Ian?" he finally asked. "I'm all confused.... I don't know what I'm supposed to be doing.... I can't see you." Hurst called an ambulance and alerted Michael Camp, who was at work at CBC Radio in Fredericton.[4]

He spent the next three weeks in Everett Chalmers Hospital in Fredericton. Fearing the end was near, his family hurriedly assembled. Linda Camp came from Toronto. Wendy Camp was in England visiting her son, and she and Christopher flew to Fredericton.

David Camp did some quick detective work to locate Donna Leggatt. A year earlier, Camp had gone to Vancouver to see David and his grandchildren and to get his lawyer son's help in writing a new will. The will provided for a $50,000 bequest to an unnamed legatee. David had no idea who it was.

Camp did not divulge much on that visit. He told David there was "a woman of importance" in his life. He did not reveal her name. He mentioned that she was married and that he had proposed the toast to the bride at her wedding. "What did you say?

Were there any funny lines?" David asked. The one thing that stuck in his mind was his father saying, "'Her initials are D.M.L.' And I made fun of that by saying, 'I always thought they stood for Don't Marry a Liberal.'" That made her initials easy to remember.[5]

When David was paying his telephone bill after Camp left Vancouver, he noticed his father had made several long distance calls to a number in Ottawa. Finally, when Camp was hospitalized, David recalled having listened to a recording of the speech his father had made at his eightieth birthday celebration in Woodstock in the fall of 2000, and he remembered a passing reference: "Donna and I came to Woodstock…"

So he had the woman's initials and a probable first name and phone number. "When Gail called me and said it looked like it might be fatal—that he was in a coma and might never regain consciousness—I put down the phone, and I made some calls," David said. "One of them was to what I thought was Donna in Ottawa. I wasn't sure, but I called this number, and I said, 'Hi, this is David Camp, and you're Donna, and I think you might be interested to know that my father's had a stroke, and it's very serious.' And she said, 'Thank you for telling me, and I am concerned to hear that, and I'm going to go down there.'"[6]

At the hospital, the family divided the day into two-hour blocks with each person assigned to a shift in Camp's hospital room. As he came out of his coma and began recovering his faculties, the three main women in his life shuttled in and out of his room, with care being taken to keep their paths from crossing. As David told it, the scene had some of the slapstick elements of a French farce, with women entering and leaving and Camp struggling to keep them straight: "I'd go in after one of these women had left and he'd say, 'David, I really feel the most beautiful thing is happening. I really think I'm going to be able to have the love in my life that I need.' And I'd say, 'But Dad, that was Wendy.' And he'd say, 'Wendy? That was Wendy? Now, which one is she?' I'd say, 'You married Linda first. Let's call her number 1. Then you married Wendy, she's number 2. And Donna is here, that's number 3. Let's try and get that straight.'"

Getting it straight was not so easy. "I'd come in afterward," David recalled, "and he'd say, 'I just had the most beautiful time,' and I'd say, 'Who was it?' He'd say, 'Well, it was number 3, wasn't it?' And I'd say, 'No, it was number 2.' He'd say, 'Oh God, was it really number 2?' And I'd say, 'Yeah, it was number 2,' and he'd say, 'Well, where's number 3?' 'She's coming in the morning.' It was all very confused, and had its funny moments."[7]

Camp's friend Jackie Webster was in the hospital at the same time for treatment of a heart condition. "He got seven calls from Brian Mulroney while he was there, three that first night," she recalled. But Camp grumbled that Prime Minister Jean Chrétien had not called. "You've had several calls from Mulroney," Webster pointed out. "Humpf," Camp said. "He calls everyone who has a sprained ankle." But then Chrétien did call. "There was a moment," Webster also remembered, with a hearty laugh, "when Linda and I were alone with him and the nurse comes barreling into the room and says, 'Mrs. Camp is on the phone from London.' Linda took the call. That's when I knew Dalton could hear because he laughed. There was this guffaw from him. Then he lapsed back. That's the amusement value of the two wives."[8]

As Camp was making what seemed to be a miraculous recovery, he was devastated by the news that Finlay MacDonald, his closest friend for many years, had died of a sudden heart attack. The doctors would not permit him to travel to Halifax for the funeral, although he propped a manual typewriter on his knees and struggled to write an obituary for his friend. The doctors did allow him to make daytime excursions out of the hospital. His daughters Gail and Cherie took him to inspect an assisted living residence with the view to renting a suite there until he was well enough to resume life at Northwood. Camp did not want any part of a place like that. "We were met by this woman from hell," Gail remembered. "She was the local manager of the franchise." Looking at Camp, she said, "Well, I guess you're here about this young fella, aren'tcha?" As Camp started laughing, she promised, "Oh, you're gonna make so many friends here! You're not gonna be lonely for a minute." She told them about the bingo games for residents and explained the institution's point system—a resident collected 50 points for climbing the stairs instead of using the elevator and another 50 points for carrying his or her own tray in the cafeteria. And there were gold stars, too, for other demonstrations of approved behaviour.

The assumption that he was gaga because he had suffered what amounted to a stroke was terribly demeaning, and Camp grew annoyed. He wandered around, examining the hunting pictures that lined the corridors of the residence. Then he started to interview the manager: "Do the people in here have a lot of guns 'n stuff? Do they walk around with rifles?" She was outraged, and uncomprehending. "No, they certainly do not! Where did that come from?" she demanded. "Oh," Camp said, tongue firmly in cheek, "It's just that there's all these dead animals here." Camp and his daughters left. They managed to get out of the driveway before they collapsed in laughter.[9]

Another day, his friend Nancy Southam took him from the hospital on three errands that he wanted to run: the dry cleaner, the liquor store and martinis at Camp's Corner in the Sheraton. The nurses told him before he left that he was to limit himself to just one martini. Camp promised to behave. At the hotel, he ordered the largest martini Southam had ever seen. "It looked like a pail of liquid with a few ice cubes floating in it," Nancy recalled. "When he finished, he called the waiter over and said, 'I'll have the second half now. The first one wasn't full. It had all that ice in it.' He got his second pail."[10]

On March 8, 2002, Camp was discharged from hospital. The doctors were astonished by the way he seemed to have bounced all the way back from his devastating attack three weeks earlier. He returned home to Northwood, and the question hanging over him was not whether he would live but whether he would be able to continue writing his newspaper column. When Eric Kierans, his fellow panelist from "Kierans, Camp and Lewis," called to wish him well, Camp's daughter Connie took the call and tried to put him off, telling Kierans her father was too tired to talk. Camp intervened: "Eric Kierans is 88. He's too old to call back." The two friends had a warm chat.[11]

Believing the worst to be over, Camp's family scattered. While Connie stayed with her father, Christopher returned to London and Wendy to Ottawa. Cherie took her children to Florida. Linda went to Mexico with David and his children. Donna Leggatt went back to Ottawa. Their optimism was ill founded. Within three days, Camp suffered a second devastating attack. "Holy moly!" he cried to Connie as he collapsed. She managed to get him back to hospital by ambulance. But he never really recovered consciousness as, over the next several days, he suffered a series of attacks, then contracted pneumonia. On March 18, 2002, he died. He was 81.

His Tuesday Club friend Harry Bagley, a rare book dealer in Fredericton, was in a quandary. Having had a heavy cold for the past week, Bagley had deliberately stayed away from the hospital. When he heard on the radio that Camp had died, he did not know what to do. Finally, he got in his car and drove to the Sheraton. He found a flower arrangement in Camp's Corner and a card of condolence from the staff. Camp's favourite waitress, a little redhead, was in tears.[12] The hotel announced that no one would be permitted to eat or drink in Camp's Corner until after the funeral.

As the family reassembled, there were some matters of practical protocol that had to be resolved. How to accommodate three special women at one funeral without slighting any of them? The family turned to Camp's old and, until recently, estranged friend, Dan Skaling, to organize the seating in Fredericton's Christ Church Anglican Cathedral. "Deputy Dan," as he had been known since his days as deputy minister of tourism in New Brunswick, was a born organizer. He figured out an arrangement that everyone could live with. None of the women in Camp's life—including Skaling's own wife, Donna Leggatt—would be seated in the front family pew. Instead, Christopher Camp, the son of Wendy and Dalton, was seated in the front row with four Camp grandchildren—the children of Gail and Cherie; the rationale was that all of them would be doing readings in the course of the service. The two older sons, David and Michael, both of whom were to deliver eulogies, were seated in the second row with their mother, Linda, and their sisters. Finally, in the pew behind them, Skaling seated Wendy Camp and

Dalton's mentally handicapped brother, Red, at one end of the row with Donna and himself at the other end.[13]

David's eulogy also required finesse. He gave respectful recognition to Linda and Wendy and slipped in a diplomatic few words that he had negotiated before the service with Donna Leggatt: "He [Camp] went to bed late, night after night, and got up early every single morning, and was busy all day long in the business of thinking. Only a person half his age could keep up with him. I honestly couldn't, but younger people did; his close and valued friend Donna Leggatt did."

They called the service on March 23 a "Celebration of the Life of Dalton Kingsley Camp." Led by the bishop of Fredericton—although born a Baptist, Camp had come to prefer the Anglican Church—the service drew Governor General Adrienne Clarkson, the lieutenant-governor, the premier, the mayor of Fredericton, Tory leader Joe Clark, and a cross-section of MPs, senators and journalists.

David Camp's eulogy was masterful. He captured the essence of his father:

> Feeling the country and the values that he loved under attack, he became, in defence of moderation, a radical, more outspoken and contrarian with every passing year. He was a columnist like no other. He challenged the accepted wisdom of the moment, challenged you to think again, to not lose sight of common sense and common decency, while he infuriated and tormented those wrongheaded, hardhearted people so determined to make Canada into something alien to his heart. All written in a style that was unmistakably his own.
>
> Had he stayed in the advertising business he might have been a wealthy man, as once he was. But he backed away from it, 30 years ago; for him there was more to life than making money: he wanted to be free, and to write, and to live in his own particular way.
>
> He had a genius for language and made his living as a successful writer, and spent what he earned, not long after he earned it—sometimes before he earned it—and here and there ran up some pretty sizeable bills, often in the care and feeding of other people....
>
> I listened to Stephen Lewis on the CBC, talking to Shelagh Rogers from Africa, and his voice was choking with emotion as he talked

about losing Dalton Camp, and the void it would leave in this country and our lives.

And I wept to have had such a father.

And when the religious celebration of his life was over, the mourners took up an invitation to adjourn to a secular celebration—at Camp's Corner in the Sheraton.

ENDNOTES

Chapter 1—An American Canadian

[1] Dalton Camp, draft of uncompleted memoir.

[2] Over a period of eight days in 1999, Terence Macartney-Filgate interviewed Camp for an episode of the television show *Life and Times*, which was never aired. Terry Macartney-Filgate kindly made his videotapes available to the author.

[3] Camp, draft of memoir.

[4] Camp, draft of memoir.

[5] Dalton Camp, interview with James Cullingham, VisionTV, aired March 22 and 23, 2002.

[6] Terence Macartney-Filgate, interview with author, February 2003.

Chapter 2—The Camps of New Brunswick

[1] The first Camp in the New World was one Edward Camp, who, as a young man in his early 20s, emigrated from Hertford County to New Haven colony in or about 1640. There, he married, sired five children and was recruited into the colonial militia. He also became the first Camp to appear in the public records of North America on September 6, 1643, when he was fined for "coming late the last trayning day" of the militia. Edward took the colony's oath of fidelity on July 1, 1644, and received a land grant at Chestnut Hill in New Haven in May 1650. He was the great-great-grandfather of Abiathar Camp, who would become the first Camp in Canada.

Edward had a son, also named Edward, who had a distinguished career in the militia, was credited with destroying an Indian fort and, in 1712, became the first Camp to venture into politics when he was chosen to represent Milford in the General Assembly of Connecticut.

2   Much of the information in this chapter about the early history of the Camp family has been assembled by genealogical researcher Henry A. Berg, of Palm Springs, California. The author gratefully acknowledges his assistance.

3   Dalton Camp, draft of uncompleted memoir.

4   Camp talked to New Brunswick oral history archivist Janet Toole about his family and career in extended interviews in 1992, 1993 and 1998. The transcripts may be found in the Provincial Archives of New Brunswick in Fredericton. This interview was recorded on July 9, 1998.

5   Dalton Camp, "End of the Dream," *Saturday Night*, November 1980.

6   Camp, draft of memoir.

7   Camp gave essentially the same account in *Saturday Night*, November 1980, and to Janet Toole, July 9, 1998.

8   Camp, *Saturday Night*.

9   Camp, draft of memoir.

10 Dalton Camp, *Whose Country Is This Anyway?* (Vancouver: Douglas & McIntyre, 1995), page 17.

11 Camp, draft of memoir.

12 Camp, draft of memoir.

13 David Camp, interview with author, September 2002.

14 Camp, interview with Toole.

15 Camp, draft of memoir.

16 Camp, interview with Toole.

17 Camp, draft of memoir.

18 David Camp, interview.

Chapter 3—*Growing Up Canadian*

1   Dalton Camp, draft of uncompleted memoir.

2   Dalton Camp, oral history interview with Janet Toole, September 28, 1992.

3   David Camp, interview with author, September 2002.

4   Camp, draft of memoir.

5   Camp, draft of memoir.

6   Camp, draft of memoir.

7   Camp, draft of memoir.
8   Camp, draft of memoir.
9   Dalton Camp, speech to the graduating class, Acadia University, May 8, 1994.
10 Camp, draft of memoir.
11 Camp, draft of memoir.
12 Linda Camp, interview with author, July 2002.
13 Linda Camp, interview.
14 Camp, draft of memoir.
15 Camp, draft of memoir.

Chapter 4—War and Marriage

1   Dalton Camp, draft of uncompleted memoir.
2   Linda Camp, interview with author, July 2002.
3   Linda Camp, interview.
4   Camp, draft of memoir.
5   Dalton Camp, oral history interview with Janet Toole, September 28, 1992.
6   Finlay MacDonald died two weeks before his best friend, Dalton Camp. Shortly before his death, MacDonald was interviewed by Hugh Winsor of the *Globe and Mail*. The interview was taped in February 2002.
7   Camp, draft of memoir.
8   Harry Bagley, interview with author, October 28, 2002.

Chapter 5—Years of Self-Discovery

1   It never hurts to have a friend review one's performance. Desmond Pacey, the reviewer for the *Brunswickan*, gushed over Camp's acting: "When Camp ambled on to the bare stage to set the play in motion, it was not the Camp as I see him day after day in English lectures but a thoroughly Yankee stage-manager, with a new voice, a new accent, a new posture, a new personality. Everything depended on that opening scene, and Camp came through magnificently. Under his persuasive voice and hands, a whole town sprang into life, more vivid than any sets could have made it."

2   Dalton Camp, oral history interview with Janet Toole, July 9, 1998.

3   Not that Camp lacked for references. "I have known this young man upwards of five years and can say that he is, in every respect, mature, well oriented, realistic and brilliant," wrote his philosophy professor, David A. Stewart, in a letter dated October 24, 1949. "...Mr. Camp is a man of sincerity, decency and high ideals. These qualities are fortunately fused with a keen sense of humour. He has an inbred sense of good form which bears acquaintance. Already a good citizen, he is an outstanding one in the making."

4   Frank Mankiewicz, interviews with author, September/October 2002.

5   Mankiewicz, interviews.

6   Mankiewicz, interviews.

7   Among the Canadian students in England attending the LSE that year was Pierre Elliott Trudeau, but the two men did not cross paths—"I never saw him there," Camp said. "Clearly he found better things to do."

8   Camp, taped interviews with documentary-maker Terence Macartney-Filgate, 1999.

9   Dalton Camp, speech to 1978 Atlantic Studies conference.

10 Camp, Macartney-Filgate interviews.

11 Camp, Macartney-Filgate interviews.

12 Dalton Camp, oral history interview with Janet Toole, March 17, 1993.

13 Camp, Macartney-Filgate interviews.

14 Camp, Macartney-Filgate interviews.

Chapter 6—The Young Politician

1   Rod McQueen, "The Man Who Knows Too Much," *Quest*, May 1984.

2   Dalton Camp, *Gentlemen, Players and Politicians* (Toronto: McClelland and Stewart, 1970), page 14.

3   *Montreal Star*, August 7, 1948, quoted in *Gentlemen, Players and Politicians*, page 3.

4   Camp, *Gentlemen, Players and Politicians*, page 25.
5   Dalton Camp, "A College Man Looks At Politics," *Liberal Review*, September–October 1946.
6   Dalton Camp, address on radio station CFNB, December 5, 1949.
7   Camp, *Gentlemen, Players and Politicians*, pages 33–34.
8   In 1968 and 1969, Camp was interviewed by historians Denis Smith and William Neville for Smith's fine book, *Rogue Tory: The Life and Legend of John G. Diefenbaker* (Toronto: Macfarlane Walter & Ross, 1995). The interview transcript may be found in the archives of Trent University in Peterborough, Ontario. This interview was recorded on December 3, 1968.
9   Camp, interview with Smith, December 3, 1968.
10   Dalton Camp, oral history interview with Janet Toole, August 27, 1998.
11   Dalton Camp, article in *New Brunswick Reader*, May 29, 1999.
12   Camp, *Gentlemen, Players and Politicians*, page 50.
13   Camp, *New Brunswick Reader*.
14   In late 1967, Camp was interviewed at length about the Conservative party in the Diefenbaker years by historian J.L. Granatstein and his colleagues Paul Stevens and Peter Oliver. The transcript of this oral history interview, which runs to 329 pages, is archived at York University in Toronto.
15   Camp, interview with Granatstein, December 14, 1967.
16   Camp, *Gentlemen, Players and Politicians*, page 140.

Chapter 7—Not Bright Enough for Two
1   Prior to Hugh John Flemming's win in New Brunswick, there was only one Conservative government in Canada. That was in Ontario.
2   Dalton Camp, *Gentlemen, Players and Politicians*, page 177.

Chapter 8—The Alter Ego
1   Dalton Camp, *Gentlemen, Players and Politicians* (Toronto: McClelland and Stewart, 1970), page 110.
2   Robert Stanfield, quoted by Alexander Ross in "Dalton Camp: The Man Who Finally Belled the Cat," *Maclean's*, February 1967.

3 Flora MacDonald, interview with author, August 12, 2002.
4 Camp, *Gentlemen, Players and Politicians*, page 110.
5 Camp, *Gentlemen, Players and Politicians*, page 111.
6 Camp, *Gentlemen, Players and Politicians*, page 122.
7 Camp, *Gentlemen, Players and Politicians*, page 124.
8 Camp, *Gentlemen, Players and Politicians*, page 123.
9 David Camp, interview with author, September 2002.
10 Finlay MacDonald, interview with Hugh Winsor, February 2002.

Chapter 9—On to Ottawa

1 Dalton Camp, interview with Denis Smith, December 3, 1968.
2 Dalton Camp, *Gentlemen, Players and Politicians* (Toronto: McClelland and Stewart, 1970), page 139.
3 Camp, *Gentlemen, Players and Politicians*, page 104.
4 Camp, interview with Smith, December 3, 1968.
5 Camp, interview with Smith, February 3, 1969.
6 Camp, interview with Smith, February 3, 1969.
7 Camp, interview with Smith, February 3, 1969.
8 Dalton Camp, oral history interview with J.L. Granatstein, December 14, 1967.
9 Camp, interview with Granatstein.
10 Camp, interview with Smith, February 3, 1969.

Chapter 10—Kempton

1 William Davis, quoted by Ron Graham in "The Unlikely Godfather," *Saturday Night*, May 1985.
2 Norman Atkins, interview with author, July 2002.
3 Atkins, interview.
4 Dalton Camp, quoted by Ron Graham in "The Unlikely Godfather," *Saturday Night*, May 1985.
5 Dianne Axmith, interview with author, October 23, 2002.

Chapter 11—Disillusion and Alienation

1 Dalton Camp, interview with Denis Smith, February 3, 1969.
2 Dalton Camp, oral history interview with J.L. Granatstein, December 14, 1967.

[3]   Similar accounts of the Hees incident are found in the Granatstein and Smith interviews.

[4]   Camp, interview with Smith, February 3, 1969.

[5]   Camp, interview with Smith, February 3, 1969.

[6]   Camp, interview with Granatstein.

[7]   Camp, interview with Granatstein.

[8]   Camp, interview with Granatstein.

[9]   Flora MacDonald, interview with author, August 12, 2002.

[10] Camp, interview with Smith, February 4, 1969.

[11] MacDonald, interview.

[12] Camp, interview with Granatstein.

[13] Camp, interview with Smith, February 4, 1969.

[14] Peter C. Newman, *The Distemper of Our Times* (Toronto: McClelland and Stewart, 1968), page 95.

[15] Camp, interview with Granatstein.

[16] MacDonald, interview.

[17] MacDonald, interview.

[18] Camp, interview with Granatstein.

[19] Camp, interview with Granatstein.

[20] Camp, interview with Granatstein.

[21] Camp, interview with Granatstein.

[22] Richard Gwyn, *Smallwood: The Unlikely Revolutionary* (Toronto: McClelland and Stewart, 1965), page 284.

[23] Gwyn, page 284.

[24] MacDonald, interview.

[25] MacDonald, interview.

Chapter 12—An Uncivil War

[1]   Gordon Fairweather, oral history interview with J.L. Granatstein, March 13, 1969.

[2]   Edwin Goodman, oral history interview with J.L. Granatstein, February 7, 1970.

[3]   Davie Fulton, oral history interview with J.L. Granatstein, April 9, 1969.

[4]   Dalton Camp, interview with Denis Smith, February 3, 1969.

[5]   Camp, interview with Smith.

6   Camp, interview with Smith.

7   Dalton Camp, oral history interview with J.L. Granatstein, December 14, 1967.

8   Camp, interview with Smith.

9   Camp, interview with Granatstein.

10   Flora MacDonald, interview with author, August 12, 2002.

11   The Tories were shut out in Toronto in 1963. In fact, they won just one seat in the three largest cities—Toronto, Montreal and Vancouver.

12   Camp, interview with Granatstein.

13   Camp, interview with Granatstein.

14   Camp, interview with Smith.

15   Camp, interview with Smith.

16   Dalton Camp, *Points of Departure* (Ottawa: Deneau & Greenberg, 1979), page 181.

17   Camp, *Points of Departure*, page 187.

18   MacDonald, interview.

19   It was an impressive crew. Clark went on to become Tory national leader (twice) and prime minister (once); MacDonald became national secretary of the party and a cabinet minister in both the Clark and Brian Mulroney governments; Murray became a senator and cabinet minister; and Atkins, who also became a senator, was the architect of the Mulroney election triumphs in 1984 and 1988.

20   MacDonald, interview.

21   Transcript of proceedings, National Conference on Canadian Goals, 1964.

22   Flora MacDonald, interview.

23   Camp, interview with Granatstein.

24   MacDonald, interview. Lest anyone think McLuhan was infallible, his assessment of a popular new singing group, the Beatles, is worth noting: "I don't think that their appeal is quite as universal as newspapers might like them to think," he said in Fredericton. "They would have no appeal in South America. They'd fall flat in any other continent, except this one."

25   Camp, interview with Granatstein.

26   Camp, interview with Granatstein.

27   Camp, interview with Granatstein.

28   MacDonald, interview.

29   Camp, interview with Granatstein.

30   Goodman, interview with Granatstein.

31   Camp, interview with Granatstein.

32   Camp, interview with Granatstein.

Chapter 13—The Ace of Spades

1   Chad Bark, interview with author, November 4, 2002.

2   Bill Saunderson, interview with author, November 13, 2002.

3   Roy McMurtry, interview with author, October 24, 2002.

4   Dalton Camp, oral history interview with J.L. Granatstein, December 14, 1967.

5   Camp, interview with Granatstein.

6   Bark, interview.

7   Flora MacDonald, quoted by Barry Conn Hughes in "Inside Dalton Camp," *The Financial Post Magazine*, February 1977.

8   Bark, interview.

9   Camp, interview with Granatstein.

10   Edwin Goodman, oral history interview with J.L. Granatstein, February 7, 1970.

11   Flora MacDonald, interview with author, August 12, 2002.

12   Displeased with this state of affairs, Diefenbaker ordered that under no circumstances was Lowell Murray, in particular, to be allowed to enter party headquarters.

13   Goodman, interview with Granatstein.

14   Camp, interview with Granatstein.

Chapter 14—Bearding the Chief

1   John Bassett, quoted by Rod McQueen in "The Man Who Knows Too Much," *Quest*, May 1984.

2   Dalton Camp, oral history interview with J.L. Granatstein, December 14, 1967.

3   Camp, interview with Granatstein.

4   Camp, interview with Granatstein.

5   Camp, interview with Granatstein.

6   Camp, interview with Granatstein.

7   Camp, interview with Granatstein.

8   Camp, interview with Granatstein.

9   Dalton Camp, quoted by Alexander Ross in "Dalton Camp: The Man Who Finally Belled the Cat," *Maclean's*, February 1967.

10 In fact, Camp did not use Diefenbaker's name at all during the leadership-review campaign that followed. Whenever he and his fellow Spades discussed strategy, as they did often in the ensuing months, they always referred to the leader as "Charlie."

11 Chad Bark, interview with author, November 4, 2002.

12 Flora MacDonald, interview with author, August 12, 2002.

13 Flora MacDonald, interview.

14 Camp, interview with Granatstein.

15 Camp, interview with Granatstein.

16 Camp, interview with Granatstein.

17 Roy McMurtry, interview with author, October 24, 2002.

18 McMurtry, interview.

19 As it turned out, the Spence report was published two weeks after Camp's Junior Board of Trade speech.

20 Camp, interview with Granatstein.

21 Peter C. Newman, *Distemper of Our Times* (Toronto: McClelland and Stewart, 1965), page 127.

22 David MacDonald, interview with author, November 24, 2002.

23 David MacDonald, interview.

24 It was the start of a close relationship between David MacDonald and Camp. Thirty years later, when Alexa McDonough was leader of the New Democratic Party, she met MacDonald. She liked him, but was apprehensive about dating a Tory. McDonough was also a friend of Camp and, as his female friends sometimes did, she called him for advice on a matter of the heart. "I asked him," she said in an interview with the author, "'Is there one former member of the Tory parliamentary caucus that you would approve of if I told you I was seeing him socially?'" Without hesitation, Camp replied, "Only one: David MacDonald."

25 Camp, interview with Granatstein.

26 Lowell Murray, interview with author, September 23, 2002.

27 Camp, interview with Granatstein. As it transpired, Korchinski's fear was premature. He would survive to win five more elections under the leadership of Robert Stanfield and Joe Clark.

28 Newman, *Distemper of Our Times*, page 141.

29 Patrick Nowlan, quoted by Alexander Ross in "Dalton Camp: The Man Who Finally Belled the Cat," *Maclean's*, February 1967.

30 David MacDonald, interview.

31 Gail Camp McIntyre, interview with author, August 18, 2002.

32 Connie Camp, interview with author, August 17, 2002.

33 Camp, interview with Granatstein.

34 The other memorable line from that meeting came the next day from Diefenbaker when, mobbed by cheering supporters, he quoted from the ballad "Sir Andrew Barton": "I am wounded, but I am not slain. I'll lay me down and rest awhile and then I'll rise and fight again."

35 Flora MacDonald, interview.

36 In the confusion, the annual meeting failed to deal with a proposal to amend the party constitution to mandate an automatic review of the leadership at the first meeting after every election. That came later. The Liberals followed suit. Joe Clark would feel the sting of this Camp-inspired amendment when Brian Mulroney pushed him out of the leadership in 1983. So would Jean Chrétien when confronted with the leadership ambitions of Paul Martin two decades later.

37 Robert C. Coates, *The Night of the Knives* (Fredericton: Brunswick Press, 1969), page 64.

38 David MacDonald, interview.

39 David Camp, interview.

Chapter 15—Richard

1   Richard Hatfield, quoted by Michel Cormier and Achille Michaud in *Richard Hatfield: Power and Disobedience* (Fredericton: Goose Lane Editions, 1992), page 30.
2   Dalton Camp, in *Remembering Richard*, Nancy Southam, ed. (Halifax: Formac Publishing Co., 1993), page 106.
3   Michael Cormier and Achille Michaud, *Richard Hatfield: Power and Disobebience* (Fredericton: Goose Lane Editions, 1992), page 22.
4   Cormier and Michaud, page 47.
5   Lowell Murray, in *Remembering Richard*, page 30.
6   Camp, in *Remembering Richard*, page 135.
7   Connie Camp, interview with author, August 17, 2002.
8   Camp, in *Remembering Richard*, page 135.
9   Camp, in *Remembering Richard*, page 17.
10 Flora MacDonald, interview with author, August 12, 2002.
11 Dalton Camp, oral history interview with Janet Toole, March 31, 1993.

Chapter 16—Ambition Denied

1   Lowell Murray, interview with author, September 23, 2002.
2   Dalton Camp, oral history interview with J.L. Granatstein, December 14, 1967.
3   Murray, interview.
4   Flora MacDonald, interview with author, August 12, 2002.
5   Davie Fulton, oral history interview with J.L. Granatstein, April 9, 1969.
6   Camp, interview with Granatstein.
7   Camp, interview with Granatstein.
8   Camp, interview with Granatstein.
9   Camp, interview with Granatstein.
10 Subsequent events would prove Smith prescient on both counts.
11 Dalton Camp, oral history interview with Janet Toole, March 24, 1993.
12 Flora MacDonald, interview.

13 Flora MacDonald, interview.

14 David MacDonald, interview with author, November 24, 2002.

15 David MacDonald, interview.

16 Andrew Stark, interview with author, October 11, 2002.

17 Murray, interview.

18 Allan Fotheringham, interview with author, October 15, 2002.

19 David MacDonald, interview.

20 Murray, interview.

21 Hugh Segal, interview with author, November 18, 2002.

22 Dalton Camp, quoted by Geoffrey Stevens in *Stanfield* (Toronto: McClelland and Stewart, 1973), page 181.

23 Finlay MacDonald, quoted in *Stanfield*, page 185.

24 It was a variation of the strategy Camp and Atkins had used at the annual meeting in November 1966 when they had their supporters arrive early on opening night to pack the front rows of the hall before Diefenbaker spoke.

25 Claude Ryan, quoted by Stevens in *Stanfield*, page 190.

26 Denis Smith, *Rogue Tory: The Life and Legend of John G. Diefenbaker* (Toronto: Macfarlane Walter & Ross, 1995), pages 560–61.

27 Robert Stanfield, quoted by Rod McQueen in "The Man Who Knows Too Much," *Quest*, May 1984.

28 In one of those small coincidences that pepper politics, 10 years later Anne Austin would marry Bob Stanfield, then a widower.

29 Dalton Camp, *Telegram*, June 29, 1968.

30 Smith, *Rogue Tory*, page 563.

31 Dalton Camp, interview with James Cullingham, VisionTV, aired March 22 and 23, 2002.

32 Connie Camp, interview with author, August 17, 2002.

33 Norman Atkins, interview with author, July 2002.

Chapter 17—Not a Conventional Father

1 Norman Atkins, interview with author, July 2002.

2 Linda Camp, interview with author, July 2002.

3 Wendy Cameron, whom Camp would marry in 1984, arranged to have her friend Giovanni Mowinckel decorate and furnish

the apartment. Mowinckel was the expensive interior designer who redid 24 Sussex Drive for Brian and Mila Mulroney.

4 David Camp, interview with author, September 2002.

5 Connie Camp, interview with author, August 17, 2002.

6 Dalton Camp, journal, December 18, 1968.

7 Michael Camp, interview with author, July 26, 2002. Although it sent Michael home to Toronto, the school allowed him to graduate with his class. He went on to Trent University in Peterborough, Ontario.

8 Wendy Camp, interview with author, September 24, 2002.

9 Cherie Camp, interview with author, August 17, 2002.

10 Cherie Camp, interview.

11 Connie Camp, interview.

12 Connie Camp, interview.

13 David Camp, interview with author.

14 Connie Camp, interview.

15 Gail Camp McIntyre, interview with author, August 18, 2002.

16 Cherie Camp, interview. The horse was a superannuated race-horse that was all skin and bone when Cherie got it. It had been rescued from the knackers by Isabel Bassett, wife of the publisher of the Toronto *Telegram* and later CEO of TVOntario and companion to Ernie Eves, the Conservative premier of Ontario.

17 Michael Camp, interview.

18 David Camp, interview.

Chapter 18—The Writer

1 Nancy Morrison, interview with author, October 3, 2002.

2 Dalton Camp, oral history interview with Janet Toole, July 9, 1998.

3 Dalton Camp, journal, October 17, 1968.

4 Camp, journal, September 4, 1968.

5 Camp, journal, October 23, 1968.

6 Camp, journal, November 1, 1968.

7 Camp, journal, January 23, 1969.

8 Camp, journal, January 24, 1969.

9   Camp, journal, February 20, 1969.
10 Dalton Camp, *Gentlemen, Players and Politicians* (Toronto: McClelland and Stewart, 1970), page 171.
11 Camp, *Gentlemen, Players and Politicians*, page 138.
12 Camp, journal, November 14, 1968.
13 Camp, journal, December 16, 1968.
14 Dalton Camp, *Whose Country Is This Anyway?* (Vancouver: Douglas & McIntyre, 1995), page 9.
15 Dalton Camp, *Telegram*, March 16, 1966.
16 John Honderich, interview with author, October 25, 2002.
17 Connie Camp, interview with author, August 17, 2002.
18 Camp, *Telegram*, October 26, 1970.
19 Camp, *Whose Country Is This Anyway?*, page 10.
20 Dalton Camp, *Toronto Star*, November 8, 1971.
21 Dalton Camp, *Toronto Sun*, January 16, 1980.
22 Jean Chrétien, interview with author, January 22, 2003.
23 Denise Morrison, interview with author, October 25, 2002.
24 Camp, *Toronto Sun*, December 12, 1980.
25 Camp, *Toronto Star*, May 6, 2001.
26 Dalton Camp, *Points of Departure* (Ottawa: Deneau & Greenberg, 1979), page 116.

Chapter 19—Stopping Spadina

1   Although Macaulay lost the leadership to Robarts, the new premier made him his trade minister. Macaulay helped Dalton K. Camp and Associates get off the ground by awarding the fledgling agency the advertising contract for Ontario's Trade Crusade—a campaign to encourage people to "buy Ontario," for example to purchase fashions from Toronto's Spadina Avenue rather than Paris or New York. As part of the campaign, Macaulay, a dynamo in an otherwise sluggish government, opened trade offices in such centres as Dusseldorf, Germany, Milan, Mexico City, Paris, Tokyo, Beijing and Singapore.
2   Clare Westcott, interview with author, April 18, 2003.
3   Roy McMurtry, interview with author, October 24, 2002.
4   McMurtry, interview.

5   Norman Atkins, interview with author, July 2002.
6   William Davis, interview with author, December 6, 2002.
7   David Camp, interview with author, September 2002.
8   Davis, interview.
9   Ontario Royal Commission on Book Publishing, *Final Report*, page 219.
10   Polling data from Environics Research Group.
11   Davis, interview.

Chapter 20—The Skunkworks
1   J. Murray Beck, quoted by Geoffrey Stevens in *Stanfield* (Toronto: McClelland and Stewart, 1973), page 252.
2   Robert Stanfield, quoted in *Stanfield*, page 252.
3   Connie Camp, interview with author, August 17, 2002.
4   William Grogan, interview with author, November 4, 2002.
5   Grogan, interview.
6   Dalton Camp, journal, February 20, 1969.
7   As it turned out, Gillies himself attempted to disown the policy when he discovered how badly it was playing in Don Valley. "We put Stanfield on a plane out of Moose Jaw and flew him into Toronto to ream Gillies's ass out," Grogan recalled. But it was too late; the damage had been done. The Tories had muddled their message.
8   Keith Davey, *The Rainmaker: A Passion for Politics* (Toronto: Stoddart, 1986), page 177. Despite the campaign rhetoric, the Trudeau government subsequently bowed to the inevitable and imposed wage and price controls in the fall of 1975.
9   Grogan, interview.
10   Ron Collister won the Conservative nomination in the Toronto riding of York-Scarborough for the 1974 election. He was defeated by nearly 9,000 votes.
11   Grogan, interview.
12   Hugh Segal, interview with author, November 18, 2002.
13   Linda Camp, interview with author, July 2002.
14   Segal, interview.
15   Flora MacDonald, interview with author, August 12, 2002.

16 Jackie Webster, interview with author, October 26, 2002.
17 Cherie Camp, interview with author, August 17, 2002.
18 David Camp, interview with author, September 2002.
19 David Camp, interview.
20 David Camp, interview.
21 Dalton Camp, journal, May 29, 1976.
22 Dalton Camp, draft of novel, pages C4–5.

Chapter 21—Northwood

1 After his death, his executors put Northwood on the market at $195,000. The best offer they could get was for $175,000.
2 Dalton Camp, journal, November 26, 1977.
3 Rilla Camp lived at Northwood until she had to be moved to a nursing home a few years later. Red was there for 15 years, until Dalton's heart transplant made it necessary to move him to a special-care home nearby.
4 Linda Camp, interview with author, July 2002.
5 David Camp, interview with author, September 2002.
6 David Camp, interview.
7 David Camp, interview.
8 Wendy Camp, letter to Dalton Camp, December 2, 1977.
9 Dalton Camp, letter to David Camp, January 11, 1978.
10 Jackie Webster, interview with author, October 26, 2002.
11 Dalton Camp, letter to David Camp, March 13, 1978.
12 Dalton Camp, *Globe and Mail*, September 20, 1980.
13 Wendy Camp, interview with author, September 24, 2002.
14 David Camp, interview.
15 David Camp, interview.
16 Wendy Camp, interview.

Chapter 22—Kierans, Camp and Lewis

1 Talin Vartanian, interview with Patricia Treble, February 3, 2003.
2 Dalton Camp, "Introduction," in Peter Gzowski, *The Morningside Years* (Toronto: McClelland and Stewart, 1997), page x.

[3] Michael Camp, interview with author, July 26, 2002.
[4] Connie Camp, interview with author, August 17, 2002.
[5] Camp, in *The Morningside Years*, page ix.
[6] Camp, in *The Morningside Years*, page x.
[7] Camp, in *The Morningside Years*, page x.
[8] Eric Kierans, *Remembering* (Toronto: Stoddart, 2001), page 226.

Chapter 23—The Ottawa Debacle

[1] Dalton Camp, draft of uncompleted memoir.
[2] Wendy Camp, interview with author, September 24, 2002.
[3] Camp, draft of memoir.
[4] Connie Camp, interview with author, August 17, 2002.
[5] Camp, draft of memoir.
[6] Dalton Camp, interview with John Sawatsky, August 9–10, 1989.
[7] Camp, interview with Sawatsky.
[8] Dalton Camp, letter to David Camp, March 12, 1983.
[9] Connie Camp, interview.
[10] Eric Kierans and Dave Barrett, quoted in the *Globe and Mail*, September 4, 1986.
[11] David Camp, interview with author, September 2002.
[12] Stevie Cameron, *Globe and Mail*, September 4, 1986.
[13] Confidential interview with author.
[14] Andrew Stark, interview with author, October 11, 2002.
[15] Flora MacDonald, interview with author, August 12, 2002.
[16] Dalton Camp, lecture to political science students, St. Thomas University, Fredericton, November 16, 2000.
[17] Hugh Segal, interview with author, November 18, 2002.
[18] Camp, interview with Sawatsky.
[19] Camp, interview with Sawatsky.
[20] Elizabeth E. May, *Paradise Won: The Struggle for South Moresby* (Toronto: McClelland and Stewart, 1990).
[21] VanderZalm was essentially trying to blackmail the federal government. He would not consent to the park unless Ottawa came up with millions of dollars in subsidies for a ferry service to carry additional tourists to the Queen Charlottes.

22 Lowell Murray, interview with author, September 23, 2002.
23 May, *Paradise Won*, page 299.
24 Camp, interview with Sawatsky.
25 Camp, interview with Sawatsky.
26 Segal, interview.
27 Camp, interview with Sawatsky.
28 Wendy Camp, interview.
29 Segal, interview.
30 David Camp, interview.
31 Connie Camp, interview.
32 Jackie Webster, interview with author, October 26, 2002.
33 Webster, interview.

Chapter 24—A New Heart
1   Michael Camp, interview with author, July 26, 2002.
2   Hugh Segal, interview with author, November 18, 2002.
3   Janet Brooks, "The Heart of the Matter: Dalton Camp and His
    Controversial Transplant," *Canadian Medical Association Journal*,
    1993: 149 (7), October 1, 1993.
4   Connie Camp, interview with author, August 17, 2002.
5   Connie Camp, interview.
6   Connie Camp, interview.
7   Norman Atkins, interview with author, July 2002.
8   Wendy Camp, interview with author, September 24, 2002.
9   Wendy Camp, interview.
10 Michael Camp, interview.
11 Wilbert Keon, interview with author, August 12, 2002.
12 Keon, interview.
13 John Honderich, interview with author, October 25, 2002.
14 Dalton Camp, interview with Pamela Wallin, December 1995.
15 The identity of organ donors is not normally made public. In
    this case, however, Natalie Young's name, age and other infor-
    mation became part of the public record during an inquest into
    her death. As he recovered, Camp, who felt guilty about the
    distress that the *Star* story had caused her family, wrote an elo-
    quent letter of commiseration and gratitude to Young's parents.

16   Michael Camp, interview.
17   Keon, interview.
18   Keon, interview.
19   David Camp, interview with author, September 2002.
20   David Camp, interview.

Chapter 25—A New Man
1   Dalton Camp, interview with James Cullingham, VisionTV, aired March 22 and 23, 2003.
2   Cherie Camp, interview with author, August 17, 2002.
3   He would have eight grandchildren, two each from Gail, David, Cherie and Michael.
4   Cherie Camp, interview.
5   Emma McIntyre, interview with author, August 29, 2002.
6   Emma McIntyre, interview.
7   Dalton Camp, *Toronto Star*, November 20, 1994.
8   Camp, *Toronto Star*, November 23, 1994.
9   Camp, *Toronto Star*, October 3, 1999.
10   Camp, *Toronto Star*, November 26, 2000.
11   Camp, *Toronto Star*, November 22, 2000.
12   Camp, *Toronto Star*, November 8, 2000.
13   Camp, *Toronto Star*, April 5, 2000.
14   Camp, *Toronto Star*, November 8, 2000.
15   Dalton Camp, *Hill Times*, February 18, 2002.
16   Camp, *Toronto Star*, December 22, 1999.
17   Confidential interview with author.
18   Dalton Camp, oral history interview with Janet Toole.
19   Terry Macartney-Filgate spent eight days in New Brunswick in 1999 talking to Camp for a *Life and Times* documentary for CBC television. Although there is some fascinating footage in his six hours of videotape, the CBC decided not to proceed with the project. Macartney-Filgate said he was told that the broadcaster wanted to do a show about someone more important, like Tim Horton. Camp thought that was funny.
20   Dalton Camp, letter to Ralph Costello, Saint John *Telegraph Journal*, November 29, 1972.

21   Dalton Camp's notes for testimony.
22   Camp, Macartney-Filgate interviews.
23   Camp, *Toronto Star*, September 29, 1996.
24   Donna Leggatt, interview with author, October 21, 2002.
25   Deb Nobes, interview with author, October 28, 2002.
26   Philip Lee, interview with author, October 28, 2002.
27   J.D.'s son, Jamie Irving, the great-grandson of K.C. and a university student at the time, subsequently became a good friend and protégé of Camp's. Camp encouraged Jamie to become a journalist and helped him get into Columbia University's Graduate School of Journalism in New York, which Camp had attended a half-century earlier. In an interview with the author on October 29, 2002, Jamie said his father was not pleased when he went to work at the *TJ* in the summer. "I don't want you there," J.D. Irving told him. "Those bastards write bad stuff about us. We sign their paycheques and they piss all over us. It's no good."
28   Lee, interview.
29   Nobes, interview.
30   Lee, interview.
31   Nobes, interview.
32   Lee, interview.
33   Michael Camp, interview with author, July 26, 2002.
34   Camp, *Toronto Star*, July 12, 1998.
35   Camp, *Toronto Star*, June 13, 2001.
36   Dalton Camp, *Maclean's*, April 21, 1997.
37   Camp, *Maclean's*, March 29, 1999.
38   Dalton Camp, speech, Woodstock, New Brunswick, October 18, 2000.
39   Graham Scott, interview with author, December 6, 2002.
40   Hugh Segal, interview with author, November 18, 2002.
41   Segal, interview.
42   Elizabeth Weir, interview with author, November 15, 2002.
43   Alexa McDonough, interview with author, November 24, 2002.
44   Sandra Estey and Jackie Webster, interviews with author, October 2002.

45 Jamie Irving, interview with author, October 29, 2002.
46 Amy Cameron, *Maclean's*, April 1, 2002.
47 Leggatt, interview.
48 Leggatt, interview.
49 Dalton Camp, as told to David Camp.
50 Jackie Webster, interview with author, October 26, 2002.
51 David Camp, interview with author, September 2002.
52 Leggatt, interview.
53 Leggatt, interview.
54 David Camp, interview.
55 Sandra Estey, interview with author, October 2002.
56 Wendy Camp, letter to Dalton Camp, October 25, 1994.
57 Wendy Camp, letter to Dalton Camp, November 2, 1994.
58 Interviews with David Camp, Donna Leggatt and others.
59 David Camp, interview.
60 Cherie Camp, interview.
61 David Camp, interview.

Chapter 26—Camp's Corner
1   Donna Leggatt, interview with author, October 21, 2002.
2   Michael Camp, interview with author, July 26, 2002.
3   Connie Camp, interview with author, August 17, 2002.
4   Ian Hurst, interview with author, October 29, 2002.
5   David Camp, interview with author, September 2002.
6   David Camp, interview.
7   David Camp, interview.
8   Jackie Webster, interview with author, October 26, 2002.
9   Gail Camp McIntyre, interview with author, August 18, 2002.
10 Nancy Southam, interview with author, November 8, 2002.
11 Connie Camp, interview.
12 Harry Bagley, interview with author, October 28, 2002.
13 David Camp, interview.

Acknowledgments

W HEN IT COMES TIME TO PAY tribute those who helped them, many authors feel compelled to start by saying there are so many people to thank they just do not know where to begin. I do not have that problem. I know precisely where to begin—by expressing my gratitude to the two people who are the keepers of the flame: David Camp and his uncle Norman Atkins.

David, the eldest of Dalton Camp's three sons, was a fine journalist for the Saint John *Telegraph Journal* before he decided to be a lawyer in Vancouver. He shared his memories of his father, opened his files and gave me complete access to speeches, journals, letters and other personal papers. He patiently answered dozens of follow-up questions I sent him and, most important, he persuaded his still-grieving siblings to help me, too. Thank you, David.

Senator Norman Atkins, Camp's brother-in-law by his first marriage, was the turnkey on the political side. He welcomed me to his cottage at Robertson's Point, spent hours talking to me about his friend and partner in business and politics, and made the phone calls that opened doors across the country. He and his indefatigable assistant in the Senate, Christine Corrigan, cheerfully tracked down all of the arcane scraps of information I discovered I needed as the writing proceeded. Thank you, Norman.

To single out two is not to downplay others. Linda Camp, Dalton's first wife, talked to me openly about the man she knew and loved. Her daughters, Gail McIntyre, Connie Camp and Cherie Camp, were a delight to interview about the man they adored as a thoroughly unconventional father. His son Michael generously filled in many blanks about Dalton's life in New Brunswick. Emma McIntyre told me about the grandfather she knew not as a big-time adman or a political guru but as a reclusive writer with mismatched socks.

In Ottawa, Wendy Camp talked about the joy and heartache of her 14 years with the man who made her his second wife and fathered their child. Donna Leggatt, the woman he loved "in the autumn of his life" (as Donna put it), talked about their very special friendship. In New Brunswick, his old Tuesday Club friends lined up to help: Dan Skaling, Jackie Webster, Janet and Barry Toole, Harry Bagley, Jim Ross and Tim Andrew. And so did his younger friends: Philip Lee, Deb Nobes, Jamie Irving and Amy Cameron.

Flora MacDonald, the most amazing septuagenarian in the country, actually sat still for a day between trips to Tibet and Afghanistan (or was it Antarctica?) to talk about the man she had known since their early years in the Tory trenches of Nova Scotia. Senator Lowell Murray spent the better part of a day reconstructing campaigns that he and Camp had fought together. There were others—friends, associates and comrades-in-arms—from across Canada and beyond: Nancy Morrison in Vancouver; Nate Nurgitz in Winnipeg; Andy Stark, Talin Vartanian, Dianne Axmith, Bill Davis, Clare Westcott, Graham Scott, Allan Fotheringham and Larry Zolf in Toronto; Senator Wilbert Keon, Thom Ouellette and Willie Jobin in Ottawa; Hugh Segal in Montreal; Bill Grogan in Bella Vista, Arkansas; Elizabeth Weir, Sandra Estey and Ian Hurst in Fredericton; Fred Chase and Norvel Robertson in Jemseg, N.B.; Frank Mankiewicz in Washington; and genealogical researcher Henry A. Berg in Palm Springs, California. Members of the "Spades," Camp's personal political organization, relived the days when they worked with him in the campaign that won for Tories the democratic right to change their leaders: Roy McMurtry, Don Guthrie, Bill Saunderson and Pat Vernon were in Toronto; another "Spade," Chad Bark, came off the golf course in the Florida Panhandle to talk about the man he recruited to run for the Conservatives against Mitchell Sharp in the 1965 federal election.

David MacDonald, Alexa McDonough and Nancy Southam talked to me in Toronto. Jean Chrétien—by his own admission a "secret fan" of Dalton Camp—reminisced about him over the phone from Ottawa.

Everyone at the Toronto Star pitched in: Camp's publisher, John

Honderich; his former editor Haroon Siddiqui; his good friend Denise Morrison; and Joan Sweeney Marsh, the supervisor of research services in the *Star* library, who made sure I got everything he wrote for the newspaper over a 30-year span.

Special thanks to Terence Macartney-Filgate of Tiffin Productions Inc., who gave me six hours of unaired videotaped interviews with Camp. My friend Pamela Wallin loaned me the tapes of five television programs she did with Camp. Another old friend, Hugh Winsor, of the *Globe and Mail*, sent along the recording of an interview with Camp's best buddy, Finlay MacDonald, conducted just before both men died. VisionTV gave me permission to use an interview of Camp by James Cullingham. Researcher Patricia Treble searched libraries and newspaper morgues for articles by and about Camp, as well as interviewing people at CBC for the chapter on "Kierans, Camp and Lewis." Robert Hoshowsky and Sue Gariepy set aside other work to type transcripts. Environics Research Group shared polling data.

Some of the most revealing information about Dalton Camp came from three sets of oral history interviews that are now open to the public. I am indebted to Ken Hernden and his staff at the York University archives for access to interviews done by Jack Granatstein and his colleagues; to Bernadine Dodge, who runs the archives at Trent University, for help with the Denis Smith/William Neville interviews; and to Marion Beyea, director, and Fred Farrell, manager of private sector records, at the Provincial Archives of New Brunswick. They gave me access to interviews done over a period of many years by oral history archivist Janet Toole; in addition, PANB is the repository for Camp's personal papers, and Beyea and her staff helped to sort and select the material I wanted, and then copied it. Thanks also to Judy Hiscock and Wanda Lyons at PANB. Brian Murphy at the National Archives of Canada helped me find material there. And my pal John Fraser, the master of Massey College at the University of Toronto, kindly found a quiet place for me to work at Massey.

At Key Porter Books, boss lady Anna Porter, a friend and admirer of Dalton, was determined that the story of his life be told.

Her senior editor, Meg Taylor, was a pleasure to work with; she kept the manuscript on track. Marjan Farahbaksh and Sue Sumeraj were attentive and diligent as copy editor and proofreader, respectively.

I take full responsibility for the interpretations I have placed on events recounted in this book. It goes without saying that any errors or omissions are also mine alone.

G.S.

Index

The Player

anger over treatment of
Camp, 208
anticipation of Camp's return,
274
in Brockville, 45
Camp's death, 350
Camp's declining health, 346
at Camp's funeral, 351
Camp's promise to, 173, 200,
201
Camp's short stories, gift of,
236
cottage at Robertson's Point,
106–7
first encounter with Camp,
38–39
on Gold Floor with Camp,
309
life in England, 57
lifestyle with Camp, 337–38
marital tension, 267
marriage, 43–45
marriage breakdown, 274
Montreal weekend during
war, 47–48
reconciliation of sorts with
Camp, 340
role in Camp's life, 222
Camp, Michael (son)
on Camp and computers, 341
on Camp's arteries, 305
Camp's death, 350
Camp's declining health, 346
as Camp's driver, 303
Camp's heart transplant,
309–10
career of, 225, 231
childhood of, 225, 327
memories of Camp as father,
228–29
relationship with Camp, 277
similarity to Camp, 225
worries about Camp's driving,
283, 302, 345
Camp, Rebecca, 16
Camp, Sanborn ("Sandy")
(brother), 10, 11–12, 20, 27,
28, 31
Camp, Wendy (née Cameron)
(second wife)
birth of Christopher, 225–26,
276
Camp's children, relations
with, 226, 267–69
Camp's death, 350
Camp's declining health, 346
denial of affair, 300
financial circumstances of,
338–39

initial meeting with Camp,
259
marriage to Camp, 279–80
New Brunswick election of
1974, 266–67
Northwood, building of,
272–73
pregnancy, 271, 273–74, 276
relationship with Camp,
264–71
rural living, 275–76
separation from Camp, 226
shock at Camp's condition in
1992, 304–5
trouble in marriage, 299–301
view on Mulroney's offer to
Camp, 288
Camp Associates Advertising,
109, 111, 223, 238, 260, 330
Campbell, Alex, 171–73
Campbell, Kim, 310–11
Camp Commission, 253–54, 255
Camp's Corner, 312, 327, 349,
350, 352
Canada's first mod premier,
191–92
Canadian Alliance, 297, 318
Canadian Civil Liberties
Association, 24
Canadian Constitution, patria-
tion of, 195
Canadian dollar, devaluation of,
122
Canadian Grill, 90
Canadian Javelin Ltd., 125
Canadian National Railways,
135–36
candidacy for Parliament, 110,
118, 150, 153–56, 217
Cannon, Jimmy, 54
CanWest Global, 323
capital punishment debate, 285
Capote, Truman, 192
Capp, Al, 258
Cardin, Lucien, 239
Carleton University, 333
Carney, Pat, 296
Carriage House, 155
Carson, Ken, 69, 99
Carter, Jimmy, 56
Carter, John, 179
CBC Radio, 5, 238, 244, 260,
278, 281, 286
CF-18 maintenance contract,
Mulroney's award of, 296–97
CFNB (radio station), 70
Chambers, Egan, 139
Charest, Jean, 56, 330, 341
Charlottetown Accord, 294

Charlottetown *Guardian*, 75
Charter of Rights and Freedoms,
195
Chase, Buddy, 32–33, 46–47
Chase, Fred, 43
Chateau Laurier Hotel
annual party meeting of 1966,
183
campaign planning commit-
tee meeting, 90
"Evening with Dalton," 341
Gold Floor, Camp's weeks on,
307–9
rooms for annual meeting in
1966, 170
secret meeting with Stanfield,
257
Cherie Camp and Friends, 224
Cherkley, 60
the Chief. *See* Diefenbaker, John
CHNS (radio station), 81–82
Chrétien, Jean, 243, 319, 341,
348, 363n
Churchill, Gordon, 97, 115,
129–30, 144, 176, 190
Churchill, Winston, 41, 61–62,
68, 121, 137, 145, 317, 320
Citizen Kane, 53
CJCH (radio station), 82
Clairtone Sound Corporation,
109
Clam Shack, 4, 335–36, 344–45
Clark, Catherine, 314
Clark, Joe
abolitionist position of, 330
anti-Clark campaign, 289–90
Atkins' support in 1983, 110
automatic leadership review,
impact of, 363n
Camp's criticism of, 277
Camp's delight at behaviour
of, 328
at Camp's eightieth birthday
celebrations, 341
at Camp's funeral, 351
Camp's ranking of, 329
Camp's view of, 138
"community of communities,"
321
election campaign strategy of
1979, 245
at executive meeting in 1965,
147
Fredericton conference, 109,
141
on fringe of Camp inner circle, 189
Fulton's leadership campaign,
202

The Player
_____

for honorary doctorate, 303–4
national president speech,
186
for Robert Stanfield, 262
Spadina Expressway speech,
246–48
Stanfield's leadership candidacy speech, 212–13
throne speeches for Mulroney
government, 294
Toronto Junior Board of
Trade speech, 173, 175–78
valedictory address (May
1947), 51–52
Spence, Wishart, 175
Spence Report, 362n
sports, interest in, 13, 51, 54, 57,
235
St. Laurent, Louis, 63, 65, 89,
98, 101
St. Thomas University, 111,
303–4, 326, 341
Stanfield, Robert
Camp, relations with, 149,
211, 215–16, 257
Camp as adviser and speechwriter, 262
Camp as guru to, 2
Camp's advice on personnel,
238
Camp's changed views on
regionalism, 320
Camp's introduction of, 56
on Camp's national president
candidacy, 138
Camp's speechwriting, 262
Canadian News Relations
joke, 214
candidacy for federal leadership, 199, 202–3, 206–7,
208, 210, 211–15
convention press luncheon,
214
convention strategy, 212
convention-week organiza-
tion, 212
Diefenbaker, relations with,
215
Diefenbaker's speech, reaction to, 183–84
Diefenbaker's view of, as
potential successor, 162
dinner for, 314
favourable first impression on
delegates, 212
federal election of 1958, role
in, 114
federal election of 1972,
256–60

federal leadership campaign,
106
federal leadership candidacy,
199, 202–3, 206–7, 208,
210, 211–15
federal leadership review
campaign, 182, 183–84, 204
and Flora MacDonald's list,
170
honesty of, 80
keynote speaker at 1956 leadership convention, 96–97
language issue, 213
leadership candidacy speech,
212–13
leadership convention of
1967, 110
leadership review campaign,
support for, 180, 182,
183–84, 204
as new federal party leader,
214–15
political campaigns of, 85
provincial election of 1953,
78–83
provincial election of 1956,
72
provincial re-election in
1967, 206
real power in Conservative
party, 139
regret over relations with
Camp, 216
retirement, 275
the Spades, support of, 151
strength in provinces, 94
Trudeau, assessment of, 256
wedge in relationship with
Camp, 211
Stark, Andrew, 209, 291–92, 303
Starr, Mike, 174
Stevens, Paul, 116, 357n
Stewart, David, 76
Stewart, David A., 356n
Stormy Nights Productions, 223
The Strawberry Statement
(Kunen), 192
Summerside Patriot, 75
Suzuki, David, 223
Symons, Tom, 258

teeth, bad, 42
television, impact of, 69, 126,
127
television work, 237–38, 281–86
Tellier, Paul, 291, 292
Telus, 109
Thériault, Camille, 324–25, 326
Thompson, Robert, 132

"Three Wise Men," 158
Time magazine, 64
Toole, Barry, 312, 346
Toole, Janet, 233, 312, 321, 346,
354n
Tories. See Conservative party
Toronto, and anti-Diefenbaker
sentiment, 135, 154–55
Toronto Junior Board of Trade
speech, 173, 175–78
Toronto Star
Camp, and not reading the
Star, 342
Camp, relations with, 241–44
Camp's columns, 222, 239–40
Camp's principal client, 282
David Macdonald's criticism
of Diefenbaker, 177
heart transplant article,
306–7
readers of Camp's columns, 5
Toronto Sun, 222, 242
Toronto Telegram
Camp's challenge of
Diefenbaker headline, 175
Camp's columns, 222, 238–39
editorial on end of
Diefenbaker's reign, 184
support for Stanfield's leader-
ship candidacy, 213
Trudeau's mastery of the
media, 217
tourism advertising accounts,
72–73, 108, 109, 114
Trainor, Howie, 325
TransCanada PipeLines Ltd. See
pipeline debate
Travel Direction Limited, 222
"treating," 76
Trent University, 116–17, 258
tributes, 340–41
Trinity College School, 227
Troyer, Warner, 238
Trudeau, Pierre Elliott
and Camp, clash of personalities, 141
Camp's column about,
241–42
Camp's ranking of, 328
Camp's views on, 256
election as Liberal leader, 217
federal election of 1965, 158
federation, concept of,
321–22
and London School of
Economics, 356n
majority government in 1968,
232, 248, 255–56
mastery of media, 217